WAKING UP HAPPY

A HANDBOOK OF CHANGE WITH MEMOIRS OF RECOVERY AND HOPE

JILL MUEHRCKE

Copyright 2012 by Juliana O. Muehrcke
muehrcke@charter.net
All rights reserved.

ISBN 0960297871
ISBN 13: 9780960297870
Library of Congress (LCCN) 2011925975
Createspace, North Charleston, SC

Published by the Recovery Foundation, Inc.
Madison, Wisconsin
recoveryfoundation.net

Without limiting the rights under copyright reserved above, no part of this publication may be reproduced, stored in or introduced into a retrieval system, or transmitted in any form or by any means (electronic, mechanical, photocopying, recording or otherwise) without the prior written permission of the copyright owner and the above publisher of this book.

For you who suffer and seek a better way.

CONTENTS

PREFACE
Where Can You Begin? Begin with Your Heart 7

BEGINNINGS
You Are the Sculptor and the Stone 11

1 Trust Your Inner Guide: My Story 15

Jill Muehrcke is a writer and editor who began her recovery journey in 1984. Since then, she has collected resources and exercises to help herself and others enlarge their horizons and craft joyful lives. These lessons are woven throughout this book, and she shares her story here.

Words of Wisdom and Light 66

2 Connect to the Earth: Shelly's Story 69

Shelly Dutch quit using cocaine in 1983. Twenty years later, she started Connections Counseling Center, a clinic for recovering addicts and alcoholics. This chapter shows how she prevailed through multiple addictions to find hope and peace. Her journey is about her discovery of personal growth and purpose in life, one day at a time.

Words of Wisdom and Light 107

3 Humbly Ask for Help: Adam's Story 111

Adam's life revolves around recovery. A forty-year-old recovering alcoholic who has been sober since 2005, he believes he owes his life to lessons learned from support groups and dogs. He summarizes those lessons here.

Words of Wisdom and Light 137

4 Make Yourself Happy: Skye's Story 141

Thirty-one-year-old Skye, who began her recovery from heroin, cocaine, and crystal meth addiction in 2003, is a counselor at Connections and recently earned her master's in mental health. Her most fervent wish is to help others learn what it means to wake up happy every day.

Words of Wisdom and Light 161

5 Just Connect: Shyloh's Story **165**

Shyloh, the author's twenty-three-year-old granddaughter, gave up heroin in 2008. Since then she has relapsed and once again recovered. She believes that addiction can be a blessing, and so can relapse, as she explains in this chapter.

Words of Wisdom and Light **192**

6 Courage Doesn't Always Roar: Andrea's Story **195**

Andrea, the author's daughter, quit drugs in her twenties. But only recently, in her forties, did she begin confronting the problems caused by her drug use and exploring the underlying issues. While she says she has "no answers" and is uncomfortable giving advice, she has a powerful story to tell.

Words of Wisdom and Light **208**

7 Make Room for Miracles: Marilyn's Story **211**

Marilyn and the author are close friends who met early in their recoveries. Marilyn quit drinking in 1983 and began an odyssey of self-discovery that continues today. Here are her hard-won keys to serenity and fulfillment.

Words of Wisdom and Light **247**

SUMMARY
What Works and What Doesn't **251**

CONCLUSION
Never, Never, Never Give Up **253**

365 STEPS ON YOUR JOURNEY **255**

Here is a strategy for every day of the year to help keep you on your path. Remember, that's all you need to do—take one small step every day. Each one will take you closer to a new life.

APPENDIX
Resources to Guide and Inspire You **277**

A Note of Thanks **283**

Index to Tips, Exercises, and Resources **285**

PREFACE

WHERE CAN YOU BEGIN? BEGIN WITH YOUR HEART

This is a workbook for changing your life. It contains true stories of people who have overturned their lives, along with exercises you can do to make your own miraculous changes. If you want to give up an addiction to a drug, person, or behavior, or simply to live the best life you can, you'll find revelations, guidance, and hope in these pages.

If your family member has an addiction, this book is for you, too. If you've watched a child, partner, or sibling struggle, you know the anguish of wanting to help but not knowing how. Here are concrete tools to guide your loved one onto a new path.

If you're a counselor, sponsor, or coach, you can assign readings to usher people toward breakthrough thinking. If you're in a support group, you and the others in your group can complete the activities together. The book's hands-on style, focusing on tools for self-reflection, reinforced with examples of how others have prevailed, will be helpful in any recovery program.

We who tell our stories here do so in hope that our struggles will make your change journey easier. To distill the messages embedded in each person's memoir, I've woven exercises throughout the stories and at the end of chapters (I've added my initials J.M. at the end of exercises that are in my words rather than the voices of the other storytellers).

This is the book I wish had existed when I quit drinking. I wanted to know how others had built new lives so that I could try what they'd found helpful.

Since there was no such book, I gathered information wherever I could—by reading, talking to others, going to meetings, taking courses, and learning different approaches. Many of the activities in this book are based on tactics I developed in my own recovery.

But since everything that benefited me may not work for you, I've included the stories of a variety of other people with different backgrounds, personalities, and learning styles. Some strategies worked for almost all of us, while others are unique. Make these lessons your own by testing them to see which ones are true for you.

WHO WE ARE

Those of us who share our stories are rebuilding our lives after years of addiction to alcohol, opiates, cocaine, and other substances—even from compulsive sex and unhealthy eating. We're young and old, male and female, gay and straight. We all have tales to tell of shaping lives of sheer joy.

Although we come from all over the country, most of us now live in or near Madison, Wisconsin, and are affiliated with Connections Counseling as clients, counselors, or volunteers. You'll read more about Connections in Chapter 2 (the story of Shelly Dutch, who founded Connections) and learn (in "Beginnings: You Are the Sculptor and the Stone") how all of us came together.

We vary in age. Shyloh, my granddaughter, is the youngest at twenty-three, and I'm the oldest at sixty-six. Andrea (Shyloh's mother and my daughter) appears in both our memoirs and also provides her own narrative. Together, our stories highlight three generations of women with similar—yet very different—addictions, recovery tools, and routes to happiness.

Shelly and Marilyn began their voyages of recovery in 1983, and I started mine in 1984. Shyloh gave up heroin four years ago and has since relapsed but once again recovered. The others fall somewhere in between in terms of years of sobriety. Several went to in-patient centers, while others recovered without such treatment. Some, but not all, found AA useful. A few began by attending twelve-step meetings and then moved on to other forms of support.

Since we used such different ingredients to stitch new lives, our diverse threads create a tapestry of many textures and colors. Somewhere in those patterns, we hope you'll find strategies that work for you.

HOW I WROTE THE BOOK

While I began this book by interviewing people, that was only a small part of the process. A number of unique circumstances gave me a distinct advantage: I was good friends with most of the storytellers and spent a great deal of time with them. Thus, much of the information for their memoirs came from questions I asked casually while doing other things—taking walks, eating lunch together, emailing back and forth.

I endured a lot of teasing for my constant scribbling of scraps of conversation every time I got together with these friends, but I think my technique ultimately led to far more nuanced tales than I could have elicited from formal interviews alone. Also, since I shared history with half these people, I was able to use my own journals to remind them of key points in their journeys and tease out buried memories.

HOW THE BOOK IS ORGANIZED

I begin with my own story in Chapter 1, followed in Chapters 2 through 7 by the stories of six others. I introduce these people at the beginning of each chapter so you'll understand how I know them and how our tales are intertwined (I use my initials J.M. at the end of these introductions to differentiate them from the words of the other storytellers).

The names of the storytellers in the seven chapters haven't been changed (except for Adam, who wants to preserve his anonymity as a member of AA). Some of us have altered a few names and details in our stories to protect the privacy of other people in our lives.

I've titled people's chapters with the core lessons they've learned, and the exercises show how you can use their approaches in your own life. While the exercises are inspired by each person's narrative, I created them through my own reading, research, and experience.

Some people with vital lessons to share didn't want to tell their stories in detail or use their real names. I've included their insights in "Words of Wisdom and Light," which appear between the longer chapters. To guard their anonymity, I've changed identifying details and in some cases merged several narratives to avoid redundancy and promote clarity. Again, I've added my own research to their lessons.

Two important keys are "Things to Do Today" at the end of each chapter and "365 Steps on Your Journey" at the end of the book. Both underscore the central message: Do just a few simple things each day, and those tiny actions will evolve into profound change.

HOW TO USE THIS BOOK

Jump into this book wherever you like. You needn't read it from beginning to end to absorb its lessons. Take what you need from it. Interact with it. Jot down your thoughts. Keep it with you and re-read it, because it will mean different things at different times.

At the end of the book, I've included an index to tips, exercises, and resources. If you need guidance on an issue, you can look it up there.

This book is a conversation between us and you. Allow the memoirs to evoke your own responses, and try the exercises that appeal to you (or put stars next to the ones you want to come back to later). Then get in touch with us at jill@snpo.org, Waking Up Happy's Facebook Page, or wakinguphappybook.com to share your insights and connect with others on the same journey.

The tales told here are evidence that others have struggled through the same upward steps you're taking. As you'll see, we've all faltered and fallen back, but, grain by grain, we've prevailed in unimagined ways. So can you, by following these same steps.

The seed that is to grow must lose itself as seed;
And they that creep may graduate through chrysalis to wings.
   —Wu Ming Fu

BEGINNINGS

YOU ARE THE SCULPTOR AND THE STONE

It began with a dream. One night I dreamed of climbing a mountain with several other women, passing through fierce storms, and arriving at a sunlit peak where we could see the paths we'd taken, gleaming below us. We realized we could help others find their own trails, supporting them on their climb, and helping them avoid the obstacles that had made our ascent so painful.

Because of this dream, I was sure I was meant to join with other women to write a book, using our experiences to help others. I waited for the book to take shape in my mind. Before I went to sleep, I asked my dream sherpa to offer guidance. But I had no more revelatory dreams, and in time I put the idea aside.

Then one day I was talking to my granddaughter, Shyloh, a beautiful young woman who had just turned twenty-one and was one of the brightest lights of my life. She'd recently been to rehab, gotten off drugs, and was telling me about a place called Connections, where she was receiving the support she needed to lead a new, sober life.

As it happened, the woman who'd started Connections, Shelly Dutch, was profiled that month in the magazine *Wisconsin Woman*, and Shyloh gave me the piece to read. She also talked about her counselor at Connections, Skye, who had an idea for a book relating the stories of people who'd come to Connections. These amazing men and women were, like phoenixes, rising up from the fires of addiction and fashioning brand-new lives.

This, I realized, was the book I was meant to write, and Shyloh, Shelly, and Skye were the climbing companions of my dream. We each had a powerful spark within us, but it took the synchrony of my talk with Shyloh to drive our energies toward a common purpose.

For years, I'd been collecting ideas about the process of change because of my own recovery journey. I realized that all the research I'd done after I stopped drinking and the strategies I'd used to turn my life around could be woven into this book of memoirs to help others on their voyages of change.

Skye already had the book's title—*Waking Up Happy*—and its premise—focusing not on the misery of people's addictions but on the joyous journey of recovery. Shelly donated Connections' meeting rooms, where we began strategizing and found people whose stories were begging to be told.

Like Skye, I'd read many memoirs of addiction and finished each one wishing there had been less immersion in the years of addiction, relapse, and anguish and more on the gratifying process of recovering and building a new life. *But what happened next?* I always found myself asking. *How did these tortured souls go on to lead meaningful lives? What were their secrets?* The title Skye chose for the book resounded with us because we'd all had the experience of waking up miserable, detesting ourselves for what we'd become. The crowning splendor of a new life is that feeling you have upon waking—that all's right with the world and that you have a productive place in it.

Connections Counseling Center—the haven Shelly has designed for people in recovery—is itself a place of joy. Those who enter the warm, cozy space feel welcomed and embraced.

On my first visit there, Skye showed me two walls—one of sorrow and one of jubilation. The first wall is covered with pictures of Connections' clients who have died—of overdoses, in car crashes, and in all the other ways people kill themselves, by design or accident, when they've forgotten how to love themselves.

The second wall is made up of collages of people who have lived to celebrate one or more years of sobriety. Each collage has been created with photos of the person laughing with friends and pictures symbolizing key points on the person's journey.

"Both walls have powerful messages," Skye said. "The first makes it clear that addiction is a serious disease. People die from it, and many others come close to dying. But my work isn't depressing. It's a joyous job, counseling people who are changing their lives. The second wall reflects that miracle of transformation."

> *Tale as old as time,*
> *Tune as old as song,*
> *Bittersweet and strange,*
> *Finding you can change,*
> *Learning you were wrong.*
> —Howard Ashman and Alan Menken, *Beauty and the Beast*

✧ ✧ ✧

There are many reasons why you may want to change your life. If you have an addiction, habit, or intolerable situation that's devastating your life, you may realize you must make a drastic shift. If you're in a relationship that's diminishing rather than enhancing your best self, or if you're eating the wrong foods, hurting your body, or doing other self-destructive things, you know, deep inside, that you can't continue on that path. As you pass through different phases in your life—as you become a parent, for example, or an empty-nester or a retiree—radical adjustments are necessary.

Changing your life isn't easy. It means learning to know yourself. It means creating yourself anew. Because you're both the sculptor and the stone, it's a wrenching task.

Yet every sculptor knows that the piece of art that's meant to be exists already: It's a matter of carving its essence from material that's already there. When asked how the granite bear came to be, the sculptor says, "I just cut away everything that wasn't a bear."

All of us in this book have worked long hours stripping away the false, burdensome, excess parts of ourselves to bring our truest spirits into being. Because we're all addicts of one sort or another, it's those addictions—to drugs, to habits that suffocated our authentic selves, to people who hurt and abused us and quelled our power—it's those addictions we chisel at every day.

You needn't be an addict to feel the clarion call to remold yourself. Everyone's life cries out for transformation. If you don't change and grow, you die; bit by bit, day by day, your innermost soul dwindles and perishes. The cost of not continuing to grow is ultimately feeling half-dead.

There came a time when the risk to remain tight in the bud was more painful than the risk it took to blossom.
—Anais Nin

Change doesn't happen in a moment. But often there's an instant that signals the need for an evolution into something new. Buried in that instant you'll often find the power of synchronicity.

Synchronicity may be a vague concept for you until one day events come together in an "Aha!" moment and it becomes crystal clear how everything's connected. Synchronicity is all about connection. It's about turning points, signposts that signal a new route. It's about the way life surprises you when your heart's open to the universe of possibilities.

This book was born through a series of synchronous events—circumstances too filled with significance to be mere coincidence. The psychologist Carl Jung described synchronicity as a link that goes beyond simple cause and effect to become meaningful, a fusion of elements that, when they merge, turn into something new. Sometimes a synchronous moment causes a major shift, pointing the way toward a deeper purpose. That's our hope for you—that as you peruse this book, you'll find a story, suggestion, or life lesson that resonates in just the right way, touching you at a moment when you're ready to take a leap toward a new life.

There is no such thing as a problem without a gift for you in its hand.
—Helen Schucman

You're the artist of your own life. All you need do is pick up the tools for change and begin to use them. Each false start is a carving crucial to the final piece of art, paving the way for you to sculpt your greatest creation: the beautiful self that lies within the stone.

1
TRUST YOUR INNER GUIDE: MY STORY

Quitting was easy. The hard part was learning to live again. The excruciating, daily, never-ending part was discovering how to lead an authentic life, without alcohol or any other screens to soften the glare of reality.

I thought I was prepared for the process. I'd spent years reading everything on addiction I could find. I knew the steps to take, and at first I simply followed them mechanically. Sometimes, when you don't know the way, all you can do is keep walking, map in hand, and trust that you'll reach your destination. That's what I did.

All the books concurred: You can't stop drinking without learning to live in a new way, which means you need a therapist and a support group. So I spent that morning—April 8, 1984, at the age of thirty-nine—on the phone searching for both.

It wasn't that I'd hit bottom in a traditional sense. My life was going well. I adored my husband, my home, the town I lived in, my career as a freelance writer and editor. My eighteen-year-old daughter, after a tumultuous adolescence and battle with drugs, was getting her life together. I had everything I'd ever wanted. On the surface, things could hardly have been better.

Yet there was a film over it all, keeping me from enjoying any of it fully. For years I'd known, deep inside, that I needed to change my life. Five years earlier, I'd quit smoking after a fifteen-year, two-pack-a-day habit, but that didn't transform my life the way I'd hoped. I tried cutting my long hair shockingly short and piercing my ears, but those weren't the transformations I needed, either.

I was dying inside. Every morning, I'd look in the mirror and hate the face that peered back at me.

Today would be different, I'd tell myself. I wouldn't pick up that glass of wine with dinner. I'd get through the evening without drinking. I'd do it the way I'd managed to quit smoking, by convincing myself to get through just one day and one evening, and then it would get easier, and my life would change.

And every evening, or afternoon, or sometimes even later that same morning, I'd pour myself a glass of wine and drink it down quickly so that I could bear to live with the person I'd become.

One night, I dreamed of a goat clinging to my back, its legs tight around my chest, crippling me, making it an agony to move, look upward, or even breathe. You didn't have to be a devotee of Freud to interpret that. It was time to take that last sip of Chablis and throw the bottle in the trash.

Good ideas must come welling up into you. Wait for them. They come from the dreamy idleness of children.
—Brenda Ueland

✧ ✧ ✧

My dreams were always touchstones for me. My first memories are of dreams I had when I was still in a crib. In one of these early dreams, my Raggedy Andy doll was chasing me with a grotesque grin and evil eyes. I woke screaming, and threw the doll out of my crib. I remember my mother coming in and handing the doll to me, thinking I was crying because I wanted it back. I was so young I didn't have the words to explain.

This sort of miscommunication set the stage for life with my family. Even after I learned to talk, I couldn't find the words to tell anyone how I was feeling. I didn't think those were words I was allowed to say.

Maybe that's because everything in our family revolved around my father. I didn't understand that he was mentally ill. What I knew was that my mother's time and energy were consumed by him and his needs. My father and my older sister, Janey, were both loudly emotional, and I needed to be quiet so I wouldn't add to my mother's anguish.

Because my mother was so preoccupied with my dad, most of my time was spent with Janey. Though she was only six years older, she was given the role of "acting mother" to me, a role she didn't relish. I didn't blame her in the least. If I were her, I wouldn't have wanted to be saddled with me, either.

I believed Janey had the answer to everything. Not all her advice was sound (she was, after all, a child herself), but much of it was helpful.

For example, her mandate about dreams has stayed with me my whole life.

It happened when I was four. I dreamed I was walking along the beach with a beautiful, goddess-like, golden-haired woman with loving eyes and the sweetest smile. Telling me she'd be right back, she dove into the ocean. Hours later, long after the sun went down, I was still on the sand, waiting for her but knowing she was gone and I'd be alone forever. I woke up sobbing. My parents were unavailable, which was common, so I told Janey my dream. She said all I had to do was go back to sleep and dream that I found my goddess friend again.

I did exactly that. I fell asleep, and I did dream that I found the goddess again. Unfortunately, she then turned into a ghastly witch. Still, Janey's directive was amazingly insightful for a ten-year-old, and I've used it many times throughout the years. My greatest insights have come from dreams. Whenever I ignored them, new dreams arrived with even stronger messages.

✧ ✧ ✧

While the goat dream wasn't my first better-quit-drinking wake-up call, it was the one that finally got my attention. The feeling the dream evoked in me—of being so hobbled and incapacitated that I might as well be dead—was more powerful than any conscious thought.

I'd known for a long time that I had to quit. I used to tell myself I'd stop smoking and drinking when I was thirty years old. On the morning I turned thirty, I woke up cranky and short-tempered and realized I didn't want to quit. The truth was, in the back of my mind I hadn't believed I'd live to be thirty. Since I was very sick with asthma as a child, I thought I'd probably die young. But as the years went on and I didn't die, just got less and less healthy by living such a toxic lifestyle, it became clear to me that I couldn't go on like that. When I stopped smoking at thirty-two, I knew I'd have to stop drinking, too, but it took me a few more years to find the courage.

What was the defining moment? I think I was at a point where I could see a future for myself, and I wanted to be alive to experience that future. There was no instant in which fate tapped me on the shoulder and said, "It's time"—unless you consider my goat dream the hand of fate. The morning after I had that dream, I woke up knowing I couldn't go through another day of such misery and self-sabotage.

In my reading, I'd learned about Women for Sobriety, which recasts the tenets of AA to meet women's needs. Jean Kirkpatrick, the group's founder, had tried AA but couldn't make it work for her, so she adapted the twelve steps for women. The step about being powerless was antithetical to women's needs, she believed. Women already felt powerless; what they needed was to get in touch with their inner strength and put the past behind them so they could build a new sense of self.

✵ ✵ ✵

I don't remember all their names, but I recall every one of their faces. In my mind I can see them now, a group of eight women at a small, round, battered table in a cavernous church basement.

It had taken a while to make contact with the Women for Sobriety group, but somehow I made it through those first sober days. Drinking had ceased to be pleasurable long ago, so it was mostly a matter of filling the time that was once consumed by drinking. Whenever I thought about having a glass of wine (my "drug of choice"), I remembered the awful feeling I'd had in my goat-on-the-back dream. That memory, along with the hopes I was pinning on the Women for Sobriety meeting, lifted me through the long hours.

When the night of the meeting arrived, I was nervous, but the women in the group made me feel at home right away. They couldn't have been more different, yet all were struggling with the same things, seeking a new balance in their lives.

One woman, with sparkling brown eyes, looked like a teenager. Another, her face etched with canyon-like lines, appeared to be a hundred years old.

Alice, a gorgeous, olive-skinned woman with long, silky black hair, described how she grew up in a wealthy family with no emotional support. She spoke of a book she'd read that advised saying, "I approve of myself," throughout the day.

"I have to keep going back to the book to remember what to say," she told us. "I can remember 'I like myself' and 'I love myself,' but I just can't remember 'I approve of myself.'"

"Approving of yourself—what a concept," someone said, and we all laughed.

"I went to a wounded child weekend," Alice went on, "but I just couldn't relate to what they said about getting in touch with your spontaneity."

"I know what you mean," said a woman named Marilyn. "I have to write it down in my calendar: Be spontaneous."

We laughed again.

One of the women shared her philosophy that "yesterday's a memory, tomorrow's a dream, but today's a real bitch."

"That's for sure," we all agreed.

"But, you know what?" she continued.. "As long as I concentrate all my energies on today, I can make it through."

Another woman, Cassie, hadn't quit drinking yet; she was going to cut down, she said.

"I've been trying to cut down for years," I said, "and it just didn't work for me. I found books with advice on cutting down, and I followed all the steps—measuring my wine and drinking just six ounces an hour. That worked pretty well when I was home, but when I went to a party, I couldn't very well take my timer and measuring cup with me."

The women responded with laughter, and I felt welcomed into the group.

I told them about my life as the wife of a professor and mother of a teenager. Although I'd divorced my first husband, John, when Andrea was two years old, I'd married Phil shortly afterwards and he'd been a wonderful father to her.

I confessed how worried I was that Phil would think less of me now that I'd stopped drinking. "It's so nice having a glass of wine together," he'd said several times over the past few years. "I'd hate your drinking to get to the point where you'd have to quit completely."

I felt I was disappointing him, but I knew that having a glass of wine with him once in a while, while a lovely idea, just wouldn't work.

"He loves you, right? He's gonna support you," Alice said.

I nodded. Yes, we loved each other, and he'd always stood by me. The women's words reassured me, as did the fact that they understood my irrational concerns, my all-or-nothing nature, and my fear of being rejected and abandoned. Those were the reasons we drank—or, at least, a few of the reasons.

I realized how secluded I'd been—how good it felt to be with people whose stories were so like mine. My heart went out to the women and the tough challenges they were facing. My struggles seemed minuscule compared to many of theirs. Yet I never for an instant felt like an outsider in that group. My life may have looked sunny, but I was haunted by the same shadows.

> **It is the paradoxical secret of transformation itself, since it is in fact in and through the shadow that lead is transformed into gold.**
> —Carl Jung

Toward the end of that first Women for Sobriety meeting, Alice said, "I've made such good friends here and found such support, I'm actually glad I'm an alcoholic."

That's one thing I'll never say, I thought.

It's funny how life changes your mind about things. Within a year, I'd be able to say, "I'm an alcoholic" with a sense of gratitude, pride, and wholehearted gladness to be part of a close, loving sisterhood of sobriety. I have a pretty vivid imagination, but I never imagined how completely my life would be upended.

After the meeting, Marilyn gave me her phone number, telling me she was available any time I needed to talk. I had no idea that Marilyn would become my friend for life nor any inkling of how many times we would laugh and cry together through the years to come.

Indeed, the journey I was beginning was still a total mystery. I hadn't a clue about what was in store. All I knew as I left that first meeting was that my heart felt a little lighter.

TURNING POINT

Join a group of people who share your interests, whether it's a support group, exercise class, book club, or mentoring society. A wonderful tool is the online site Meetup (www.meetup.com), which lists groups in your area that meet your criteria and gives you the tools to start your own groups. In our small community, my friends and I found and joined (or started) the following: a vegetarian group that gets together for specially-prepared vegan fare, a group that meets at a non-drinking place for board games, a crafting circle, a philosophical gathering, an alcohol-free dining-out group, and a variety of non-drinking book clubs. That's just a fraction of what's available.

–JM

✵ ✵ ✵

During the next few days, I often returned in my mind to that meeting. Remembering the women I'd met, the conversations we'd had, helped keep me going. Life seemed so much the same, the changes I was making so microscopic. Where was the transformation I'd expected? Rather than feeling strong and empowered, I felt raw and vulnerable.

My asthma started bothering me, too, as it hadn't in decades. I'd battled asthma all my life, but I'd thought I had it under control. This felt like a big setback.

I'd been reading books on depressives and alcoholics; both are trying to "depress" anxiety. Another way to depress such feelings is through illness. So it made sense that my asthma was back in full force.

Certainly I didn't want to be sick all the time. But I was positive I never wanted to drink again. For some reason, drinking was simply not an option anymore. I felt about it as I did about smoking: Now that I'd quit, I'd be crazy to start again.

So I did the only thing I could, which was just to keep going, day by day, step by step, like an inchworm along a leaf.

Only that which changes remains true.
—Carl Jung

✫ ✫ ✫

I was still waiting to start therapy. For my insurance to pay for treatment, I needed a psychiatrist to certify that I had a legitimate reason to go to therapy and then be referred to a therapist. Each step of the process took weeks. In the meantime, I threw myself into work even more than usual, going to the office early and bringing home manuscripts to edit.

I had worked as a freelance writer since Andrea was small so that I could be home with her as much as possible, but the life of a freelancer wasn't good for me. The unpredictability of it, the constant rejections, the cycle of impossible deadlines followed by periods of complete lack of work—all of it had fueled drinking and depression.

A year earlier, I'd become the full-time editor of a magazine in addition to my freelancing work, and that gave a much-needed structure to my days. Since it was a brand-new magazine, I got to design it myself and put it together from scratch. I was in my element.

The only downside of being part of a startup magazine was that its survival was shaky, and I didn't handle uncertainty well. I worried constantly that the magazine wouldn't survive, and I'd lose the best job I'd ever had. But now that a year had passed and the magazine was still going strong, I began to think it might actually last.

I didn't think of it at the time but, rather than hitting bottom, as many of the other women described, perhaps I'd hit "top." Maybe it was only when I saw how fulfilling life could be for me, how much I had to live for, that I mustered the courage to stop killing myself with alcohol. Perhaps I needed to feel some steadiness beneath my feet before I could take that first step onto the high wire. With my skeptical nature, it had taken me a year to assure myself that my job wasn't too good to be true, that it was something I could count on.

Until you are willing to be confused about what you already know, what you know will never grow bigger, better, or more useful.
—Milton Erickson

✫ ✫ ✫

A STEP ON THE JOURNEY

The best cure—words from your heart. There's no better remedy for whatever's bothering you than to write. You can write in a beautiful journal, on scraps of paper, or on your computer. You can draft a few words or dozens of pages. You can write twice a day, once a week, or just when you need an outlet.

You can also keep a journal by talking into a digital recorder or video cam. But even if you do, it's still a good idea to get into the habit of jotting things down. If writing feels foreign to you, keep penning a few lines every day until it feels more natural. It's a practice that will benefit you throughout your life.

There are no rules, but you can use the following tips:
- Start by jotting down a few tetherings—the date, what's going on in the news or in your life, whatever will anchor your words to a specific time. When you look back on your writing, these hooks may give you insights into why you were feeling the way you were.
- Don't worry about grammar, spelling, or writing in complete sentences. Just let the words flow.
- If you don't know what to say, begin by answering questions such as these: Where are you in your life? How did you get there? Where would you like to go next? What do you wish you were doing? What's the most important thing in the world to you?
- You needn't restrict yourself to words. Draw your ideas. Doodle. Paste in photos, cut-out pictures, objects from nature, or anything that will remind you of special moments in your life. Print out the lyrics of your favorite songs, and use those as springboards to clarify your feelings. Make collages, or sketch or paint. Tinker with colors and shapes. Let the creative child within you come out to play.
- Every few months, look back over your journal. Certain patterns will become clear—threads that occur and reoccur—and give you insights into your truest self.

– J.M.

✫ ✫ ✫

I'd grown accustomed, over the years, to having a few glasses of wine with dinner, then more wine as I sat in bed reading till the world grew fuzzy and friendly and I drifted into a welcoming sleep. Now I tried to stay so busy that sleep came from exhaustion and I had no time to miss that state of blurred, negligent bliss.

I began adding things to my life, things I'd loved to do as a kid but hadn't done during my drinking years—singing, dancing, swimming, or, rather, playing in the water, because I was a poor swimmer. I joined a gym, something I never would have done while I was drinking, and went there every afternoon after work.

I also started attending lectures where I learned a great deal about the disease of alcoholism. I'd always thought of alcohol as a more benign substance than "hard" drugs like cocaine and heroin. But I learned that alcohol is actually far more dangerous. While we often hear about people dying of overdoses from cocaine and heroin, the many thousands of alcohol-related deaths that occur each year rarely appear on our radar.

One scale that ranks drugs in terms of damage to users and to society shows that alcohol is the most harmful with a score of 72 out of 100, followed by heroin with 55, crack cocaine with 54, and crystal meth with 33. Alcohol is the third leading risk factor for premature death and disabilities. Such information reinforced my certainty that staying on the sober road was the best thing I could possibly do.

During this time, I turned to my journal every evening. Pinning down each day in words, exploring the fears and joys, despair and triumph, clarified my mind and helped me navigate this unfamiliar landscape.

JOURNAL—April 19, 1984

After work today, I took a water aerobics class at the gym. I haven't had so much fun since I was a kid, just splashing in the water.

Going to the gym is freeing in another way, too. I was surprised that the locker room—which I dreaded in high school because it exposed all my body's defects—can be a place of wonderful camaraderie. Seeing how different the women's bodies are, so beautiful in their glorious variety, helps me accept my imperfections.

After water aerobics, I joined a choir that's taking a singing tour of Greece this summer. I haven't sung with a group since college, and I'd forgotten the joy of it, how the sound grabs you up and makes your spirit sail.

I also signed up for yoga, pilates, and something called movement therapy, which again reminds me of my childhood. I find myself twirling around to the music till I'm almost dizzy, something I loved to do as a kid. Exercise is energizing, and you really do get a high from it that's better than alcohol because it doesn't impair the brain.

Trying all these new things was intimidating at first. For so long, I've avoided anything new for fear of failing. But I'm trying to see each challenge as a chance to practice acceptance of my faults. Living with more of a child's attitude, getting in touch with joy within me, is the best way I know to reach for this acceptance, at least for now.

A STEP ON THE JOURNEY

List things you loved to do as a kid, and find ways to incorporate them into your life. Look to your list for clues to the route that will take you to your inmost self. Begin your list here: _____

_____

_____

– J.M.

✫ ✫ ✫

When I talked at Women for Sobriety about all the new things I was doing, Marilyn asked, "Aren't you tired?"

"Exhausted!" I replied.

Everyone chuckled, and I asked, "Do you think I'm trying to do too much?"

"Maybe," said Alice. "You're the only one who can say for sure. That could be what you need right now—to fill your days with so many things you don't have time to think about drinking."

"That's how it was in rehab," said Linda, who had just graduated from in-patient treatment. "They gave us tons of chores to do, and if we weren't working we were in some type of support group or therapy. Maybe what you're doing serves the same purpose."

"Yes, and after you've sampled lots of different things, you can start eliminating the ones that don't serve you well," Marilyn said.

The women were the best teachers I'd ever had, and they put me in touch with the person I wanted to be. I loved the way we supported one another, offered comfort spiked with gentle teasing, and assured each other that we were doing the best we could. When I saw my own foibles mirrored in them, I could accept them in myself for the first time.

They, in turn, stood up for me, bolstered me. "You're too hard on yourself," they told me again and again, and while it took a while for the words to penetrate, I did begin to ask for less than perfection from myself.

It was the first time I'd discussed feelings in such depth. Like me, most of the women had grown up in homes where emotions were denied, so we all had a lot to learn about expressing what was inside us.

Before we could verbalize our feelings, we had to identify them. Marilyn brought a list of emotions to the group one night, and we were all surprised by how many there were. Using the list as our guide, we began figuring out what we felt and then talking about it.

TURNING POINT

How do you feel? It's helpful to pinpoint your emotions and describe how you're feeling, both to yourself and others. The more you deal with each emotion—feeling it fully and trying to understand its origins—the less overwhelming it will be. Soon you'll find that, no matter how strong a feeling is, it won't kill you. There's nothing more freeing than that knowledge.

Also remember that it's common to feel more than one emotion at once. Here's a partial list of emotions.

Challenging ("Negative") Emotions
   Sad: desperate, melancholy, anguished, hopeless, disappointed, lonely, bored, hurt, self-pitying, empty, desolate, lethargic, discouraged, pessimistic, devastated, heartbroken, defeated, needy
   Scared: worried, anxious, timid, uneasy, nervous, apprehensive, panicky, terrified, doubtful, tense, suspicious, wary, alarmed, edgy, horrified, dismayed, insecure, intimidated, paranoid
   Angry: bitter, resentful, annoyed, disgusted, irritated, exasperated, frustrated, tormented, aggravated, jealous, envious, hostile, enraged, repulsed, furious, impatient, vindictive, offended

Uplifting ("Positive") Emotions
   Happy: contented, amused, optimistic, proud, pleased, triumphant, ecstatic, glad, delighted, hopeful, eager, enthusiastic, peaceful, excited, exhilarated, serene, satisfied, relieved, inspired, joyful
   Loved and Loving: accepted, cared for, understood, cherished, caring, affectionate, connected, forgiving, grateful, passionate, trusting, appreciative, warm, friendly, safe
   Confident: courageous, purposeful, determined, empowered, creative, capable, self-reliant, strong, worthwhile, validated, positive, independent, whole

> Pick out the words that define how you're feeling right now. _____
> _____
> _____
> _____
>
> – J.M.

✣ ✣ ✣

It turned out I was right to worry that Cassie's cutting-down strategy wouldn't work; soon she was drinking full-time again and dropped out of our Women for Sobriety meetings. It also turned out that Alma, the woman with the hundred-year-old face, wasn't that much older than I was. But the struggles of her many relapses were etched into her cheeks.

When she smiled, though, she lit up like the sun, and her eyes were as bright as a girl's. That was true of all the women in the group: No matter how weary and debilitated they looked, their faces changed as they told their stories, and they were beautiful.

We didn't talk much about our histories of drinking and drugging; that was one of the things I liked about Women for Sobriety. The focus wasn't on our pasts but our futures.

We discussed the need for a higher power to move our minds away from ourselves to something greater. We agreed it was important to believe in such a power, although that force was different for each of us.

My higher power, I decided, was the group itself, the energy and hope we created as we helped each other and brought out the best in ourselves. I saw the miracle of it every week when the group's insights metamorphosed into wisdom far beyond the sum of our parts. So many times, I'd come with a problem that seemed insurmountable, or feel disgusted with myself for not handling things better, and the group would give me the gift of fresh perspectives, affirming that there was always an answer and that I was stronger than I realized.

The group was giving me wings, and I saw glimpses of how life might be if I learned to unfurl them. For now, I carefully folded them back, keeping them safe until I was ready to fly.

✣ ✣ ✣

A GOOD QUESTION

How do you define your higher power (H.P.)? Many of the people in recovery at Connections don't believe in the personal, all-powerful God of traditional religion. But they all have some sort of universal energy they tap into when needed. Here's what they had to say when asked to define their higher power:

- My higher power is my creativity. There's something miraculous about building something with your mind, heart, and hands.
- I equate my H.P. to the way a doting mom holds her newborn. Nothing but love!
- My higher power is the best and wisest part of myself. I've learned that when I'm desperate for help, the best thing I can do is look deep inside, and the right answers come. I believe we all have a piece of the divine within us.
- I think of my higher power as laughter. You can't look around this world without coming to believe that God has a sense of humor. I try to laugh at the ironies my higher power keeps pointing out to me. It's when I'm laughing that I feel closest to the angels.
- My H.P. is all that's inexplicable in this world. I can wonder how the world began and how it will end, but I'll never know for sure, and there's no use worrying about it. I leave it in the hands of my H.P.
- My higher power is embodied in my friends. I have a box of file cards, and on each card I've written a friend's name. When I'm feeling low, I pull a name out of the box. Then I email, call, or text that person—or sometimes just thinking about my friend is enough to raise my spirits. Even if I don't contact the person right then, I usually tell them later how their friendship helped me. I've found that solidifies our connection with one another.
- Mother Nature is my H.P. The greatest boon of recovery is that you can appreciate the simple joys of nature, like sunshine, cricket song, clouds drifting across the sky.
- I'm not sure who or what my higher power is. I've struggled with the concept and have never figured it out. All I know is that when I say, "Hey, H.P., I could use some help here," help always comes.

How do you define your higher power? _____
_____
_____
_____

– J.M

Sandy, one of the women in the support group, was going through a divorce, and I identified with her pain. I told her the story of my own divorce, and she seemed to find it helpful.

I'd met my first husband John when we were both sophomores at the University of Colorado in Boulder, and I loved him as I'd never loved anyone before. A year after we started dating, I discovered I was pregnant and married John a few weeks later. I'd just turned twenty.

When Andrea was born that spring, she introduced me to a kind of boundless love I'd never dreamed existed. I had worried I'd view her as a duty, as my mother had seen me, and I was elated to find that wasn't true. From the first moment I looked into her beautiful face, being Andrea's mother was my greatest joy.

After John graduated from the University of Colorado in 1967, we moved to Ann Arbor, where John entered grad school at the University of Michigan. I'd taken a semester off when Andrea was born, so I was a few credits shy of graduating, but I figured I could get my degree later. The important thing was keeping the family together.

Despite my best efforts, John asked for a divorce a year later. I was devastated. I don't know how I could have made it through this period without a therapist. That once-a-week opportunity to talk to someone was a lifeline.

So now, in our Women for Sobriety meetings, I empathized as Sandy wrestled with all the emotions a divorce elicits. I'd felt them myself and believed my life was over, when the truth was that a better life was waiting. If John hadn't left me, I wouldn't be married to Phil, and he'd thrown me an even stronger lifeline, one that offered me something I wasn't sure I deserved—a second chance.

It's a fine life, rich with misfortune.
—Larry McMurtry

✯ ✯ ✯

I was way too serious a child, my mother often told me, and she was right. Death preoccupied me. My parents were in their late thirties when I was born, so when I was ten, they were nearing fifty. I'd lie awake at night, doing the math. Fifty years isn't far from sixty, I thought, and after sixty comes—well—death. I couldn't bear the thought of them dying.

I worried just as much about life. What was it all about, really? Why were we here?

It didn't help to ask my mother or sister. If they weren't too busy to answer, they would respond with a few dismissive words or a deflective quip.

I could talk to my father, but he was rarely available. When he wasn't at work, he was in his bedroom with the door closed, his air conditioner on high while he lay under an electric blanket (also set on high), cut off from the world. On weekends, he would come out of his bedroom only for very brief periods, never speaking. I didn't realize he was on heavy-duty psychiatric medications.

Each evening when Dad got home from work (he was a magazine editor and took the train to Chicago from our suburb of Naperville), he and my mom went into his bedroom, where he ranted about everything that had gone wrong at the office while Mom murmured assurances in her calm, gentle voice.

I longed to be like my mother, cool, composed, competent. My deepest fear was that I was like my father, wildly emotional, passionate, overly sensitive.

✯ ✯ ✯

The most important things I learned growing up weren't things I discovered by asking. I learned them by spying. I'd sit at the top of the stairs outside my bedroom, just out of sight, where I could monitor everything that went on below.

Once, eavesdropping on Janey while she talked on the phone to a friend, I heard her say that she'd had an older brother, but he died. He would have been eight years older than she was, she said, but he was stillborn.

After she got off the phone, I asked her about it. She was mad that I'd overheard her and refused to give me any more information. She warned me that Mom and Dad didn't want to talk about it, so I should never bring it up.

I never did. I never mentioned my brother to anyone, but he became part of my dreams and fantasies. I thought about him often and imagined how different life might be if he'd lived.

That wasn't the only secret Janey was guarding. Later, when I learned that a family's dysfunction is measured by the secrets it keeps, I understood the depth of the sickness Janey and I grew up with.

When I was in my teens, I discovered I had an aunt I'd never met or even heard of. My father's older sister had been in a mental institution since the age of sixteen. Again, Janey told me not to speak of her, and I never did.

Those were some of the hidden truths I'd uncovered in my life as a spy. But I had no glimmer of the profound secrets yet to be discovered.

✯ ✯ ✯

Everything changed when I was fourteen. Late one night, I woke from a deep sleep with my heart thudding, hearing a loud, unfamiliar voice downstairs. At first I thought someone had broken in, but then I heard my mother's calm voice.

Mystified, I crept down the stairs and peeked into the living room. It was my sister making those fiendish, inhuman noises.

My racing heart calmed down a bit, but I was still frightened and confused. What was Janey doing here? Twenty years old, she'd gotten married a year before and lived with her husband on a farm an hour away. She'd had a baby daughter a month ago, and the last time I'd seen her, she'd been as beautiful and competent as ever.

Now she was bellowing as if a demon had taken possession of her. What she was saying made no sense at all.

I was too scared after my first glimpse to watch what was happening, but as I huddled in the stairwell, I heard sirens and then men coming in and carrying Janey out as she thrashed and howled. It was the first of countless episodes of Janey appearing at our house in the middle of the night, being wrestled into a police car, and taken to the mental hospital, but the experience never got easier to bear.

When I mustered the courage to come downstairs and ask what was wrong, my mother said, "Nothing's wrong. Go back to bed."

No one ever explained to me what had happened, but I eventually pieced together the fact that Janey was in the psychiatric hospital, diagnosed with paranoid schizophrenia. She'd had a complete break with reality. This psychotic break was the first of many, as she went in and out of mental wards.

Whenever I looked back on the night of that first breakdown, it was Janey's voice I remembered most, the sound of the stranger she'd become. After I went back to bed that night, I lay awake till almost dawn, then fell into a fitful sleep, where that voice chased me through my dreams, that monstrous roar that was like the distillation of horror itself.

After Janey's first breakdown, we never talked about her at home, except obliquely, as when my mother told me, "You are my sunshine. Janey used to be my sunshine, but now you are." It was what I'd always wanted, to be first in my mother's heart, so I didn't understand why those words made me so sad.

✺ ✺ ✺

"Come on, Jill, have a beer."

I smiled and shook my head. "No thanks, Janey," I said for the tenth time since I'd arrived. She never listened—or if she did, she chose to ignore what she didn't want to hear.

It was a few weeks since I'd quit drinking. I'd known it wouldn't be easy seeing my sister, but I always stopped at her apartment in Elgin, Illinois, on my way from Madison, Wisconsin, to visit my mom in Naperville. This trip had turned out to be even harder than I'd expected.

I'd told Janey that I'd quit drinking, of course, but she refused to believe me. I tried not to take it personally as she pressed me to drink beer with her. I knew she was this way with everyone, ignoring or discounting much of what people said. At the same time, she couldn't be dissuaded from her own irrational convictions. Today, she was insisting that she hadn't received any of my letters because her neighbors were stealing her mail.

Puffing frenetically on a cigarette while two others burned in the ashtray, Janey leaned forward and confided, "I haven't eaten in five days. All we can afford is noodles. Paul keeps telling me, just eat noodles."

I felt terrible for her but at a loss for what to do or say, especially when she opened the refrigerator to get more beer and I saw plenty of food—a whole package of carrots, bunches of greens, bags of apples and cherries. Probably her husband Paul was trying to get her to eat more healthfully, and she was resisting because she was devoted to fried food. If he was keeping junk food away from her, maybe it was true that noodles were the only things in the house that she was willing to eat.

It was clear to me that Janey was an alcoholic, although Mom refused to believe it. Of course Mom also denied that Dad had been an alcoholic. She idealized him in death so that the person she described was totally unfamiliar to me. And of course we never discussed, or even mentioned, how he had died, eleven years earlier.

Now, sitting at Janey's kitchen table, heaped with beer bottles and overflowing ashtrays, I couldn't help thinking of the big sister I'd worshiped as a kid. Looking at her now—toothless, unbathed, a hundred pounds overweight, her hair an implausible orangey-red, I still saw the gorgeous, perfectly coiffed girl with the dazzling smile that she'd been before everything went askew.

When I told Janey I had to leave, she exploded. "You didn't finish your coffee! After all my work fixing it for you! You can't go yet! You haven't even had a beer!"

Leaving was always the hardest part. I recalled how after one visit she'd grabbed my car's door handle and let herself be dragged for twenty feet rather than say good-bye. After such partings, I sometimes discovered my palms bleeding from clenching my fingernails so tightly into my hands.

As always, I took deep breaths as I left Janey's apartment. There was a sense of relief but, at the same time, a heavy feeling of remorse, as if I'd committed a crime.

✱ ✱ ✱

A week after that trip to Janey's, I was finally able to start therapy. Right away I could tell this experience would be different from my past attempts. Not only was I more motivated to change than ever before, but I felt an immediate rapport with my psychologist, Nancy. She was the first therapist in my experience who acted like a human being, who told stories about herself and gave common-sense advice. This kind of warmth helped me enormously.

I brought up things I'd never spoken of because they seemed so mean and shameful, like my jealousy when some friends got together without me and my resentment toward a woman at work because she never said hello to me.

"They seem like such petty emotions," I said.

Nancy smiled. "They're *human* emotions," she said.

✱ ✱ ✱

The spring I quit drinking was like waking up from a long nap. I felt disoriented, blinking in the sudden sunlight. A sober life still didn't feel natural to me, but I was beginning to see that one day it would.

I don't know why I'd been so worried about Phil's reaction to my giving up our nightly wine together. It was true that he found the whole concept of addiction baffling, but as I shared with him what I was learning, he was nothing but supportive.

That first alcohol-free summer, we celebrated our fifteenth wedding anniversary at our favorite Himalayan restaurant. Smiling at him across the table, I thought about the winter we started dating, in 1969. John had recently left me, Andrea was two years old, I was constantly sick with the worst allergy symptoms I'd had since childhood, and I'd started drinking hot toddies at bedtime so I could sleep.

Phil was getting a Ph.D. in the geography department at the University of Michigan, where I worked, and I was first attracted by how smart he was. My mother had stressed the importance of intelligence so much that it never occurred to me that there were more valuable characteristics. Even my first marriage to a guy who was brilliant but emotionally distant hadn't taught me that lesson.

Luckily, Phil had many other, more vital traits than intelligence—like kindness, thoughtfulness, a cheerful optimism, a buoyant sense of humor, and a steadiness that helped keep me grounded.

As that long-ago winter melted into spring, I began to tell Phil things I'd never said aloud before, and he listened without judging me. One June night, five months after we started dating, I decided I had to tell him my greatest secret. I was convinced no one could love me if they knew, but I wanted to be utterly honest with him.

So I whispered a secret I'd never told a soul before—that deep inside, at my core, was a black hole. On the surface, I looked fine, but it was just a costume, a sham. Underneath were layers of other surfaces, all the roles I'd played in my life, as mother, wife, daughter, lover. If you stripped away all those guises, there was nothing, just that blackness at my center.

My heart pounded when I told him this, but he didn't flinch or turn away. He didn't reject me, just comforted me and told me I was beautiful, competent, and strong, and for the first time I believed that someday it might be true.

We talked all night. and when the sun rose, I knew I'd spend the rest of my life with him. We were married a month later, six months after our first date.

Over the years, Phil has taught me so many things—just about everything I wish I'd learned as a child—not to carry the world's burdens on my shoulders, not to take things so much to heart, not always to expect the worst. He taught me that telling stories was the best way to make a point and that the best stories emerge when things don't go as planned.

Phil also gave me a name for something that had bothered me all my life. I never understood how I could get lost almost daily in the town where I grew up. My mother didn't understand either, so I never told her about the times I wandered helplessly for hours, sometimes becoming so desperate that I accepted rides from strangers. (She never warned me against the practice, and luckily none of the drivers who picked me up ever hurt me.)

Phil explained that I had the symptoms of a brain problem called dyscalculia—the mathematical and spatial equivalent of dyslexia. At last I understood why I could get so turned around on a route I'd traveled many times and why I had such problems with numbers, frequently reversing them.

Growing up, I'd kept these problems as secret as I could, hoping no one would realize how stupid I was. Although I got good grades by studying hard in math class and getting by on my aptitude for writing and reading, I felt incompetent and was terrified someone would find out how inept I truly was.

Like my mom, Phil was so fluent with directions that he could, at any given moment, tell you which way was north. But he never made me feel like a failure because of my directional problems, and he helped me accept them as just another interesting aspect of myself.

When we'd begun dating, Phil and I had started sampling wine together. I thought it was such a sophisticated thing to do that there could be nothing wrong with it.

After we married, we moved to Seattle, where, at the University of Washington, Phil taught cartography and I finished my degree in English. Three years later, in 1973, we moved to Madison when Phil got a job at the University of Wisconsin.

Now, three months into sobriety, I could see our marriage getting stronger. We began to have fun again, taking dancing lessons, going to concerts, hiking alongside Madison's lakes.

He said he could see how hard I was working to make positive changes in my life, and he told me he was proud of me.

I get up. I walk. I fall down. Meanwhile, I keep dancing.
—Hillel

✻ ✻ ✻

The summer after I gave up drinking was full of revelations. My meetings with Nancy, my therapist, were opening my eyes. For one thing, I began to see my mother in a different light.

When I told Nancy, "I have to spend my birthday at my mom's," she asked, "Why?"

The answer seemed obvious. My mother expected me to come, as I had every year, so I needed to do it.

But when I thought about it, I realized that maybe that's not the way it was for everybody. Phil's mother, for instance, would miss us if we couldn't come for Thanksgiving, but it wouldn't be the end of the world.

Nancy began to gently point out ways my mom had hurt me. She noted that Mom had left the parenting to my sister, who used me to fulfill her needs—and she was a very needy, demanding person. So, rather than being mothered, I'd been the one taking care of her.

"What can I do about it?" I asked.

"Just grieve," she said. "Grieve for what you missed. Then you can go on."

TURNING POINT

Grieve the losses in your life—not just the obvious ones like the people you lose to death and divorce but the ones that occur every time you make a change—by moving, leaving a job, or quitting an old habit. Even positive change involves loss, and you need to acknowledge it before you can embrace the good things.

Grieve, too, for losses from your early life. Feel the lack of the childhood you wish you'd had as well as dreams that have died and fantasies that won't come true.

Don't forget to mourn the death of your addiction. Your drug was your friend, always there when your feelings became too much to bear, and you need to lament its loss just as if a friend has died. You also need to feel sorrow for your old life, the years you lost to your addiction, and the person you used to be. You can miss your drug of choice without using again. Feel the feelings, talk about them, then release them.

What losses might you need to mourn?_____
_____
_____

– J.M.

✧ ✧ ✧

That summer, as the time for the singing tour of Greece drew near, my anxieties escalated. I'd signed up for the tour in April, just eleven days after I quit drinking, back when I was adding everything interesting I could find to fill up the sober hours. Now, three months later, I realized that such a long, complicated excursion probably wasn't the smartest thing to undertake so early in sobriety.

My Women for Sobriety group must have wondered, too, if it was the best thing for me, but they never said so. They supported me wholeheartedly, were excited for me, and listened as I poured out my worries about the trip.

I told them I'd always wanted to travel and explore other cultures but wouldn't have even considered this expedition to Greece while I was drinking. I joked that I couldn't have fit all the wine bottles I needed into my suitcase.

"That says it all, doesn't it?" said Marilyn. "None of us was able to travel any distance when we had those bottles weighing us down."

"Exactly." My fears and insecurities would have burdened me too much to take such a leap. The journey to Greece was emblematic of a far greater distance I was traveling in my own psyche.

Rehearsing for our singing tour became more time-consuming as we came closer to leaving, and I was exhausted from practicing our songs every night as well as packing, unpacking, and repacking my suitcase.

I began to wish I'd never signed up to go. But it was too late to turn back.

Then, a few days before our trip, we held a concert as a dress rehearsal. After endless hours of plodding away at our separate parts, suddenly our voices melded together to create a transcendent, soaring harmony that might have been spun by angels. It was like the feeling I had in my support groups, a sense that the whole was infinitely more powerful than its pieces. The music floated, and so did I, certain for the first time that everything was as it should be.

We must accept finite disappointment, but we must never lose infinite hope.
—Martin Luther King

✧ ✧ ✧

The singing tour of Greece was like an SAT test for a recovering addict who'd spent a lifetime worrying about all the things that could go wrong. All our modes of travel, whether planes, boats, or buses, were invariably late, and the trip was a nightmare of missed connections, hours waiting in cramped spaces, and heart-pounding rushes to get places on time. I soon realized worrying didn't help things go more smoothly and there was no choice but to relax, let go, and embrace the uniqueness of every moment.

Wine flowed wherever we went, but I rarely felt tempted. There was too much to see, too much to do, too many people to get to know. For so long, I'd thought I couldn't enjoy myself without alcohol, and here I was dancing and laughing and having a marvelous time. Suddenly, alcohol was irrelevant.

In the mountain villages where we sang, the whole town would turn out for our concerts. As I watched the local people, whose lives were worlds away from my own, smiling and tapping their feet to our music, I felt a bone-deep sense of connection that reached beyond cultures and rocketed me far beyond the narrow, circumscribed life I'd led for so long.

I held on to that feeling after I got home, through the much larger journey of remaking myself. It helped me navigate the hard times to come, reminding me of what was possible.

> *The true mystery of the world is the visible, not the invisible.*
> —Oscar Wilde

✶ ✶ ✶

That fall, Marilyn asked if I'd go with her to an Adult Children of Alcoholics (ACOA) workshop. I was happy to go along to support her, but I didn't think I'd get much out of it myself. Although Dad had considered himself an alcoholic (I knew because I'd read his journals after he died), he'd quit by the time I was a toddler, so I didn't have any memories of him drinking. It didn't occur to me that he was addicted to psychotropic drugs throughout my life, so I was well-qualified to attend the workshop.

From the moment we arrived, I was dumbfounded at how much I had in common with the hundreds of other people there. Though the details varied, their stories were mine.

It was here that I talked for the first time about my father's death. It was still as clear to me as if it had happened yesterday, though I'd never spoken of it in depth before.

He was sixty-five and had just retired. His anxieties had been getting worse, and he'd been talking more persistently about suicide. He was taking a new anxiety medication, and my mother had to dole it out to him to be sure he wouldn't take too much.

On October 2, 1973, she had an especially busy day at North Central College, where she worked. She'd been coming home at noon every day to give Dad his pill, but today, she told him she might be late because she had to attend a meeting.

"Just give me the bottle," he insisted, as he did every day, and, late for work and unable to go through one more argument, she handed him the bottle of pills.

She found him when she returned home not long after noon. Though she never told me the details, I've lived them in my mind many times, imagining the horror and guilt she must have felt when she discovered his body.

I couldn't ever talk to my mother, or anyone else, about how Dad died. Whenever I mentioned his suicide, there was always a sharp silence, then an abrupt change of subject.

But now, eleven years later, I could talk about it openly, and saying the words I'd kept inside for so many years felt like heaving a long sigh. Here, at the ACOA workshop, people understood. Those who'd lived with drugs in their families had lived with suicide, too. If loved ones hadn't killed themselves, they'd threatened it often enough to make suicide a vivid reality. I could finally talk about my father's death and see people nod with understanding rather than watch their faces freeze.

In addition to being able to talk freely, I found the exercises we performed at the workshop illuminating. One speaker had us draw our family of origin, using circles to represent each family member. I depicted myself as a small circle near the middle of the page, Janey as a big circle about halfway across the page, and my parents as two bigger circles, together at the farthest corner of the paper.

When we shared our pictures, I was stunned to see how many people's drawings looked like mine, with huge distances between the circles, showing a dearth of emotional connection. Either that, or the circles were actually inside one another, indicating a lack of proper boundaries between family members.

Someone asked, "But what does a normal family look like?" The speaker answered by sketching a line of circles, all the family members right next to one another but not quite touching.

Later, when I tried to explain to Phil what insights I'd gained about growing up in a dysfunctional family, he said "I think all families are dysfunctional." I asked him to use circles to portray his family, and he drew a line of circles exactly like the normal family the speaker had drawn on the blackboard.

When I showed him my circles in comparison, I could see the light go on in his mind. From that moment on, he was a companion on my journey to understanding.

TURNING POINT

Use talking to heal your soul. If you have a problem with alcohol or other drugs, it's likely you grew up in a home with problems such as drinking, abuse, and buried secrets. You may also have ended up in an unhealthy relationship with someone else.

That's why twelve-step meetings for alcoholism and drug abuse may not be enough. You may find AlAnon meetings useful, as they can help you detach from hurtful relationships and empower yourself rather than let yourself be a victim.

Adult Children of Alcoholics meetings may also help you. If you grew up in a dysfunctional home, you're likely to share some of the following characteristics: isolation, approval seeking, fear of criticism, an overdeveloped sense of responsibility, feelings of guilt associated with standing up for your rights, an attraction to people you can "rescue" and care for, avoidance of feelings, fear of abandonment, low self-esteem, and a tendency to be what others want rather than being yourself. Talking about these symptoms with those who understand is medicine for your soul.

– J.M.

✫ ✫ ✫

Shortly after I celebrated my first year of sobriety, something happened that altered my life forever. Although I was feeling good about the healthy changes I was making, my progress still seemed way too slow. I often became inundated with feelings of sadness, and I didn't know what to do about it.

Then one day, talking with a woman from my support group, I mentioned how guilty I felt about not having been a better mother to Andrea.

"Have you told Andrea how you feel?" she asked.

It was such a simple suggestion, yet it turned out to be the most powerful advice I'd ever received.

When Andrea stopped by the next day, I seized the chance. "There's something I want to tell you," I said. "I wasn't the mother to you I wish I'd been. I did so many things wrong, and I wish I'd done a much, much better job. You deserved the best mother in the world, and I let you down. I love you so much, and I'm so sorry."

"That's okay, Mom," she said. "You did the best you could, and I think you did a good job. I'm glad you're my mother."

Her words took my breath away.

Those quiet words of forgiveness opened the door for us to talk more directly than ever before. We had an honest dialogue about my drinking, and I told her I knew that alcohol had made me unpredictable, inconsistent, and dishonest. I'd lied to her, pretending there was nothing wrong, just as my parents had lied to me when they told me, "Don't worry about it. Everything's fine." Because I was constantly lying to myself, I'd been incapable of the honesty Andrea deserved.

I'd vowed to do a better job with her than my parents did with me, and yet I'd repeated all their mistakes—sending her mixed messages like my mother did, being moody and hard to live with like my father, trying to control everything, including Andrea, rather than accepting her the way she was and simply loving her.

"I always knew you loved me," she said. "Whenever I was hurt or had a really bad problem, you were always the one I came to. Your love was the one thing I was always sure of."

Those words were a balm to my heart.

We talked all afternoon, and it was as if she lifted a mountain from my shoulders. I'd never felt so light and free. Her forgiveness was a huge step toward forgiving myself. That would take much longer, but my healing began that day.

TURNING POINT

Do you need to apologize to someone in your life? Here's how to be sure your apology is effective:
- Be specific about what you did and whom you hurt.
- Begin with the word "I." Use active rather than passive voice ("I'm sorry I misunderstood," rather than "I regret that this misunderstanding happened.")
- Take responsibility for your behavior. Express remorse. Include a promise that you won't repeat the offense. Offer restitution—a concrete act that will help mend the relationship.
- Make the apology in person if you can. If that's impossible, a phone call followed by a letter is often the best alternative. If you must use email, follow up as soon as possible with an in-person, phone, or letter apology.

- Practice your apology, writing it down and going over it aloud a few times before delivering it.

   —from *Effective Apology* by John Kador

– J.M.

✲ ✲ ✲

More than anything else, confiding my worries to the women in my support group heartened me and gave me the courage to take more risks. I chipped away at my phobias, forcing myself to go new places despite my fear of becoming irretrievably lost, to take elevators even though I was claustrophobic, to face the many things that scared me.

The biggest challenge came during my second year of sobriety when I was asked to lead a writing workshop in Nashville. I'd been terrified of public speaking since seventh grade when I won a writing contest, stood in front of the whole school to give my acceptance speech, and froze. As my blood thundered in my ears and I struggled to keep from fainting, I jettisoned my talk, said a quick thank-you, and collapsed into my chair.

That debacle colored my entire life. It dictated that I would never become a teacher, a trial lawyer, or any of the other tempting jobs that required standing in front of a group. I'd even declined a number of awards because they required acceptance speeches, and nothing was worth reliving that near-death experience.

Now, however, I was tired of hiding away in fear. I knew the way to grow was to keep trying things, stretching myself a little more each time. The best way to strengthen myself, I thought, was to test myself by doing something that seemed way too hard and surviving—assuming that I did survive.

Luckily, I had two months to get ready for the workshop. I started planning and writing my script immediately, and I also signed up for a public-speaking course.

On the first night of the course, the instructor asked each of us to give a short speech. When it was my turn, my heart thudded against my chest like the wings of a desperate bird against its cage. I had to gasp out the words because I couldn't get enough breath. It was torture. I decided then and there not to come back.

But over the next week, I changed my mind. I had to try this. I needed to conquer this phobia. I showed up for the second class, and the one after that.

That course was my savior. What I learned there was helpful far beyond the Nashville workshop. Our teacher imparted many useful tips, like using breathing exercises to calm down and viewing butterflies in the stomach as excitement and anticipation rather than fear. On the last night of class, while still nervous when I rose to give my speech, I was thrilled to find that I could speak with confidence and without the dread of throwing up or passing out.

✲ ✲ ✲

A STEP ON THE JOURNEY

Practice square breathing. Inhale while silently counting to four. Hold for a count of four. Exhale for four counts. Hold for a count of four. Keep repeating. You can do this anytime—while in a meeting, while driving, while pumping gas. Once it comes naturally, you can use this technique to calm yourself any time you feel nervous or unsettled in any way.

– J.M.

In the week before the workshop, I spent every spare minute going over the words I would use, honing them, practicing till I knew every one by heart. I relied heavily on my friends and my therapist, Nancy, to help me with my worries.

At my last therapy session before leaving for Nashville, Nancy reminded me to use my new message to myself: Life is to be enjoyed rather than endured. Have fun with it, she said. Look forward to the new people you'll meet. Relish the experience!

"You carry your goodness, resourcefulness, and smartness with you wherever you go. You can handle whatever comes along," she said.

The day before I left, I had lunch with Marilyn, my friend from Women for Sobriety. "You're going to do great," she told me.

"You really think so?"

"I *know* so. I believe in you," she said.

With words like that, I thought, a person could do anything.

> *The trick is not to rid your stomach of butterflies but to make them fly in formation.*
> —Outward Bound

✻ ✻ ✻

In Nashville, all the hours of writing and rewriting, rehearsing and re-rehearsing slid into place, and the workshop went without a hitch. Most surprising of all, I found that I was having fun. It was a thrill when the audience laughed at my jokes and when I saw lights going on in their eyes as a result of my words. I realized how much I enjoyed sharing insights with other people and decided that I wanted to add more such experiences to my life.

I couldn't wait to get home and tell my friends about my adventure.

That workshop in Nashville gave me the confidence to start reaching out to nonprofit leaders in my community. They were inspiring people whose lives were given over to helping others and improving the world, and they became role models for me.

I started speaking at more meetings and to more diverse groups. With every speech, I gained far more than I gave. I could almost feel my brain changing and expanding as I stretched myself into doing new things.

✯ ✯ ✯

The spring of 1988 brought two epic changes that would resound throughout my life. First, Andrea's daughter, Shyloh, was born. From the beginning, I adored being a grandmother. I could love her without the dread of fatal error that had weighed me down as a mother. It was the opening of an unexpected new world.

The second transformation occurred when my therapist, Nancy, asked me to keep a feelings log. "When your mood swings low," she said, "see what messages you gave yourself to make you feel that way. Once you isolate those thoughts, you can replace them with more positive ones."

After keeping the feelings journal for a few weeks, I told Nancy it had helped me more than anything else in keeping my depression at bay. She gave me some books by Albert Ellis, who wrote about rational emotive therapy. The method goes by many names, like cognitive therapy, solution focused therapy, and rational emotive living. The point is to find the irrational messages you're giving yourself and replace them with rational ones.

It may sound simple, but when you have a lifetime of illogical messages to undo, it's harder than it seems. For me, the toughest part was recognizing the messages crowding my head as irrational in the first place. My brain was a kaleidoscope of crazy thoughts, mostly in my mother's voice, such as "You should do things the right way." It was a big step for me to realize, first, that "should" statements weren't rational and, second, that there was no "right" or "wrong," just a plethora of different perspectives.

I could see that changing my thoughts could change my emotions, which could alter my behavior. If I changed my behavior, I could change my world.

But making that switch required practice. I was still working on it one day in October when, on the way home from work, it started snowing so hard I had to turn the windshield wipers and defroster on high and still could barely see.

I felt anger and depression wash over me. It shouldn't be snowing like this so early in the season.

Then I reminded myself to think differently. First I told myself I shouldn't feel so bad about the snow, that it was beautiful, and I should enjoy it. Instantly I realized I was using "should" statements. So, instead, I told myself, "I'd feel better if I let myself see the good things about the snow," and I could feel my energy shift and become more positive.

I was taking control of my thoughts, and that seemed like the most powerful thing I'd ever done.

MOMENT OF TRUTH

Listen to the self-talk in your mind, and replace negative messages with positive ones. Here are some self-talk do's and don'ts:

- Don't label yourself with thoughts like "I'm a failure." Tell yourself, "I've accomplished many things and can continue to do so."
- Avoid words like never, always, or can't. Rather than "I always screw up, I can't do anything right, I'll never succeed," try "I made a mistake, and I'll learn from it. I can do things differently next time. I'll keep improving."
- Don't compare yourself to others. Instead of "She's more successful than I am," recognize that we're all good at some things, and concentrate on your strong points.
- Eliminate "should" and "ought to" from your vocabulary. If you find yourself making "should" statements, write them down, then rewrite them in ways that leave room for choice and flexibility. For example: Instead of "I should have gone to bed earlier," you might say, "I plan to go to bed earlier in the future so I won't be so tired the next day." Rather than "I should study," consider, "I think I'll study now because I want to learn this material." Replace "I ought to quit smoking" with "I'd most likely feel better if I quit smoking."
- Don't think of anyone making you feel a certain way, as in "She makes me so angry." A better way to look at it: "I let myself feel angry when she does that."

Write down a negative message you received growing up and replace it with a more self-affirming one: _____
_____
_____
_____

– J.M.

✧ ✧ ✧

Soon after that breakthrough, Nancy invited me to join a women's therapy group she led. I immediately liked and identified with the five other women.

At one meeting, a few months after I joined the group, Nancy asked me to tell the others about an assignment she'd given me, to record five things a day I felt good about. I said that often all I could think of were negatives—I didn't drink, didn't let Andrea's bad mood upset me, didn't let myself get depressed when I came home to a dark, empty house. I was amazed at how reassuring everyone was, telling me that those weren't really negatives, that they represented big shifts in my life and it was okay to still be working through these changes.

Beth, another woman in our group, talked about the pain of a recent break-up. "What's a co-dependent to do when she has no one to co-depend with?" she asked. "I've been so concentrated on this relationship that there's a huge void within me now."

I felt a jolt as I realized that the void Beth mentioned was the "black hole" I'd felt inside as I tried to be what others wanted me to be—the secret I'd confided to Phil with such apprehension all those years ago. So I wasn't the only one with that emptiness within. Nor was I alone in trying to fill that cavern in misguided ways. I felt a rush of gratitude toward Beth for putting into words what I'd hidden for so long.

Others in the circle were nodding. "Yeah," someone said. "That's a good question. I'm actually unclear about what co-dependency is anyway."

"You don't need to be in a relationship to be a co-dependent," Nancy said. "Your behavior alone makes you co-dependent. You're a co-dependent when you see yourself only as you relate to others."

"But what's the solution?" Beth asked. "How do I stop the co-dependency?"

"The answer," Nancy said, "is to nurture yourself. You have to put the same energy into yourself that you put into the most intense, consuming relationship you've ever had. It won't be easy. It'll take time. But you've made a good start, just by coming here."

A STEP ON THE JOURNEY

The road toward self-esteem:

Write down three things you like about yourself (examples: a friendly personality, a kind heart, a good brain, a sense of humor, an active imagination). _____
_____
_____

Write down three ways you could nurture yourself (examples: go to a concert, get a massage, talk to a friend). _____
_____
_____

Every day this week, write down five accomplishments. It needn't be something big. It can be any positive thing you've done, anything you feel good about. It can be as simple as eating nutritious food, going to a support group, flossing your teeth, keeping a promise, wearing your seatbelt, asking for help, or being honest with yourself. It may simply be not doing drugs or not overeating—anything that keeps you on the path to your goals. You may find you're doing more positive things with your life than you're giving yourself credit for.

– J.M.

Toward the end of the therapy group meeting, I mentioned a dream I'd had in which I became angry when my mother told me I should pay more attention. "*You're* the one who wasn't listening," I said, so furious that I flung an expensive, fragile necklace onto the floor. Instead of breaking, as I feared, the beads miraculously turned from crystal into strong, indestructible metal and became even more beautiful and luminous.

"That's a powerful dream," Nancy said, and I sensed that she was right. That dream gave me my first clue that my anger could actually be a gift. If I started expressing that anger in constructive ways rather than turning it inward, perhaps it could make me, like the beads in my dream, stronger and more resilient.

Therapy helps you go from life being the same damn thing over and over to life being one damn thing after another.
—John Weakland

✲ ✲ ✲

I had a chance soon enough to test my new knowledge. It was time for a trip to Illinois to see my mother and sister.

These visits continued to be hard. But I'd begun to see them less as torture sessions than as scientific expeditions to study an odd tribe. If nothing else, at least they provided good material for my therapy and support groups.

As usual, I stopped at Janey's on the way to Mom's. Janey and I were able to laugh about Mom's ways in a kind of family shorthand no one knew but my sister and me.

"Mom bought me a new mattress," Janey said, "but then she got mad because I wouldn't buy a cover for it. I kept telling her I couldn't afford it, and she got madder and madder. So then I repeated to her all the disparaging things she'd said to me that day, like 'I'd hoped you'd be rid of that big belly.'"

I could just hear Mom saying that. Laughing, I said, "When you said that, you sounded exactly like her!"

She laughed, too. "You just can't please that woman."

"Amen." We laughed again. Then we looked at each other and laughed even harder. No matter what, Janey and I always ended up laughing over some absurdity or other.

Later, at Mom's house, Mom brought up the fight with Janey and said it happened because she tried to tease Janey, "and Janey never gets the joke." Mom often claimed she was "just teasing," but it never seemed like it to me.

Throughout the visit, I was able to stand up to Mom when she made unreasonable statements in a way I'd never done before. Better yet, I could *see* the insanity of her words for the first time.

When she said, "You're too skinny!" I told her how hard I'd been working at the gym and that I was happy with my body.

When I showed her the latest issue of the magazine I edited, and she responded, "You're wasting your talents with that little magazine in Madison; you should be in New York editing *The New Yorker*," I said I loved my job, was happy in Madison, and didn't feel my life was a waste.

After reading the letter Andrea had given me to pass on to her, Mom said, "So Andrea's still into tattooing."

"Yes," I said. In her twenties now, Andrea had learned tattooing, and her unique, colorful designs decorated her arms and legs.

"Don't you ever get a tattoo!" Mom ordered me.

"It's my life," I shot back. I wished I'd been able to say that to her a long time before.

She looked startled but not upset. I realized that I'd always feared my anger would destroy her. But, just as the necklace in my dream survived my anger, it seemed that she—and I—could survive it too.

Break a vase and the love that reassembles the fragments is stronger than the love which took its symmetry for granted when it was whole.
—Derek Walcott

✲ ✲ ✲

Mom had invited Janey for dinner, but when Janey arrived she said she could only stay a minute. Mom had prepared the special dinner Janey had ordered (hot dogs, macaroni and cheese, and chocolate cake), so she insisted that Janey stay.

That set Janey off. "Don't tell me what to do!" she roared, gathering up her things and storming out.

In the silence that followed, I hugged Mom and said, "I know she can't help it, but it hurts to see her like that."

Mom didn't say anything, but as I held her I felt I was receiving what I'd needed when Janey had her first breakdown and I was so confused and scared. Those were the very words I wished Mom had said to me then. "She can't help it, but I know it hurts to see her like that."

I knew my mother couldn't help, either, the fact that she hadn't been able to give me what I'd longed for.

Like me, she was imperfect, but she'd done her best. There was no way to change the past, and at that moment, I forgave her everything.

Nothing worth doing is completed in our lifetime;
Therefore, we are saved by hope.
Nothing true or beautiful or good makes complete sense in any immediate context of history;
Therefore, we are saved by faith.
Nothing we do, however virtuous, can be accomplished alone;
Therefore, we are saved by love.
No virtuous act is quite as virtuous from the standpoint of our friend or foe as from our own;
Therefore, we are saved by the final form of love, which is forgiveness.
—Reinhold Niebuhr

✲ ✲ ✲

My life was full, but I knew there was something left undone: I needed to confront the fear of mental illness that had haunted me for so long. I decided to attend a support group for family members of people who were mentally ill. It would be hard, because I'd never discussed that part of my life in any depth, but those deeply rooted feelings were something I had to explore.

The Alliance on Mental Illness office was downtown, and I needed to park several blocks away. I had that nervous feeling I always got in parking structures at night. Out on the street, my anxiety escalated as a group of teenage boys started following me, calling out jeers.

I kept my eyes straight ahead, walked briskly, and tried to draw myself up tall (not easy when you're only five feet in height). The boys got closer and some of them ran ahead so that they could look back into my face. I glared into their eyes, willing them to leave.

"Hey, baby, don't you want to party with us?" one of the boys demanded, and they all hooted with laughter.

My heart jackhammering, I hugged my purse tighter to my side, hoping they wouldn't notice and take it as a challenge.

"Come on, don't be shy," another boy taunted. They were closing in, forming a circle around me, all a good foot taller than me. My whole body was shivering.

Thank God, the building I was looking for was just ahead, and the number on the side was big enough to read. If I'd had to search around for the right address, my attempt to appear confident and unintimidated would have crumbled.

Slipping into the building, I merged quickly with a group waiting for the elevator. I glanced back and saw that the boys hadn't followed me inside, and I sighed with relief.

When I found the room where the meeting was being held, two other women were already seated at the long table. They were deep in conversation, and it was clear that they were friends.

I wanted to tell them about my hair-raising walk from the parking structure, but their chatter excluded me. So I sat across the table from them, breathing deeply and letting my heartbeat begin to slow.

The group facilitator arrived a few minutes later and had us introduce ourselves. It turned out that the two women, Kathy and Joy, both had mentally ill sons.

Joy started talking about Cheryl, her daughter, and Ted, her mentally ill son. "Cheryl seems to resent the time I spend trying to help Ted. I get so mad at her. I have enough on my mind without worrying about her, too."

That was the very message I'd received growing up—that I'd best be trouble-free so that Mom could devote all her energy to my father's and sister's mental problems. She'd never said it aloud, but now, hearing it put into words like this, shame and guilt flooded me.

"I know," Kathy said, nodding at Joy and leaning closer to her. "Blake's sister, Jennie, is the same way. She wants *me* to spend more time with *her*! As if I don't have enough to do with all Blake's problems."

"Yes, and Cheryl's troubles are so minor compared to what Ted is going through. I just have no patience for her whining," said Joy.

I'd always suspected that's what my mother thought about me, that I was too greedy for attention, that I should have been more unselfish and unassuming.

"I know! Guess what Jennie said to me: 'I have needs too'! I felt like saying, 'Oh, shut up. You think you've got it bad? You have no idea.'"

Their words awakened a fear that had stalked me all my life—that I'd been such a burden to my family that they would have been better off without me. That dread was so deep it made my fear of the gang on the street seem insignificant.

It was so hard to keep listening that I let my mind drift away from the room. I looked out the window at the crescent moon, golden against the black sky.

I continued watching the moon as I walked back to the parking structure after the meeting. I found myself wishing that the taunting boys would return and that this time they would kill me.

I thought of the oblivion wine used to provide me, and I wanted a drink, but, even more, I wanted to die.

Perhaps everything terrible in us is, in its deepest being, something helpless that wants help from us.
—Rainer Maria Rilke

When I got home from the meeting, I went straight to bed. I'd found that when I ran out of ways to keep going when life staggered me, sleep was one thing that always worked.

The women's conversation had underscored my worst feelings about myself. I couldn't bear to think about it, much less discuss it. It would be quite a while before I told anyone about that night.

There is a time, when passing through light, that you walk in your own shadow.
—Keri Hulme

✭ ✭ ✭

In the days that followed, I tried to put the meeting out of my mind and concentrate on other things.

One thing I wanted to do was find a place to worship. "Alcoholism is a void of spirituality," the psychiatrist Carl Jung once said, and I knew it was true. To fill that vacuum, I needed to get in touch with something infinite, with my truest self, and with other people on the same seekers' path.

After sampling a variety of churches, I was drawn to the Unitarian Society and began to attend regularly. Even better than the Sunday services, I enjoyed the classes held at the Unitarian Meeting House, everything from a course on philosophy to a group that focused on women's creativity.

As always, meeting with like-minded people, talking about common problems, was the best nourishment for my spirit. I also received practical advice, like the value of using affirmations to comfort myself when I hit a tough patch. One of my favorites was, "There is joy and purpose."

TURNING POINT

Use affirmations to claim your power. Affirmations are positive statements you tell yourself to change your life for the better. Here are a few examples of affirmations you can use or adapt to fit your life. Say them many times a day, especially at bedtime so they'll implant themselves firmly in your subconscious mind.

- I love and accept myself just the way I am today.
- I am confident and capable.
- I love life and value every moment.
- All is as it's meant to be.
- I accept what is now and what is to come.

An affirmation is a strong, positive statement that something is *already* so.
—Shakti Gawain

Write down an affirmation for yourself, and plan to repeat it at least ten times today: ____
____

–J.M.

☆ ☆ ☆

Even with the progress I'd made, sometimes I still felt a great weight pressing down on me. I couldn't help feeling I was missing something. Somewhere was a door I hadn't opened.

I didn't realize that door was right in front of me. But I wouldn't find the key to unlock it in any of the places I was looking, not at Adult Children of Alcoholics meetings or through affirmations, or even at church.

No, the answer came from another direction altogether.

☆ ☆ ☆

Dreams are often most profound when they seem the most crazy.
—Sigmund Freud

It was a year later that I had two dreams. Something told me they were important and I'd better listen to what they were telling me. But, as with so many dreams, their meaning wasn't immediately clear.

In the first dream, I had two fluffy, light-as-air pets who were very precious to me. They were about the size of a golf ball and a baseball, as delicate as dandelion fluff, and just as likely to blow away with the wind. So I was looking for cages in which to keep them safe.

I searched for a long time and was becoming discouraged when a sleazy man sidled up and whispered that he had some cages he would give me. He led me down a dark, smelly alley, filled with rotting garbage, jagged edges of broken glass, and the putrid carcasses of dead animals.

I would never have followed such a creepy guy into such a squalid place if I hadn't needed so badly to protect my pets.

At the end of the alley, the sleazy man showed me the cages and said casually, "This is where I put my aunt's body after I killed her."

My revulsion wasn't as great as my joy at finding a way to keep my beloved pets safe. As I gently placed them in their new homes, they were as warm, vulnerable, and soft in my hands as newly hatched chicks.

The dream ended with me hurrying to the car with my pets in their new cages, feeling utter relief and a fluttering of hope.

In the second dream, Phil told me he had a wonderful present for me—something I wanted more than anything else in the world. I followed him across a snowy campus into a building and down a hallway. As we neared the door at the end of the hall, however, I felt a stab of doom so overpowering that I could hardly move. Phil pulled me along and flung the door open. I only glimpsed the room before panic overtook me and I whirled and fled. I kept running till my breath was gone and I collapsed in the snow.

Phil caught up to me and asked what was wrong. I didn't know what to say, because the room that had terrified me had looked quite ordinary. All I'd seen were walls of file cabinets and shelves filled with books.

Phil told me that his gift to me was this library, where I had access to all the wisdom in the world, not only through books but through expert counselors, psychiatrists, and teachers, who would answer any question in the world for me.

It did sound like the perfect gift. So why was I still so scared? Why did I feel sure that I couldn't bear to enter that room again?

> *The road that has always been open to that place of wisdom is the dream.*
> —Rhianon Haniman

Both dreams puzzled me. I wrote them down and decided I'd wait awhile before trying to decipher them.

Then, a few months later, the Unitarian Society offered a course in dream analysis, and I began to attend. Every night in class, we each shared several dreams, and the rest of the group took turns describing what the dreams meant to them. What amazed me—what still had the power to astound me even after all my experiences in support groups—was the group's insight. No matter how simple or complex a dream seemed, it gained incredible, revelatory meaning when we combined our many points of view.

A STEP ON THE JOURNEY

Trust your inner guide—your dreams. Listen to that wise voice inside you. Sign up for a class on dreams to train yourself to remember, record, and analyze your dreams, and use them as your best advisors. No one else knows you as well as your dream self does.

> Dreams give you access to all the layers of your subconscious, everything you've known and sensed since you were born, to things you heard only peripherally and didn't register at the time. All these veins of meaning come together in a form that's unconstrained by the limits of time or space.
>
> Your dreams apply the greatest wisdom about yourself to whatever difficulties you're facing today. Often dreams will alert you to problems your conscious mind doesn't detect. There are many instances of dreams spurring people to go to the doctor, where they discover they have a life-threatening illness.
>
> Some tips: Before going to sleep, spend a few minutes considering what you'd like to dream about. Open your mind to welcome your dream guide. When you wake from a dream, hold your head as still as possible as you reach for a pen and write down whatever you can remember, or speak into a voice recorder. Be sure to describe how the dream made you feel, as dreams are all about connecting with your deepest emotions. Be especially alert to things that seem to make no sense, for those coded messages often contain the most important keys. As you look for your dreams' meanings, consider all the figures in your dreams as parts of yourself.
>
> Don't discount the power of your dreams. Albert Einstein's theory of relativity came to him in a dream. Who knows what treasures your subconscious holds? Take the time to dig for those riches, and you'll embark on the greatest adventure of your life—the journey that will take you to your authentic self.
>
> – J.M.

Before class one evening, I started reading through my dream diary, and I came upon the two mysterious dreams. This time, though, I saw they were both telling me the same thing, and it truly was a message I needed to hear.

The first dream—the two-creatures dream—was saying that, to find what I needed, I had to walk a path that terrified me and face the worst part of myself.

The second dream—the library dream—was telling me that the thing I wanted most in the world—to know myself—was also what tormented and frightened me the most. Every molecule of my being resisted looking into the hidden parts of myself. Yet I couldn't go on living as I was, with so much of myself buried and unexamined.

That night at class, I described the two dreams. With everyone's input, I gained even more insights. I realized that the two creatures represented me as a child and as an adult. Both needed me to protect them, nurture them, and care for them by ceasing to hide from my fears.

I realized I was the sleazy guy, too. I was the one who murdered my aunt, which stood for the worst thing a person could do (probably because even my dream self couldn't accept the idea of murdering my mother). Once I stopped fearing these dark regions of my soul, I could take care of the vulnerable parts of myself.

I suddenly recognized the room in the second dream—the room with all the books, counselors, and people to answer my deepest questions. It was the office of the Alliance on Mental Illness, where there were support groups, meetings, and an extensive library of resources.

It was indeed the thing that scared me to my core. I'd lived most of my life hiding from my dread that I would become mentally ill like my father and sister. The hellishness of that possibility was so great that I'd buried it where only my dream self could unearth it.

I remembered something I'd read years ago that had stuck with me: The most important thing you can do in life is to find the thing that frightens you the most and then run toward it.

My greatest fear was finally clear to me. All I had to do now was to take a deep breath and start running.

Healing is embracing what is most feared; healing is opening what has been closed, softening what has hardened into obstruction; healing is learning to trust life.
—Jeanne Achterberg

✵ ✵ ✵

Gathering my courage, I called Vicki, a woman I'd met at a lecture about mental illness, and asked if she'd go with me to an Alliance on Mental Illness support group. If there were two of us, I figured, it wouldn't be so scary walking down the dark streets from the parking structure.

"I haven't been to an AMI support group in over a year," I told Vicki when I called her. "I only went once, and it was such a disaster I thought I'd never go again." I explained about the pack of teenagers harassing me and, even worse, the angry mothers.

"Listening to them made me feel so small," I said. "Yet it was as if I should be even smaller—as if I shouldn't take up so much room or have so many needs of my own."

I'll never forget the compassion in Vicki's voice as she told me, "I'm so sorry you went through that, but guess what—they moved the support-group meetings to a place with a parking lot so you don't have to walk in the dark. And they changed the composition of the groups. Now there's one for parents and spouses and another for siblings and children of the mentally ill. Believe me, it's a much better match."

A STEP ON THE JOURNEY

Discover what you fear the most, and put your arms around it. The thing that frightens you is never as bad as the fear of it. The key is to look that fear in the face, feel it, and move forward in spite of it.

Confide your fear to your journal and to a friend or therapist. Write it out, and talk it out.

Every step toward that menacing thing will lessen the fear and build your courage. Eventually, you'll be braver than you ever thought possible.

What is your deepest fear? Write it here:_____
_____

– J.M.

✢ ✢ ✢

That second Alliance support group was light years away from the first. While the mothers in the earlier group had deepened my feelings of remorse and worthlessness, this group did just the opposite. They listened, and they understood.

I spoke of things that had seemed beyond the power of language—my guilt for becoming the favored daughter that Janey once was and for having a good life while hers was in tatters, my revulsion and fear of ending up like her, my anger at her for manipulating and controlling me and the whole family. I could almost feel myself get lighter and lighter as I let out the burdens of these secrets.

I told them how Janey sometimes called me on the phone twenty times a day—drunk, incoherent, yelling words at me that I couldn't decipher. She'd told me how upset she got when people didn't understand her, so I pretended to understand. It didn't matter, because the next day she wouldn't remember having talked to me.

"I know what you mean," said Lena, whose sister, like Janey, was schizophrenic. "Sometimes I wonder if anything I say to my sister matters. There's no way I can help her, no way I can cure her; she's going to be crazy forever, no matter what I do."

Kate, who had a bipolar brother, said she didn't have any intimate friendships because she couldn't feel close to anyone who didn't understand about her brother. And nobody understood—except for people like us.

Hearing how hard the others were on themselves, how they couldn't forgive themselves for things that clearly weren't their fault, made me feel kinder toward myself. Many of the stories they told were heartbreaking. But we also shared the funny moments, and there were many of those, too. Absurdity and irony are built into life with someone who's mentally ill. All of us were well acquainted with the need for black humor to deal with heartache.

Sometimes we erupted into bursts of laughter at things that wouldn't seem the least bit amusing to most people. What a relief to be able to laugh instead of cry.

When the meeting was over, I hated to leave. At the door, I said good-bye to people who had been strangers just two hours before but now felt like friends.

Starting toward my car at the other end of the parking lot, I smiled up at the starry sky, and I flew.

> *Listening is a magnetic and strange thing, a creative force. The friends who listen to us are the ones we move toward. When we are listened to, it creates us, makes us unfold and expand.*
> —Karl Menninger

✢ ✢ ✢

I knew even then, soaring across the parking lot, that I'd reached a juncture in my life's journey. It was like that moment driving to college from Illinois to Colorado when, after days crossing those unchanging, never-ending plains, I came to the top of a hill and, suddenly, stretched out before me to the horizon were those majestic, snow-capped Rocky Mountains. That view had so stirred my younger, teenaged self that I think it was the main reason I decided to go to college in Boulder—to change the landscape of my life.

Now I'd come upon a landscape even more breathtaking and life-altering. It was as if all the steps I'd been taking had been in a series of concentric circles, each a little larger than the one before but always in the same winding pattern. Every breakthrough I'd made had expanded the circles outward, but no matter how giant the strides I took, they moved me around and around instead of forward.

All at once the walls surrounding those circles fell away and I could see the rest of my life laid out in striking detail, all the way to a new horizon. Up until that moment, since the day I quit drinking, I'd discovered myriad reasons why I drank. I'd learned I had a genetic disposition to be an alcoholic and that drinking took my mind off the terrifying abyss I'd felt at the center of my being. But the true source of that awful hollow had eluded me.

Now it was plain—so obvious I was shocked I hadn't seen it before—that the source of that chasm within me, the root cause I'd been refusing to face, was the mental illness in my family. The gaping wound I'd been trying to heal with alcohol stemmed from that night when I was fourteen and woke in the middle of my sister's psychotic break to find that I'd lost the person who meant the most to me in the world to the cruelest disease imaginable.

I'd built a cage around me to protect myself from the impact of that memory, and my dreams had been tapping on that cage, offering me the key that would release me. It was my dreams that had led me here, to this run-of-the-mill building and this ordinary parking lot.

Because I'd finally listened to those dreams, it was now a simple matter to reach out, take that key, and slide it into the lock. As quickly as that, the door swung open and I stepped out into a new life. From that instant on, the laborious steps I'd been taking became ridiculously easy.

> *Blackbird singing in the dead of night*
> *Take these broken wings and learn to fly*
> *All your life*
> *You were only waiting*
> *For this moment to arrive.*
> —The Beatles, "Blackbird"

✣ ✣ ✣

Almost immediately, the anger I'd harbored toward Janey melted away, replaced by a dawning empathy and the desire to help her as much as I could. That's because I'd begun spending many hours in the Alliance's library, devouring the books, videos, and other resources there.

Education is power, and the more time I spent at the Alliance offices, the more powerful I felt. I'd read a lot of books about mental illness in the past, but they'd only confused me. Books like *David and Lisa* and *I Never Promised You a Rose Garden* romanticized mental illness, while others painted the mentally ill as serial killers and monsters. It wasn't till I brought home *Surviving Schizophrenia* from the Alliance library that I understood the disease for the first time.

This landmark book was written by the psychiatrist E. Fuller Torrey, who himself had a schizophrenic sister. In language both scientific and readable, factual and empathetic, he describes exactly what it's like to have the disease of schizophrenia.

Ask yourself, Torrey says, how you would feel if your brain played tricks on you and unseen voices shouted at you. Imagine trying to have a conversation while dozens of TV sets blared different messages at the same time. That's what Janey was going through all those times she disrupted family gatherings by taking an overdose of pills and being rushed to the hospital. Those weren't bids for attention as I'd assumed but desperate attempts to make the nonsensical voices and delusions stop.

"If a worse disease than schizophrenia exists," Torrey writes, "it has not come to light."

I was astounded at how little I'd known about mental illness beyond common myths and stereotypes. It reminded me of one of Stephen Colbert's great lines on *The Colbert Report*: "In order to maintain an untenable position, you have to be actively ignorant."

But fear will do that to you, encourage you to live with blinders on. Now that I could see the big picture, the world was a whole new place.

Every page in Torrey's book opened that world more for me. I learned that schizophrenia almost always starts in early adulthood, as it had for Janey. The chances of my acquiring it now, in my forties, were minuscule. Finally, I could put aside my terror that I'd end up like her.

I realized that I, like my father, was prone to the emotional disease of depression, which was far different from the brain disease of schizophrenia. Dreadful as depression was, at least I was able to make meaningful connections with others, and to me that's what life was all about.

As Torrey points out in his book, "Compassion follows understanding." Now that I understood the disease for the first time, I was able to view Janey with real compassion.

There's no way to describe how life-changing that book was for me. To understand schizophrenia was to understand myself. Where so often in the past I'd felt there was no place for me, now I found my place everywhere.

I have always imagined that Paradise will be a kind of library.
—Jorge Luis Borges

A STEP ON THE JOURNEY

Keep learning. Education is never wasted. It renews you. It helps you discover who you are. If your education was interrupted, consider going back to school, either full-time or part-time. Getting a degree is self-affirming, but you don't need to work toward degrees to educate yourself. There are all kinds of online courses, evening classes, and offerings through local community organizations. Even a class that lasts just one or two evenings can transform your life. A painting class can open up a well of creativity you never knew was inside you. A class in literature or philosophy can connect you to people in other generations who felt and thought as you do. You can always learn on your own, by reading, exploring the Internet, asking questions. Teachers are all around you, every day.

What would you like to learn about?_____

_____

_____

– J.M.

✼ ✼ ✼

The people in my Alliance support group, especially Lena and Kate, became fast friends. With their support, I was able to set limits with Janey for the first time. I told Janey I had a hard time dealing with her constant phone calls, especially the ones that woke me throughout the night. Please, I said, don't call me more than five times a day, and don't call before 7 a.m. or after 10 p.m.

We had a good laugh over the results at the next support group. "Now she calls me every morning at precisely 7:01 and every night at 9:59," I said.

"We should have predicted that!" said Lena.

"And of course she calls me exactly five times a day."

"But what a huge improvement over the twenty daily calls you used to get," said Kate.

"Absolutely," I agreed. "It makes all the difference, knowing I can go to bed and I won't be awakened by Janey obsessing about something or other. But I think the biggest change is my own attitude. I can see now that she's not trying to annoy me. She simply can't help herself. She needs these boundaries as much as I do. I can't believe it didn't occur to me earlier that I had the right to set such limits."

A STEP ON THE JOURNEY

Care for yourself by setting boundaries. A vital part of taking care of yourself is to set limits with other people. These steps will make the process easier:

- Look closely at any relationship that makes you feel uncomfortable. Is it too intrusive or too distant? Boundary needs are different for each of us, and it's important to find a balance that feels right for you.
- Speak with the other person, explaining your needs with clarity and compassion. Make it clear what you will and won't tolerate.
- Don't back down. You have every right to make the choices that are best for you. Give the other person time to adjust to the new boundaries, but don't let them take advantage of you.
- If the other person refuses to respect your needs, you may need to take a break from that person. During that break, notice whether you feel less stress and more energy, purpose, and passion in your life. Perhaps you'll decide that you can find healthier relationships elsewhere.

Is there a relationship in which you could create new boundaries? To whom would you like to talk about boundary issues? _____

_____
_____
_____

– J.M.

✿ ✿ ✿

Kate, Lena, and I started reading and discussing *Hidden Victims* by Julie Tallard, who says it's typical in families of the mentally ill not to talk, because no one understands what's happening. Not talking leads to a sense of hopelessness, because feelings are never addressed, nor are possible solutions ever suggested.

When you lose a family member to death as a child or adolescent, she says, your ability to cope is damaged. In a way mental illness is worse than death because it's a chronic loss. You keep losing the person over and over.

All of us identified with that. We all felt as if our sibling had died and been replaced with a stranger. Yet we never stopped hoping that our loved one would be returned to us one day.

One of the exercises in the book was to write an autobiography and then read it aloud, and each of us in the group did so. When I wrote mine, I realized how big a part of my life suicide was, beginning with one of my first memories when I was around four years old. Janey was babysitting me and was furious because I wasn't behaving the way she wanted. "If you don't mind me, I'm going to kill myself," she'd said, taking a knife out of the drawer. I promised I'd be good, and she put the knife away, warning me not to tell Mom and Dad. It would be our secret.

That was the first of innumerable times she said she was going to kill herself. All my life, I was petrified I'd do something wrong and cause someone I loved to die.

When I read my autobiography to the group, it was such a relief that they understood. For them, too, the threat of suicide was very real.

Kate, Lena, and I put together a reading list of books about mental illness, and I began going to schools to give out the list and talk to the kids about my experiences. It was the most healing thing I'd ever done. It was as if I were giving myself the gift I wish someone had given me at that age—the realization that I was not alone.

TURNING POINT

Give someone what you wish had been given to you. There's no better way to mend feelings of resentment, bitterness, and longing than to think about what you need and then give it to someone else. If you wish someone had given you helpful information when you were young, gather resources for others who need such information now. If you want to be nurtured, find a person or creature you can care for. If you want someone to forgive you, give your forgiveness to them.

What do you wish had been given to you? To whom could you give that same thing now? _____
_____
_____
_____

– J.M.

> *A person should live, if only for curiosity's sake.*
> —Yiddish saying

✫ ✫ ✫

One day that summer, Janey called to say she was "off the beers." Her doctor had told her she had cirrhosis of the liver and would die if she didn't stop drinking.

She'd said many times in the past that she'd quit, but this time I could tell it was true. Her mind was clearer than it had been since she was a teenager. She remembered things from the last time we talked, and even her long-term memory, which had been burned away by electric shock treatments, was sharper. She no longer slurred her words or rambled. She made sense.

We began to have longer talks, and I found myself looking forward to her calls and staying on the phone longer. When I hung up now, it was with a smile.

After yearning for a connection with Janey my whole life, a connection I'd decided was impossible, the simple pleasure of talking like two friends, like two sisters, was almost too sweet to bear.

She started writing me several letters a day. Email hadn't been invented yet, so these were actual letters, two or three in my mailbox every morning. Most of them detailed the minute-by-minute trivialities of living. Getting papers ready for recycling. Vacuuming the living room floor. Listening to a country song. Taking a nap. Walking to the store and buying something that gave her a lift. I found something vaguely comforting in all these details.

In one letter, she said she'd decided to make a skirt. She bought the green material and cut it out but then had trouble threading the machine so her husband Paul helped her. She finished sewing the skirt and made a scarf to match. Now she was ready for her doctor's appointment Monday, where she planned to wear her new skirt and scarf. "I'm proud of myself!" she wrote.

I felt proud of her, too. This chronicling of completing something and feeling proud of doing a good job—it encapsulated life. How else do we build self-reliance except by taking on a task, doing our best, and feeling good about it afterwards?

I looked forward to seeing Janey, but she didn't want me to stop by while she was so sick and looked, she said, so ugly. The cirrhosis had given her a huge stomach, and it was so embarrassing that she didn't want me to see her.

I argued that I didn't care how she looked and that maybe I could help make her feel better. I wanted to try. But she adamantly refused, and when Janey took a stand, there was no changing her mind.

> *The only real meaning of life is the experience of it.*
> —Mark Salzman

✫ ✫ ✫

The call, when it came, took me by surprise. Phil had just returned from a fishing trip to Alaska, and we were getting ready for bed while he recounted his adventures, so I was laughing when I picked up the phone. It was Lois, Paul's mother and Janey's mother-in-law. Janey had died an hour earlier. She was fifty years old.

My heart ached when I thought of the pain she endured those last few months. I remembered how she complained yet how brave she was.

I'd always thought she would die by her own hand, but she hadn't committed suicide after all—except for the long, slow way that alcoholics kill themselves ("Suicide on the installment plan," as Laurence Peter described alcoholism). It was cirrhosis of the liver that had killed her—a combination of the alcohol and anti-psychotic medications she'd taken for most of her life.

At the end, she'd quit drinking when it was the hardest thing in the world to do. On some level, despite everything, she'd wanted to live.

How glad I was that I had made peace with my conflicted feelings about her before she died. How I would miss the one person who had known me all my life in a way no one else ever could, who had been biologically closer to me than anyone else in the world.

Do you know that disease and death must needs overtake us, no matter what we are doing? What do you wish to be doing when it overtakes you? If you have anything better to be doing when you are so overtaken, get to work on that.
—Epictetus

✧ ✧ ✧

A few months later, I turned a corner with my mother. In my therapy session one day, Nancy gave me a book called *Toxic Parents*. "You still haven't sorted out your relationship with your mom," she said. "You won't be able to move on till you do."

After reading the book, I wrote a letter, using the technique the book described. I put everything into it, all that I'd learned about myself, all the feelings I'd uncovered.

> Dear Mom,
>
> I'm going to say some things to you that I've never said before. In fact, when I started to write this letter, or even considered writing it, I told myself I couldn't tell you these things. When I thought about why, I realized that deep inside I believed that telling you the truth about my feelings would hurt you too badly, would in fact destroy you. I know that's not true, because another part of me has always admired you for your strength of character and how courageously you stand up to things. This dichotomy comes from the fact that I saw you withstand so much from Dad that I came to feel that I couldn't put any additional emotional burden on you—you had too much to bear already, putting up with his moods and emotional tirades and neediness. There was no room left for any of my feelings. I had to protect you from emotional overload.
>
> But now I realize that wasn't a job for a child. If I'd been able to discuss my feelings honestly, I wouldn't have carried so much pain inside me all my life.
>
> Many times you told me, "You are my sunshine. Janey used to be my sunshine, but now you are." Hearing that, I felt I had to always be pleasant and happy for you, that if I weren't exactly what you wanted me to be, then I, like Janey, would no longer be your "sunshine," that you wouldn't love me if I ever expressed anything negative.
>
> Of course, my feelings came out in other ways. In physical illness, in pain inside myself that I couldn't get out. Even now, I have a terrible time talking about anything negative, especially with you. The feelings don't even have to be what most people would call "negative" for me to have trouble articulating

them—just anything I fear you might disapprove of, and that includes any preference that's different from yours. You have such strong opinions, and when I try to give an alternate viewpoint, your beliefs engulf mine and make me wish I'd never spoken up.

I love you so much. It's because of my love that I tried so desperately to please you that I lost my own needs and desires in the process. If what I like or feel is different from you, I end up feeling guilty. I even feel put down because I like Mexican food!

Now you're doing with Andrea what you did with Janey. You castigate Andrea because she has tattoos, wears quirky clothes, pursues her artistic talents rather than going to college, and isn't your image of what she should be. I admire my daughter for being herself, and I feel angry and upset when you reject her. It validates all my fears and makes me even more sure that you couldn't love the real me—only the picture of me as you thought I was, the me who never expressed her anger, conveyed her needs, or voiced her beliefs, likes, and dislikes unless they were the same as yours.

What I need now is for you to acknowledge this letter and my feelings and let me know that you can love me and my daughter the way we are. Let me know that I don't have to be perfect for you.

I'd like for us to talk about this more. I want to spend time with you, but it has gotten hard for me to do so. I still feel you reject much of what I do and that I can never accomplish enough for you. You belittle my job, even though I've told you many times how much I love it and how proud I am of what I do. You do the same with Andrea, disparaging her although you know how much I love and admire her and how much I want the two of you to love and appreciate each other.

But the relationship between you and Andrea is only a symptom of the problem I see between you and me. We've never openly clashed, because I've always swallowed my feelings, and this has made me sick and unhappy. I need to get this out in the open and know that I can be honest with you and that it's okay. I need to be sure you won't stop loving me.

It would also mean a lot to me if we could speak honestly about Dad—the fact that he was an alcoholic, drug-addicted, and committed suicide. We have to acknowledge these painful things if we're to get past them. All those things about him affected my life—and so did the fact that I was given the message not to talk about them, to pretend they weren't true. Sometimes I feel as if my whole life ended up a pretense because of that, because I spent all my energy trying to keep you happy, and that meant never acknowledging that any of these "bad" things were going on.

Yes, I'm different from you, and I wish you could support and encourage and applaud those differences. That's what I'm trying to do for Andrea—celebrate her distinctiveness. That's what I'm now beginning to try to do for myself as well—honor my differences from you, not be afraid to speak up about them, not to feel guilty about them, begin to be free. As I say, I'm just beginning this process, but telling you all this—how I've felt all these years—is, I believe, a necessary step. I pray you'll understand.

Please write soon and acknowledge my letter. That's all I ask, and I'll then feel much better. I love you very much always.

Love, Jill

> ***In search of my mother's garden, I found my own.***
> —Alice Walker

I sent the letter off with some trepidation but a firm sense that it was something I needed to do. I hoped against hope that she would understand.

Her response was typical Mom:

"Relax! Letter received; I haven't suffered a heart attack or a stroke as a result of reading it. I still love you."

She went on to say that I was mistaken about Dad, that he wasn't an alcoholic. "He was prescribed too many pills and they weren't helpful, and I was too stupid to understand what was going on."

She said, "I think sometimes you don't 'get' the fact that I'm teasing you, as when I suggested you write me an essay on why you like Mexican food. I was joking, plus I really can't imagine what's so attractive about it for you."

She advised, "Remember the generation gap and the benighted age in which I grew up," and noted, "It's a family trait not to complain, discuss illness or symptoms."

She said she was sorry for the unhappiness she caused me and ended, "So don't worry any more about pleasing me; just be yourself and remember I love you."

My whole body exhaled when I read that letter. From then on, there was an honesty and acceptance between us that I'd never imagined. Of course, she continued to be her judgmental, critical, largely-in-denial self, and she would never change. But something fundamental had shifted. I could speak up now and say exactly how I felt, and she accepted my views with more respect and less condemnation than ever before.

TURNING POINT

Write a letter to your parent. This exercise is powerful even if your parent is dead. Tell your parent how she or he hurt you, and ask for an acknowledgment of what happened and how you feel.

You don't need to send the letter, and you can write it over and over. You'll find that if you rewrite this letter every week for several months, it will evolve, and so will your feelings.

– J.M.

✳ ✳ ✳

In 1992, my mother was diagnosed with brain cancer. The bitter task of moving her into a nursing home was balanced by Andrea's news that she was expecting a second child. She wanted her daughter, Shyloh, as well as her husband, to attend the birth, and asked if I would be there as Shyloh's companion. I told her I'd be honored.

Once I would have been consumed with concerns about all the ways this plan about the birth could go awry. But it was a measure of how far I'd come that I was able to relax, realize I had no control over the outcome, and put it all in the hands of the higher power who took care of such things.

> *None of us got here by control. We got here because our parents loved each other enough to lose control; that is part of the universe's ecstacy.*
> —Matthew Fox

The birth went more smoothly than I could have hoped, and I felt none of the empathetic pain I'd feared. If ever I had a final exam on the matter of separating from Andrea, this was it. As I watched her giving birth, I could view her with love and admiration without agonizing over her suffering. It was like having all the excitement and wonder of childbirth without the pain.

Shyloh slept through most of it. At the end, when we could see the baby's head, I woke her, and we held each other as we watched, mesmerized. The instant when we saw his face was pure magic.

I'd watched Andrea being born, through a mirror above me, and I'd thought that was the most miraculous moment possible. This was even more wondrous.

Andrea held her son as we crowded around, kissing and hugging the two of them. Shyloh was beaming. "Isn't my baby brother beautiful?" she asked.

✫ ✫ ✫

Two months later, my mother died. I arranged her memorial service and gave the eulogy, two things that, a scant few years ago, I never fathomed I could do. Writing and giving that eulogy put me in touch with all my mom had given me. Even if she didn't encourage me to speak my feelings, her support of my writing had blessed me with a priceless alternative—to release those feelings onto paper—which has helped me my whole life.

> *Hold on to what is good*
> *even if it is a handful of earth.*
> *Hold on to what you believe*
> *even if it is a tree which stands by itself.*
> *Hold on to what you must do*
> *even if it is a long way from here.*
> *Hold on to life*
> *even when it is easier letting go.*
> *Hold on to my hand*
> *even when I have gone away from you.*
> —Pueblo Blessing

✫ ✫ ✫

The next spring, just after I celebrated my tenth year of sobriety, I was asked to speak at a conference on nonprofit leadership in California. This time, I set off on my trip without analyzing every possible eventuality. I'd begun to trust that when things went wrong I'd find a way to handle them. I didn't obsess over the details of the trip or the speech, and I was amazed at how well everything went and how much fun I had.

But that trip stays in my mind for another reason. I'd arranged to get together with my cousin Jeane, who lived near the hotel where I was staying.

I hadn't seen her since I was five. She was twenty years older than I was, so she remembered things about the family from before I was born. Also, she came from the Obright side—my father's branch of the tree, which was more open and communicative than my mother's side, the Rennels family. So I had a feeling she would cast some new light on things. I had no idea.

Family faces are magic mirrors. Looking at people who belong to us, we see the past, present, and future.
   —Gail Lumet Buckley

✳ ✳ ✳

The warmth I felt for Jeane was immediate. She was sensitive, creative, and caring—all the traits I liked best in my dad's family and was beginning to value in myself.

Our discussion ranged wide but focused mostly on the family we shared, especially our grandma. Like me, Jeane felt that the only unconditional love she'd received growing up came from Grandma Obright.

Then she mentioned Grandpa, about whom I knew nearly nothing. "We got our turned-up noses from Grandpa Obright," she said with a laugh.

"Really? I never met him or even saw pictures of him. He died before I was born."

"No, he didn't die till 1957. You would have been—what?—about ten or eleven?"

I nodded. "But, then, why didn't I ever meet him?"

"He moved to Chicago when your dad was a little boy, and he had a whole other family there, kids and everything, although he and Grandma never got a divorce."

"Wow. I can't believe he was alive all that time. I could actually have known him, if only—"

My voice trailed off, and Jeane nodded knowingly. "Your mom didn't like to talk about it. She never thought much of the Obrights, anyway. I suppose she felt it was good riddance when Grandpa Obright left. And then, well, you know, out of sight, out of mind." She smiled and squeezed my hand.

I barely had time to comprehend this buried secret before Jeane disclosed another one. She brought up our aunt, Bessie, my father's older sister, who'd been in a mental institution since she was a teenager. I'd heard about her from Janey, but I knew no details.

"I remember visiting Aunt Bessie a few times in the institution before we moved to California," she said. "She was beautiful and seemed very sweet, but she didn't say much."

"Where was the institution, do you remember?" I asked.

"Sure," she said. "It wasn't far from Naperville. Your mother always visited Aunt Bessie once a month."

"She did?"

"Yes. Aunt Bessie died around the same time your sister did. Your mom arranged the funeral."

My mind was spinning. I tried to imagine my mother doing all that—driving to the mental institution every month, making arrangements for a funeral—all without a whisper to me.

"So Aunt Bessie was alive just a few years ago?"

Jeane nodded. "I didn't make it to the funeral. Your mom was the only one in the family at the funeral service."

For a minute, I fantasized what it might have been like if my mother had asked me to attend the funeral with her or to visit Bessie with her all those years. A chance to know an aunt and grandfather I'd never met—what kind of difference would it have made in my life?

And what if my dad had talked to me about his own father and the pain of his leaving? What kind of healing might have begun? Had that unresolved wound somehow reverberated through the generations to infect my daughter and granddaughter? Could it have something to do with why Andrea's and Shyloh's fathers both disappeared from their lives when they were children?

> *The past isn't dead. It isn't even past.*
> —William Faulkner

I knew I'd dwell on those questions for a long time to come. But now I focused on learning all I could from Jeane while I had the chance, for I sensed there were still more mysteries to unravel. I asked her about my stillborn brother, whom I'd never mentioned to anyone but who had haunted my dreams for most of my life.

"That was such a sad time for your mom," Jeane said. "First of all, getting pregnant like she did, without being married, was kind of a scandal at the time."

"She wasn't married?"

"You didn't know that?"

I shook my head. I thought of how ashamed I'd been to tell Mom I was pregnant before John and I got married. How comforting it would have been to know she'd been through the same thing herself. Here was another unexpected strand from the past weaving its way through the generations—Mom, me, and Andrea, all unmarried when we became pregnant.

"Yes, they got married when they did because of the pregnancy, and then to have the baby die like that…"

"It must have been a terrible time for them," I said. Had they wondered if their son's death was repayment for their "sin" of unwed pregnancy? What guilt they must have felt in addition to the sadness and loss.

"Of course it was even harder on your mom when you were born," Jeane said.

"It was?"

"Yes, right after she got pregnant with you, your dad had his first really bad nervous breakdown. He quit his job, so there she was with two kids to support and no money. He had to go into a sanitarium for almost a year."

"Wow," I said. I'd always had the sense that there was chaos around me as a baby, and this certainly accounted for it.

"When you were born, your dad was just getting out of the hospital and in no shape to look for a new job," Jeane went on. "Your mom had to borrow money from relatives to get by."

"That must have been awful. Mom hated owing money." My eyes were riveted to Jeane's face as she continued.

"She paid it all back five years later when your dad won all that money at the race track."

"The race track?" I'd never heard about this.

"He was quite the gambler back then. That's where he got the money for that house he designed and built in the woods."

"Oh, that was a beautiful house," I recalled. "We only lived there a year, when I was six."

"As I remember it, they had to sell that house when he lost a lot of money playing poker. That devastated him. I think that's when he quit gambling altogether."

I'd never seen my dad as happy as when he was overseeing the building of his dream house. I never understood why we moved from that gorgeous home on acres of wild land at the edge of town. At the time, my parents told me it was because I was allergic to so many things in the woods.

I was in a sort of daze, trying to process all this new information about my family, when Jeane said something that snapped me to attention.

"There was one thing I'll never forget that your mom did to you when you were a baby that always bothered me."

A shiver went through me. I had a feeling she was about to give me some sort of key.

"What was it?"

"She kept you in a bag, tied tight, up to the chin so you couldn't move your arms. She said it was to keep you from sucking your thumb. Even then, I knew it was wrong," she said. "I mean, that's how a baby gets so much of its comfort, by sucking its thumb."

"That explains a lot," I said.

I could hardly wait to tell Phil. He always said if he ever wanted to drive me mad, all he'd have to do was restrain my arms. I'd overcome most of my claustrophobic tendencies through the years, except for that one. Not being able to move my arms did drive me practically insane.

It also explained why I got frustrated so easily. Once I calmed down, I was always able to accomplish what I set out to do. But my first reaction to any problem was a panicky feeling, just as if I were tied in a bag, unable to move or take action toward a solution. My first thought was always, *I can never do this, it's impossible.* As a baby, it actually was impossible to free my hands, which are of course the tools for getting things done.

> *Just being with your fear, just being it, is the most powerful form of fearlessness.*
> —Jerry Granelli

✧ ✧ ✧

How grateful I was to Jeane for all she told me. I returned from that trip to California carrying one of the greatest treasures anyone had ever given me—the gift of my history, or at least a huge chunk of it that had been lost to me, and all the self-knowledge that a person's history unearths. I felt as if the truths she'd granted me were what I'd been thirsting for my whole life.

After the baby-in-the-bag revelation, as I called it to myself, I felt a new kind of freedom. Throughout each day, I found myself getting up from my desk, extending my arms, stretching, and breathing deeply. Each time, I felt I was loosening the grip of that bag over me a bit more, becoming a little less shackled by the secrets of the past.

> *Free from clutching at themselves, the hands can handle; free from looking after themselves, the eyes can see; free from trying to understand itself, thought can think.*
> —Alan Watts

✧ ✧ ✧

Today, when I look back over my twenty-eight years of sobriety, it's plain how everything that happened to me strengthened me. I can see that none of my journey was about drinking, not really. It was about getting at the root of why I drank.

That meant reaching into that emptiness I'd always felt and filling it with love—love for myself, then love for other people, for the community, the world around me, the universe, and the greater power that connects us all with the best parts of ourselves.

As I gave more of myself to others, I discovered it was the best way to heal and help myself. Devoting time and money to causes I believed in was the most gratifying thing I'd ever done. My volunteer work for mental health and suicide prevention groups deepened my understanding of those issues, and, somewhere in the process, I found a healing peace about my father's suicide.

My favorite forms of volunteering involved teaching, as when I taught writing, editing, and English as a second language. I began leading a yoga class twice a week, and the work I did to prepare for it gave me a greater understanding of the practice than all the yoga classes I'd taken.

Everything we do counts. That was brought home to me when people would mention things I'd said—little things I didn't even recall—that had helped them. All the small acts of volunteerism, the everyday acts of compassion, even more than the big things, taught me how intimate our universe really is.

MOMENT OF TRUTH

Be of service. Donating your time and money gives your life meaning. It takes you out of yourself and your own troubles, focusing you on what's important—people rather than things. Money means little if you don't share it and use it to do good in the world.

Helping others can be life-altering. When you volunteer or give money to a cause, you're living your values and declaring what's important to you. You're turning your deepest beliefs into actions you can see and experience. That's the surest passage to fulfillment.

No act of kindness, no matter how small, is ever wasted.
—Aesop

What causes are important to you?_____
_____
_____

– J.M.

✧ ✧ ✧

It's clear to me now what Alice meant, at that first support-group meeting, when she said she was glad to be an alcoholic. Having such a glaring problem forced us to take a hard look at ourselves and change our lives. We learned we had to turn to others for help and offer help in return, and in the process we gained lifelong friendships. Along the way, we learned to trust and be completely honest with ourselves and everyone else.

The path is never straight, and I've veered off course often. I think I've learned a lesson and then am startled to find I've forgotten it. I remember and forget again and again.

When I was young, I thought there was a secret to life and that I'd find it someday if I kept searching. Now I don't feel much wiser than I did back then. I still have good days and bad, but I'm able to ride out the bad days with a lot more grace. I've learned to accept myself as I am, and that makes a huge difference.

Maybe that *is* the secret to life. At least for me, it's the secret to waking up each morning with joy in my heart.

Life continues to surprise me. I begin my morning and end my evening with gratitude drenching my heart. Every day, I learn something new.

✫ ✫ ✫

TOOLS FOR THE JOURNEY

Use these tools to help put the lessons in this chapter to use in your own life:

Keep a feelings log. Throughout the day, record your emotions on a page divided into three columns. In the first column, write down how you're feeling. Then write down what was happening when that emotion came over you. In the third column, write down the message you were giving yourself just before you felt that emotion. Replace that message with one that doesn't make you feel so bad. Here's an excerpt from a feelings log:

Feeling	**What Was Happening**	**Negative Message and Revised Message**
Jealousy	Mom told me my brother won an award.	Mom likes my brother better than me. **Revised Message:** I'm doing exactly what I want with my life. There's no reason to compare myself with anyone else.
Anxiety	My boss told me he wanted me to lead a new project.	What if I screw up the project and lose my job and become bankrupt and out on the street? **Revised Message:** I've done a good job on past projects, and I'll do fine on this one. I'll do the best I can and not worry about it.

Sleep. A good night's rest is crucial to making big changes in your life. High-quality sleeping can alter your brain chemistry. Whenever you learn something new, you can consolidate it and make it part of you by getting lots of sleep the next night. If you have trouble sleeping, there are many books (for example, *Good Night* by Michael Breus) and websites (see, for instance, helpguide.org/life/sleep) with useful tips.

Pills, drugs, or sleeping medications aren't the answer. The solution is to change your habits in ways that encourage healthy, productive sleeping. Important keys: Go to bed at the same time every night, and get up at the same time each morning. Follow a regular, relaxing routine every evening before going to bed.

Remember these basic coping skills to take care of yourself no matter what life throws your way:
- Make a list of what you believe in and what's most important to you. Keep it where you'll see it frequently. Use it to remind yourself that you're on an exciting journey and that your deepest beliefs will keep you on the right path.
- Focus on your successes. Experiments show that when people spend time thinking about what they've done right, they get better at those things. When they think about what they've done wrong, they don't improve. Make a list of times you felt proud of yourself, prevailed over adversity, and kept going despite obstacles. You'll be surprised how many resources you have available.
- Take action. Doing something constructive is always an excellent way to cope. Every time you accomplish something, no matter how small, you build your self-assurance.
- Laugh. Anything is bearable if faced with a light heart. Humor heals.

Connect with mentors, role models, sponsors, and guides. Think of people who have qualities you admire and are living the kind of life you'd like to live. Make a point of connecting with them. Hang out where they hang out, take the same classes they do, join the clubs they're in, and get to know them. Support groups are ideal places to find role models, and no one there will be surprised if you ask them to mentor you. Indeed, everyone is flattered to be asked to be a mentor, and it will be a rich learning experience for you both.

Keep a datebook, appointment book, calendar, or other scheduling tool. You can find one online or buy one at the dollar store. In addition to this yearly datebook, create a weekly one. Simply divide a piece of paper into seven segments, one for each day of the week. Every Sunday, transfer your plans for the week from your yearly datebook onto your weekly schedule. Put it by your bed so you'll see it first thing in the morning. Such scheduling devices are wonderful tools for keeping your plans, goals, and dreams on track.

– *J.M.*

THINGS TO DO TODAY

Forge a path with these tangible things you can do right now:

1. Go for a walk. Tune in to your body, the swing of your arms, the stride of your feet. Hold yourself as if a balloon were tied to the top of your head, pulling you gently toward the clouds. Feel your body lengthen and lighten with each step, pushing through the balls of your feet to bring a spring to your walk. Even the shortest stroll is an occasion to feel the mind-body connection, experience joy, and be grateful for your ability to move through the world.

2. Choose one book from "Resources to Guide and Inspire You" in the Appendix, and order it from the library. Libraries are one of the true wonders of the world. Anyone can get a library card, and that little piece of paper is a pass to all the wisdom you can imagine. Librarians love to answer questions, track down books, and suggest resources to help you. If they don't have the book or DVD you want, they're happy to get it for you from another library—and all for free!

3. Put a notebook and pen (or voice recorder) by your bed. Plan to record the dreams you have tonight, using the tips in "A Step on the Journey" in this chapter.

4. Do something that will put you in touch with yourself as a child. Some examples: Play in the bathtub. Take a trip to the playground. Lie in the grass. Roll down a hill. Do a somersault or stand on your head.

5. Set one goal for yourself, and write it down. Think of one small thing you can do that will put you closer to your vision of a new life. Be sure your goal isn't too big or too vague. If it is, break it into manageable chunks, and focus on just one piece at a time. The way to make big, transformative changes is to start with one finite step. Begin today.

– J.M.

WORDS OF WISDOM AND LIGHT

Here are lessons that have transformed people who are rebuilding their lives. See if any of their advice rings true for you.

Go Back to Seventh Grade: Wisdom from Carlo

Someone in my support group told me that you quit maturing at the age you start drinking and drugging, because you never have the chance to develop the life skills you would normally be learning. That means I'm twelve years old.

I started using drugs to escape life's troubles when I was twelve. So, although I'm thirty years old chronologically, my maturity level is that of a pre-adolescent. No wonder I feel so inadequate so much of the time. Sometimes I feel too weird and damaged to be part of this universe.

But once I understood that I was a twelve-year-old trying to live in a thirty-year-old's world, I saw why I struggled to get through the days. That insight gave me a new perspective on how I could reconstruct my life.

I started out by imagining what skills I'd be acquiring if I were twelve again. I'd be in seventh grade, discovering basic things like how to make decisions, form good work habits, and make plans for the future. I can go back to that time in my mind and begin again. I have the facilities now to learn all that I missed. I can take mini-courses, read books to help me develop those skills, and seek guidance from other people. I can keep my eyes open and see how others navigate the world, and when I see people I admire, I can ask them how they do it.

As I started asking questions and sorting through information people gave me, I discovered that one core skill I had to learn was how to weigh priorities. I learned to start each day with a to-do list, putting a "1" next to the things that were most important, a "2" next to the second most important, and so on. I tried to finish all the high-priority tasks before I started on the second tier. That was a huge step for me and calmed a lot of the confusion and turmoil in my life.

From there, I moved on to doing exercises to help me control my emotions and impulses, tune out distractions, organize ideas, make short-term and long-term plans, and forge meaningful relationships. Those things are still hard but they're getting easier, and in the process I'm learning who I am and what I want to do with my life. Progress isn't as fast as I'd like, but it's not as slow as I feared, either. I can see myself changing, and I notice my fears diminishing.

In addition to learning basic skills, I've had to firm up my own opinions. I'd never formed beliefs for myself, because I'd been too busy doing drugs to figure out how I felt about anything. To others, it looked like I had solid convictions, but I was only reiterating what my parents had told me or what I'd heard others say. Whenever I heard or read something that sounded good, I would repeat it to others as if it was what I thought. But I never took time to think deeply about it to see if it truly made sense to me.

Now I take that time, and it's one of the best parts of being sober. I ask myself: Do I really like *Moby Dick* or do I just say I do because it's supposed to be a great book? Do I enjoy *Pretty Woman* or am I just aping what everyone else says about it? I can read the book and see the movie now and make up my own mind. Every day I can solidify a new belief for myself.

Change is always frightening, and it's especially formidable when you have to make so many shifts at once, bounding across years that were lost. But the good thing is, I can learn. I can always keep learning.

Carlo's best advice: Take time to learn all the things you missed while you were a mindless slave to your addictions. Experts on disease talk about DALYs (disability-adjusted life-years) to refer to years that are lost due to illness. You can't gain those years back overnight, but you can recapture them if you're patient, methodical, and motivated. Be gentle with yourself, and enjoy the journey.

Act As If: Wisdom from Ben

When I was first in recovery, I knew I should reach out to others, but it was hard to do. Someone told me to act *as if* I felt comfortable reaching out, so, even though my impulse was to isolate myself, I went to support-group meetings, smiled hello, talked to people, and shared my experiences.

At first it was agonizing, but each time it felt more natural and less like torture. People responded to my reaching out and became my friends. I was amazed at how well this simple advice worked. Since then, I've used it countless times. Whenever I feel anxious, I act as if I have the self-assurance I wish I had, and I grow into that confidence. When I'm full of self-blame, I act as if I deserve the best, and I start to feel that maybe I'm a worthy person after all.

Time after time, this technique has helped me learn new, positive behaviors. When I act *as if* I feel a certain way often enough, my feelings and behaviors actually change.

> **It's easier to act your way into a new way of thinking than to think your way into a new way of acting.**
> —Millard Fuller

Ben's best advice: Sometimes, especially early in sobriety, it's useful to let your action precede your thought. For instance, "I'm skipping the meeting tonight because I'm lazy" is backwards. Instead, tell yourself, "I'd be acting lazy if I skipped the meeting tonight." Then go to the meeting, acting as if you're not lazy. String enough of these actions together, and pretty soon you'll think of yourself as a competent person who gets things done.

Put Past, Present, and Future in their Proper Places: Wisdom from B.J.

People talk about the importance of living in the moment. I've found that it's true: Living without guilt about the past or worry about the future is wonderfully freeing.

But that's a whole different thing from the "living in the moment" life I lived while I was doing drugs. All I cared about then was my next fix, and it was a careless, meaningless existence. It wasn't really living at all.

Now I've learned to balance my past and future around my present. I've made peace with what happened in the past and started planning a purposeful future for myself. First I had to believe I deserved a productive future; then I had to envision the life I wanted; and, finally, I had to devise strategies to make it a reality.

Now I enjoy making plans. Every morning I write down one or two actions to advance me toward my goals. Every evening, I check how well I did in completing those tasks. Often I'll find that when I take an action, I learn something new, and that changes my plans. I've found that I must be flexible enough to adapt my plans as circumstances change.

B.J.'s best advice: Create a clear, simple plan that furthers a long-term purpose. Having a blueprint for your life will make all the difference as you move forward.

2

CONNECT TO THE EARTH: SHELLY'S STORY

Shelly Dutch quit using cocaine in 1983. Twenty years later, she started Connections Counseling Center, a clinic for recovering addicts and alcoholics. This chapter shows how she prevailed through multiple addictions to find hope and peace. Her journey is about her discovery of personal growth and purpose in life, one day at a time.

Author's Note:

When Shelly started Connections Counseling Clinic in 2003, it was something she passionately believed in, but she wasn't sure her idea would be sustainable. A few years later, her clinic was booming. In addition to running Connections, she's started a foundation to help struggling addicts who can't afford treatment.

After hearing about her accomplishments, I could hardly wait to meet her and find out how she moved from a life of pain, drugs, arrests, and hopelessness to one of service, success, and joy. My granddaughter Shyloh and her counselor at Connections, Skye, had arranged for me to meet Shelly. My hope was that she would support the idea of this book, introduce me to Connections clients who would share their stories, and perhaps tell her own story. I had no idea what "support" could mean!

In her office, we sat on plump, soft couches to talk. A petite woman with short dark hair and luminous brown eyes, Shelly was a bundle of energy with a warm smile. "My clinic has just evolved," she said. "I started Connections with just two teenagers as clients, and now we have fifteen groups, including a teen group, women's group, couples' group, and a group for families. The cool thing is the teenagers have grown older but they've never left me. We're like a family, so they keep coming back to volunteer at Connections and mentor others."

Shelly's creativity, energy, and warmth make her a perfect fit for the task of running Connections Counseling Clinic. Her caring comes through, inspiring her staff as much as her clients. Her ability to give great quantities of love draws in those who desperately lack esteem. They thrive on her hugs.

"I couldn't have accomplished what I have if it weren't for people who believed in me," Shelly said. "I wanted to create a place where people would have that same feeling, a place where they feel safe, understood, and not alone.

"My therapist, Bobbi, saved my life. I've been going to her for over twenty years. To her, I'm the most important person in the world. Or at least that's how I feel when I'm with her. That's how I want our clients at Connections to feel."

Within an hour of hearing my ideas for writing this book, Shelly offered to let me read her journals—twenty-five years of her most private feelings. Although she'd never let a soul see her journals before, she trusted me and my vision for Waking up Happy so much that she was able to take an awe-inspiring leap of faith.

She also invited me and everyone interested in being part of the book to a weekend retreat at her cabin in northern Wisconsin. There, overlooking Spider Lake, I began interviewing people as we celebrated life and got into the book's spirit.

"One reason my cabin is so special to me is that I get to share it with other people on weekends like this," Shelly said. "My journey to recovery began when a therapist looked at me like I mattered, and I want to give that gift to others. That's what life's all about."

The following is Shelly's story in her own words.

– J.M.

✧ ✧ ✧

Stories shape our lives, and the stories in my family growing up were all about appearances. As the only girl, with two brothers, I was the one my mother loved to dress up and show off. I felt like she was always comparing me with her friends' daughters. I got the message that having a husband, kids, and a lovely home was what would fulfill me in life. Boys go to college and get good jobs; girls get married and taken care of, so they need to put their energy into looking perfect.

"You have a pretty face. The rest is up to you," my mama always said. Translation: "You're heavy, but we can't help you lose weight. You have to deal with it yourself."

My weight has preoccupied me nearly all my life. I'm a compulsive overeater. I started gaining a lot of weight in sixth grade, and that hurt my feelings of self-worth. I inherited my mother's addictions to sugar and carbs. Even when my mom was dying from complications of diabetes at age sixty-seven, she still couldn't eat healthy or give up the lifestyle that had damaged her health.

My addictions could kill me, too. I have to be careful whenever I face any addictive substance—including M & Ms. I'm addicted to practically everything—alcohol, drugs, men, shopping, chocolate—food of all kinds, really, but especially sugar.

A drug is a drug is a drug—and that includes alcohol. So many times drug addicts (including me) will think they have no problem with alcohol and decide, now that they're clean, they can start drinking wine or beer. That can be so seductive—and it's just another form of denying and lying to oneself.

An addict is like a diabetic, and going to meetings and connecting with other people is like insulin. Without that saving medicine of connection, you risk getting sick and even dying.

I'm amazed that some people still believe that addiction is a moral defect and don't understand that it's a disease. When I was in the depths of my addiction and went to in-patient treatment at age twenty-eight, I realized I wasn't a bad person trying to get good, I was a sick person trying to get well.

My family never understood that. They couldn't comprehend why I was lying and stealing and making a mess of my life. They didn't realize I was afflicted with a horrible illness. Then, when I went into treatment, I met people who saw the good in me. That's what turned everything around.

It's crucial to understand that the reason people do drugs and drink is different from why they're addicts. I drank and did drugs because of poor self-esteem and the issues from my past, such as sexual abuse. But those aren't the reasons I'm an addict. I'm an addict because I inherited this disease of chemical dependency.

CONNECT TO THE EARTH: SHELLY'S STORY

✧ ✧ ✧

If I was my mama's girl, my brothers and dad had a special relationship that shut me out. I longed to be close to all of them but never felt accepted.

I started using drugs when I was twelve. My mom was on amphetamines for weight loss, and I started stealing her pills. I thought if I were thin I'd be happy. That's why cocaine became my drug of choice, because it helped suppress my appetite.

When I was sexually abused by a family friend as a teenager and told my parents, I got the message that I should put it behind me and not talk about it. My feeling of separation grew, along with a sense of shame.

Somehow, I managed to get through high school and college. I never enjoyed school, but I liked children, so I got a degree in elementary education. After college, I roamed the country teaching grade school. I thought the geographical cure—escaping problems by moving somewhere else—would work, but of course it didn't. Everywhere I went, I carried myself with me.

I bounced from Madison, Wisconsin, to Eugene, Oregon, to Davis, California, to Lexington, Kentucky. In each new place, my problems caught up with me and I got in trouble again, due to drugs as well as sexual and shoplifting compulsions. During those years, I was fired from jobs, married and divorced, incredibly alone and lonely.

Over and over I would break down crying and praying, "Please, God, I don't want to die. What's wrong with me? I fail at everything I do. I can't stick with a job. No relationship works. I go to therapists and lie. I lie to everyone. I use men to feel loved, but it doesn't work. The only people who ever loved me were my family, and I've let them down."

The only reason I didn't kill myself was because of my family. Whenever I thought of how my suicide would hurt my parents, I just couldn't do it, even though I was in so much pain.

In 1983, while in Lexington, I was fired again for stealing and went to a new therapist. She looked at me and said, "I can't help you." No one had ever said that to me, so I sat up and listened. She told me I was sick and I had to go into an in-patient hospital.

Because I didn't know what else to do, I followed her advice. During my month in rehab, my self-hatred and despair were gradually lightened by a ray of possibility. When I saw that someone believed in me and thought I was worth saving, that started me on the long road to real change.

Millions and millions of years would still not give me half enough time to describe that tiny instant of all eternity when you put your arms around me and I put my arms around you.
—Jacques Prevert

✧ ✧ ✧

When I left the in-patient program, they told me they would give me a job if I stayed sober for a year. So that became my goal. I worked at odd jobs in Lexington until the year was up and then was hired as a mental health associate at the rehab center while working to earn a counseling certificate. Becoming a counselor was my next goal.

During this time, I began to separate what I wanted from what I'd been told was important. I realized that I loved counseling and had a knack for it.

When I received my counseling certificate and was able to work as a counselor at the treatment center, I was thrilled. I'd never felt so happy and proud of myself. But my life didn't change overnight. Not by any means.

✫ ✫ ✫

JOURNAL—September 15, 1984

I'm feeling tired and angry and resentful. Work isn't going the way I want. People aren't doing what I want. There's too much in my brain.

People at work keep leaving, and I have such a hard time with that. I feel so hollow and alone when they leave.

I have a job I like most of the time, yet I feel dissatisfied and anxious. I'm staying sober but dependent and selfish in my relationships.

I'm thirty years old and long to have my own family, a husband and kids to share my life. But there seems no hope of that happening. I'm afraid I'll be alone forever.

Stressed out and eating all the time. Weight 133 pounds.

I'd been numbing my emotions with drugs for half my life, so when feelings started bubbling up, I had no idea how to deal with them. I was like a kid just learning to know herself and her place in the world, still confused about the difference between what I wanted and what I needed. I had a lot of growing up to do.

A year after I abstained from all drugs and alcohol, I made a grave mistake. I'd always thought of myself as a drug addict, not an alcoholic, so I decided it would be okay for me to have a glass of wine now and then. The problem was that I often ended up drinking way too many glasses of wine, waking up the next morning feeling horrible about myself, sometimes having blacked out so I didn't remember what I'd done the night before. Eventually it dawned on me that I was an alcoholic—that most addicts are alcoholics, just as every alcoholic is an addict.

One of my other addictions when I first quit cocaine was shopping. At the time I didn't recognize it as addiction in another guise. I was buying way too many things, spending too much money. I couldn't get a handle on it till I talked about it in therapy and in my journal. I realized that I felt I needed material things to make up for what was taken from me when I was sexually abused and my parents minimized it.

What I needed to learn was how to love and accept myself. Of course, that's a lot harder than taking a trip to the mall. But it's also lasting in a way material possessions can never be.

Closely related to shopping was shoplifting, and that was the addiction that worried me most. I had to speak to that lost little girl and tell her that stealing wasn't going to heal the wound within her and that I would do my best to heal and comfort her.

Overeating was the hardest addiction for me to break, and I continue to struggle with it today. You can't give up food the way you give up drugs. Because you have to eat, you have to learn healthy ways of relating to food.

Men were an addiction, too, in those early days. I didn't think I could be happy without a man in my life, but no matter how many men I dated, I was always disappointed. Miserable and lonely, I was obsessed with finding the man who would fill that desperate need inside me. Because of that obsession, I wasn't appreciating each day or pursuing my talents.

But I would receive glimpses of what a full life, centered on helping others, could be like, and I knew that's the life I wanted. So I kept striving to eliminate all the addictions that were weighing me down. I knew the answer was charity, love, and giving to those around me.

In those early months, I held on tight, went to twelve-step meetings, and told myself to trust that things would get better. But I felt vulnerable, scared, and out of control. Writing in my journal was one thing that grounded me and helped me start to identify, manage, and make peace with my emotions.

> JOURNAL—December 23, 1984
>
> What does my mother want from me? Why doesn't she love me? Why isn't she proud of me? Why does she keep wanting more from me—a better-paying job, better grammar, neater? It breaks my heart. I desperately love her and want to be close to her.
>
> Mom, I'm doing the best I can. I want your approval and love more than anyone's. You have never been proud of me. All my life you've compared me to all your friends' kids and you wonder why I'm insecure and have low self-esteem.
>
> I had great hopes for this trip to Madison to see my family for the holidays, but it's bringing up all the bad feelings between my parents and me. I also feel sad about my brothers being so close to each other and doing things together without me. I feel like that left-out little girl again.
>
> I've been so dishonest lately with everyone, especially myself. I'm so desperate to be loved that I forget to love myself. What am I supposed to be learning? I have a good job, money, a nice home, so where is all the dissatisfaction coming from? I have little to give to anyone now. I must have faith that God will give me good things if I'm honest and loving.
>
> I always eat more when I'm with my mom, especially during Hanukkah. I'm not happy with my weight and my overeating. Up to 135 pounds.

I worked hard to strengthen my body, mind, and soul. I started exercising regularly and especially enjoyed running, which made me feel free and strong. I spent time reading and developing new interests.

I began to pick up coping skills that helped me deal with uncomfortable situations. Instead of turning to addictive substances when I felt anxious, I learned to do other things, like going for walks or calling a friend.

For my spirit, I found I felt closest to the goodness in the world and in myself when I was in nature, so I took every chance to get out of town and into the wilderness. Those were the best times, the times I could get in touch with my gratitude for all the good things in life.

A GOOD QUESTION

Bad hair day? We all have days that go far beyond unruly hair, when everything seems to go wrong and we feel at our wits' end. If we have addictions to drugs, food, sex, or anything else that's bad for us, it's important to have a list of "Ways to Cope with a Bad Day" handy so we can quickly launch into one of these alternatives.

Here's what clients and counselors at Connections said when asked how they cope with those days:

- When I'm having a bad day, I go directly to gratitude. I make a list of all the things I'm thankful for. If that doesn't work, I ask my higher power for direction or support.

- I call my sponsor, a friend, or my therapist.
- I write in my journal and try to get to the sunlight of the spirit.
- I go outside and look around. Nature helps me appreciate the abundance in my life.
- I cuddle with my sweetheart if he's around. If not, I cuddle with my dog.
- I put on funky music and fling myself around my bedroom singing and shouting out all my frustrations.
- A good cry always does me a world of good. Pity parties are fine as long as they're short. I set my timer for fifteen minutes and feel sorry for myself until the bell goes off. Then I usually feel refreshed and able to get on with my day, having got all those yucky feelings out of me.
- I look outside myself to see what the world is asking of me. When I act to help others, I replace my bad mood with a feeling of good will. I've found that happiness comes by helping others.
- There's a shop where you can pick out chocolates with different flavors. My favorites are the spicy ones, like chili, turmeric, curry, and cayenne. Each of these hand-crafted chocolates is a work of art. They're fairly expensive (about two dollars apiece) but a bargain compared to what I used to spend on booze. If I don't have time to get to the chocolate store, a Snickers bar will do in a pinch.
- I write down—or tell a friend—all the things that are bothering me. Often when I see how small those things are, compared to all the goodness in my life, I'm able to laugh at my troubles and at myself. Laughter does wonders.

– J.M.

JOURNAL—January 28, 1985

Two years ago today I went into in-patient treatment. I was stealing money, drugs, anything else I could take. I'd been fired from my job. I had no self-love. I took every drug I could get my hands on.

Now I'm a counselor. I speak on cocaine abuse and addiction. I'm running every day and feeling good about my body and my work. My weight is down to 129.

Shel, the fact that you're still struggling doesn't mean there's something wrong with you. It's a hard road you're on, and you're asking a lot of yourself. Look how far you've come!

✼ ✼ ✼

In 1985 I ran my first race—3.1 miles in 26 minutes, 42 seconds. It was such a high. I was hot and exhausted, but I survived. Running gave me something magical—a sense of accomplishment and fulfillment. I ran for me, not for anyone else but purely for the sense of satisfaction it gave me. It was one of the first things I did for myself. My self-assurance increased.

I finally built my confidence to the point that I was ready to move back to Madison, Wisconsin, where my family was—my mom, dad, and grandma. I realized I had to stop blaming everybody else and using geography to distance myself from the people I thought had caused all my problems. I needed to take responsibility. By returning home, I felt like all the hiding, lying, and insanity were coming to an end. Finally I was going to face everything I'd been fleeing.

I hadn't been able to find a job in Madison, but I took the chance anyway, trusting it would turn out for the best.

> *And the trouble is, if you don't risk anything, you risk even more.*
> —Erica Jong

JOURNAL—July 2, 1985

I'm glad to be living in Madison, but it was hard leaving Lexington and all the people there who loved, respected, and believed in me. It's great being able to see my parents every day, but I worry that I'm doing things for them instead of for myself. I get confused about what's for me and what's for them.

Weight is 130 pounds. I know I eat to fill that loneliness inside me. I must get onto a diet and exercise program. I vow to do better.

I'll remember what I've learned—that I'm a worthwhile, loving, and good woman. I have to hang on to that, know I have a gift of giving, caring, and touching others. That's what scares some people—my intensity. I want to talk about things like relationships and tell people all about my past when I first meet them, and they're scared off by that.

Yet I've learned the true meaning of friendship and joy. There are people who like my intensity, who like me the way I am. But I do need to lighten up more!

Sometimes I feel like a blossom just beginning to unfurl.

✻ ✻ ✻

In Madison, I worked in low-paying jobs at various treatment centers and at the university hospital with patients who had cirrhosis of the liver due to alcoholism. I got a taste of how awful this disease of addiction truly is.

Meanwhile, I was looking for love in all the worst possible places and the most counter-productive ways—letting myself be picked up by strangers in bars and clubs—not the best plan for meeting a good Jewish man. I did want a nice Jewish husband, although I wasn't sure whether it was to please my parents or myself.

It seemed as if I was always interested in men who weren't interested in me, men who were insensitive and inconsiderate and didn't include me in their plans. I told men lies, like saying I was getting a master's degree, to impress them. Because I was so insecure and felt I wasn't smart or clever enough, I needed to pretend to be someone else.

I was unbearably lonely, and my neediness kept scaring men away. As each new man told me he'd call and then didn't, I felt worse about myself and more hopeless about the future. How many hours I wasted waiting for those calls, and how shattered I was when they never came.

✻ ✻ ✻

I never had to try so hard to succeed as when I moved to Madison. I couldn't get a job as a counselor—what I'd loved doing in Lexington—without more education and experience. I felt inferior intellectually and because I was female.

I'd never felt I was smart, but when it came to people, perceptions, feelings, and psychological factors, I had a lifetime of experience. It was frustrating not to be able to use those talents in my work. Instead of counseling people, my jobs involved screening and interviewing patients when they arrived for treatment.

Sometimes I felt I was learning how to tread water when I wanted to dive deep and swim. I'd been alienated and sick for so long that getting back into the mainstream was a challenge.

Although I'd moved to Madison to be near my parents, my relationship with them didn't seem to be improving. They couldn't put my past of partying, drug use, and promiscuity behind them. They still didn't believe in me or trust me, and I felt I would never be what they wanted me to be—or what I wished I were. My mom treated me the way she used to—putting me down in subtle ways, making oblique references to every pound I put on. I didn't mind when she kidded me, but her barbed comments seemed aimed straight for my heart, undermining me and making me feel awful about myself.

My brothers no longer lived in Madison, but they visited fairly often, and I'd looked forward to seeing them again. I'd hoped our relationship would be different now that I was a sober, responsible adult, but I still felt incompetent when I was with them, like I would never measure up, and I was still jealous of the close relationship they had. I felt I didn't fit in anywhere, at work or with my family.

I knew my dad loved me in spite of my shortcomings. But, as always, he was distant and unavailable much of the time.

I still had trouble making women friends, but I decided to try harder. I found that focusing on others, rather than myself, made me feel better.

> JOURNAL—December 30, 1985
> My hope is to do something with my life, to make something of myself, to help others, to be a spiritual person. I must stop trying to be loved and just submit, surrender to what life wants for me.
> Shel, be careful with your eating. Today you're up to 136 pounds. You need to keep your weight going down, not up.
> Anyone who has accomplished anything significant has done so with sacrifice and pain. If I spend my time wanting what I don't have, I'll miss all the blessed moments. I must give the universe time to thread a bright ribbon through my life.

I was still looking for someone to love, but I'd smartened up a bit. I'd stopped obsessing about finding a man and, instead, resolved to let it happen in its own time. Rather than seeking someone to fill me, I concentrated on filling myself by strengthening my talents and trying to become the person I aspired to be. As I gained more self-possession, I began doing more public speaking about drug addiction and more reaching out to help others.

Once I shifted my focus and became less self-involved, I felt much better. I was still lonely, but I came to see that I could be lonely without feeling empty. That was a big revelation, to realize that I could feel comfortable with loneliness. I could upend those stories implanted in me as a child—that only a husband and children would fulfill me, that making myself look good on the outside was more important than becoming self-sufficient and competent.

I saw that developing my spiritual side was central to this process of self-discovery and growth. I did more walking in the woods and along the lakes, where I felt closest to my higher power. I stopped cruising the bars and, instead, I would occasionally go to temple as well as to Jewish singles events.

I concentrated on doing things I loved, such as dancing. It was by following my passion for dancing that I finally met the man of my dreams.

That night, the music pulled me in, and I couldn't sit still, so I went up to a nice-looking guy and asked him to dance. I found out he liked kids, animals, and nature. And he was Jewish.

I think it's because of my change of attitude that when I met Peter, things fell into place. I didn't scare him off by being too needy, the way I'd done with other men. Because I felt balanced and secure—well, fairly secure; I still had a long way to go—I was ready for the give-and-take of a real relationship.

> *The miracle is not to walk on water but to walk on the Earth.*
> —Lin Chi

Peter was kind, loving, and good to me. We laughed together and had a great deal in common, including our Jewish upbringings. We both enjoyed the outdoors—hiking, camping, and swimming.

But, preoccupied with his job in the computer business, he was seldom around. He didn't give of himself the way I gave myself to him. That worried me and kept me feeling insecure.

> JOURNAL—May 1, 1986
> I've decided to go into therapy because I'm so emotional and unhappy. I haven't been exercising, have been overeating, and not developing friends.
>
> I worry so much and project my fears for the future onto other people. I cried and went crazy when Peter said he was interviewing for a job in St. Louis, imagining how I would lose him just after I'd found him. I felt I would die if he left. That's when I knew I had to get help.
>
> I binge almost every day on cookies, candy, chips, whatever. I swear I've stopped and then I go back to it. I see the beautiful spring—rebirth, flowers, fragrance, blossoms—but I'm too miserable about my weight to enjoy it. Thank God that ninety-five percent of the time I'm not bingeing on sugar or I would be obese or dead, or both.
>
> The main thing is to persevere. I know I can do it.
>
> I need a massage, whirlpool, and sleep. How about a hot bath and sleep? That will do.

> *Sometimes I go about in pity for myself and all the while a great wind is carrying me across the sky.*
> —Ojibway saying

I'd been in therapy before, but I'd learned that I needed to keep going back. This whole excursion into the self was never-ending, and there were always new caverns to excavate, deeper layers to unearth.

My new therapist helped me make inroads in that long process of accepting myself as I was—moods, wild emotions, imperfections, and all. She pointed out how many challenges I'd met in the past and how experiences that seemed awful at the time turned out for the best. There wasn't anything I'd been unable to accomplish or overcome when I put my mind to it, and I could continue to solve problems and improve myself, just as I'd done before.

With her guidance I learned to get in touch with my emotions without overreacting. I learned to take a "time out" and cease interactions that were getting out of hand. I learned to self-soothe.

I realized I couldn't build a partnership with anyone else till I had a loving relationship with myself. That meant being honest, confronting my past, and forgiving my mistakes. It meant giving up my attempts to control the way my life would go and, instead, just letting things unfold. I began to feel hopeful.

> ### A STEP ON THE JOURNEY
>
> **Take time to find the right therapist for you.** It doesn't always happen the first time, or even the fifth time. Keep trying. Therapy is a lot like a marriage, so you need to find someone who's compatible with your personality and needs.
>
> *Never go to a doctor whose office plants have died.*
> —Erma Bombeck
>
> For example, some therapists want to delve deeply into people's pasts. But you may not need to revisit painful childhood experiences unless they're intruding on your present and keeping you from living a full life today. The important thing for you may be to leave the past behind and learn what you can do to make your current life better.
>
> With the right therapist, therapy can be a life-saver. Yes, it's difficult, but it's also a joyous adventure. It's a way to understand and express your feelings so you can take control of them instead of letting them rule your life.
>
> – J.M.

✻ ✻ ✻

Peter and I were married later that year. For our honeymoon, we backpacked for ten miles and camped in the woods by Lake Michigan, surrounded by white pebbles and lush green pines. I relaxed for the first time in months—no plans to make, no worries, no concerns. The lake was so meditative and soothing. It was like a dream.

I'd hoped and prayed for a good man to marry, and I'd received everything I'd asked for. But if I thought a man would transform my life, I soon learned how wrong I was. I was the only one who could transform myself.

✻ ✻ ✻

The honeymoon was over in the blink of an eye, and Peter was always working. Right from the first, I wasn't sure how important I was to him, as he spent very little time at home. Being married didn't cure my loneliness.

At the time, and for years afterwards, I didn't see that in a way I'd married my father—someone who loved me but was inaccessible. I fell into the role my mom had taken with my dad—criticizing Peter, wanting to change him, nagging him to spend more time with me, and trying to bend him to my will.

Peter lived for his work. I knew that, of course, before I married him, so I shouldn't have been surprised when I saw him so infrequently. I had to relearn the lesson of relying on myself for my own happiness.

This was, however, a difficult lesson to learn.

I turned almost immediately from longing for a husband to wanting kids. When months passed and I didn't get pregnant, I started getting anxious and worried that I would never have the family I wanted so badly.

But I had tools now I could use to calm myself. I had my journal and therapist to talk to. By making an effort to reach out and share my feelings, I'd begun making women friends, and they gave me support, compassion, love, and understanding.

I continued to focus on self-improvement and earned a certification in Alcohol and Other Drug Addiction (AODA) counseling so that I could get higher-paying, more meaningful work doing what I really loved to do—counseling people suffering from substance abuse problems. In one of my jobs in a rehab clinic, I was put in charge of two teen programs and found that teenagers and I connected with each other in a special way. That was a turning point, although I didn't realize at the time how profoundly it would change my life.

> JOURNAL—January 28, 1988
>
> Five years ago today, I went into in-patient treatment in Lexington and gave up cocaine for good. I was sick, poor, alone, lying, cheating, stealing, with no job, no friends, and no confidence. Today I have a great career, husband, friendships, and zest for life. I feel stable, secure, healthy, and joyful. I'm close to my parents again. I no longer feel like a dumb girl when I'm with my brothers—at least most of the time—and they seem to respect me more, now that years have passed and I've continued to live a responsible life. There's more give-and-take between us, as I stand up for myself and project more assurance.
>
> I wrote a letter to the Lexington clinic to thank them for giving me my life back. Expressing my gratitude to as many people as possible, as often as possible, is, for me, the key to everything.
>
> I'm on a good diet and eating healthily. I've cut way down on sugar and carbs and my weight is 127½ pounds.
>
> Work is stressful but gratifying. The teens I work with are difficult, but when I get through to them it's exhilarating. I'm truly helping them and having an impact on their lives. There's nothing like that feeling.

Blessed is the influence of one true, loving human soul to another.
—George Eliot

✯ ✯ ✯

That spring, I found out I was pregnant. I was ecstatic.

But the fears and worries about the future that bubbled up were overwhelming. At thirty-five years old, I was a candidate for all kinds of complications during pregnancy and birth.

To keep my mind away from everything that could go wrong, I turned to meditation and affirmations. They helped me relax and give up my desire to control everything. Over and over, I repeated to myself, "I'm grateful and trusting, believing in the goodness at the core of the universe."

I started going to OA (Overeaters Anonymous) meetings, and they were a big help. As long as I kept going to meetings, I didn't overeat, and I felt good about myself every time I made it through a day of healthy eating. The OA meetings and my sponsor kept reminding me that I was an addict and couldn't take food for granted. Managing my food issues helped free me of my addiction to overspending as well. I was learning what had once seemed impossible—to find balance in my life.

A STEP ON THE JOURNEY

Learn to meditate. Meditation can help you turn your mind away from the past and future and be present in the moment. You don't need any special equipment or training to meditate. Just sit quietly and still your mind. When a thought comes, label it "thinking" and let it go. Don't become involved in the content of the thought. When the next thought comes, do the same thing. You'll feel an exquisite freedom as you disengage from the busyness of your thoughts. You'll realize you're much more than your thoughts; you're an integral part of the universe.

– J.M.

✧ ✧ ✧

On December 31, 1988, Alexander was born. My little boy was such a joy to me. Seeing the world through a baby's eyes was the most rewarding experience of my life.

I exulted in introducing Alex to the wonders of the natural world. He and I spent most of our time outdoors, where I was always happiest. Walking along Madison's lakes with Alex in my backpack, I felt connected to the peace of the universe.

> *Healing is to give a person the skills to see the miracle of their own existence and that of a flower's. And, even further, how the two are connected.*
> —Shawn May

JOURNAL—January 1, 1990
   Resolutions: Be healthy, exercise, get pregnant with a second child, be a good role model for Alex, don't overeat, do more volunteer work, help the needy. Get more involved at temple. Diversify, learn more, get involved with politics, cooking, and artwork. Stretch myself into new interests. Be more patient and less demanding.
   My weight is better than it's ever been. I'm down to 124 pounds. I'm staying away from sugar and carbs.
   These last two years have been the best of my life. Each day is a precious gift.

> *Heaven is right where you are standing and that is the place to practice.*
> —Morehei Ueshiba

Peter and I started going to an AA-Al-Anon couples meeting, which helped our relationship immensely. Peter had a hard time talking about feelings—another way in which he was just like my dad—but he was making progress in expressing himself. I saw that I was taking out my frustrations and projecting my fears onto Peter—one more way I was like my mom. Sometimes he couldn't do anything right in my eyes, and I realized those were the times I wasn't happy with myself.

So we both kept trying.

> JOURNAL—September 6, 1990
> I've started teaching half time at the university medical school, educating interns, residents, and physicians about addiction. It's a stimulating, challenging position and hard to believe these things are happening to me! Such great opportunities are coming my way because of the changes I've made in my life, my sobriety, and the work I do every day to become a better person.
> It's hard putting Alex in daycare and I miss him lots, but I enjoy working, and Alex needs to not be the center of the universe all the time.
> Shelly Dutch, recovering addict, teaches at the Med School!
> Life is very good! I'm trying to get pregnant again but am not obsessing about it. It will happen when—or if—it happens.
> Weight 129½ pounds.
> Thank you, H.P.

✶ ✶ ✶

I began going to temple more regularly. It was something I could share with my mom that didn't revolve around food. Being with her at temple took me back to my childhood when I had a firm relationship with God.

I had a habit of taking Peter's inventory—cataloguing his failings, which seemed so much clearer than my own. It was easy for me to see where others needed to improve. I decided I would be better served, whenever I found a fault in someone else, to look at myself instead. If I could become happy with myself and accept my own imperfections, I wouldn't have the need to criticize Peter.

> JOURNAL—November 6, 1990
> This could be a turning point. I started with a new therapist, whom I like a lot, and I've learned so much about myself. First of all is the fact that I've never been disciplined because the adults didn't set limits with me and I got away with everything as a child and teenager. When I overate or overindulged with boys, no one stopped me. So I can't be a good parent or role model till I learn to be honest, face up to consequences, and discipline myself.
> Now when I feel like overeating, I ask the adult Shelly to say no. I'm taking control of my weight and my body, exercising daily and eating healthily—no food diets. I realize now that diets don't work; they just make me feel deprived and set me up to overeat even more. Instead, I must find a plan I can stick with, and for me that means going to a twelve-step group (Overeaters Anonymous). As long as I have to report to others and be honest with them, I'm honest with myself.
> My therapist is also teaching me to slowly detach from Alex. I'm getting healthier.
> Thank you, H.P., for making me teachable.

> ## MOMENT OF TRUTH
>
> **Live-it, don't die-it.** Rather than going on a diet (a "die-it"), go on a "live-it"—a joyous celebration of healthy, nurturing food. Instead of denying yourself—which may make you rebel and overeat—eat what you want but in moderation, while experimenting with new recipes that are tasty and nutritious. Don't count calories or weigh yourself. Remember to indulge yourself on occasion. If you're kind to yourself, you'll eat more consciously and will soon train yourself to stop eating when you're full.
>
> – J.M.

There are so many things in human living that we should regard not as traumatic learning but as incomplete learning, unfinished learning.
   —Milton Erickson

✧ ✧ ✧

Shortly before Alex turned two, toward the end of 1990, I found I was pregnant with our second child. I was in seventh heaven.

When I learned our child would be a girl, I started getting nervous about Mom taking over and trying to make her into a little doll, like she did with me. I didn't want my daughter to grow up like I did, insecure, addicted, and out of control. I wanted her to be independent, confident, and to love life.

But I'd learned not to project my fears into the future. I was able to contain my anxieties with lots of prayer, meditation, and an attitude of acceptance.

When Carly was born on July 29, 1991, I was happy beyond belief to have two healthy, beautiful children. I was frustrated, however, because Peter assumed I would take care of all the parental roles while he worked day and night on his computer job or played hockey. I had no one to open up to, no one with whom to share the overwhelming challenges of raising two little ones.

When I went back to teaching part-time at the Med School, I felt ripped in two between wanting to work and longing to be with my children. The teaching job was hard for me, and I felt inadequate and not smart enough sometimes. I missed counseling young people, which I loved and knew I was good at.

I was worried about my mom, who was fifty pounds overweight and taking twelve pills a day for various conditions, including diabetes and heart disease. Her eating disorders were killing her, and yet she still insisted on taking diet pills, which were exacerbating her physical problems. I feared that she would die, that I was following in her self-destructive footsteps, and that my daughter would take that same fatal path unless I did something drastic to end the craziness.

I had a long talk with my higher power. Knowing my higher power was walking with me every minute gave me the resolve to keep going, counting my blessings and focusing on all the positives in my life.

> *Diamonds are nothing more than chunks of coal that stuck to their jobs.*
> —Malcolm Forbes

✱ ✱ ✱

In 1992, I started working with recovering teens at a counseling service. It was deeply fulfilling to hurl myself again into my passion. I felt in my bones that this was what I was meant to be doing.

Life was full and busy, but I made a point of slowing things down so I could be present for my family. I committed myself to planning getaways for the four of us, because otherwise we rarely saw Peter.

I lived for those times when Peter, Alex, Carly, and I were together as a family, relaxing and connecting. Trips to northern Wisconsin, where we camped, backpacked, and stayed on the beautiful shores of Lake Michigan, filled a special place in my heart.

A STEP ON THE JOURNEY

Let nature teach and comfort you. Here are ways to deepen your connection with nature:
- Use all your senses in the out-of-doors. Look around you and absorb the colors and shadings. Listen to the soothing sounds—birds singing, frogs croaking, wind whooshing through the trees, waves lapping the shore. Smell the scent of the earth after a storm. Hold a raindrop or snowflake on your tongue. Pick a radish straight from the garden and taste the essence of springtime. Feel the texture of the grass underfoot, the icy shock of a fresh stream on your toes.
- Get on your hands and knees to check out the earth, the grass, the insects in your yard or in a park. It's helpful to ask a child to join you. Children, so open to the wonders of nature, often see things we overlook.
- Watch the sky. During the daytime, see how the clouds move and change. At dusk and dawn, notice all the colors of the sky. At night, look at the stars and feel your connection to the universe.
- Plant some seeds—flowers or vegetables, in or outside your house—and watch life unfold before your eyes.
- Take a camping trip. Not only will you see nature in a new way, but in the process you'll strengthen your self-reliance.
- Bring arrangements of leaves, grasses, and flowers into your home and office.
- Always make time for sunrises and sunsets.

– J.M.

JOURNAL—January 28, 1993

Ten years ago today I entered treatment. Without my sobriety I would have none of the things I treasure today—my wonderful family, friends, and a career that lets me make a difference in the world. Today I feel especially grateful for my progress and ability to handle problems without using. I'm taking care of myself, exercising, and eating right.

Peter and I don't have a romantic relationship or intimate conversations, but I must remember all he has done to encourage me and how empty my life was before I met him. I waited so long for my own special family, and now I have it.

Somehow, just being alive and healthy, I'm able to cope with all the little troubles of life.

MOMENT OF TRUTH

Appreciate and trust your body. Take these steps to be sure you're giving your body the unconditional acceptance it deserves.
- Notice your breathing. Count how many breaths (one inhale, one exhale) you take per minute. Try taking fewer, deeper breaths—five to ten full breaths a minute is optimal, but don't force it. Accept your breathing as it is. Spend some time every day being aware of your breath. Imagine it as an ocean wave caressing you.
- Recognize that people with different body types experience life very differently. One body type will always be cold, while another will be constantly perspiring. Let your understanding of different bodies make you less judgmental and more compassionate toward your own body as well as others.
- Use tools such as massage, exercise, meditation, yoga, pilates, swimming, or relaxing in a hot tub to celebrate all your body does for you. Move beyond your aches, pains, and concerns for appearance to find a gentle peace with your body. Explore new physical challenges such as line dancing, rock climbing, or swinging on a trapeze. Appreciate how much your body is capable of doing, how much pleasure it can give you, and how well it manages to get you where you want to go.
- Take time to feel the feelings in your body. Speak your feelings out loud (for example, "I feel tense and tight"). Don't judge your emotions and sensations. Observe and appreciate them. Breathe into them.

– J.M.

✳ ✳ ✳

Having children shifted my perspective in unforeseen ways. I spent a great deal of time thinking about healthy families—what they were, how to achieve one if you'd never seen one, what ingredients were necessary, and what needed to be left behind.

Thinking about my parents, I felt sad at times that they seemed so disconnected, although they would have insisted that they had a great marriage. Reflecting on my own marriage, I wondered if it was better to stay with someone and be unhappy or leave and break a family apart. Which would be wiser in the long run? I struggled to find answers so that I could teach my children about good relationships.

Mom was always hard on Dad, very critical and not very kind. Maybe part of the reason he was never around was to escape her disapproval. Now Peter and I seemed to be re-enacting that pattern, and it wasn't what I wanted my children to see. I knew I had to be more accepting of Peter so we could show our kids what a good marriage was like and give them the right template for their lives.

> JOURNAL—June 10, 1994
> I'm thirsting for a spiritual retreat into nature and solitude, where I can turn off the distractions and listen to the inner world. I need to let God enter and fill me up because no human will ever relieve the emptiness.
> My therapist is helping me gain control of my tendency to complain, blame, and criticize, and to be more warm and reinforcing while still being honest about my needs. Instead of telling Peter, "You need to clean up your messes," I'll say, "When I see messes all over the house, I feel anxious and unhappy." I'll show more interest in hockey and in Peter's work—he has started his own computer business—since he devotes all his time to one or the other.
> I know everything will be okay if I keep asking for help. I feel I'm where I'm supposed to be in life.

✼ ✼ ✼

I wangled every chance I could to immerse myself in healing, quiet, natural environments. Sometimes that meant walking along the lake. Now and then it meant taking a long weekend and renting a cabin up north. I savored those times to get in touch with my burgeoning inner self.

Whenever I could put together the time and money, I signed up for guided retreats in the wilderness, which never failed to make me feel reborn. I reveled in everything about those experiences—learning survival skills and building independence, making connections with other people, performing self-awareness exercises, sharing the beauty of the wild, and spending alone time in stillness and silence.

TURNING POINT

Make room for silence. You nourish your brain by bringing more stillness into it. Perhaps that's why such good ideas arrive while you're in the shower or on walks, when your mind is unfocused and receptive.

> *Silence is the language God speaks and everything else is a bad translation.*
> —Thomas Keating

Not only does quieting your mind add creativity and energy to your life, it also opens you to the greatest possibilities. Deep wisdom is most likely to come to you in a whisper. Your higher power doesn't usually yell to get your attention.

> Start by spending just two minutes a day in complete silence. If you find this practice nourishing, you may want to add more such moments later.
>
> – J.M.

During the summer of 1995, I went on a spiritual retreat in northern Wisconsin, overlooking a lake, surrounded by pine trees, wildflowers, birds, deer, and other natural wonders, with twelve other women and a therapist. I didn't know any of them beforehand, but they ended up overturning my life in ways I'd never expected.

I signed up for the four-day retreat because I wanted to quit trying so hard in life and just be. I wanted to learn to live for myself instead of other people, to stop being addicted to being busy, to get in tune with myself and the natural world.

All those things happened to me there, and more. As we sat in a circle and shared what was in our hearts, I opened up and let the sadness out. I cried harder than I ever had before.

I began by talking about the pain of always needing something to fill me—alcohol, drugs, food, men, shopping. I talked about feeling empty, like something was always missing.

The therapist leading the group asked me to go way back, and I talked about little Shelly wanting love and attention, feeling that her brothers were respected and encouraged but she wasn't and that the father she adored never seemed to notice her.

I realized as I told my story that I'd never had the attention from men that I'd craved, nor did I feel I deserved it, all the way from my dad and brothers to my husband. That little girl was still alive in me, needing to be loved and filled. I'd used drugs and sweet, soothing foods as my companions, and now that they were gone all this sadness emerged.

My other letting go had to do with the sexual abuse. My parents had downplayed it, but I felt like my promiscuous behavior in my teens and twenties and all the years I was so needy for male attention resulted from that experience.

After those feelings poured out, I went down to the lake, picked up a log, slammed it against the dock, and screamed as loud as I could: "I hate you for taking away my innocence! I hate you for violating me! I hate you for taking away my dignity and self-respect!" Then I took the log and heaved it into the water.

Till then, I hadn't faced my anger and hurt over the sexual abuse, so I couldn't let go of it. But this was the beginning of moving forward and not carrying all that pain around with me. Like a freed-up logjam, something broke inside me and floated away forever.

The therapist pointed out that I'd put my deep feelings about injustice to good use in my life, work, volunteerism, and everything I did to help other people. She noted that I was drawn to children and teens, those who were powerless—as I'd been when I was violated.

Safe in that haven in the woods, I exposed my real self to those women and felt unconditionally accepted. They gave me something I'd yearned to receive from my parents—the validation that something terrible had happened to me, something that wounded me to my soul, and that I wasn't overreacting.

After the retreat I wrote a letter to my abuser, detailing all my feelings about what he'd done to me, and I let my therapist read it. She and I cried together. Then I set the letter on fire and watched it turn into ashes.

A STEP ON THE JOURNEY

Write a letter to someone who has hurt you (a parent, spouse, lover, friend, or maybe yourself or your addiction). Get out all your emotions. Read the letter to a friend or counselor if you want to share it. Then tear the letter up, throw it away, or burn it. Leave those feelings behind you, and move forward.

– J.M.

✣ ✣ ✣

JOURNAL—April 11, 1998

I'm up north at a cabin I rented on Lake Michigan. Here, watching a sunset of pure gold, I understand that the purpose of life isn't to accumulate things or be successful and admired. The purpose of life is just this—to live. To live in tune with nature and myself.

I got a beautiful little cocker spaniel, Jasper. He is my stress reducer. He teaches me so many good lessons. He grounds me, connects me to the natural world. He knows the truth I'm trying to teach myself every day—to concern myself not so much with doing as with being.

✣ ✣ ✣

Writing in my journal offered insights, especially when I took time to read back over what I'd written months and years before and saw how I was growing and changing. My journals were helpful, too, in revealing patterns so I could get a handle on my seemingly crazy moods, eating patterns, and addictive behavior. I could see what had worked before—and what hadn't worked—so that I was making better choices all the time. Each setback was a chance to learn.

Re-reading my journals gave me the chance to meditate on my own values, those I'd grown up with, those I was passing on to my children, those I lived by, and those I espoused but didn't always follow the way I wished I would. I could see my life as part of a larger whole. It showed me that I'd been through many tough times but always came out learning more about myself and finding the gift in every experience. The challenge was to look for that gift *while* I was going through the hard experience. I still had problems doing that. But I was getting better at it.

Another thing I did was to write journals for my kids. I kept these journals separately from mine, writing about what was going on in Carly's and Alex's lives—things they said to me, things they were doing, things they showed special interest in. Later, they told me those journals made them feel loved and special while giving them a way to re-experience their childhoods. The Carly and Alex journals were invaluable to me, too, reminding me every day how lucky I was to have such great kids. While raising them wasn't always easy, because they were such spirited creatures, I wouldn't have had it any other way.

WAKING UP HAPPY

JOURNAL—January 2, 1999

I must make some major changes in my life. For one thing, I have to stand up to my mother and tell her I won't eat with her anymore. It will hurt her, because eating together has always been our way of feeling close to each other. But I can't impair my life as she has.

Another thing that's become clear is that a lot of my eating has to do with feelings of not being loved and respected by my husband. I may have to leave my marriage. The things I need most—closeness, true communication, a spiritual partner, affirmation, validation—none of those are part of my marriage.

Peter and I must go back into couples counseling and make some changes if we're to keep this marriage alive.

I'll stop comparing myself to others, because that leads to insecurity and overeating. If my parents feel my brothers are more successful and important than I am, that's their opinion, and it's time I stopped trying to change it. I can admire my brothers for their accomplishments without feeling "less than." I have my own strengths, which are unique, and I'll be grateful for what I have.

I'll be thankful for discomfort and conflict, letting them motivate me to a place of love.

I'll stop viewing food as my best friend. I'll quit telling myself that food will make me feel better, that I'll hurt people's feelings if I don't eat dessert with them, that if I abstain from sugar for a month I deserve extra candy the next month, and all the other lies I've told myself so often. I'll be truthful with everyone, including myself.

Instead of looking to others to take care of me, I'll turn to myself for the nurturing I need. I'll get rid of black-and-white, good-and-bad thinking. I'll stop judging myself and others. Those old thought patterns are part of my past. I can change my thinking and my behavior, starting today.

TURNING POINT

Clarify your feelings around food. Do you eat when you're not hungry? It's common for people, especially those with addiction problems, to use food to meet their needs. To break this cycle, clarify those needs and find other strategies to satisfy them.

Step 1. Write down all the things you're feeling. Usually you'll find that you're feeling more than one thing at a time. After each emotion on your list, write BECAUSE and then describe why you might be feeling that emotion. Examples:

I feel **resentful** BECAUSE my spouse hasn't done his share around the house.

I feel **sad** BECAUSE I want to be close to someone.

I feel **disappointed** BECAUSE I expected marriage to be more fulfilling.

Talk about these feelings with a therapist or friend, or write about them. Learning to express emotions rather than "eat" them is the first step to gaining control of your eating habits.

Step 2. List the needs you might be trying to fill with food. Then write down other ways you could meet that need in your life. For example:

Need for safety: I feel anxious, worried, and scared about all the uncertainties of life. SOLUTIONS OTHER THAN FOOD: Turn to soothing rituals like listening to a favorite song, lighting candles, and practicing deep-breathing exercises.

Need for nurturing: Sometimes I feel depleted and uncared for. SOLUTIONS OTHER THAN FOOD: Take care of myself with a hot bath or shower, a massage, or a yoga class. Visit Grandma and ask her for hugs.

> **Need for excitement and escape from drudgery:** Sometimes life seems dull, boring, and monotonous. SOLUTIONS OTHER THAN FOOD: **Take a class or find a new hobby. Plan a getaway. Sign up for a conference or workshop. Rent movies. Go dancing.**
> —adapted from *Life Is Hard, Food Is Easy* by Linda Spangle
>
> *– J.M.*

✫ ✫ ✫

Writing daily about my feelings surrounding food began to transform my thinking, and I made great strides in understanding and accepting myself.

One of the biggest changes was with my mom. We had the most honest talk ever when I explained why I wanted to spend time with her doing things other than eating. She was my eating buddy, and making food for me was how she showed love. So it was hard to shift this dynamic, but we both tried. We found other things to do, like playing with Jasper, whom she loved and called Puppy Boy.

One of the central reasons I overate, I realized, was to fill the need for validation I'd had ever since the sexual trauma. I had to stop looking to my parents and husband for validation that would never come. Instead, I could talk out my emotions in my journal and with my therapist, women friends, and others who valued me.

These insights into my overeating helped in other areas of my life, too. I'd been blaming myself for many things, letting guilt build up till it nearly suffocated me. I'd castigated myself for flirting and enjoying male attention, thinking it made me a bad person and faithless wife. But I hadn't cheated on Peter, just appreciated conversations with men who saw me as the interesting, whole person I aspired to be. That was a normal human response, I realized. Instead of feeling ashamed, I could decide to behave differently in the future. I could recognize my humanness, forgive myself, and leave the past behind.

> *What you do every day is as important to the soul as what your parents did to you.*
> —James Hillman

JOURNAL—March 19, 2001

I'm at Life in Balance, a program in Tucson where people come to get centered. I came to find some clarity, re-energize, and be lifted.

Tonight we entered a sweat lodge while two Native Americans drummed, prayed, and sang. They placed lava-like rocks and steam in the center of the teepee, and the steam and heat became unbearable. But we stayed with it, releasing negative energy and speaking the truth. It was cleansing, spiritual, and powerful. I felt very close to the other women, even though I didn't know them beforehand.

In the sweat lodge, I grieved for my mother, whose health is so fragile that I know she won't be with us much longer. But was she ever emotionally present? I mourned the mother I was losing and the one I'd never had.

I thought about how she is always so put together, her hair and nails perfectly done, and how she puts so much energy into her appearance while neglecting her inner health. I cried because I can't help her give up the overeating, diet pills, and denial that are killing her. All I can do is work on changing myself, breaking this cycle, teaching my children the right values, and helping them feel good about themselves for who they are, not how they look.

Life, I embrace you.

If I'm going to die, the best way to prepare is to quiet my mind and open my heart. If I'm going to live, the best way to prepare for it is to quiet my mind and open my heart.
—Ram Dass

✳ ✳ ✳

After deteriorating for several years, my mother died on June 29, 2002. I'd been slowly letting go for quite a while, but that didn't keep me from being devastated by her death. I'd been spending hours a day with her and, although she didn't always recognize me, it comforted me to hold her hand and kiss her cheeks.

I'd been keeping my food cravings under control, but after Mom died, I started eating emotionally again. It was as if I could stay close to her by getting back into the crazy eating patterns I'd shared with her for so long.

Miserable and grief-stricken as I was, though, I could feel a difference in myself. I was able to get in touch with my feelings of loss in a way I'd never done before, and that helped me get my overeating in check.

At a wilderness retreat, I did a visualization in which I closed my eyes, went to a beautiful spot in my mind, and connected with Mom. She told me I didn't have to binge anymore to feel close to her. She gave me permission to live a life different from hers—to care for myself, let go of my obsession, and enjoy food in a healthy way.

JOURNAL—August 8, 2002

I'm meditating at Indian Lake, alone except for my dog, Jasper. The wind is blowing. There are no people around. It's peaceful and beautiful here.

I need to decide whether to stay with Peter. I've been so unhappy in my marriage for so long. I've felt like a single parent almost constantly since the kids were born.

I'm trying to let my higher power help me make this decision. My therapist asked me to choose five stones to represent Peter's positive qualities and five to stand for his negatives, then reflect ten minutes on each stone and release them to the earth or water.

Five positives: good father, fun to be with, easy-going, helpful with chores, supports my career and my recovery.

Five negatives: lack of intimacy and emotional connection, critical and disrespectful of me, inattentive, never plans dates or vacations, never gives of himself at temple or to those less fortunate, plays hockey too much (whoops, that's six).

I want so much to understand my higher power's plan for me, to be content with what is—my family, my body, my life. Prayer, surrender, gratitude, and service are the answers.

Even when the obstacle of myself seems endlessly insurmountable, I continue.
—Carla Needlemann

CONNECT TO THE EARTH: SHELLY'S STORY

✭ ✭ ✭

Everything within me was telling me to leave the marriage, but I just couldn't do it. The idea of being with the kids only half-time was too painful to bear. I kept seeing the kids' faces and how they glowed when they saw Peter and me happy together. So I hung on, begging my higher power to help me trust and accept things as they were.

I continued to work on making changes in my life. Rather than rushing into my exercise routine each morning, I started the day by meditating and listing my blessings. This small shift made a huge difference, helping me feel less angry, closer to my family and higher power, and more present for life.

I was leading a support group for recovering teens and getting referrals from a lot of lawyers in town. When their teenaged clients got into legal trouble due to drug use, the lawyers sent them to my group. Many of these teens were at such a low point that they were willing to put in the energy to turn their lives around, and that was gratifying to see.

One of these lawyers, who became a mentor to me, asked me, "Why are you working for someone else?" and encouraged me to start my own clinic.

Those words were a seed that took fruit in my mind. I realized that having my own clinic was what I wanted. It seemed like a huge undertaking, but I knew if I desired it enough I could make it happen.

For months, I thought about it and bounced ideas off my friends. Everyone was encouraging, and their support propelled me forward.

Once I made the decision to go ahead with the clinic, I was energized. I knew I'd never do it if I thought about what a giant step it was. Instead, I broke it into pieces and concentrated on them one at a time—creating a business plan, finding therapists to work in my new clinic, buying office equipment and furniture, getting licenses and insurance, filling out countless forms.

I knew my strengths were counseling and working with people, not paperwork or administrative details. But I also knew I had the ability to find and engage the best minds to help me.

> JOURNAL—September 22, 2002
>
> Every day the idea of my clinic is unfolding a bit more. I've decided to call it Connections. That's what it will be about—connecting with other people, which I've come to believe is the key to sobriety. It's only through my ties with others that I have the certitude to start this clinic in the first place. It's by linking up with people who care about them that clients at my clinic will care enough about themselves to get and stay sober.
>
> I remember how scary it was to be under the influence of speed and coke—the desperation, headaches, chest pains, fear of death, inability to eat or sleep, wanting more and then being so depressed, never present, never happy, always lonely.
>
> Now my life is so full of love. I cherish my children with my entire soul. Since Mom died, I've been spending more time with my dad. Now that he's retired and without Mom, he has finally found space in his life for me. Although he still doesn't talk much about feelings, and I know he's not likely to change any time soon, just being with him is enough. I feel his love and know he feels mine.
>
> People inspire me. My friends surround me, and I'm no longer afraid to ask for what I want. It sounds simple, but sometimes simplicity is the hardest thing of all. Still, I'm learning to do it more and more. I would be in jail or dead today if I hadn't learned to let others in.

✭ ✭ ✭

TURNING POINT

Make your dreams come true. No dream is too big, but the key is to remember that fulfilling a dream takes time, patience, and persistence. It won't happen overnight. But it will happen if you follow a few basic steps:

- Create a vision of what you want. Write it down in as much detail as possible. Picturing it in your mind's eye will help you bring it to life.
- Talk about it—with the right people. Don't share your vision with naysayers, those who tend to criticize and belittle. What you need is constructive feedback, helpful support, and positive energy. Find people who will help you sustain your excitement. Meet with them regularly.
- Educate yourself. Attend seminars, search the Internet, and read books related to your vision. Join groups, either online or in person, to discuss topics in your area of interest. The more diverse stimuli you receive, the more vivid your vision will become.
- Break your vision into manageable goals. Under each goal, write down specific tasks to achieve it and realistic deadlines for each task. Make sure the first task isn't more than a few days away; that will keep you from postponing it. If you don't complete a task on time, don't despair. Planning is essential, but plans aren't meant to be followed slavishly. Keep readjusting your list of tasks and deadlines, keeping them realistic in light of what's happening in your life.
- Create a network. Few dreams are actualized by one person alone. A network of supportive people will open all kinds of opportunities for you. Help others in your network, and they'll be there when you need them.

What is your dream? What would you wish for if you knew for sure you could make it come true? Write it here:_____
_____
_____

– J.M.

Connections Counseling opened at the beginning of 2003. The night before the grand opening, I invited my friends, family, and supporters to join me in a ceremony to bless the new space.

My long-time therapist, Bobbi, facilitated the ceremony. We sat in a circle and each person lit a candle and talked about what this day meant to them. They said such eloquent, reflective, caring things about the work I do. Carly gave a moving speech, and we were all touched by her words.

I told everyone how much they meant to me and emphasized that I couldn't do this work if it weren't for their support. There were lots of tears but mostly a feeling of powerful love from people who believed in me. I'll never forget that special blessing and the excitement of opening my own clinic—truly a dream come true.

JOURNAL—January 28, 2004

It's been a year since my clinic opened, and it is magical. I love being there and bask in the energy and warmth. Everyone feels connected and happy there.

It's gratifying that the clinic is progressing financially so that we can expand our services as needed. Of course, I didn't start Connections to get rich. But I did want to make enough money so that I'd never have to depend on a man. I wanted to know I could be self-sufficient, and now I know I can, just through my own initiative, ideas, and hard work. That's a delicious feeling.

Today's the twenty-first anniversary of my going into in-patient treatment and giving up cocaine. The kids in my teen group gave me a beautiful party, each standing to speak about what I meant to them. They said I was their mentor, their role model—that I saved their lives and helped them find hope—that I make them feel valued, important, and loved. (It's much easier when it's not your own kids!)

The greatest gifts are mindfulness, a positive outlook, and gratitude. I count my blessings every day.

Follow your bliss and the universe will open doors where there were only walls.
—Joseph Campbell

QUICK QUESTION

Live each day with an attitude of gratitude. We asked some of the counselors and their clients at Connections what they're thankful for. Here's what they said:

ability to live in the moment
babies smiling
back scratches
human ingenuity
crisp, fresh fruit
cartwheels
snow days
goosebumps – love 'em
napping in the sun
each new day
the lotion I put on after my shower
and the friend who gave it to me

orgasms and chocolate
health and growth
sunshine
people who believe in me
laughter and tears
my second chance
being alive
my amazing support network
tear-jerking movies
lattes in the morning, cocoa at night
those precious moments of normalcy
my ability now to feel my feelings

– J.M.

JOURNAL—August 9, 2004

Peter, the kids, and I just returned from a two-week family trip to Europe—another dream fulfilled. For a long time I'd been wanting to experience more of the world (this was my first time outside the U.S.) and expose my children to other cultures. It was everything I'd hoped it would be, and more.

I'm so glad I decided to put so many resources—months of planning and dipping deeply into our funds—to reach this goal of mine. While I try to live a simple life, money spent on trips is worthwhile because travel opens up new worlds and restores the spirit.

I haven't written in my journal for months, and I need to get back into the routine of journaling every day or at least once a week. I journal for the same reason I go on trips and retreats—to refresh, gain perspective, and value what's important. My purpose becomes clear.

A STEP ON THE JOURNEY

Go on a retreat, either by yourself or with a group, somewhere away from your usual life. If possible, plan retreats near bodies of water; there's nothing as restorative as the murmur of a brook or the rhythmic crashing of waves.

If there isn't time for a full getaway, go on a mini-retreat. Take a quick trip outdoors to enjoy trees, sky, and sunshine. Install a small fountain in your yard, office, or home so you can appreciate the soothing quality of water whenever you need to be restored.

– J.M.

✣ ✣ ✣

My clinic was going well, and I'd been working hard to get a sober high school up and running. It was something that was badly needed, because once teens got sober it was counterproductive to send them back where they'd been using. It was vital to give them a fresh start with a chance to make new, non-using friends.

To my joy, Horizon High School opened in 2005. I incorporated it as a nonprofit organization so that parents and others who wanted to help could contribute money to keep it running. The opening ceremony was one of the most heartwarming experiences of my life. I felt proud that I'd found meaning in my pain and that my pilgrimage had taken me to a place of service and love.

It was hard to believe how huge my little teen program had become. Now, professionals were studying it, exploring what made it so unique. The answer was simple: The key to getting these kids better was to believe in them, connect to them, and teach them the secret of a healthy life—to have hope, love, and compassion for others.

JOURNAL—April 23, 2005

I'm flying home from a week in Florida ready to begin a new phase. As I danced and prayed on the seashore under the full moon, I let go of all the stress and worry about work.

Inhaling the clarity of the stars, I reflected on my life and arrived at some new resolutions. I decided to hire more people at my clinic so I won't burn out and risk doing less quality work. I reminded myself that accepting assistance is a sign of strength, not weakness, and I'll delegate more when I get back. I'll take more time for myself. Trying to do too much isn't healing.

My life has gotten very cluttered—too much of everything. Simplify rather than intensify. Let go of everything that's not essential and meaningful. Be content with small things. Appreciate a taste of chocolate, not huge quantities. Never waste time wanting. These are life's lessons.

I've started taking yoga classes, an excellent way to balance mind, body, and spirit. I especially like laughter yoga, which we practice at the end of one of my classes. We begin to chuckle, and at first it's forced and insincere, but soon it's real, straight-from-the-gut laughter, and it's wonderful to feel it bubbling up from inside us and from our yoga partners all around us. We all need belly laughs like that—they're as necessary as tears.

TURNING POINT

Try laughter yoga to reduce stress, bolster your immune system, and make happiness a choice. Research shows that laughter activates the same pleasure centers of the brain as cocaine.

There are no rules for a laughter yoga session, but here are ideas you can use to get started (for more, see laughteryoga.org):

Sit in a circle. Maintain eye contact with another person in the group.

Open your mouth wide, and laugh silently.

Close your mouth and make a humming sound while continuing to laugh.

Hold your arms out to the side and flap them like a bird while chanting, "Hoo, hoo, hoo, hoo, hoo."

Begin to giggle and then to laugh from your belly, slowly increasing the tempo and volume of your laughter.

Even if you don't genuinely laugh, it doesn't matter. Here's a good place to practice "faking it" till it becomes real.

Keep laughing as you lie on your back and close your eyes.

–J.M.

☆ ☆ ☆

That summer, another dream came true when Peter and I bought a lake cabin in northern Wisconsin—almost two acres, secluded and peaceful, a screened-in porch facing the water, no neighbors in sight, so calm and tranquil. Blue sky, loons, kayaks, canoes—everything I'd hoped, dreamed, and visualized for so long.

We couldn't afford it but we bought it anyway, taking out a one-hundred-percent loan on home equity. The cabin meant so much to me that I happily cut expenses in other areas of my life. My parents didn't take risks like that to make their dreams come true, and I saw how unhappy they were as a result. This was a gamble worth taking.

No matter how difficult life became, I always found serenity at our cabin. When the whole family went for a weekend, it was a perfect way to connect and get the kids to leave computers, video games, and TV behind. We swam, rafted in the lake, and walked in the woods together. At times it was just Carly and me, and we always had fun and laughed a lot. I brought my women friends there, and occasionally my dad, and at other times my Connections clients who needed a time out from the turmoil of life. Sometimes it was just my dog and me.

I enjoyed painting and decorating our new place, even preparing meals and washing dishes by hand—not usually my favorite chores, but there was something invigorating about doing everything "from scratch," not having all the modern conveniences. It was good for the soul to do strenuous physical work, sleep well, play hard, and revive my lost creative self.

A STEP ON THE JOURNEY

Connect to your inner creative force. Here are some ways to unlock your creative self:
- Stimulate yourself with as many different people, bits of knowledge, and viewpoints as possible. Read books and magazines outside your usual field. Take classes that open your mind to new ideas.
- Brainstorm ideas, either by yourself or with others. Write or call out as many ideas as you can, no matter how silly they may seem. Sometimes those that seem most crazy at first turn out to be the most worthwhile.
- Draw your thoughts rather than writing them out.
- Rejoice in failure. "I have not failed," Thomas Edison said. "I've just found 10,000 ways that won't work." Embracing failure will give you a sense of freedom that unlocks your creativity.
- Have fun. The more you can laugh and enjoy what you're doing, the more creative you'll be.

– J.M.

✧ ✧ ✧

Life continued to shower lessons in my path. Alex and Carly were both diagnosed with ADD (Attention Deficit Disorder), and as I took them to doctors and therapists, helping them cope with the disorder, it occurred to me that I probably had ADD, too.

Like my kids, I'd struggled with school, concentration, and follow-through. I'd always been easily distracted, impulsive, and disorganized. My teachers had chided me that I wasn't trying hard enough, even though I was trying as hard as I could. ADD wasn't recognized when I was in school the way it is today, so I'd gotten the message that I was lazy, troublesome, and inadequate. Part of the reason I became addicted to cocaine, I realized, was that I hadn't been diagnosed with ADD earlier.

I found a good doctor who put the kids on medication for their ADD, and they thrived, becoming less easily frustrated and overwhelmed. After the doctor confirmed that I also had ADD, I found many ways to address it, including nutrition, exercise, medication, and therapy, in which I explored my feelings and found new coping strategies.

Once I discovered that I'd struggled with ADD all my life, I felt more compassion for myself. I saw that, along with all its challenges, ADD had given me many gifts—my creativity, energy, and resourcefulness. While it's hard having a mind that's always racing to the next subject, that's also how I came up with a lot of good ideas. Without ADD, maybe I wouldn't have accomplished all I have in my life.

> *I sang in my chains like the sea.*
> —Dylan Thomas

✧ ✧ ✧

My beloved dog Jasper had become more and more ill-tempered as he grew old, and when he bit Carly on the nose I knew it was too dangerous to keep him. When we put him to sleep, I felt like a part of me died. Coming home to an empty house, no one excited to see me, no one to snuggle and play with—his loss was a physical ache that seemed endless.

It was hard to make that leap to love again, but after mourning Jasper for nearly a year, I got another puppy—a golden retriever I called Emmy. Her easy, happy nature soothed my heart. I relished taking her to the dog park, where just saying hello to other dogs and people was enough.

> *On beyond ideas of right doing and wrong doing there is a field. I will meet you there. When the soul lies down in that grass, the world is too full to talk about.*
> —Rumi

My next challenge at Connections was to help people who didn't have health insurance and couldn't afford treatment. I made sure we had many sliding scales because I didn't want to turn away anyone who wanted counseling. But to increase opportunities for addicts while accommodating people who wanted to donate money, I decided to start a foundation.

Recovery Foundation was launched in 2008. We earned seed money for the foundation by throwing a giant sober party with lots of music, dancing, and rock bands. The party was a success, and we raised enough funds so that we could start offering scholarships and broadening our services to help many more people. Again, a new beginning.

Time seemed to be speeding up, and it took all my energy to reduce the pace so I wouldn't be overwhelmed. Much as my job meant to me, I didn't want work to become another addiction in my life. I forced myself to take time away from Madison so I wouldn't forget to enjoy the present moment with a full heart.

TURNING POINT

Break free of digital distractions. Our constant connection to technology leads to enormous stress. *Conquer CyberOverload* by Joanne Cantor describes ways to take back our lives:
- Schedule regular breaks in which you leave technology behind and do something relaxing and fun.

- Limit TV time. Research shows that the more TV people watch, the more anxious and dissatisfied they are.
- Reduce contact with your messaging devices. Constant interruptions are so detrimental to the brain that you can begin to have symptoms of dementia. Turn off your cell phone for a few hours at a time. Change your email settings to check for messages every few hours rather than once a minute. There's nothing so important in anyone's life that it can't wait at least that long.
- Keep in touch with people physically rather than virtually whenever you can. The crucial parts of communication—the real connections—don't occur through technology. Giving and receiving smiles produce pleasurable changes in the brain that can happen only in person.
- Practice single-tasking rather than multi-tasking. What we call multi-tasking is really task-switching. Rather than doing two things at once, our brain is shifting back and forth between tasks. We end up doing neither one effectively.
- As frequently as possible, perform a cyber cleansing. Turn everything off—TVs, cell phones, computers, everything—and bask in the silence.

– J.M.

In April of 2008, I attended a retreat in Arizona. I didn't have headaches for the entire trip, so I decided I didn't have a brain tumor, as I'd been fearing. Rather, I realized, it was the stress, worry, and working too hard that had been making my head hurt for months. Even though I was accomplishing good things at work, I knew it was foolish to risk my health and my life by trying to do too much. During the retreat, I made a list of strategies to put my life in more balance:
- I'll rate my stress level daily, 1-10, and, if it's too high, I'll add more down time, more recovery meetings, and more yoga classes.
- I'll limit phone calls to five minutes, and I'll schedule a time each day when I turn off my cell phone for an hour or so. I'll keep digital distractions to a minimum.
- Every Sunday, I'll prepare healthy food for the week so it's always available. I'll have cut-up veggies ready at all times for snacks. That will keep me from mindlessly reaching for junky foods when I feel stressed, and I'll be sure I have the nutrition I need to stay healthy.
- I'll eat, go to sleep, and wake up each day at regularly scheduled times.
- I'll experiment with exercising less obsessively. I don't have to work out every single day.
- I'll say "no" to speaking requests unless they don't conflict with home time.
- Fridays will be my sacred days when I won't overextend myself or do too much. I'll give myself permission to stay home on Friday if I need a break from work.

Making that list was a fundamental step for me. Just writing down those tactics for change made me feel better, clearer, and less frantic.

Another thing I did at the retreat was even more illuminating. The facilitator asked us to write autobiographies in the third person, and the exercise opened up something deep inside of me. This is what I wrote:

> Once upon a time there was a cute little girl who was loved by her family. Her mother wanted the little girl to be perfect, clean, neat, and well-mannered. Her dad was busy with work and sports. She always wanted her dad to spend time with her and her mom to accept her as she was.
>
> As a teen, she was sexually abused by a trusted friend of the family and told her parents, but they never wanted to talk about it, and the man was never arrested or punished. She tried to forget what had happened, but she was confused and frightened. When she grew up, she never felt valued or important and had a hard time relating to men.
>
> The story changed when she became willing to surrender, to let go of that anxious child who needed to feel power. She did work that helped others and encouraged people to believe in themselves. She took good care of her body and soul. She reached out to become more effective in her career by speaking and writing about her work. She became active in her community, gave away some of what she had, and felt peaceful and grateful.
>
> She was no longer that scared, helpless kid. She was a competent adult who knew how to meet any challenge that came her way. When the little girl inside her cried out for attention, she took care of her in productive, nourishing ways rather than indulging in junk food or other hurtful behaviors. She loved, protected, and cherished that sweet child who had tried so hard for so long. She became the mother and father the little girl had always longed for. Instead of living happily ever after, she pushed forward every day and learned to love the struggle.

To begin writing from our pain eventually engenders compassion for our small and groping lives. Out of this broken state there comes a tenderness for the cement below our feet, the dried grass cracking in a terrible wind.
—Natalie Goldberg

Writing my story and then reading it over to myself was healing in so many ways. I was able to feel kinder toward the innocent child of my story than I ever felt for the adult Shelly. Feeling empathy for that little girl helped me forgive myself for being such a flawed, imperfect person.

Even more life-changing was the next exercise—reading our stories out loud to one another. Once the words were out, there was such a sweet release. The other women embraced me, soothed me, and cried with me. I felt surrounded by love.

The last day of the retreat, I hiked up Camelback Mountain. It was brutal and challenging but such euphoria when I reached the top—so much better than cocaine! One step at a time, I'd climbed much higher than I ever dreamed I could.

✯ ✯ ✯

> ## A STEP ON THE JOURNEY
>
> **Write about your life in the third person** (he or she) rather than the first person (I, me). View yourself as a character in a story. For example, instead of saying, "I was raised by an alcoholic father," you might say, "He was raised by an alcoholic father." Seeing yourself with a more objective eye is a good way to see yourself with more clarity and compassion.
>
> — J.M.

It was when I returned from that retreat that I made a major decision. Even after going to couples counseling and trying with all my strength to save our marriage, I knew I couldn't stay with Peter any longer. I'd never been a priority in his life, and I couldn't continue being treated with such disregard. Once I hadn't thought I deserved more, but now I did. Despite the piercing pain of it, I decided to go ahead with a divorce.

You spent the first half of your life becoming somebody. Now you can work on becoming nobody, which is really somebody. For when you become nobody there is no tension, no pretense, no one trying to be anyone or anything. The natural state of the mind shines through unobstructed—and the natural state of the mind is pure love.
— Ram Dass

JOURNAL—August 18, 2008

Emmy and I have been at the cabin for four days. There's no better place for me to learn to be a human being rather than always a human doing. I can go at my own pace, listen to my thoughts, and just be. I delight in getting up early and looking forward to my day, not answering my cell phone unless I want to, exploring the woods, talking to myself or enjoying pure silence, not having to please anyone but me.

I'm sitting on my orange Adirondack chair watching the lake, sky, and trees, listening to the bird sounds, A caterpillar is slowly inching along. I enjoy his calm, unhurried demeanor. This stillness is more valuable than psychiatrists, workshops, or self-help books.

When I think about divorcing Peter after twenty-two years of marriage, sometimes I feel like my heart will break. But we are moving forward with the divorce, and I feel sure it's the right thing to do. I would have done it years ago if I'd been brave enough.

Once I thought Peter was my purpose in life. Now I see that another person can't be my reason for being. I'm not positive why I'm here on earth, but I do know I feel most complete when I'm working to help others and living an honest life with integrity, simplicity, and faith. I'm closest to my higher power when I spend time in nature and look for the good in people and in my life.

Here at the cabin, life is as clear and clean as pure water. Last night, watching the sun set over the lake, streaking the sky with violet, I performed a sort of letting-go ceremony in which I said good-bye to my marriage, my urge to control, the commotion of my busy mind.

I murmured words that became a chant: "The day is ending, it's time for something beautiful to be born. Let go. Watch day pass to night, and connect to the infinite. Let go. Throw off the ego, the desire for power and material things, all the useless suffering. Let go of the past. Give up the pain. Relinquish the striving. Let it go. Here, now, in the dying light, I release all sorrow, resentment, and regret. I surrender. I forgive everyone who has hurt me. I forgive myself for all the things I've done that hurt myself and others. I'm renouncing it all. I assure myself with all my heart: I love you, I'll always take good care of you and never leave you. I see your goodness. You're safe now. It's time to let go, time to stop doing, doing, doing, trying, trying, trying, and time just to be. Just to be, just be. Just be."

> *You need not do anything*
> *Remain sitting at your table and listen*
> *Just wait*
> *And you need not even wait, just become quiet and still and solitary*
> *And the world will offer itself to you to be unmasked*
> *It has no choice*
> *It will roll in ecstasy at your feet.*
> —Rainer Maria Rilke

MOMENT OF TRUTH

Balance doing with being. First and foremost, you're a human being, not a "human doing." Don't get so wrapped up in activity that you forget the power of simply being in harmony with the world around you, living with awareness and intention. Ground yourself by feeling your body and your breath, viewing yourself with kindness and without judgment.

– J.M.

✼ ✼ ✼

With my therapist's help, I formed a group I called my wild women team. Knowing those trusted friends were there when I needed guidance was a great comfort. Even more important than their advice was the knowledge that I could feel safe and secure with them and always speak my truth, whatever it might be, without being judged or abandoned.

I saw how much healthier it was to call on a group of friends than to depend on one person to fill all my needs, as I'd done with Peter. Asking a man to be my savior would never work. It would either drain him or force him to retreat. Instead, I needed to use the collective group to ground me, along with such tools as music, art, nature, and animals.

My wild women's support helped me through the heartache of my separation from my husband as well as another loss that came like a bolt from the sky. My precious dog Emmy was only three years old when she got sick with an infection and died suddenly.

I mourned for weeks and then made that plunge into the next phase of my life—another golden-retriever puppy I named Rylee. I wasn't cured of my grief. That would take much more time. But, while I'd learned I didn't need a man to complete me, I couldn't bear to live without a dog.

> ### TURNING POINT
>
> **Create your own board of nurturers.** Think of three to five people who accept you for who you are. Call on them separately or together when you need to know you're cared for, when your confidence needs bolstering, or when your life seems unmanageable. Such a board is invaluable to sustain you, support you, laugh and cry with you, and keep you on the right path by gently pointing out when you've strayed from your true self and your life's mission. Jot down the names of people you'd like to have on your board:_____
> _____
>
> – J.M.

✤ ✤ ✤

Painful as the separation from Peter was, it filled me with the kind of strength I'd always wanted for myself. It was a declaration that I could trust myself. It toppled the stories I'd absorbed growing up and was, in a way, the ending to the tale I'd written at the retreat about the frightened, neglected little girl. It was the beginning of a new narrative about a grown-up Shelly who crafted her own life and knew how to appreciate and care for herself.

When Peter and I started the divorce process, I worried that I'd have to give up the cabin as part of the settlement. The cabin had become so central to my well-being, such a sacred space to me, that I couldn't imagine life without it. But I had faith that things would turn out, and they did. Peter agreed to keep the house in town and let me have the cabin. I moved into a small apartment until I saved enough money to buy my own condo. I spent almost every weekend at the cabin and felt that as long as I had it as my special retreat I'd be all right.

> *This is the time. This is the place. This is the vastness. Right here is paradise. Always. Always.*
> —Byron Katie

✤ ✤ ✤

As the months and then years passed, I appreciated my new independence but also longed for a mate to share my life. Alex and Carly had their own lives, and I was often alone. Dating was hard, and none of the relationships I attempted seemed right.

Then, several years after my divorce, my friend Candace brought me to her house, gave me a large art board and a bin of art supplies, and told me to spend the afternoon creating a collage that would answer the questions, "If you could have anything you wanted in a mate, what would you ask for? What are the things you want to share with someone?"

It was an inspired idea, because that's the way I express myself best—with art materials in my hands. Candace knows me so well.

Time dissolved as I worked, and before I knew it the afternoon was over, and the collage was finished. In thick letters at the top I'd written out what I'd always craved: "To Be Cherished." Scattered around the board in various colors were words like intimacy, spirituality, respect, and adventure, along with action verbs like skiing, biking, swimming, kayaking, dancing, hiking, and skinny-dipping. I'd created hearts out of felt material, symbolized nature with feathers and birch bark, and sprinkled silver sparkle judiciously over it all. In the center of the board I'd added a large figure of a bicycle.

I'm not sure why I placed that bicycle there, and at the time I had no idea of all that it portended—no clue that it was a harbinger for an unimagined life.

About a month later, just by chance—who knows how these things happen as they do?—I ended up on a site called fitness.com. Since I was there, I filled out a profile describing who I was and what mattered most to me—many of the same things I'd pinpointed in my collage.

A few days later I got a call from a guy named Chuck, who had seen my profile and began by asking, "Do you want to go paddling or cycling?"

I laughed, liking the way he got right to the point but thinking we'd better get to know each other first.

"How about coffee?" I replied.

When we met and started talking, we were amazed at how much we had in common. He owned a small house in the same block as the condo I'd just bought. We'd both been in long-term marriages and were now divorced. Like me, he loved nature, travel, and the out-of-doors, and was spiritual but not religious.

He was a serious exerciser who did triathlons and especially loved road biking, and pretty soon we were spending every weekend biking together. I discovered that I shared his passion for biking, and, after months of training, I even completed the Door County Century, a hundred-mile bike ride.

If you'd told me a year earlier that I'd be pedaling for a hundred miles, I'd have said you were crazy. But that's the miracle of recovery and all it teaches you—knowing it's possible to change your life, being open to possibilities, seizing each new day, and following where it leads you. That ride was the hardest thing I'd ever done (physically at least) and also the most satisfying.

The bike image wasn't the only part of my collage that came to life for me. Every one of the words in my collage became a reality. For the first time I understood what "cherish" meant.

Before, with every potential romance, I'd tried too hard. This time, I was able to relax and be myself in a way I'd never been able to do when meeting a man. I think getting to know each other on bicycles was part of the secret. Not that I didn't have to fight against those old tapes telling me I wasn't good enough, that I needed to be more than I was, but by now I had learned how to talk back to them. This time, I let myself be cherished.

✭ ✭ ✭

Today, the list of blessings in my life is long. So many of my life's dreams have come to fruition, and I embrace each day with playfulness, curiosity, and willingness to take my life to the next level, whatever that may be. I'm content, more than I've ever been, not wanting more of anything, not rushing.

It has been years since I weighed myself or obsessed about my weight the way I once did. I've integrated healthy eating into my life, along with exercise, relaxation, and other self-loving practices.

With my friends' help, I learned to let go as Alex and then Carly left for college and started building their own lives. It was a difficult transition, but I know their lives are out of my hands, and I must trust the cosmos to take care of them.

Rylee, Chuck, and I spend every moment we can at the cabin, which has become the truest home I've ever had. There, encircled by pine trees, sky, and water, I can see that all the endings are beginnings, too—a new season, a new dog, a new boyfriend, a life without the food issues that bound my mom and me, a new kind of independence and belief in myself.

Your task is not to seek for love, but merely to seek and find all the barriers within yourself that you have built against it.
—Rumi

SHELLY'S BEST ADVICE

- Don't try to change and fix other people, just accept and love them.
- Remind yourself that misery is optional. You have the power to change your thoughts, feelings, and behavior.
- There's no need to chase happiness because it exists within you.
- Build a team of helpers and support people.
- Focus on what brings you joy.
- Find the opportunity that lives within every obstacle.
- Avoid filling life with doing rather than being.
- It's never too late to be who you are meant to be.

If stories shape our lives, and I know they do, I want to tell my children—and my clients at Connections—tales of empowerment, change, and endless possibility. I want my life to be such a story.

If I still struggle daily with my addictions, I'm now able to ask for help to manage them. They can't control me if I don't let them, and I've learned enough ways to combat them so that I can live with certitude and serenity. I go to support-group meetings five times a week, meet for an hour every week with my sponsor, and continue to work with my long-time therapist Bobbi. I have three best friends—Debi, Julie, and Andrea—who have been my constant companions and support. Women friends are a core necessity for me.

I talk to myself constantly, relaying encouraging messages. You could call them affirmations, suggestions, or even prayers. I remind myself, "Trust your relation to the universe," "Today is all you have," "Slow down; pay attention," and my favorite four-word piece of advice, "Thy will be done."

Saying "Thy will be done" is a form of surrender, another way of telling myself, "Whatever will be, will be, and I will accept it." I repeat it silently many times a day, every day. If I'm upset because someone in my group isn't "getting" it, or because I'm late and frazzled, or whatever it is, I just say to the universe, "I give up, I can't handle it, I'm turning it over to you; do whatever you want with it. Whatever you think is best."

It's a small thing, but it works. It turns me into Teflon, so the stress slides off me.

It hasn't been easy to get to this point, and I continue to grow every day. You can't help it when you're in this business, the business of changing lives.

I'm successful in my work because I feel compassion for my clients. I know what they're going through, how hard it is. I don't have all the answers, but I've been where they are. I've been through my own struggles so I can help them in theirs. It's a real privilege for me to do this work that I believe in so deeply and to help people who are suffering.

Change begins with taking myself away from clutter in order to hear what my heart needs to say. At my cabin, with Rylee at my side, my body stretches, lightens, and develops a rhythm with the earth. The busy world narrows to the simplicity of sky, wind, and water. Slowly I become still. Sitting on my cabin porch, watching the sun play on the water, listening to the wind sing, I am at peace.

✯ ✯ ✯

TOOLS FOR THE JOURNEY

Be sure your job doesn't overwhelm your life. Take breaks at work to re-energize and shift perspective. Use your lunch hour to take a walk, do some exercises, or meditate. Take time to reflect on what you're doing, why you're doing it, and why it matters.

Practice visualization. Create a mental picture of the life—or the experience—you desire. Imagine how you'll feel and how you'll look, the environment that will surround you, the people beside you. The clearer the reality you envision, the more likely that you'll make it come true.

Take time, too, to visualize moments in the past when you felt you were your best self. Use those visual memories as touchstones in your journey through change, reminding yourself that you've faced change in the past and triumphed over your fears.

Don't overextend yourself or add so many things to your life that you spread yourself too thin. Part of saying yes to life is knowing which things are essential and which you can put aside. Drop the things that sap your energy and don't bring you joy.

Treat each moment with curiosity, close attention, and awe. Zen master Shunryu Suzuki pointed out that in the beginner's mind there are many possibilities, but in the expert's there are few. Those who consider themselves authorities have whittled the world's boundless opportunities down to a few options. But when you view things as a beginner would, you open yourself fully to the moment, without assumptions, judgment, or limits.

An ideal way to cultivate a beginner's attitude is by practicing mindfulness. Next time you're standing in line, sitting at a red light, or attending a meeting, focus all your attention on the experience, noticing everything around you. Mindfulness is practically synonymous with renewal, since when you discard old certainties, you expand the world around you.

– J.M.

THINGS TO DO TODAY

1. **Stimulate your creative self** by doing something completely different—or doing something ordinary in a new way. Take a new route to work. Brush your teeth using your non-dominant hand. Practice walking backwards, standing on your head, or dancing to a new song. Doing just one small thing differently each day keeps your brain alive and opens you to the gifts of the universe.

2. **Hug someone,** or ask someone for a hug. Another person's embrace tells you more about them, and conveys more about you, than any conversation, and makes you both feel good. Hugs are indispensable, as vital as air to nourish the soul.

3. **If you'd like to explore a topic in this chapter more fully, take a look** at one of the websites or books listed in "Resources to Guide and Inspire You" at the end of this book.

4. **Buy a houseplant** (or ask a friend for a cutting of one of theirs). It will keep you connected to nature throughout your day. Research shows live plants improve people's moods.

5. **Let your calls go to voice mail** for an hour. Give yourself a chance to pause and center yourself.

– J.M.

WORDS OF WISDOM AND LIGHT

Use these lessons from others who are paving new paths to replace their old, unhealthy ones.

I Am a Spirit Trying to Be Charlie: Wisdom from Charlie

I had trouble at first understanding how to add a spiritual dimension to my life. But then it occurred to me that I was born spiritual. We all were. It's just a matter of getting back to that original purity of spirit.

So, rather than think of myself as trying to be spiritual, I think of myself as a spiritual being trying to be Charlie. Once I started knowing myself as a spiritual creature, I became connected to something universal and boundless, a source of strength that can never run dry. It has changed my life.

Charlie's best advice: Get in touch with the spirit that's always been at your core. Strip away all the pretense, striving, accumulating, and role-playing, and be who you truly are. One way to do so is to recall yourself as a child. What did you love to do? What excited you? What comforted you? What did you believe about life? Look at pictures of yourself as a child, and remember how it felt being open, curious, and alive to all the magic of the world. You're still the eager spirit you were then.

This Is a "We" Thing: Wisdom from Raoul

One of my big struggles has been discovering who I am and learning to like that person. The journey to liking myself is, of course, partly a private quest. But much of who I am revolves around being part of a whole.

As I learn about myself, I'm becoming more open-minded toward new people, ideas, beliefs, adventures. I'm learning to put myself in other people's shoes, understand other points of view, and do what I can to make each person feel valued and important.

Having empathy and listening to others benefits me as much as them. When a new person comes to my support group or into my life and shares what they've been through, I'm reaffirmed that I'm making the right decisions for myself and becoming the person I want to be. The more I discover about myself, the more open I can be to other people. The more I care about others, the more I like myself.

Raoul's best advice: When connecting to others and building relationships, listen more than you speak. Don't just pretend to listen while mentally rehearsing what you want to say. Instead, concentrate deeply on what others are saying without judging or interrupting. Validate them by recognizing their feelings and beliefs as legitimate even if you don't understand or agree with them. This is the way to make true friends—with others and with yourself.

Puzzles Saved My Life: Wisdom from Tony

After I got sober, I realized that one of the reasons I'd used drugs was to try to damp down my anxiety. Once I quit drugs, my anxiety overwhelmed me.

I realized that puzzles were the perfect solution. When I'm involved in doing a puzzle, my mind becomes concentrated. It takes up all my attention. I don't think about using drugs, and my anxiety is under control. For me, a puzzle is a form of meditation.

Tony's best advice: You never know where you'll find the magical tool to help you recover and find your best life. If you haven't tried putting jigsaw puzzles together, give it a try. If that doesn't work for you, try crosswords, solitaire, online chess, Sudoku, or other games or calming activities such as knitting, whittling, or origami. If none of those are for you, keep looking—there's something out there for everyone, and miracles hide in the most unusual places.

Sing out Your Story: Wisdom from Dave

A cathartic way to release your emotions is to compose a song and sing it. That's what I did when I was recovering from my addictions. I'd gone to a ranch out west that we lovingly called "Yella Dawg Ranch" in honor of a golden lab who lived there. There, with nature and animals as my teachers, I wrote "The Yella Dawg Ranch Song." These are the lyrics.

> Take a long look at me; take a long look at where I wanna be.
> I've lost years I can't recover, buried a treasure of wants I discover.
> Yes, I meet some needs, listen to myself screen my own pleas
> Reintroduced in a Midwestern freeze. Nobody escapes this disease.
>
> > Can I get a little bit of comfort?
> > Will you take a chance on me?
> > The odds are frightening—
> > Just a little bit of comfort
> > As I make my final stance
> > At the Yella Dawg Ranch.
>
> Found some peace, packed it away. I'm saving up for some rainy days.
> I'll take a brittle stitch of harmony, always together right in front of me.
> When I feel content, don't give myself too big a compliment.
> Serenity doesn't come with ease. There is no cure or known remedies.
>
> > Can I get a little bit of comfort?
> > Will you take a chance on me?
> > The odds are frightening—
> > Just a little bit of comfort
> > As I make my final stance
> > At the Yella Dawg Ranch.

Dave's best advice: Sing out your emotions, your pain, and your joy. Make up a song that sums up your life lesson, and sing it with gusto.

Think beyond the Law of Attraction: Wisdom from Alonzo

The best-selling book *The Secret* advocates the Law of Attraction—the idea that if you concentrate on something, you'll bring it into your life. Think hard about being rich, and you'll attract riches to you. Well, I think the best way to become rich is to work hard at something you're good at. Just thinking about something isn't enough.

But it's true that if you focus your attention, you'll see many things you'd miss if you were thinking of something else. When you're getting ready to buy a car, for instance, you notice all kinds of details about cars that normally aren't on your radar.

If you fix your thoughts on what you want and combine that focus with action, good things are likely to happen for you. You'll remove blinders that have kept you from seeing opportunities and move consistently toward what you want.

Alonzo's best advice: Wish for what you want, but realize it's only the first step. Keep focusing on that goal, with all the power of your mind and actions. Do so every day, and you'll realize your dreams.

3

HUMBLY ASK FOR HELP: ADAM'S STORY

Adam's life revolves around recovery. A forty-year-old recovering alcoholic who has been sober since 2005, he believes he owes his life to lessons learned from support groups and dogs. He summarizes those lessons in this chapter.

Author's Note:
I met Adam at the first get-together I held for those interested in being part of this book. At that gathering, we agreed collectively that we would meet each month in the Connections conference room. Only a few people came back, however. Adam was one of them.

He became the one constant at our monthly "Waking Up Happy" meetings, a strong center I could count on. After I got to know him, I realized how amazing that was, since he was a loner by nature and it was a struggle, he said, for him to go to meetings. Yet he was the one who showed up every single time and contributed the most to our discussions.

Though he wasn't much of a talker, what he said was always on target. Looking into his kind, intelligent blue eyes, you knew you could trust him.

With his red hair and innocent-looking face, it's no wonder he garnered the nickname Opie. He jokes about it, but his resemblance to the cute kid on the old Andy Griffith Show drew lots of teasing as a child.

Though Adam never brought it up, I learned that he volunteered regularly at Connections, mentoring newly sober clients, raising funds, and working quietly behind the scenes, doing what needed to be done, without fanfare. He didn't care about getting credit, as long as the work got done, things ran smoothly, and people were happy. He was rock-solid, but with a tender heart.

When Adam's friends talked about him, they used words like humble and loyal. He smiled when I told him this. "I do try to be humble," he said. "I view ego as a dangerous thing. It's extremely important for me to accept that I'll never be free of my alcoholism. Although I'll always have this disease, I can continue to work on acceptance. Asking for help is a humble act, but very important.

"And I also try to be loyal. If I give my word, I stick to it, especially with others—I'm not as successful in keeping promises to myself. It's other people—and my higher power—who keep me honest and remind me to honor the pledges I make to myself."

Here, then, is Adam's story as he told it to me.

— J.M.

✫ ✫ ✫

I can't take credit for any of it. The real accolades must go to AA, Connections Counseling, the people I met there, and two dogs named Gunnar and Kodi. They were the ones who gave me the keys I needed to transform my life.

I had no idea when I brought Gunnar home that September morning how profoundly he would change me. I'd recently stopped drinking and was groping my way through a kind of fog toward something I could barely see. My life as I knew it had been shattered into bits and swept away. It was a terrifying time.

Looking back, it's hard to explain how I arrived at that place of desperation and pain. There was nothing in my childhood to foreshadow what was to come. No one looking at me from inside or outside of the family could have predicted the way things turned out.

I grew up in Madison, where my parents were both medical researchers, my father working at the University of Wisconsin and my mother doing para-medical exams for insurance companies. My brother, sisters, and I grew up in a white frame house with a big yard and a special "suite" where Nana, my grandma, lived.

Both my parents grew up with very little. Even after they started earning good wages, they lived a simple, frugal life. While others were going to Disney World, we camped in the northern Wisconsin woods. My fondest memories are of those camping trips.

By the time I was born, my parents were in their forties. The thought of how old they were—the fear they might die—was always with me.

I was the youngest of four, with a brother six years older and sisters four and eight years older than me. Those years between us seemed pretty big to me as a kid. I was the only redhead in the family, and I guess I always felt "different." But I was basically a regular kid who spent time with neighborhood friends, playing games and riding bikes.

One thing I struggled with, being the youngest, was watching my family change as my sisters and brother grew older and into their own lives. As I approached my teens, the family dinners and vacations started to feel incomplete, as not everyone was there. It felt like they were leaving me. Perhaps that has something to do with another addiction I have, and that is isolation. It's hard for me to make the effort to connect with others, and I'm always more comfortable by myself.

As I watched my brother and sisters find their way through their teenage years, experimenting with alcohol and marijuana, I thought that was just part of growing up. They all left drugs behind as they moved into adulthood, and I expected to do the same. It never occurred to me that I might have inherited a gene that they didn't.

In high school, too, drinking was accepted. It was a social thing, and I joined in as a matter of course, without thinking anything about it. It helped me feel accepted. The more I drank, the funnier and more outgoing I was. But take me out of the crowd, and I didn't know who I was or how to act. My only answer was to take another drink.

I was a decent student and managed to get accepted to the University of Wisconsin. My friends and I drank, partied, smoked pot, and on a rare occasion experimented with things like cocaine.

It was toward the end of my college years that I started to question my use. I became involved with a woman I'd known since we were kids. Although we had a close bond, she was still with her boyfriend of many years—truly a dysfunctional situation. I decided to give up marijuana, thinking that might help our relationship. I briefly considered giving up drinking, too, or maybe slowing down. But I quickly dismissed the thought. Everyone drank, and it was just part of life.

I had no trouble quitting marijuana, but my relationship with Kathy didn't improve. Eventually we broke up.

I graduated with a degree in construction management, got my own apartment, and entered the workforce. My job—as a salesman for a window company—wasn't a good match for me. I didn't have the right personality to work in sales. Still, I tried to make the best of it.

As I started to earn a little money and adapt to life after college, drinking and partying were regular things. There was a neighborhood bar behind my apartment and I spent a lot of time there with my friends. I went in and out of a few romantic relationships with women, who lived the same life I did. I recall one of them turning me on to vodka.

I started to buy vodka in big bottles. I'd have a few drinks before going to the bar and a few more after I got home.

Kathy and I connected again when a mutual friend was in a serious accident and we both spent a lot of time at the hospital. Slowly, our relationship was rekindled, and before long we moved in together.

No longer living alone, I was forced to sneak drinks and hide my vodka bottles. Kathy had no idea how much or how often I drank. Like any good alcoholic, I was adept at hiding my drinking patterns from everyone, including—or especially—myself.

It was at that time that I was diagnosed with clinical depression. When I talked to the doctor, I minimized my alcohol use, and he prescribed several antidepressants. I tried them out but didn't stay with any of them.

Less than six months after Kathy and I moved in together, Kathy became pregnant and we got married. She gave birth to our daughter, Amy, that July.

I handled all this change the only way I knew how, and that was to drink. To my mind, vodka was my friend, helping me adjust to the curve balls life was throwing at me.

It's clear to me now what a big role my alcohol use played in the breakup of our marriage. Although Kathy didn't know how much I drank, alcohol changed me into someone different from the guy she'd known since middle school. The more I drank the more I shut Kathy out.

Our divorce, when Amy was five, was agonizing. My love for Amy was the one thing that kept me moving forward. She lived with me half time, and when she was with me things made sense. But when I was alone, my tendency was to crawl deep inside my darkest self. That was the pathway to despair.

Through the divorce, my drinking had escalated. I swore to myself that once I was living by myself again, I'd get a handle on it. Instead, what happened was quite the reverse. My depression and drinking got far worse when I was alone with no one to hold me accountable. I began drinking every evening till I blacked out. When I woke the next morning, I'd lie there trying to recall what I'd done, whom I'd called, and what I'd said the night before.

My depression deepened. It didn't occur to me that my depression was related to my drinking. I didn't realize that I was drinking to medicate myself or that, because alcohol is a depressant, I was continually intensifying my condition.

About a year after the divorce, I reached an all time low and sought help. My doctor put me on antidepressants and referred me to a therapist. Throughout therapy for the next year, my drinking came up only once, when my therapist asked if I was drinking a lot. I lied and said no.

I don't know how long things would have gone on that way, with me lying to my parents, to my therapist, to everyone. But then something happened that I never expected, turning my life upside down.

> *The ultimate dragon is within you.*
> —Joseph Campbell

✯ ✯ ✯

It was a nice Saturday in June, warm and breezy. It began like all my weekend mornings, with a cup of coffee and a few screwdrivers. Then I headed to my parents' house to do some repairs for them.

While I was there, my cell phone rang. It was my friend Ned, inviting me to a beer tent at a park near his house. I went home, drank a couple more screwdrivers, took a quick shower, and drove to the beer tent.

I don't know how much beer I had, but I'd been drinking continuously since I woke up, as I did every weekend. I vaguely recall leaving the beer tent and struggling to find my car in the parking lot. The next thing I remember I was on the other side of town, six miles from home, and there was a squad car behind me, lights flashing and siren chirping.

The police officer pulled me over. My blood alcohol level was .24 percent, three times the legal limit. I was arrested and taken to the police station.

Calling my mother from jail was one of the most excruciating things I'd ever done. I'd never felt so ashamed. She got me out of jail and, later that night, told me she wasn't surprised. I hadn't been hiding my drinking as well as I thought.

Concerned about me, my mom urged me to stay at their house that night. I refused, telling her that I wanted to go home, call some people, and share with them what had happened. The truth was that I couldn't wait to get home and have a drink.

But that was the day that started the long, slow process of change for me. I got in to see my doctor two days later. He gave me a prescription to help me with withdrawal symptoms and told me there was someone I had to see—Shelly, the head of Connections Counseling.

I was in bad shape when I entered Shelly's office the next week. She spoke to me from her own experience and from her heart, and I could identify with everything she shared about her own recovery. As I grew to trust her, I began to tell her things I'd never told anyone. I confessed that I didn't like myself very much, that I'd been dishonest with people who loved me, that I'd lied about my drinking, that I drank far more than anyone realized. She nodded and affirmed that she'd felt those same feelings and that she could help me end my pain. As the secrets poured out of me, I felt an infinity of relief.

That's not to say that my recovery was complete, just like that. Far from it. I continued to drink while I met with Shelly and went to group sessions at her clinic. She kept encouraging me to try Alcoholics Anonymous, but I was very resistant. At one point she suggested that I might need to go to in-patient treatment and that scared me to the bone. All I could think of was losing shared custody of my daughter, and I couldn't bear that thought.

So I finally took a deep breath and attended my first AA meeting. There were only four or five other people there. I was far too overwhelmed to remember that meeting, but I do recall how they welcomed me and made me feel at home.

A few days later I went to my second meeting. I still had no idea what AA was about, but I remember thinking how much like me these people were. As I left, a man named John made a point of giving me his phone number.

Going against my loner instincts, I ended up calling John. After talking with him for a while, I asked him to be my sponsor, not completely understanding what that meant. He agreed to sponsor me and stressed regular meeting attendance—"Twice a day if you can. Just show up and listen."

I did my best to follow his instructions and found that, although I still wanted to drink, I was abstaining more often. The frequent AA meetings, counseling with Shelly, group sessions at Connections, and daily phone conversations with John combined in a powerful way to get the message through to me: Just don't drink. I clung to that as John guided me through the twelve steps. He felt I needed to get to the fourth step as quickly as I could. (For details on the twelve steps, see "Tools for the Journey" at the end of this chapter.) Before long I'd strung together thirty days of sobriety, and people around me started to notice a change.

Take the first step in faith. You don't have to see the whole staircase, just take the first step.
—Martin Luther King, Jr.

✯ ✯ ✯

It was while working on my fourth step (making a "searching and moral inventory" of myself) that I relapsed. I can't say what brought it on beyond the fact that I'm truly an alcoholic. Perhaps taking my personal inventory stirred up too many feelings. I came back to AA right away and admitted what had happened. Just like the first time, they welcomed me.

Over the next months, I attended AA meetings regularly, but I discovered something I'd always known I could do—and do well. I could lie. I could go to meetings, stop at the liquor store on the way home, and get drunk. I could do it every day and no one would know.

That's when I reached the absolute bottom. For me, the bottom wasn't being arrested, painful as that was. It was a spiritual bottom I reached after lying to myself and everyone around me, day after day.

One Tuesday evening, I got home from work, looked at the bottle of vodka on the counter, and called Shelly. I told her how ashamed I was of the lies I'd been living, and she told me not to worry about the past, just dump the vodka into the sink.

And that's what I did.

With encouragement from Shelly and John, I went to the people at AA and admitted that I'd been drinking and lying about it. They accepted me back into their fellowship without blaming or condemning me. Although I felt terrible about abusing their trust in me, I made a commitment to re-earn that trust and never again to betray it.

I also asked my doctor to prescribe Antabuse. I needed everything I could find to keep me from drinking, and Antabuse would make me extremely sick if I put any alcohol into my body.

It worked. My last drink was January 10, 2005. I simply stopped resisting. I finally understood what they meant when they told me I had to completely surrender myself.

Something magical happened that day. I believe that a miracle occurred. I gave up and turned myself over to something greater. I couldn't let go of alcohol on my own and I finally, truly asked for help.

A STEP ON THE JOURNEY

Experience the epiphany of surrender. What does "surrender" mean? It's not complicated. Surrender is simply the opposite of control.

Do not seek to have events happen as you want them to, but instead want them to happen as they do happen, and your life will go well.
—Epictetus

As addicts, we have an innate desire to control. We're used to trying to manipulate every aspect of the world around us. When we surrender, we give up the struggle and admit to ourselves that our attempts at control are illusory. When we stop trying so hard and surrender our will to a greater power, miracles can happen. Things fall into place, and what seemed impossible happens effortlessly.

– J.M.

✲ ✲ ✲

While I struggled with the idea of God, I knew that at AA I found countless miracles. Every person there was a miracle, whether they had twenty-four years of sobriety or twenty-four hours. I saw God's power in those miracles of rebirth, and that's what I held onto. I had to keep holding on or alcohol would take my life, and for the first time in many years I actually wanted to live.

All I needed to do was continue going to meetings and be honest with others and, most important, with myself. I could do that as long as I did it one day, one hour, one moment at a time. I didn't have to tell myself, "I'll never drink again." All I had to do was to get my head on my pillow at night without taking a drink.

Every day you may make progress. Every step may be fruitful. Yet there will stretch out before you an ever-lengthening, ever-ascending, ever-improving path. You know you will never get to the end of the journey. But this, so far from discouraging, only adds to the joy and glory of the climb.
—Winston Churchill

I was struck at those early AA meetings by how much everyone laughed. It was the last thing I'd expected. I was astonished to see how much fun those people were having—and all without alcohol. It was so liberating to replace the tension of my old life with the release of humor. Laughter can do so much—it breaks down stress, cements the connections between people, and feels wonderful. I can't imagine a life worth living without it.

> *I think that wherever your journey takes you, there are new gods waiting there, with divine patience—and laughter.*
> —Susan M. Watkins

✦ ✦ ✦

I slowly started to become a different person. I began to see things I'd never seen before and hear things I'd never heard. Relationships improved. People started to see who I really was. For so many years that person was hidden behind the walls I built with alcohol.

In my counseling sessions with Shelly, she talked often about her dog and said it was common for newly sober people to get dogs because of all the lessons they can teach us. It was the first time I'd heard of a "sober dog," but the idea of dogs' acceptance, patience, and love helping people stay sober made sense.

With my daughter living with me only half-time, I'd been coming home to an empty house the other half of the time. The cold, cheerless house fed my desire to isolate myself, and I knew it wasn't good for me. When I thought of how a dog could help me feel less lonely and give me another being to care for, I made my decision.

> *All knowledge, the totality of all questions and all answers is contained in the dog.*
> —Franz Kafka

After researching breeds, I bought a golden-retriever puppy I called Gunnar. From the moment I brought him home, that fuzzy bundle of enthusiasm changed the energy in the house, filling it with life. Being responsible for him gave me a purpose and forced me to become active, take daily walks, and meet people at the dog park.

I learned why "sober dogs" are so valuable. Dogs live the secret of sobriety, always in the present instant. As long as you're good to them, they never hold grudges, and even if you're not good to them, they forgive you instantly.

Gunnar had an enormous impact on the spiritual part of my program. There was a part of God in the heart of this wonderful dog.

TURNING POINT

Learn from dogs. If you're open to their energy, dogs can teach you a great deal about life and about yourself. Here are just a few of the lessons they offer:
- Be playful and spontaneous. Playing with others draws you closer to them.
- Take every chance to celebrate. Rejoice in all the delights of life.

- Be curious about the world around you. Even the smallest thing can be a source of wonder.
- Travel lightly. Don't get too attached to material possessions or worry about accumulating more.
- Focus fully on what you're doing. Don't compare one experience with another, just enjoy each one as it happens.
- Love without judgment or conditions. There's incredible power in that kind of love.

It's important to add a caution here. Don't bring home a dog without putting research and thought into the decision. If you get a dog that doesn't match your personality, you can find yourself in a nightmare of unsuitability.

In *Why We Love the Dogs We Do*, Stanley Coren classifies breeds by behavioral characteristics—friendly dogs (such as golden retrievers); protective dogs (boxers); independent dogs (setters); self-assured dogs (terriers); consistent dogs (dachshunds); steady dogs (beagles); and clever dogs (poodles). After you take a personality test, he clarifies which dogs fit best with your disposition.

For example, dogs classified as "independent" are difficult to train and need lots of time outdoors, running and exploring. Someone looking for a predictable, home-loving pet would likely be overwhelmed by such a breed.

The same is true for "friendly" dogs such as goldens. In fact, the golden retriever is the breed most often surrendered to shelters, because its friendly nature demands a huge amount of time and attention. You must understand that such a dog will follow you and want to play at all times. Some people find such constant companionship smothering and unbearable.

Before bringing home a pet, you may want to volunteer at an animal shelter, taking time to experiment with different breeds. A shelter is also an ideal place to adopt a dog when you find the right one.

– J.M.

I love a dog. He does nothing for political reasons.
—Will Rogers

✫ ✫ ✫

One of the defining moments in my new life occurred in my first year of sobriety. It began like any other day. My habit was to begin each morning by waking Gunnar, who slept on the bed next to me. On this particular day, as I knelt at the edge of the bed to wake him, it dawned on me that this might be a good time to try praying.

Meditation and prayer were things I had yet to get a good grasp of, but I'd been hearing about them in AA. The principle of asking the universe for help seemed valid to me, but I felt awkward about trying it. I hadn't prayed since I was a child, and I didn't know how to begin.

Suddenly, I realized that being on my knees beside my bed offered the perfect chance to get started down that spiritual passageway. I had so much to be grateful for—my daughter, my dog, my family, my friends, my sobriety. I began by listing those things in my mind as I knelt there, thanking the universe for the new life I'd been given. Then it felt natural to ask my higher power to guide me through the day and help me see the right direction to follow.

Things fell into place, and I knew, from then on, I'd begin each day the same way. That dawn started me on a road of meditation, thanksgiving, and prayer that became a lifelong evolution. I'll never forget how Gunnar led me there.

Later, when I told this story to a friend, he nodded knowingly and told me, "It makes perfect sense. After all, dog spelled backward is God."

A STEP ON THE JOURNEY

Discover the power of prayer. In *The Year of Living Biblically*, A. J. Jacobs, Jewish by birth and agnostic in his faith, describes his attempts to live the literal word of the Bible for one full year. At first, he relies on cognitive dissonance—the idea that if you behave a certain way, your beliefs will change to conform to your behavior—and thus prays several times a day in hope that he'll start believing in the being to whom he's speaking.

He says ready-made prayers for several months till he becomes confident enough to make up his own prayers. A pastor helps him by explaining that there are four types of prayers, which you can remember with the mnemonic ACTS: Adoration (praising God), Confession (confiding your transgressions), Thanksgiving (being grateful for what you have), Supplication (asking for help and guidance).

Feeling most comfortable at first with thanking God, he says a prayer before and after every meal. He gives thanks for the farmer who grew the food, the trucker who carried it, and the grocer who sold it to him. These prayers remind him that he's lucky to have food at all.

Later, he discovers another type of prayer he likes: intercessionary prayers, those said on other people's behalf, and begins praying for others every night. He also finds websites like ePrayer.com and CyberSaint, where you can place prayer requests.

Praying begins to change him, giving him a new reverence for life. He finds himself praying spontaneously as he becomes aware of the "thousands of things that go right every day."

At the end of the year, he describes himself as a "reverent agnostic." While still unsure whether there's a God, he now believes that there's something transcendent, sacred. And he's sure of one thing: he'll never stop praying.

– J.M.

* * *

During my second year of sobriety I faced my most difficult challenge to date when Gunnar was diagnosed with leukemia. It was agony to watch the life in his eyes fade from day to day. When he stopped eating and drinking, I knew Gunnar—my best friend, my gift from God—was ready to leave this world. I made the appointment with the vet to have him put down the next day.

Several people offered to go with me for Gunnar's euthanasia. My alcoholic instincts told me to do it alone, but I resisted those thoughts and in the end accepted my dad's offer to accompany me. He was by my side when I said good-bye to my dear friend for the last time.

Afterwards, it startled me to realize that through the whole process of Gunnar's sickness and death I never considered drinking. That was a gift from my friends at AA and Connections. They'd given me the tools I needed to get through one of the hardest times of my life—the ability to ask for help, the knowledge that sharing feelings lessens pain, and the sense of gratitude that now infused my life. I'd learned I could overcome any challenge by walking through it rather than around or away from it, with my friends, family, and higher power by my side.

> ***Dogs never lie about love.***
> —Jeffrey Moussaieff Masson

* * *

My "sober dog" had meant so much to me that I couldn't imagine myself dogless and went on a waiting list for another golden-retriever puppy a few weeks after Gunnar died. Two months later, I brought Kodi home.

I see now that I tried to move on too quickly. While I claimed that I knew Kodi wouldn't "replace" Gunnar, a part of me believed he would. I had a shocking reality check in store. Although Kodi looked just like Gunnar as a pup, the two weren't anything alike, and nothing went as planned.

There I was in the middle of winter trying to housebreak a new puppy who wouldn't listen and wouldn't sleep through the night. I didn't remember Gunnar being this much work. Deprived of sleep for days, I was close to breaking down. It was agonizing, but I made it through.

It took a while, but I eventually grew to love Kodi for who he was, apart from Gunnar. I also realized that Gunnar's spirit would always be with me. I've come to believe that God is everywhere, especially inside the soul of dogs like Gunnar and Kodi. Gunnar saw me through my early sobriety, and while his body was gone, that spirit remained.

> ***If you don't have a dog—at least one—there is not necessarily anything wrong with you, but there may be something wrong with your life.***
> —Vincent van Gogh

I doubt I would have survived Gunnar's death and the traumatic integration of Kodi into my life if it weren't for Shelly, Connections, and AA. Time and again I was saved by the principles of AA, the people I met there, and the stories we shared.

From my first experiences with AA, I was riveted by the stories. Many people's narratives were heartrending, yet at the same time their wisdom awed me. How, I wondered, did so many ordinary-looking people grow so wise? How did they manage to reach so deeply into my heart and capture what I thought was mine alone? How did these people find such a sense of joy and hope?

As I listened and gained the courage to tell my own story, I found the experience incredibly healing. I saw that sharing tales of hard times—and of experiences that made me feel guilty—lessened the pain and shame, while poking fun at myself with anecdotes, laughing at my failings, gave me a wonderful sense of release.

> *All sorrows can be borne if you put them into a story. . . .*
> —Isak Dinesen

TURNING POINT

Tell it with a story. There's nothing like a story to make an unforgettable point. That's why support groups, mentoring programs, and coaching are such potent ways to produce lasting change. Stories point out the common ground we all share, drawing us together. People who attend support groups say that as they listen to stories unspool like soft yarn, they often feel they're hearing their own words in another voice.

Some of the best stories describe mistakes that turned out to be learning experiences. What episode from your life could you divulge to help people laugh and learn?

_____
_____

– J.M.

✳ ✳ ✳

During my third year of sobriety, I came to a new crossroad when my aunt Bev, my mom's older sister, died of ovarian cancer. It was a moment of truth, because I had a paralyzing fear of death.

I'm not sure why the idea of death terrified me. I had little acquaintance with it. Maybe that's one reason it scared me, because there's always something frightening about the unknown. Until Aunt Bev's death, only two people who were truly part of my life had died.

The first was Nana, my dad's mother, who died when I was seven. The image of her lying in her casket is burned into my brain. Perhaps that's when my irrational dread of death began.

My other grandma died five years later. I remember that open coffin even more clearly. I have a vivid memory of my horror as I watched my cousin reach in and touch our dead grandma.

Aunt Bev's illness and death also brought up my worries about my parents, who were forty-three and forty-eight years older than I was. My mom wasn't much younger than her sister, so I couldn't help thinking that if Bev died, my mother could die soon, too. So could my dad, who was five years older than my mom. I counted on my parents a lot, drawing great strength from them, and I wondered how I'd deal with that inevitable loss. Sometimes, lying in bed at night, my obsessive thoughts of death went round and round in my head like a hamster on a wheel.

During the five years that Bev went through surgeries and chemotherapies, I tried to come to terms with the fact that she would die, there would be a funeral, and she'd be in an open casket like my grandmothers had been. I couldn't imagine how I'd get through the experience, but I knew how hard the funeral would be for my mom, and with all my heart I wanted to be supportive of her. It would definitely be a test of my new, sober life.

I faced that difficult test in July when Mom called, telling me Bev had died. Our whole family would be driving to Ohio for the funeral. I was consumed with worry about how I'd handle it.

Before we left for Ohio, I shared my misgivings at an AA meeting. The room was full of people that day, and every one of them supported me wholeheartedly. They confirmed that funerals were always hard and that the death of loved ones was a universal fear. They shared their own experiences of death and provided guidance and perspective. One man even told me he would come with me on the trip for support. That offer meant the world to me. I told him that just knowing that he—that all of them—would be with me in spirit was all I needed.

I left that meeting knowing I'd be carried by my friends and higher power as I walked forward in the face of my anxieties.

> ***Only when we are no longer afraid do we begin to live.***
> —Dorothy Thompson

The morning of the funeral, as we got ready at our hotel, I spoke with my mom. She'd planned to eulogize her sister, but she told me she wasn't sure she'd be able to go through with it. I gave her a hug and told her to let God carry her. By her reaction, I could tell she knew what I meant and that my words comforted her.

"That's just what I needed to hear," she said.

It struck me at that moment: This is why I needed to be on this trip. Had I not been sober, I most likely wouldn't have come. I know I wouldn't have been there mentally, nor would I have had the clarity of thought to give my mom that hug and say those words to her.

At the funeral, my mom's eulogy was beautiful and brought tears and laughter to everyone there. Afterwards, I felt so much closer to my mom and my whole family. I was enveloped by a sense of peace unlike anything I'd known.

Even looking into the open casket didn't upset me as I'd feared. For the first time, I understood why we have funerals, how they can mend hearts and knit people together. I saw how confronting your worst phobias can be the best thing in the world.

> ## MOMENT OF TRUTH
>
> **Make peace with death.** The key is to embrace the knowledge that life and death are part of an infinite continuum. The idea of nothingness is frightening, but death isn't nothingness.
>
> In *No Death, No Fear*, Thich Nhat Hanh says that death, like birth, is only a door through which you pass. You, like everything on this planet, are in constant flux, moving toward a new state of being.
>
> You're like a page of this book. If you burn it, it doesn't die. It merely changes form. It becomes smoke that rises into the air and blends with the clouds and sky. It becomes ash, which merges with the earth and lives on in the grass and trees. It turns into heat, which caresses your body and becomes part of you.
>
> It's the same when your loved ones die. They, too, become part of the air, part of the earth, part of your heart. You can never lose them, because they continue to exist in your memories and dreams. They live on in you, in their descendants, in everyone who knew them, and in the universe, forever.
>
> – J.M.

✧ ✧ ✧

Several years earlier, I'd left my job selling windows and found work with a company that designed office buildings. My new job was to select the right windows for each construction project.

Looking back, I think my higher power had a role here, because it turned out to be the perfect job for me. It was a technical position, which was far more geared to my personality than the sales job.

Once I was in a job that suited me, I saw how important it was to work at something that used my unique talents. It gave me a feeling of purpose that I'd lacked.

Growing in my job was part of a greater journey toward knowing and liking myself—who I really was, not who people expected me to be. I realized that before getting sober I'd played different roles depending on the stage I was on and who was in my audience. Then, when I was alone, I was lost. Finding myself lost, I drank. To play the roles I felt people wanted me to play, I needed to prep myself. That always involved another drink. It was an endless cycle that left me drinking every chance I got.

In my new life, there were still many audiences. The difference was that I could now be, simply, who I was. How people saw me was up to them, and I had no control over their reactions. All I could do was be true to myself.

At first I was mystified about why I was the only one in my family to become an alcoholic. How did I, with no family history of addiction or alcoholism, end up in the depths of despair, gripping a bottle of vodka? How did someone like me, raised in a stable, loving family, end up a classic alcoholic? But when I started talking to my mom about my disease, she told me her brother was an alcoholic. That stunned me. He lived in California, and I'd only seen him a handful of times throughout my life. I knew he liked to drink, but learning he was an alcoholic was a revelation.

Mom also told me her father had suffered from debilitating depression. That knowledge threw my own diseases of alcoholism and depression into a new light. Knowing that addiction and depression walk side by side, and neither one grows in a vacuum, I could now see myself as part of a bigger picture that was taking form for me. Those talks with my mom gave me the puzzle pieces I needed to make sense of it all.

> *When you really want to have wisdom, open all the doors, and listen.*
> —Barry Lopez

With these pieces in place, I launched fully into a journey of self-discovery. I found that writing down my thoughts and feelings was an important step in the discovery process. At first I thought I needed to be in the right mindset to write. But when I waited for that perfect writing moment, it never came. I finally learned that if I just sat down and started writing, even if I didn't know what I wanted to say, it turned out to be a cathartic release as well as a learning experience.

As I wrote about myself and my early life, I realized I'd grown up believing that a successful life would be based on my own accomplishments. But I realized I had to overturn that message. I now knew I needed other people's help if I was to succeed, or even to survive.

In AA, we often spoke about the masks we wore when we were drinking. It was one thing for me to let my masks fall away. The next step was to make an active effort to let others into my life, and that was the hardest part for me.

Gradually, however, I began to open up. If I had a problem, I'd call my AA friends, my sponsor, or my siblings or stop by my parents' house and ask for help—something I was too uncomfortable to do in my old life. Whether I was facing an emotional challenge or trying to hang drywall on the ceiling, I once would have wrestled with it on my own. It was such a relief to see how easy life became when I no longer took it all on myself.

TURNING POINT

Ask for help. When you ask someone for a favor, make your request as specific as you can, and make it clear that it's okay to say no. People enjoy being asked for help as long as they understand they have the option of refusing. Be willing to hear "no" without taking it as a personal rejection.

> Also ask the universe for support. Then be on the lookout for help to arrive—not necessarily in the form you intended.
>
> With what do you need help? Whom could you ask for assistance?_____
> _____
>
> – J.M.

I used to hide so much from my family. I'd told them to call before they stopped by. Now I was happy to have them drop in anytime and see how I lived. That, too, was a bottomless relief, as comforting as a deep sigh. Hiding a huge chunk of yourself and your life takes untold amounts of energy.

Amy was eight when I got sober and could finally be the father she deserved. To make our relationship grow, I had to let go of the past and the awful things I'd done—drinking in her presence, driving drunk with her in the car, putting her life in danger. I had to leave my guilt for those things behind and focus on setting the best example I could.

I liked the saying, "Show, don't tell." Role models are so important, and we learn by watching.

Having Amy in my life helped my sobriety by making me accountable. If I didn't go to enough support-group meetings, my mood dipped and Amy felt the brunt. It took a while, but I discovered I couldn't get or stay sober for Amy, no matter how much I wanted to. That was a hard concept for me and perhaps played a role in my early relapses. I needed to stay sober for myself, and then Amy would feel the benefit.

Sobriety taught me to be honest with Amy. We had long conversations about making choices, "doing the next right thing," and other principles that applied not only to a recovering alcoholic but to a pre-teen and teen (which she has now become).

Daily, I told Amy I loved her. I tried to make sure she knew I was proud of her and that she was okay just the way she was. I stressed that the material things we had were just stuff and that what mattered was what we gave to others. I educated her about the dangers of alcoholism, explaining that she ran a greater risk than someone who didn't have addiction in the family.

We talked about the importance of a belief in something beyond our own small selves, and I described how my views had evolved. I was raised Catholic but hadn't been a practicing Catholic in a long time. I don't think of myself as religious. I've come to believe that religion is God as someone else understands Him, while spirituality is God as I understand him (or her?). I can find God anywhere—in sunlight, a quiet snow, a child's laughter. Miracles are everywhere.

Amy and I talked about lessons I'd been learning from my reading. I especially liked this story:

One evening an old Cherokee told his grandson about a battle that goes on inside people. He said, "The battle is between two wolves that live inside us all.

"One is Evil. It is anger, envy, jealousy, regret, greed, arrogance, self-pity, guilt, resentment, inferiority, lies, false pride, superiority, and ego.

"The other is Good. It is joy, peace, love, hope, serenity, humility, kindness, benevolence, empathy, generosity, truth, compassion, and faith."

The grandson thought for a minute and then asked, "Which one wins?"

The old Cherokee smiled and replied, "The one you feed."

☆ ☆ ☆

One great blessing sobriety gave me was friends. Through AA and Connections Counseling, I built the strongest friendships I'd ever had. My friends and I counted on each other, day in and day out. Somewhere along the way, my sponsor became my best friend, a true friend unlike any I'd ever known.

My relationships changed diametrically from the ones I had before I became sober. I lost touch with most of those who were in my life when I was drinking. They were no longer healthy for me, and I had to let those friendships go.

A STEP ON THE JOURNEY

Find new friends. When you're recovering from a harmful habit or addiction and starting anew, one crucial piece of the puzzle is to leave behind unhealthy friends—even family members if they're part of the problem. This step may seem almost impossible at first, but it will become easier as time goes on. You need to surround yourself with people who are eager to support your growth, not pull you down. Your former friends' agenda is likely to be to keep you beside them as they continue the self-destructive ways you want to give up. So, at least for now, look for new friends. There are innumerable ways to form healthy new friendships. Just a sampling:

- Support groups are an excellent place to meet others striving to build friendships. These can be groups, such as AA or NA, geared specifically for recovering addicts and alcoholics. Or they can focus on other problems, such as dealing with grief, overeating, or chronic illness. While you may not make friends right away, you'll build strong connections if you attend meetings regularly, listen attentively, and share your own perceptions.
- Interest groups can link you with people who care about the things you do, such as gardens, animals, birds, reading, architecture, music, art, or movies. Many organizations have newcomer groups, which are ideal for meeting those looking for friends. Check out local newspapers, magazines, and bulletin boards at libraries, health stores, and other community gathering places, as well as meetup.com.
- Volunteering at nonprofit organizations will connect you with those who want to meet people while getting out of their own heads and helping others.
- Courses at local colleges, trade schools, recreational centers, or hospitals can link you with others interested in learning everything from how to dance, meditate, or give massages to painting, creative writing, and cooking.

- Sports and exercise groups are always looking for people who want to join in such activities as golf, basketball, aerobics, and cycling.
- Houses of worship are excellent gathering places even if you aren't religious. Most churches, temples, mosques, and other spiritual congregations offer classes, social groups, and volunteer opportunities. They're good drug-free opportunities to meet caring people.
- Online discussion groups aren't as helpful as face-to-face meetings or even phone conversations. There's something about hearing the voice and feeling the touch of a real live person that provides the courage we need to move forward with our lives. Sometimes, though, online groups can fill the gap and assuage the loneliness during the transition between old, destructive friendships and new, nurturing ones.

– J.M.

I had a rule: Never go two days without speaking to one of my sober friends. It was another reminder for me that I wasn't alone.

There were some relationships I wouldn't have chosen, but my job or other parts of my life put them on the path I walked. I learned to accept such people, even if I didn't agree with them. With practice, I learned to look past our differences without the tension and arrogant confrontation that was part of my drinking life. I became far more diplomatic than I used to be. I learned to give in when I felt a battle wasn't worth fighting, and I admitted fault when I made mistakes. Those were mammoth changes from my old self.

Four years into sobriety, I went through a program of group sessions at Connections called Stage Two Recovery. Designed for people with a significant amount of sobriety time, it dealt with the question, "Okay, I'm sober. Now what?" For twelve weeks, ten of us exposed our deepest childhood wounds to one another and shared our struggles, fears, accomplishments, and hopes. Through this process, we grew together and forged powerful ties with one another.

After finishing the Stage Two Recovery sessions, I volunteered to become a mentor at Connections. Foolishly, I thought I knew what it would be like—letting go of expectations and just letting things unfold was something I was still struggling with—and I imagined how I'd come in and help all these people.

What I found was how much they helped me. The newcomers were the ones who gave me the most, reminding me how far I'd come and how precious my recovery was to me. I discovered that if I was there for someone who needed me, I felt better myself.

I didn't have any answers for them. It was a process of sharing rather than a prescription. What was important was delving into the questions together.

The best way to find yourself is to lose yourself in the service of others.
—Mahatma Gandhi

Giving myself to others provided endless returns for me. It was difficult, and sometimes I had to force myself to do it, but the feeling that came from making a difference in someone's life was incomparable.

Awakening every day, I had innumerable choices. I could pick the right path or the wrong one. I could elect to change my attitude when my thoughts, stemming from my old behaviors, rose up. I could decide to share my thoughts and struggles with another person or I could let them fester in my mind.

I didn't always make the right choices. But I knew that when I made the wrong one, I needed to admit it, move on, and let it go. In the grip of my disease, I had none of these choices.

✺ ✺ ✺

Just when I thought I had the sobriety thing down, I realized the road wasn't going to be as smooth as I'd hoped. Six years after I'd quit drinking, I was plunged into the worst hell I'd encountered yet.

Quite simply, life happened. I faced increased uncertainty in my job. There was a huge strain on the relationship with my daughter, and I was struggling with how to be a parent of a teenage girl. I'd been in a relationship with a woman, and that ended. This all landed in front of me at the same time, and I plummeted into a depression so deep I was unsure I'd survive.

More than I've ever wanted anything, I wanted the pain to stop. I knew alcohol couldn't remove the pain. Only death could. How desperate was I? To say that I feared for my life wouldn't be a stretch. I'm not sure if I've ever been more frightened.

I can't explain exactly how I survived. But I know one thing: I never wavered in attending AA meetings. Instead of one or two meetings a week, I stepped up my program to eight, nine, and then ten meetings every week.

I did my best to share my feelings, but part of me—the addict in me—couldn't help thinking I was unique and no one could understand my feelings. That made it hard to be open and honest, even with my closest friends. It was easier to isolate myself, both physically—staying home alone—and mentally—hiding who I was and how I felt.

I fought those voices within me and tried to listen to messages from outside myself. I listened as people told me I'd get through this, and I tried to believe them. With my intensified AA program, I read, prayed, and meditated every day. I knew the solution was spiritual, but I was struggling to find it.

After a month of groping through the dark, I came across an article—"The Next Frontier: Emotional Sobriety" by Bill Wilson, one of AA's co-founders. In the article, published in 1958, Bill explained that staying sober from alcohol wasn't enough. The next step was to achieve emotional equilibrium, or what he called "emotional sobriety."

Many years after he quit drinking, Bill W. went through a harrowing depression similar to mine. Like me, he wondered why the twelve steps failed to cut through the black despair.

I'd learned many times in the rooms of AA that I wasn't unique in my struggles. But hearing it from Bill W., at the very moment I was desperate for guidance, was a miracle as great as the one that helped me quit drinking years earlier.

Once again, the lesson was all about letting go. Bill W. wrote that he reached emotional sobriety only when he let go of his expectations of others. Reading his words, I realized that my downward spiral was linked to my beliefs about how other people ought to behave. I was expecting people to do what *I* thought was the right thing. I grew depressed because they weren't living up to standards *I* had set for them.

It was electrifying to realize that Bill W. had lived through the same things I was facing and that I could trace my key problem back to the same origins. At that moment, I realized that I would survive, just as he did.

I can't say that I changed my strategies in any way. I continued doing the same things I'd been doing—going to meetings, reaching out, praying, and meditating. The only change was that now I was doing these things with an attitude of hope. That made all the difference.

This sense of hope renewed my connection to my higher power, helping me let go of my demands of others. I saw that I could give of myself without expecting anything in return. I could share my experience with people, knowing that what they chose to do with it was completely up to them.

My next challenge was to face the fact that, while I'd made it through a huge crisis, my struggle wasn't over. This thing called sobriety was a never-ending process. It would take daily work for the rest of my life.

Fortunately, the only thing I can work on is what's in front of me right now. If I focus on that thing, and then the next one, and share the gifts I've been given, I'll continue on the right path.

I used to think there would be a point at which I'd be happy. I'd have the right job, right house, right woman, and then everything would be good. Now I know it's about growing in the right direction, not arriving anywhere. I'll never graduate from AA or get a diploma in how to live. It's a gradual thing, an unfolding voyage.

> *There are only two ways to live your life. One is as though nothing is a miracle. The other is as though everything is a miracle.*
> —Albert Einstein

What I've learned in my recovery is far beyond my ability to measure. There are lessons everywhere. The alcoholic inside me has the ability to block out these gifts, even though it's been a long time since I've had a drink. It takes hard work to keep the disease at bay.

So many people have helped me, people who've shown tremendous bravery and compassion. I'm awed by those brave enough to come to a support-group meeting for the first time—that first step is such a giant one—and anyone who has the courage to ask for help. I have great respect for all those who keep working on themselves, growing and learning every day.

Most of all, I admire people who give back and make a difference in the world—people like my parents and Shelly at Connections. I want to emulate them by living a humble, unpretentious life filled with service and simple caring. Like them, I want to show others that there's a beautiful world out there that can give so many gifts to anyone who chooses to accept them.

Every day, I continue to be amazed by what Shelly has created at Connections. When I first sat down with her years ago, I wasn't sure I wanted to live. I'll bet there are hundreds, if not thousands, of others who wouldn't be alive today if Shelly hadn't started Connections. She teaches people to live.

As far as a plan for the future, I'm not sure except that I want to grow. I want to stay sober, find the path I was meant to follow, and be the person I was meant to be. I want to continue to learn how to like myself, and I think the best way to do that is to continue to give as much as I can to others.

Whether a person is an addict or not, life deals good things and bad. Good or bad, these situations can be learning experiences, and new opportunities arise from each challenge.

Sometimes the pathway is steep, and it can be a struggle to keep going, but that's what gives it meaning. The most important thing to remember, the thing that can keep us going no matter how difficult the path, is this: We don't travel it alone.

✶ ✶ ✶

TOOLS FOR THE JOURNEY

Here are suggestions you can put into practice in your own life to mirror the lessons in this chapter:

Deal with depression. Many—it wouldn't be a stretch to say "most"—people who drink and use other drugs do so, in part, because they're depressed, but they often go a long time without being diagnosed.

The first step is to realize that depression is a disease, not a weakness, lack of strength, or something to be endured. The next step is to go to a psychiatrist, who can test you, determine if you suffer from depression, and prescribe medication. Some recovering alcoholics believe that if they take any medication, even for depression, they risk relapse and can't honestly call themselves "sober." This may have been true decades ago when antidepressants were indeed addictive. But the new antidepressants work quite differently and don't have the potential to cause addiction or relapse to drug-seeking behavior. You can find an excellent explanation of how modern antidepressants work in Peter Kramer's *Listening to Prozac*.

There are three vital ingredients for recovering from depression—medication, talk therapy, and hope. Hope is the most elusive and also the most essential. It comes when you combine the first two and add a little time. Here are a few tools to help you through the days until hope arrives:
- Concentrate on tangible objects close at hand. Focus on parts of your body—your fingers, the palm of your hand—or the simple things around you, in your bedroom, in your kitchen, in your office. If abstract thoughts and feelings overwhelm you, turn your attention back to these concrete things.
- Find a small task, and complete it. Clean off the top of your desk. Scramble some eggs for dinner. Wash one sinkful of dishes. When you've finished the job, congratulate yourself for what you've accomplished.
- Be kind to your body. Eat healthy meals. Do some walking or other exercises.

- Look around, and count the things you have to be grateful for—your special mug filled with morning coffee or afternoon tea, the phone that connects you to other people, the parts of your body that are healthy, a place to sleep at night.
- Forgive mistakes—your own and others'. Remind yourself how insignificant they are when measured against infinite time and space.

Take the giving challenge. Try the ritual Cami Walker describes in *29 Gifts*: Give with mindful intention once a day for twenty-nine consecutive days. These tips may help deepen the experience for you:

- Before you begin the ritual, rid yourself of assumptions. Be ready to be surprised.
- Your gift can be simple. Grand gestures aren't required. Sometimes the smallest action carries the most meaning.
- Don't worry whether your gift "counts." Anything counts as a gift as long as you offer it mindfully, with the deliberate purpose of giving. A few examples: Take time to smile and greet a neighbor. Give to the earth by recycling. Give your family the gift of a healthy meal. Give the gift of patience to the driver ahead of you who's moving too slowly. Give yourself the gift of letting go of old burdens.
- Practice receiving with a glad heart. The more you give, the more you'll receive, and there's an art to acknowledging gifts gratefully. Remember that a closed hand can't receive. That's an important part of the lesson this ritual teaches.
- Consider parting with something you feel you can't live without—or something that feels scarce. It could be money, an object, or a belief that no longer serves you.

What makes this ritual so compelling is that it opens your eyes to the world. Having an "assignment" alerts you to those around you and what they might need. As you take advantage of little opportunities to give, your life expands.

– J.M.

Learn from the twelve steps. These steps, which originated in Alcoholics Anonymous, can be—and have been—adapted to many other support groups. The principles have been proven, over and over again, to help people change.
Here's what Adam has to say about the steps and what he has learned from them:

1. We admitted we were powerless over alcohol—that our lives had become unmanageable. When I entered AA, I knew I was powerless over my drinking. At that point I couldn't go a single day without it. But as far as my life being unmanageable, I had a harder time accepting that. I had a job, house, and car. I thought I was managing fine. I ignored the fact that there were consequences to my drinking. I was miserable, but I thought that was a card life had dealt me.

Then, from the people around me in AA, I learned that my misery was actually a choice. The first word of the first step is *"We."* That meant I couldn't do this myself. Asking for help goes against the primary instincts of every alcoholic, but I fought those instincts, surrendered completely, and admitted I needed help if I was to survive.

2. Came to believe that a power greater than ourselves could restore us to sanity. Coming into AA, I made a great effort to mesh the God and religion of my upbringing with the higher power referred to in the second step. AA taught me that I didn't have to marry those two. My AA group could be my higher power if I wished. That group of alcoholics could restore me to sanity. It started to click. Something far greater than myself or any one person was saving these people—and could save me.

3. Made a decision to turn our will and our lives over to the care of God *as we understood him.* Left to my own will, I can easily fall back into the darkness I lived in when drinking. Every day I must let go and offer myself to that power greater than myself. I must open my heart and get outside of my selfish, manipulative, isolating, alcoholic self. That means daily surrender and turning my will over to a greater force.

4. Made a searching and moral inventory of ourselves. Early on in my AA career, I heard many discussions about the fourth step and how important it was. I didn't understand what writing down all my fears, resentments, and wrongs would do for me. I did, however, hear many times that there was no wrong way to do this step. I also heard that I didn't have to dig up everything from my past. If I only rooted out the "tall weeds" in my garden, that was fine for now. I could always come back later and do another fourth step. That advice helped make the fourth step less intimidating for me. I opted not to follow the format in the *AA Big Book* and instead decided to write out the fourth step in longhand format.

The act of putting pen to paper was galvanizing. Writing about the demons of my past was completely different from thinking about them. It wasn't easy, and, in fact, I relapsed the first time I tried doing the fourth step.

I had to write that I resented myself for the mess I'd made of my life, my ex-wife for her role in the demise of our marriage, and my own daughter for wanting to be with her mother when it was "my time" for custody. I wrote of my fear of getting close to others and of guilt I carried—guilt over being an alcoholic, over my failed marriage, over my daughter having to live as the child of divorced parents.

What helped me complete my fourth step was to schedule a time and day to do my fifth step. That set the deadline for me.

5. Admitted to God, to ourselves and to another human being the exact nature of our wrongs. I'd set the day with my sponsor and completed Step 4. Now it was time to share with him what I'd written.

It was extremely emotional. Admitting not only my actions but my thoughts and feelings was foreign to me. But by this time I felt comfortable with my sponsor, who acted as a mentor, coach, and friend to me, and that made the process a bit easier.

We sat on his couch while I read everything I'd written. He commented occasionally, and I found that he'd had many of the same dark thoughts I did. The experience was more cleansing than I ever imagined.

When we were finished, I asked him, "Now, how do I admit these things to God?" He said, "You just did."

As I left his apartment that night and walked to my car, I had to look down to see if my feet were on the ground. I felt like I was floating, like a huge burden had been lifted.

Step 5 is simple: It's all about getting regrets and feelings such as guilt, anger, and fear out of your head. Left unaddressed, those things will haunt you.

6. Were entirely ready to have God remove all these defects of character. At first glance, I thought this would be easy. Why wouldn't I want to let go of those things I'd written about and admitted in the previous two steps? But I discovered that when a person has been hanging on to a fear or anger about something, it's hard to let go. Those feelings were part of what made me the person I was. Leaving those things behind meant that I would change, and I didn't know who would come out of that. That scared me.

But I could see how all those emotions had been weighing me down. I had to learn not to have so much anger toward myself. I couldn't change the fact that my marriage was over and my daughter was split between two homes. I couldn't dwell on the people I'd hurt. Resenting what happened in the past gained me nothing. Only through a willingness to change could I move forward.

7. Humbly asked him to remove our shortcomings. This step went hand in hand with Step 6. As long as I was willing to change and to accept my higher power's role in my life, I could begin freeing myself of my character defects. In Steps 4, 5 and 6, I'd identified those weaknesses, including self-pity, self-hatred, and a resentful, unforgiving heart. I had to ask the universe to help rid me of those flaws.

Are they all removed? No. I think maybe the universe wants me to learn something first. For example, I still care too much what others think of me. Perhaps the lesson is that I need to practice the art of self-acceptance before I can reveal myself to others without fearing their reactions.

8. Made a list of all persons we had harmed, and became willing to make amends to them all. To perform this activity, I returned to what I'd written in my fourth step. Item by item, I went through and identified the people I'd harmed. It was all laid out for me in black and white.

9. Made direct amends to such people wherever possible, except when to do so would injure them or others. My friends at AA warned me not to go into this step with expectations—not to anticipate people reacting in a certain way. If I did, there was a good chance I'd be disappointed.

When I began making amends, I purposely started with those I knew would be less challenging and worked my way to more difficult ones. The hardest was my daughter. How could I possibly make amends to an eight-year-old whose whole life had been overturned by my actions? My friends gave me direction: She was too young to understand direct amends from me. I had to make living amends—focusing on being a good father every day, abiding by my deepest values, and showing her who I was becoming. That's how I began making amends to my daughter and how I'll continue to do so for the rest of my life.

When it came to other people I'd hurt, I found most apologies went best when done face-to-face. I also discovered that I could always re-do one. I made amends to my ex-wife a second time about three years after my first attempt. I froze the first time and didn't say all the things I needed to say.

Each reparation was different. To some, I explained why I was doing this—that it was part of my program of sobriety. To others, I simply said I was sorry for the things I'd done. I told my parents how sorry I was for the worry I'd caused them and for distancing myself from them.

I never asked for forgiveness. The point of the ninth step was to clean up my side of the street. Whether people forgave me was completely up to them. I could only do my part.

10. Continued to take personal inventory and when we were wrong promptly admitted it. I practice this step daily. Before going to sleep at night, I trace through the day: Where was I hurtful, resentful, dishonest, or selfish? If I hurt someone, I resolve to make amends as soon as possible. Carrying mistakes inside can eventually take someone like me down a dark road.

11. Sought through prayer and meditation to improve our conscious contact with God as we understood him, praying only for knowledge of his will for us and the power to carry that out. My mood depends on my connection with my higher power. Some days that contact is prayer. Other times it's simply opening my eyes to something bigger than myself—a sunrise or a sky full of stars—or just sitting in the grass on a warm summer evening watching the world go by. When I meditate, it's most often a meditation in motion. It's the time I spend every day with my dog. We walk before dawn when life is quiet. We play in the yard or hike in the park. It's there that I relearn the lessons my dog teaches me: Live in the moment, play hard, and have fun.

12. Having had a spiritual awakening as a result of these steps, we tried to carry this message to alcoholics, and to practice these principles in all our affairs. That spiritual awakening happened for me, though I can't say exactly when. It wasn't after one or even two years of sobriety. It's a process that's still occurring. I carry the message every time I speak in a meeting or mentor other people, sharing what has worked for me and admitting that I still struggle every day. The second half of this step—practicing these principles in all our affairs—is simple—not always easy, but simple. We can apply the principles of this program—honesty, faith, hope, willingness, compassion, and humility—with our families, our work, our relationships, and whenever we interact with others. The people I admire most do try to practice these principles in all their affairs. That's the direction I hope my growth takes me.

✣ ✣ ✣

Believe in what you've been promised. The *AA Big Book* makes some promises about what will happen if you follow the twelve steps. These are the promises:

"If we are painstaking about this phase of our development, we will be amazed before we are halfway through. We are going to know a new freedom and a new happiness. We will not regret the past nor wish to shut the door on it. We will comprehend the word serenity and we will know peace. No matter how far down the scale we have gone, we will see how our experience can benefit others. That feeling of uselessness and self-pity will disappear. We will lose interest in selfish things and gain interest in our fellows. Self-seeking will slip away. Our whole attitude and outlook upon life will change. Fear of people and of economic insecurity will leave us. We will intuitively know how to handle situations which used to baffle us. We will suddenly realize that God is doing for us what we could not do for ourselves.

"Are these extravagant promises? We think not. They are being fulfilled among us—sometimes quickly, sometimes slowly. They will always materialize if we work for them."

I heard these promises many times in early sobriety. It all sounded like an unreachable state of Nirvana at the time. I wasn't sure I could ever let go of past regrets or feel like a useful member of society. The self-pity that fueled my disease would be hard to shake from my being.

Over the years, though, just as the promises state, my "whole attitude and outlook on life" changed. That's the promise that stands out the most to me.

There was no turning point when the promises were suddenly fulfilled. Moment by moment, I continue to grow and find new freedom. With that freedom comes happiness. Today, on this very day, I'm happier than I've ever been. I'm so far from the place that brought new misery with each day. It's through Alcoholics Anonymous that I was pulled from that misery and despair. That program and my higher power have given me a path and tools to continue growing.

Do the promises come true? Absolutely. That far-away state of Nirvana described to me years ago is here, in my life, today.

THINGS TO DO TODAY

Here are six actions you can take right now to begin transforming your life:

1. Write your obituary. Turn it into a story about your life, the way you want others to think of you. Include all the little things that characterize you, the tales that will make people laugh and cry when they eulogize you, the way you've touched people's lives, the memories you'll leave behind. Ask yourself: What do you want your obituary to say? How do you want to be remembered? What might you do differently to make sure your obituary will capture the person you want to be?

2. Scan the resources in the Appendix, and put stars next to the ones you want to follow up on.

3. Do something ridiculous—something you would ordinarily never do. Skip around the block. Do some somersaults. Dress in your partner's clothes. Dance to a wild song. Ask your children or your friends' children for suggestions. They'll have lots of ideas. The theory is that it breaks down the ego to be silly, to laugh at yourself, to do the thing you never dreamed of doing. It teaches you to be humble, and humility is a necessary part of the healing process.

4. Call your local United Way or other volunteer matching service. Finding a way to give of yourself will open up amazing possibilities, take your mind off your problems, and help you find your life's purpose.

5. Close your eyes, and speak to the universe. If you don't want to call it a prayer, call it an affirmation. Just say what's on your mind. Ask for strength, love, or whatever you need more of. Give thanks for the good things in your life. If you can't think of what to say, check out all the prayers and affirmations on the Internet (prayers.org, bmindful.com, beliefnet.com, for example). Find one you like, and repeat it.

6. Give one small gift to someone else.

–J.M.

WORDS OF WISDOM AND LIGHT

Use these beacons of hope and change to illuminate your own life.

Become Your Authentic Self: Wisdom from Tony

For so long, I lived for other people. If I'd met you then, I would have summed you up quickly, figured out what I thought you wanted from me, and given it to you full-force. You probably would have liked me. Most people did, at least at first. But eventually, you would have realized I wasn't who you thought I was. It was all pretense, an ugly sham, a hoax.

Now, I still lie constantly, but I own up to it. I might say to you, "I finished reading that book you gave me. No, sorry! That's a total lie! I meant to finish it, but I didn't."

Or I might say, "I went to a meeting yesterday—no, forget that! That's my lying self talking!"

My friends are used to me confessing to my lies on a pretty constant basis now. It may seem ridiculous, but I would rather be a foolish-sounding truth-teller than a smooth-talking fraud.

Sometimes I lie to make myself look better—smarter, kinder, more competent. Sometimes I might make things up because I think it will make you like me more. Most of the time, I can't tell you, or myself, why I lie. It's just an ingrained habit.

Everyone who's ever abused a substance or had an addiction has had a lot of practice with lying. If the people who loved us had known how much we were drinking and using, they would have tried to stop us, and that's the last thing we wanted. So we lied.

By the time I got sober, I was so sick of all the pretense. I made a vow to myself: No more pretending. Rather than tailoring myself to be liked and validated from the outside, I decided to work from the inside out.

Self-acceptance is the key. It's okay for me not to always look like I know what's going on. It's okay to feel awful and talk about it. It's okay to show my vulnerability. And it's okay for me to disagree with you and not be exactly the person you want me to be. I don't have to look the part, or talk the talk, as long as I walk the walk of authenticity, as much as I possibly can, every day.

I'll probably always be a liar. But by admitting it, to myself and to you, I'm taking control of it. I'm not letting pretense rule me. That's the only way I can get in touch with my bona fide self.

Addiction saved me. I know that sounds strange, but it's true. Using drugs, entering recovery, and then starting over from scratch, with people by my side to help me—that whole process was what introduced me to myself. If I hadn't gone through it, I would still be the glib, heedless person I once was. I'm still getting to know who I am, and becoming true to that self will be a lifelong journey. But I know now that if I don't keep looking at myself with unflinching honesty and unblinking eyes, I'll never get where I need to be.

Tony's best advice: Come to terms with your lying. It's important to understand that everyone lies. In *The Liar in Your Life: The Way to Truthful Relationships*, Robert Feldman describes research revealing that in ten-minute conversations with strangers, people tell an average of three lies. Other studies show we start lying when we're babies, crying and making a fuss to get attention, and there's a hereditary advantage to lying. We're born to lie.

Addicts make lying and manipulating others a way of life. When they stop using, they're often consumed with guilt about all the lies they've told and the trust they've broken. The first step to forgiving yourself is to understand that lying is a common part of life. Perhaps you've raised it to a fine art, but that doesn't make you a bad person.

If you resolve never to lie again, you're setting yourself up for failure. Instead, commit yourself to trying to lie less. Before you speak, think for a second, because it's easy to lie automatically if you aren't careful.

Don't use a commitment to honesty as a reason to rub harsh truths in people's faces. Balance a sincere effort to be candid with sensitivity to people's feelings.

Realize that the person who is hurt most when you lie is you. Every time you tell the truth, you'll feel better about yourself.

Learn to be comfortable with uncertainty and ambiguity. You're not either honest or dishonest. You're a human being who lies sometimes, like everyone else, but who is moving away from a life of deception.

Most of all, try not to lie to yourself. You need to act differently with different people and in various situations. That's part of being a social creature and getting along with others. But don't let these different social stances confuse you about who you really are. Being true to yourself is the most important thing of all.

Let It All Out: Wisdom from Jack

Recently I went on a men's retreat. I almost changed my mind at the last minute. The idea of spending a weekend with people I didn't know, talking about intimate issues, was terrifying. But I told myself to turn the fear around. The fact that I didn't know these people meant that I didn't have to worry about ever seeing them again if I didn't want to. It was an opportunity to talk about things I'd never spoken of because I was afraid to puncture people's opinions of me.

I was surprised at how quickly I bonded with the twelve other men at the retreat. It became clear that we were all wounded in some way. I had quit drinking a year earlier, and most of the other men were also addicts of one kind or another. We had a lot in common.

On the last night of the retreat, it was my turn to talk about the worst thing that ever happened to me. I told the group about a time in high school that I'd never mentioned to anyone before.

It happened when I was sixteen. I'd just admitted to myself that I was gay, but I wasn't ready to come out to anyone. In the high school gym that day, a boy called me something that means "gay" but has ugly, sickening connotations.

Those words were an ice pick that pierced my heart. They lodged there and never left. I carried them inside me throughout the twenty-five years that elapsed between that day in the gym and the evening at the retreat. During that time, I'd lived all over the world, unable to find peace or a place that felt like home. I'd searched for love but never found it. I'd struggled with depression and suicidal thoughts. Life hadn't seemed worth living.

When I told the group about that high school experience, all the pain and anger, the shame and self-hatred I'd kept within me came pouring out. The other men surrounded me and hugged me, and I felt their acceptance and caring soothe me like a healing salve.

Getting out those feelings, putting into words what had hurt me, and being accepted despite my shame—that was a life-changing moment. I felt my heart thaw and open up.

I had let those terrible words define me. I'd let the judgment of another person override my acceptance of myself. I'd been too young at the time to understand what I was doing, how I was hiding the truest part of who I was.

Once I got those hateful words out from inside, I could suddenly see that the boy who said them was speaking out of his own insecurity. It was about his brokenness, not mine.

The acceptance of those men on the retreat helped me begin to accept myself, including my dark, angry, shameful emotions. The experience didn't transform me all at once, but it was a turning point. I know I'll have to go back and face those feelings again, but next time will be easier. I still have work to do on myself to find peace in my life. But my heart is open now. I think I'm finally ready to find someone to love.

Jack's best advice: Find a safe place, with people you can trust. Talk to them, share your emotions, and let out everything you've held inside. Until you feel that breathtaking sense of catharsis, you have no idea how curative it is.

4

MAKE YOURSELF HAPPY: SKYE'S STORY

Thirty-one-year-old **Skye**, who began her recovery from heroin, cocaine, and crystal meth addiction in 2003, is a counselor at Connections and recently earned her master's in mental health. Her most fervent wish is to help others learn what it means to wake up happy every day.

Author's Note:
I liked Skye the minute I met her. I'd heard a great deal about her since she'd become my granddaughter Shyloh's counselor at Connections six months earlier. But I hadn't expected such a contagious effervescence. Petite, red-haired, with an impish grin, Skye could pass for a cheerleader rather than a thirty-one-year-old substance-abuse counselor and recovering heroin addict.

"I don't look like a heroin addict, and it shocks people when they find out I am," she said. "I tell them: This is what a heroin addict looks like.

"When they find out my story, some people judge me harshly," she went on. "Other people actually think my background as a heroin addict is cool and want to glamorize the lifestyle.

"But every once in a while someone 'gets' it and realizes it's not about who I once was but about how far I've come."

Another frustration, Skye told me, is that people are always asking how she can be so upbeat when she works with addicts every day. "I tell them I'm happy because I'm alive and I have the greatest job in the world. I have the privilege and joy of watching people find their true potential, every single day. I can't imagine anything better."

As I got to know Skye, I found that cheery was her default setting. But I also learned that under her look of elfin mischief was an inner ferocity, determination, and remarkable strength.

On our second meeting, when I asked what her goals were, having babies was at the top of her list. Two months later, when she told me she was pregnant, she was the pure essence of excitement.

She finally had everything she'd dreamed of. The distance she'd traveled over the past few years was almost impossible to fathom.

The following is Skye's story.

– J.M.

✱ ✱ ✱

Feeling a sense of permanence was always hard for me. We moved often when I was young, and, while it made me adaptable, it also unmoored me. I never felt like I belonged.

The oldest of three kids, I had to fight for every inch of space and freedom. My parents loved me, but my mom is controlling and a perfectionist. If she can't control something, she works harder until she can. So when I started to pull away as a teen, she fought me like a demon.

My mom is a brilliant, talented woman. She's a doctor of biology and a respected professor. I'm proud of her for being strong and independent, but when I was growing up I also resented that she wasn't like other moms.

My family was always different. We were atheists, environmentalists, and feminists. We ate pumpernickel and gouda, not American cheese on Wonder bread. We didn't fit in.

I never felt I could measure up. My mom always strives for something better, so I constantly felt pressure from her to improve, to never be satisfied.

My dad was my rock. I could always count on him. But I felt I would disappoint him, too, if I didn't live up to the special person he thought I was.

In third grade, I had an anxiety attack and thought I was going to throw up because I was afraid I wasn't going to get an A on a test. I constantly made myself sick with fear that I would disappoint my parents. If I got a B instead of an A, I felt the world would end. Nobody would think I was smart anymore.

In my teen years, I rebelled against all those expectations. I stopped paying attention in school and cut class. I said to myself, "I won't be ruled by my grades any longer." That could have been a helpful insight, but I didn't put it to use in an effective way. I went from caring too much to not caring at all. I hadn't yet found that middle place where it was okay to make a mistake.

Being accepted was all I cared about as a teenager. So I started using drugs. For a while I did feel accepted and cool and beautiful, but it didn't last. Pretty soon the only thing that mattered was getting more drugs.

I was in seventh grade the first time I smoked pot. Soon I was drinking, smoking, and sneaking out of the house to party with older kids. I started taking acid in ninth grade and cocaine, meth, and ecstasy in tenth grade. In twelfth grade my boyfriend introduced me to heroin.

I loved the counterculture and sense of unity in the rave scene. I didn't feel like I was good enough or that I belonged, and drugs made me good enough and gave me something to belong to.

I also was pretty pissed at the way the world works. I hated that no one paid attention to how we were destroying our planet. In grade school and middle school, I spoke up, started petitions, and tried to change things. But nothing changed and it all seemed so useless.

If some people are pulled into drugs by their peers, and some are pushed in by needing to escape problems, I don't feel like either of those is true for me. I wasn't pushed or pulled. I stepped in. For me, it was entirely self-will, my own decision to do drugs.

I kept using because I loved it. Then, when I no longer loved it, I kept using because I was an addict.

Even though my grades dropped in high school, I did well enough to get into college. I was offered a scholarship to Iona College but turned it down because I wanted to stay with my boyfriend. I moved in with him and went to a community college in Annapolis.

By that time, my parents had moved to Vancouver, so I spent some of my time in Canada and some with my boyfriend in Annapolis. He and I continued to shoot up heroin together every day.

Here's something no one ever tells you: When you first use drugs, they're great, but then they stop working. Everything that seemed so wonderful turns ugly and keeps getting worse. Bit by bit, your addiction steals your soul.

To restore my soul and my sanity, I had to get off drugs, and I knew I couldn't do it unless I left my boyfriend. So I moved out of our apartment and tried staying clean.

Even though I had good intentions, I didn't set up the proper support system for myself, so I quickly relapsed. Instead of starting a new life, as I'd hoped, I ended up sleeping on people's couches and using drugs with friends. Eventually, I went back to my boyfriend.

My relationship with him had deteriorated years before. He was mean and angry. He stole from me, cheated on me, and degraded me. He hurt me emotionally and sometimes physically. But he had convinced me that I couldn't make it without him.

I only half believed that.

But I also half believed that he would commit suicide if I left. So I stayed.

During those years, I saw such ugliness. I was often homeless, and I lived with violence and poverty all around me. Many days, getting my fix required me to engage in despicable criminal acts that only someone desperate for drugs could rationalize.

The lowest point came when my best friend, Ian, died from a heroin overdose. He was one of the sweetest guys I've ever known. I was the one who'd introduced him to heroin. Although I believe we're all responsible for our own lives, I couldn't help blaming myself for his death. He wouldn't have used, and he wouldn't have died, if he hadn't met me.

When Ian died, I tried to get clean, but after a few months I started using again. It felt like I was dishonoring his memory to go back to using, but that's the insanity of addiction. I swallowed myself up in drugs so I wouldn't have to confront the guilt, grief, and despair I felt.

Who knows how long it would have taken for me to follow him into death? But fate intervened, and I was arrested when I tried to take a little trip from Canada to the United States. When they checked my visa, they found I'd overstayed my Canadian visitor's visa. I was also charged with possessing drugs.

I spent over a month in jail and then was deported back to the United States.

All I can say is thank God for the Canadian border patrol.

During those weeks in jail, I had no option but to get clean. Without that intervention, I shudder to think how I would have ended up. Getting arrested and deported was the best thing that could have happened to me.

When they sent me back to the United States, I was a wreck with no place to go, no idea what to do. Thankfully, my parents, who now lived in Wisconsin, took me in. Their nonjudgmental love at this time of my life was a touch of grace.

A GOOD QUESTION

What is grace? It's hard to define, but it's an intrinsic part of recovering, starting a new life, and thriving. Most of us have heard of "God's grace"—the fact that God loves us no matter what we do or who we are. But not everyone in recovery has embraced the idea of a personal God. Many of the counselors and clients at Connections have been turned off, even traumatized, by organized religion. They've all struggled to find their own definition of grace. Here's how some of them described it:

- Grace is an unexpected gift from the universe—often something you didn't even know you needed, like sobriety, or patience, or a new friend.
- It's what lets you forgive yourself.
- Grace connects you to the energy of something bigger than yourself when your own energy is depleted. It comes in those moments of epiphany when you understand at a gut level how perfect and beautiful life is and how lucky you are to be alive.
- Grace is what saves you when you least expect it and when you feel you least deserve it.
- Grace is a gift we receive simply for being human and alive. This gift isn't something earned or deserved. If we're aware, and grateful, we notice there are many moments of grace in our lives. We often miss them because we're remembering the past or planning the future rather than being in the now.
- It's the strength you didn't know you had, the spark of self-preservation and belief in yourself that can save your life.
- Grace comes when you need it most, but it's also around you all the time, even when you don't realize it.

– J.M.

To live completely, wholly, every day as if it were a new loveliness, there must be dying to everything of yesterday.
—Jiddu Krishnamurti

✣ ✣ ✣

When I arrived at my parents' house, I was like a new baby, defenseless and vulnerable. I put myself in their hands, and they found a sober house where I could live. When my mom took me there for the intake interview, the counselor asked me to relate my drug history. For the first time, I did so honestly, leaving nothing out. My mother was sitting beside me. I knew it would devastate her, but only truth could set me on the right path. I had no doubt of that.

It was shattering, the hardest thing I'd ever done—telling my perfectionist mom, whom I admired and respected more than anything in the world, that I was an IV-drug user. But I realized if I lied, as I'd done so many times before, I'd go back to using. Being totally honest was the only way I could make this time different. If I was to stick with recovery, I had to put everything out there.

I could see the horror in her eyes, and then she started crying, and so did I. It was a nightmare made real.

Yet those tears were cleansing, washing away all the sick secrets and falsehoods of the past, freeing me to start again.

I would be honest, for there are those who trust me.
—Howard Arnold Walter

✧ ✧ ✧

This wasn't the first time I'd quit drugs. I'd gotten clean three times before and then relapsed. I didn't have little relapses. Each time, I went back to using for about a year before I tried once again to sober up. It seemed like everything had to fall apart before I was ready to try again.

Someone asked me recently to describe my attempts to sober up. I must admit it's pretty fuzzy in my memory, but I think the timeline went like this: The first time I got clean, I was in Maryland when a "friend" borrowed my car and totaled it. Without a car, there was no way for me to get to school, so I moved to Vancouver to live with my folks.

My parents didn't berate me for the life I'd lived or all the gifts I'd thrown away. Instead, they told me I was strong and that they loved me but that they were scared for me. That was the best thing anyone could have said to me, the one thing that got through to me and kept me sober the whole time I was there.

But after four months with my parents, I moved back to Maryland to return to college. A month later, I started seeing my ex, who'd never stopped using drugs. Soon I was back to doing drugs, too.

Then one day, my girlfriend took me aside. She said she'd always thought of me as a strong person, and it made her sad that, because of my addiction, I was letting my boyfriend treat me like crap. We cried together, and then decided to get help, and we signed up to go into in-patient treatment together.

I was in treatment for three weeks. When I got out, I foolishly went back to live with my ex. He used heroin in front of me the day I got out, so of course I started shooting up again too, that very first night.

My girlfriend also relapsed that time, but about a year later she got clean. She graduated from college and works as a nurse now.

After another horrible year of using, I developed a blood infection caused by my IV use. It was so bad that I nearly died and the doctors almost had to amputate my leg. I was unbelievably lucky to recover with my life and limbs intact.

That scared me enough that I stopped using needles for good. I moved back to Vancouver to make a new start. But within a few weeks of moving there, I met one of the biggest meth dealers in the city and started snorting meth.

That's what I was doing when the Canadian border patrol arrested me, threw me in jail, and deported me.

I'm listing my relapse history here not to glorify the lifestyle but to reassure everyone who has relapsed that it's not the end of the world. There's always another chance.

Why do some attempts to get clean result in relapses and some don't? What's different about the times that people stay sober for good?

For me, there were a couple of things that made this time different. For one thing, I'd been forced out of my using environment and into new surroundings. Instead of being with my using friends, I was with my family, who were willing to do whatever they could to help me get clean.

The other big difference was that, this time, I realized I had to tell the truth—not only to everyone close to me but to myself. I knew how easy it was for me to fool myself—telling myself, for example, "It's okay to snort heroin because at least I'm not using needles," or "Drinking is fine because at least I'm not doing heroin, cocaine, or meth."

This time, I gave myself to recovery with all my heart, and it transformed me. Every day was a revelation. I discovered things about myself. I was exposed to other people who were in recovery. I learned.

Till then, whenever I'd felt sad, lonely, or angry, I'd tried to get away from those feelings as quickly as possible. But avoiding those emotions didn't make them go away; it just buried them inside, where they took on an even greater power to hurt.

Now I discovered it was okay to feel bad. The only way to make a feeling go away is to feel it. You have to be there and let yourself feel crappy for a while.

Feelings are the universal language and are to be honored. They are the authentic expression of who you are at your deepest place.
—Judith Wright

There was a time in early sobriety when my mind raced all the time, and I worried that feeling all these emotions would break my psyche. I felt as if I was dying. It wasn't till much later that I realized I *was* dying. The old me had to die so I could start again.

During those days, I was bombarded by the memory of all the traumatic events that had happened. I'd never mourned the death of my best friend, Ian, or the others who'd overdosed while I was in that lifestyle. Once I was no longer deadened by drugs, those deaths hit me, one after another.

I was completely broken for a while. But every day I called my sister, who'd gotten sober shortly before I did. She shared her strength and wisdom with me, and I survived.

Each day I survived was a clue that I was tougher than I thought. This was a new kind of strength. For a long time I felt I was strong to endure the using lifestyle and push away my emotions. Now I saw that real strength lay in dealing with life sober and confronting my feelings.

Every time I faced one of those long-buried emotions, I felt braver. Then, when one of those feelings came up for me again, I was able to deal with it a little better.

When I realized it was okay to feel like that, everything changed. One day I realized: I *am* strong enough to face all the awful things I did when I was using. That was a transforming moment.

> ***The unconscious wants truth. It ceases to speak to those who want something else more than truth.***
> —Adrienne Rich

✣ ✣ ✣

The second stage of sobriety—after getting clean—was much harder than I expected. It's that way for everyone, and if you aren't prepared, it can derail you. You're newly sober and pleased about your recovery, but you're rudderless. It's easy to get stalled at this point and slip back into old habits.

Years later, I read a book called *Repotting* by Diana Holman and Ginger Pape, and it reminded me of how I felt during those early days of sobriety. Imagine, the authors write, that you're a plant in a pot and you're suddenly transplanted into a garden. Your roots, strangled and cramped for so long, all at once have room to spread out. What a strange feeling that would be. That uneasiness is natural when your whole life opens after being scrunched up for so long.

Such an enormous change is threatening. People will suffer unimaginable things to evade the unknown. But accepting the new and different is the only way you can stretch out your roots and grow. It's the only way you can become a healthy, whole human being.

> ***Look, the wind vane fluttering in the autumn breeze***
> ***Takes hold of certain things that cannot be held.***
> —Feng Chih

I started looking for a job and found a management position at a bank. It felt good to give structure to my days, but I still felt lost and adrift. I was nervous, unsure of myself, and worried that I wouldn't be able to hold down such a responsible job.

Why was it all so hard? Much of the time I felt that, rather than making progress, I was barely holding on.

Then it occurred to me that I was having a hard time moving forward because I was unsure of who I was. For a huge chunk of my life, I was a criminal and an addict, so if I wasn't those things anymore, who was I? I wanted to be honest with myself, but who was "myself"?

The way I answered that question was to list what I called "My Truths." I started with the only thing I knew for sure: People are born good. Even at my lowest point, when I was using heavily and unhappy with who I was and what I was doing with my life, I still believed in people's basic goodness.

That belief was enough to fortify me as I tried to put myself together out of a jumble of pieces. Soon I was adding more to my list every day. As my list of truths became longer, it became clearer to me who I was.

One tactic I used to ferret out my truths was to say to myself, "I did such-and-such because…" and then add the reason I did it. Often I wasn't sure why I did something, so I would ask myself what I would surmise about other people if they did it. For instance, when I stayed late at work, at first I wasn't sure why. So I asked myself: What would I think about someone who stayed late? I would guess that they valued hard work and responsibility. So then that became something I knew for sure about myself: I valued hard work and responsibility. I could add that to my list of truths.

Another truth had to do with personal accountability. I believed I needed to take total responsibility for myself and my decisions. That conviction gave me a big boost on my road to recovery. I didn't waste time blaming others, which saved me a lot of misery.

MOMENT OF TRUTH

What do you value? To live an authentic life, you need to connect with your core values—the truths you want to live by. Which of the following values do you want to put at the center of your life? Place a 1 by the three values that are most important to you, a 2 by the next three most important, and so on. If you think of others, add them to the list.

__Honesty __Fairness __Accountability for your actions
__Creativity __Security __Respect for the environment
__Compassion __Loyalty __Courage in the face of obstacles
__Learning __Gratitude __Service to others
__Kindness __Generosity __Industriousness and hard work
__Belonging __Love __Inner peace
__Friendship __Beauty __Communication with others
__Spirituality __Justice __Personal Growth
__Adventure __Teamwork __Independence
__Others:_____

– J.M.

✻ ✻ ✻

I remembered things I knew but had forgotten—that my family loved me, that the world was filled with reasons to laugh and rejoice, that I had a million blessings in my life. Gratitude saved me every day.

It was such a relief to wake up and worry about being late to work instead of scoring a fix. I loved having the same everyday problems as everyone else.

Best of all, I was starting to like the person I was. For so long I'd despised myself and what I was doing with my life. To turn that self-hate to self-love took time. I did it by surrounding myself with people who cared about me and my recovery. I set goals and felt proud when I achieved them, even if they were only tiny things at first. I did ordinary things like gardening, playing tennis, and spending time with my goddaughter and her siblings. I took walks with my friends, laughed at nothing with my sister, and took a hip-hop class. I showed up for work every day and did the best job I could, even when it was the last thing I felt like doing. I came to believe that the day was a success if I made one contact with another person and shared at least one laugh.

I learned that when I felt "stuck," the best thing was to do something, take some action. Rather than ruminate over things, it was better to get moving.

Part of healing was apologizing to people I'd hurt and repairing relationships I'd broken. I told Ian's mother how sorry I was for bringing him into the life that ended up killing him. I couldn't imagine the amount of strength and goodness it took to be in her position and not blame me, because I blamed myself so much. But she told me it wasn't my fault. I was so grateful to her for not thinking I was a horrible person.

Hardest of all was to face my parents and tell them how sorry I was to have disappointed them. I vowed I would make it up to them, and they told me they believed in me and forgave me.

Receiving forgiveness like that was such a gift. It led me to the most essential step of all—forgiving myself.

✻ ✻ ✻

My sister, who was my rock through early recovery, introduced me to Connections Counseling. Connections had helped her get clean, and she wanted me to check it out. That's how I met Shelly, the founder and head of Connections, and my whole life changed.

Everyone at Connections was so warm, welcoming, and understanding. Talking to others who'd been through experiences like mine soothed the loneliness I'd felt for so long.

It was like coming home.

I began speaking up in groups and sharing some of what I'd learned. At a meeting one evening, I offered feedback to a teenager who was struggling. Afterwards, Shelly took me aside. She'd always encouraged me to share my experiences, but this time she went even further.

"That was great input," she said. "You know, you would be a good counselor. Have you considered going back to school and getting a certificate in substance-abuse counseling?"

I was stunned. "Not really."

"Well, think about it. You're great with these kids. If you finish your education, I'll hire you as a counselor here at Connections."

I thought she was crazy. I could barely keep my own life together! Who was I to be giving advice to others?

But Shelly never gave up on me. She kept championing me, mentoring me, coaxing me to continue my education and consider a career in counseling.

A year later I registered for classes.

The idea of becoming a counselor was new to me, but it turned out to be a perfect fit. I enrolled at a technical college, where my teachers' encouragement vitalized me and strengthened my belief in myself.

Give me everything mangled and bruised, and I will make a light of it to make you weep, and we will have rain and we will have begun again.
—Deena Metzgar

During that year, I continued going to meetings at Connections and learning about myself. I did something that, when I look back on it, seems reckless and unwise. I went back to Baltimore, where all my problems had begun.

I told myself I was going there to see my grandparents and some of my old friends. But once I got there, I realized I had to see my ex-boyfriend, who'd been with me through all the insane, drug-infested times. Somehow, I couldn't move on till I laid that relationship to rest.

Now if someone I was counseling told me they were planning such a trip, I would tell them it was a dreadful idea, that the chance of them relapsing was high. I would be so worried for them.

But I was smart enough not to go alone. My dad was by my side on the trip to Baltimore, and an old friend went with me to see my ex. Those safeguards lowered my risk of relapse.

Seeing my ex opened my eyes to how poisonous our relationship had been. He'd been another addiction for me, and our relationship had been based on an obsessive need.

Now that I was feeling better about myself, I could face him without being sucked back into the craziness. We had a good talk, and I told him I forgave him for everything. That helped me get rid of a lot of anger.

I felt so strong when I got back from that trip. I'd proven to myself that I would never return to that life.

An ancient tree
Too fibrous for a logger's saw,
Too trusted to fit a carpenter's square,
Outlasts the whole forest.
—Lao Tzu

✧ ✧ ✧

Going back to school was scary. I worried that I would put that same pressure on myself I'd felt as a child, thinking I had to get straight A's.

I did. I couldn't help it.

But the saving grace for me was a class I took on solution focused therapy (also known as cognitive therapy and rational emotive therapy). My teacher emphasized the fact that you have to let go of anxiety about what you can't control.

So I started making lists. Every time I got stressed about something, I'd list what I could control in that situation and what I couldn't. That simple exercise helped me tremendously. I realized, for instance, that I didn't give myself the grades, so that was something I couldn't control and might as well stop worrying about. What I could control was showing up for class, doing my homework, and getting my assignments in on time. When I concentrated on those things and let go of the rest, my stress level dropped dramatically.

Those cognitive strategies helped me pinpoint and supplant many harmful messages from my childhood. I didn't even realize these messages were in my brain, yet they were directing my thoughts and actions.

> ### TURNING POINT
>
> **Change the messages of childhood.** When you're growing up, you internalize many "truths" without realizing it. As you grow older, it's a good idea to seek out those hidden messages and decide whether they're true. If not, replace them with new advice that you believe is true. Here's what some counselors and clients at Connections came up with when they did this exercise:
>
> *Message from my childhood:* There is only success or failure, and failure is unacceptable. *What I replaced it with:* The best way to prevail is by making mistakes and learning from them.
>
> *Message from my childhood:* People grow by focusing on what they're doing wrong. *What I replaced it with:* People grow by immersing themselves in what they're great at doing.
>
> *Message from my childhood:* Having fun is frivolous. *What I replaced it with:* Play as often as possible; it's what makes life worthwhile.
>
> What messages did you receive as a child? Do they enhance your life? If not, what can you tell yourself instead? (For more on cognitive therapy, see "Moment of Truth: Listen to the Self-Talk in Your Mind" in Chapter 1.) _____
> _____
> _____
>
> – J.M.

✻ ✻ ✻

In addition to my schoolwork, I still had my bank position. Although it was exhilarating to discover that I could hold my own in such a high-powered job, I didn't enjoy it. I was working fifty hours a week and felt overwhelmed, but I kept at it to show myself I could do it.

I also started volunteering two or three hours a week at Connections, and that work sustained me. I loved working with people who, like me, were rebuilding their lives after giving up their addictions.

> *We are not what we know but what we are willing to learn.*
> —Mary Catherine Bateson

✳ ✳ ✳

I learned to trust again. When I was using, I always had my guard up. I had to. When we use drugs, we avoid the people who love us, because they see us self-destructing and try to stop us, and we don't want to be stopped. So, instead, we surround ourselves with people who don't care if we destroy ourselves.

That's not to say they're bad people. But they're addicts, which means that using is more important than maintaining a friendship; using is more important than anything else. So it would be foolish to trust them.

In sobriety I had to learn that this rule no longer applied. I began making friends who didn't need anything from me but simply liked me for myself. As I opened up to them, I found that they wouldn't hurt or betray me. They were friends in the true sense of the word.

> **Life is partly what we make it, and partly what is made by the friends whom we choose.**
> —Tehyi Hsieh

✳ ✳ ✳

At first I was bothered by the emphasis on "God as you understand Him" in the recovery groups I attended. I grew up in a family of atheists, and I'm still an atheist to this day. The idea of surrendering to this God was especially hard for me, because I believed so strongly that I was responsible for everything that happened in my life. I didn't like the word "surrender," since one of the fundamental values of my family is independence, especially for women.

As I struggled with how to relate the higher-power concept to my life, I learned some vital things about myself. I realized I have a spiritual dimension even if I don't believe in God. To me, spirituality is taking care of your mind, body, other people, and the environment. My higher power is people's innate goodness. As long as I hold true to that basic tenet, I'm okay.

I also came to understand that surrender doesn't mean giving up personal responsibility, not at all. I can believe I'm accountable for my actions and still submit to things I can't change. I can try as hard as possible to do my best and then yield to the outcome. I can help someone by giving them my love, understanding, and the tools for a new life—and then leave it up to them to be responsible for their life, just as I'm responsible for mine. I must do my part and then stop analyzing the situation and embrace whatever happens.

> **Help us to be the always-hopeful gardeners of the spirit who know that without darkness nothing comes to birth, as without light nothing flowers.**
> —May Sarton

✳ ✳ ✳

Two years after I got sober, I took the biggest leap of all: I got a boyfriend.

Dating someone like Mason was a huge shift for me. I'd never dated a nice guy before. With my ex, I'd allowed myself to be treated in ways that were unthinkable. At the time I thought I deserved to be treated poorly. When I got sober and started to like myself, I began to change what I thought I deserved.

I was upfront with Mason from the beginning. When he asked me out the first time, I said, "I just got out of this abusive relationship, and I don't want a romance with anyone, and I'm a recovering drug addict and criminal, and I've been a homeless intravenous-heroin user living on the street, and I've been incarcerated and deported…"

He said, "I just wanted to take you to dinner."

So we laughed, and that was good. I'd always wanted to be with someone who made me laugh. Even better, he didn't judge me for any of the shameful things I'd done. His reaction to my history was, "It's amazing you've come as far as you have," which was the perfect response.

For our first few years together, he had to prove to me every day that he wasn't going to hurt me. He was so patient with me.

Five years later, he asked me to marry him, and I accepted. He proposed in January, and we were married in August. That winter and spring, I was working ten hours a week at Connections and fifty hours a week at my bank job while going to school and planning the wedding. It was an incredibly busy and happy time. I was seeing all my hopes realized, and I knew it was only because of my sobriety.

I still remember the day my mom and I went to pick out my wedding dress. It was such a landmark day, and I'd never felt so close to her. We talked about how tumultuous our relationship had been and what good friends we'd become. It was clear to both of us that without our relationship falling apart while I was using we wouldn't have been able to build such a close friendship.

That was true of so many of the good things in my life. All my relationships became stronger because they shattered and had to be rebuilt. It made me realize that my addiction, while a terrible curse, was also an incredible gift. It was what had fractured everything so that I had no option but to change. It was the crucible that forced me to strip away everything that wasn't me and become wholly and authentically myself.

Someone once told me, "In chaos, we're closest to the divine." How true that is—particularly for those of us in recovery. Because our lives disintegrated, we had the opportunity to refashion ourselves the way we wanted, to make ourselves better. Few people get that chance. It takes such courage to remake yourself that you're unlikely to do it unless forced by the chaos in your life. That makes us lucky.

I felt especially fortunate to have found Mason when I was strong enough to forge a healthy relationship with a man. If I'd met him earlier, when my self-esteem was nonexistent, I wouldn't have given our relationship a chance.

> *Barn's burnt down—*
> *Now I can see the moon.*
> —Masahide

✵ ✵ ✵

Our wedding was everything I'd dreamed. Several weeks beforehand, I'd quit my bank job, and afterwards I was finally able to start working at Connections full time. It was so satisfying to finally achieve what I wanted both personally and professionally. Such a fulfilling life was galaxies beyond anything I could have fathomed back in my using days or early sobriety. I'd accomplished it simply by taking one step, one venture, one breath, at a time.

Mason and I wanted kids and decided to start trying as soon as I got my degree. By this time, I'd transferred from the technical school to a four-year college in Madison. I had three supportive teachers there who broadened my understanding of social work, psychology, and substance-abuse counseling. I could almost feel my roots expanding as I eagerly reached out for all there was to learn.

I finished my bachelor's in a little over a year. By that time, I knew I wanted to treat people's mental-health concerns as well as their substance-abuse issues. For that I needed a master's degree. So two weeks after I finished my bachelor's I started my master's.

> *It is in changing that things find meaning.*
> —Heraclitus

Six months later, I found out I was pregnant. Soon after that, we learned the baby was going to be a girl.

I'd always wanted a daughter. I'd actually picked out her name—Siela—in ninth grade. That's what I was called in Spanish class, since it comes from the word for "sky." I loved the sound of it and knew, even as a teenager, that someday I wanted a daughter named Siela.

Our beautiful baby girl was born that spring. She was a dream come true and taught me how deep love can be.

I'll never forget one morning when she was about four months old and I was making faces at her. Suddenly she started laughing, not little giggles but a big belly laugh. I was flooded with a sense of euphoria beyond any high I'd ever had. At last I knew what life was all about—just being present for the simple, everyday ecstasies of life.

> *Be tough in the way a blade of grass is rooted, willing to lean, and at peace with what is around it.*
> —Natalie Goldberg

✧ ✧ ✧

Hard as it was to leave Siela when I returned to work, I found immense satisfaction in my job. Working as a substance-abuse counselor with teens and young adults, especially those with opiate addictions similar to my own, I found my purpose.

I remember one client at Connections who was always so morose. I couldn't get through to him. Then he was in a terrible motorcycle wreck. When he returned to Connections, he was in a wheelchair, bandaged from head to toe, but he was beaming, just beaming, because he finally got it. He finally understood how precious his life was and how he'd been destroying it with drugs.

Each time I see someone turn their life around it's like magic. I'm filled with joy.

My work allows me to use my greatest strengths. I've always been good at connecting with people, and when I was living negatively I was a harmful influence on others. Now that I'm living positively, I have a healthy impact on the people around me. Seeing this reaffirms to me daily that this is the right way for me to live.

I love the people I meet at Connections, not just my clients and the other counselors, but the people who come in to give talks and share their wisdom. I recall an epiphany I had when an expert on tobacco use spoke to a group of us. He said that more of us would eventually die from smoking cigarettes than from using other drugs. That floored me. I had considered cigarettes the lesser evil, but from that moment on, helping people quit using tobacco was my new crusade.

I'd smoked for many years myself and had just recently quit, so I knew how hard it was to give up cigarettes. I also knew that those of us who are addicts have to be on guard against replacing one addiction with another. Food, shopping, caffeine—anything has the possibility of becoming my next addiction.

Addictions are so sneaky. They creep up on us when our backs are turned. I learned to be cautious whenever I saw that I was using something outside of myself to fix something on the inside. That was a red flag. It meant I should take a closer look to see if that behavior benefited me. In the case of using tobacco, there were absolutely no advantages and lots of drawbacks.

MOMENT OF TRUTH

The other addiction: If you're addicted to alcohol or other drugs, it's likely you're addicted to smoking, too. Here are some tried-and-true strategies for kicking the compulsion:

- Identify your triggers. When are you most likely to smoke? After a meal? When you first wake up? List those triggers. For each one, write down what you'll do at that specific time instead of smoking. For instance, if you feel you must smoke after a meal, consider taking a walk or chewing gum instead. If you usually need a cigarette first thing in the morning, try exercising rather than smoking.
- Write down your goals. What do you want to accomplish in your life? Where do you want to be in ten years, thirty years, fifty years? Ask yourself if your goals are compatible with continuing to smoke. Do you want to be a role model to others? Have healthy children and grandchildren and watch them grow up? Do your goals fit with a life chained to tobacco?
- Talk to a doctor or other healthcare professional, who will be happy to help you decide on a quitting plan, prescribe helpful medication, enroll you in quitting classes, and put you in touch with countless other resources to make quitting easier.
- Think of your tobacco as a best friend who has died, and mourn that death. Hold a memorial service and say good-bye.
- Find a counselor or group that will hold you accountable, sustaining you through your cravings.

– J.M.

✫ ✫ ✫

My entire approach to life has turned upside down. Now I absolutely believe that one person can change the world. I believe everything you do ripples outward. If you help those around you, they act on those changes and make a difference in the lives of others. One small act can create waves that go on forever.

The first time this truth was brought home to me was early in my career as a counselor when I mentored a girl who had just quit using drugs and was in a rehab center. Scared and desperate, she decided to kill herself and took an overdose of pills. She and I had built a close relationship, and she felt she couldn't die without saying good-bye to me, so she snuck out of her room to call me. A guard saw her and took her to the hospital, and she survived.

That girl is alive today because of me. I remind myself of her whenever I start feeling like I'm not doing enough or that what I do doesn't count.

We shall find peace. We shall hear the angels, we shall see the sky sparkling with diamonds.
—Anton Chekhov

I often think about what the author Anne Lamott once said: Meet a person where they are but don't leave them where you found them. That's true for everyone but especially people suffering from addiction.

The very framework of recovery work is changing. It used to be that a person would go into recovery for thirty days, and that was it. Now we see addiction as a chronic illness like dyslexia or asthma that needs maintenance for the rest of your life.

That's why if my clients go back to using, I never judge them. Nor do any of the other Connections counselors. Most of us have been there ourselves, so we know lecturing them won't do any good. Instead, we support them wholeheartedly every time they decide to make a new start.

The key for me is to live joyfully and mindfully. I don't meditate in the traditional sense because I find it impossible to empty my mind of thoughts. So I've adapted a practice called loving-kindness meditation. I give loving-kindness to myself and then pick some other people and give loving-kindness to them. Next, I write about what I'm grateful for. Sometimes it's just a sentence, like "I'm glad it's sunny today," or "I'm thankful that my check-up went well and I'm healthy." Sometimes I write more, especially when I make a point of remembering how low I once was and how far I've come. Here's what I wrote one morning not too long ago:

A TIME TO REMEMBER
When I woke up I always had two thoughts. The first was: How am I going to score?
After I had a plan for scoring, the second thought would come: I hate my life.
And I did. Most nights I would wait till my boyfriend was asleep and then cry. I had to wait for him to fall asleep because my crying made him angry and violent.
Our town house was spattered with drops of blood and cigarette burns—standard junky decor. My family was in a different country and if they knew how I was living they'd be ashamed. My real friends wanted me to get off the dope so I drove them away. The only people I saw most days were the boyfriend and the guy in the ghetto who copped for us.
Nine years ago I quit. I left the boyfriend, and my family took me back. I was an addict and a liar, and my family took me back. I was arrested and deported, and my family took me back.
My family took me back.

My family took me back but it wouldn't have been enough. It was the last time; I knew, they knew, that it was the last time. If I used, I was alone. If I was alone, I was dead. To survive I had to stay sober. So I did.

I stayed sober, but each day was a struggle. I went through the motions, but I had no sense of direction or purpose. Nothing seemed real. My old "using" self was gone, but I had no new self to take her place. I was in limbo, in purgatory.

Then something happened.

Four months after quitting, I woke up without the two thoughts. I woke up and I didn't need a drug or a man or anything outside of myself. I was enough to make me happy. Just me, myself. I was free.

SKYE'S BEST ADVICE

- Always remember that instant gratification doesn't mean long-term contentment.
- Fail fast. The sooner you plunge in, the sooner you can move past mistakes to find success.
- Feel your feelings. The secret to happiness is to let yourself feel shitty. Without the bitter, you can't savor the sweetness.
- Have fun! If sobriety sucks, nobody stays sober.
- You can deal with almost anything by concentrating on four things: breathing, hugging, laughing, and talking.
- The best way out is always through. You can't get to the next step by trying to go around problems. You have to look squarely at the problem and work through it. That's how you grow and move forward in your life.
- Look for happiness within yourself. Don't expect others to make you happy. You hold the key to rapture in your own heart.

✫ ✫ ✫

Recovery has taught me so much. I always felt like something was missing in my life—that I couldn't be happy until this or that happened. Now I've learned to accept myself and others as we are, instead of trying to make us into something we're not or something we could be in the future. I've learned that happiness doesn't come from the outside; it comes from within.

We all have the power to make ourselves happy. To find fulfillment we have to start in the dark emotions, facing our fear, anger, loneliness, guilt, and remorse. It's crucial to feel bad because that's what provides the definition of feeling good.

A friend of mine gave me a framed piece of calligraphy, which I have on my office wall:

Life isn't about waiting for the storm to pass. It's about learning to dance in the rain.

I look at that message every day and remind myself how true it is. I'm happy now, and I wasn't happy when I was using, so the decision to stay sober seems pretty simple.

My sobriety is the foundation for my career, my relationships, my marriage, my self-worth. I know that if I take away that foundation, everything crumbles.

I love myself now. It's still hard for me to say that, because for so long loving myself wasn't okay. But I've learned to know myself, and I like the person I am. My life is dedicated to helping others realize that they can get sober and build a new life. They can start loving themselves. They can wake up happy.

✣ ✣ ✣

TOOLS FOR THE JOURNEY

Every morning, write down the first thoughts that come to you when you awake (or speak them into a recorder or video cam). Later, take a look at those thoughts and ask: Are they happy thoughts, or do they suggest changes you could make to improve your life? Those first thoughts of the morning, like dreams, hold valuable clues to whether you're living the life you're meant to live.

Don't search for happiness. It's not something you can find by chasing it. It's not a goal. It's something that may come to you if you shift the focus of your life. Research points to factors that often lead to happiness—and those that don't. Here, for example, are some things that have been proven *not* to lead to happiness:
- Money. When countries are ranked on a happiness scale, people in the richest countries are, on average, no happier than those in poor countries (as long as the average income in a nation exceeds $8,000).
- Material possessions. The more "stuff" you have, the less likely you are to be happy.
- Your health, race, or educational level.
- A life free of pain and hardship. Suffering is necessary before you can know true happiness.
- A pleasant, sunny climate. Indeed, the regions with the happiest people (Switzerland, Iceland, the Scandinavian countries) all have cold climates with long, dark winters.

Since external circumstances don't affect happiness very much, it's better to turn your attention to your inner environment. Here are ways to make an enduring difference in your happiness by changing yourself:
- Understand your signature strengths (assess yourself at www.authentichappiness.org). Research has identified twenty-four strengths that are common to a successful, happy life: curiosity, love of learning, critical thinking, ingenuity, emotional intelligence, perspective, bravery, perseverance, integrity, kindness, loving, loyalty, fairness, leadership, self-control, prudence, humility, appreciation of beauty, gratitude, optimism, sense of purpose, mercy, humor, and enthusiasm. Pinpoint your greatest strengths, and spend time building them rather than trying to eliminate your weaknesses.
- Choose gratification over pleasure—reading a book or writing in your journal, for instance, rather than watching TV. Pleasure is a powerful motivator, but it builds

nothing for the future. Gratification isn't always pleasant, but it's rewarding. Gratifications challenge and absorb you. Whether it's painting, rock-climbing, or listening to someone's troubles, find gratifications that deeply involve you. Fix your mind on the happiness of others and on improving the world.
- Plan regular times to connect with others. One study shows that having a group to attend once a month will boost happiness as much as doubling your salary.
- Foster a feeling of being successful, whatever "success" means to you. Sometimes money is a byproduct of doing what you love, but those who think money equals happiness become disappointed later in life when they discover it isn't true.
- Cultivate gratitude. Thank people (and your higher power) verbally, in letters, on sticky notes, in as many ways as you can, as often as you can.

—adapted from *The Geography of Bliss*, *Authentic Happiness*, and *Gross National Happiness*

Develop a strategic plan for your life. Since you can't do everything, you need to identify the most pivotal aspects of your life and focus on them. Picture yourself three years from now, and write down what you see. _____
_____
_____

What could you do now that would lead to the results you want? Write your answer here: _____
_____
_____

It's Time to Recover from the Disease of Perfectionism
Perfectionism can be as debilitating as other diseases and addictions. Here's how to become a "recovering perfectionist":
- Understand that human beings are fallible, make mistakes, and fail constantly. Accept these frailties in yourself and others.
- Let go of expectations. Nothing is more restrictive than expecting things to turn out a certain way. Broaden your definition of what's possible and acceptable.
- Every day if possible, tell someone about a mistake you've made or an imperfection in yourself. Doing so will build connections with other people, and you'll find they like you more, not less, when you share your foibles.
- Set time limits for each task. If it's an important activity, you might schedule two hours to do it. If it's not as high a priority, give it less time. Do the best job you can within that time frame, realizing that there's always more you could do, but you must move on. It will never be perfect, and that's okay.
- Each time you have a critical thought, write it down, and balance it with three positive, noncritical thoughts.
- List times in your life that you felt you failed. What did you learn from those experiences? Can you see each "failure" as an education, a chance to change, a time to try something new?

Every evening, think of three good things about your day. Ask your partner, children, or others in your life to do the same thing, and share your thoughts.

Look at your newspaper as your to-do list. Every few weeks, respond to something in the paper. You could write a letter to the newspaper's editor. Or write to a politician to express your views. If you're moved by a person's or country's problems, send a check to a charity that deals with those issues. The more you reach out to do something, the more power you'll have over the world around you, and the more you'll like yourself.

Learn to be great. *The Genius in All of Us* by David Shenk has far-reaching implications for anyone who wants to fulfill a dream. The key to greatness is to discipline yourself, which is a skill you can learn. Here are some tools:
- Persevere. The greatest lesson from high achievers isn't how easily things come to them but how persistent they are.
- Find your motivation. You have to want it so badly you'll never give up, so badly that you'll sacrifice time and money, so badly that you'll actually revel in failure so that you can learn from it.
- Practice. The way to achieve greatness is through deliberate practice, which requires a daily commitment to being better and a resolve to keep trying.
- Identify your limitations–and then ignore them. To be great, you need to look beyond your shortcomings, believing you can grow, change, and triumph.
- Have heroes. Heroes inspire not just by their achievements but by their humble beginnings, hard work, and the dogged patience that leads to success.

– *J.M.*

THINGS TO DO TODAY

Here are some ways to get started right now.

1. Create a "Waking Up Happy" box. Find and decorate an old shoebox. Fill it with things that make you happy: photos of those you love, funny cartoons, postcards from places you've been or want to go. Look through it whenever you need to remind yourself of life's joys.

2. Write your own personal mission statement—one sentence that describes what you want your life to be. Put it where you'll see it every day.

3. Title a page "Things I Love." List things that make you feel contented, cared for, or blissful. Plan to nurture yourself with one of these activities every day for the next week.

4. Visit one of the websites in the Appendix.

– *J.M.*

WORDS OF WISDOM AND LIGHT

Here are more grains of wisdom from those on the road to new lives.

Listen to the Ancients: Wisdom from Nita

I found words to live by in a book called *The Four Agreements*. The author, Don Miguel Ruiz, says there are four principles which, if followed, make for a good life.

1. Be impeccable with your words. Do what you say you're going to do.
2. Don't take anything personally. Most of what happens doesn't have much, if anything, to do with you.
3. Don't assume anything. Live your life based on what you know is happening rather than what you think might happen.
4. Do your best. But remember that your best can be different on different days and at different times.

Nita's best advice: Be open to guidance from ancient seers. *The Four Agreements* is based on wisdom from the Toltec Empire, an ancient Mexican civilization. It may resonate with you as it did for me. If not, seek out advice from other cultures and creeds, such as Taoism or Confucianism. People throughout the ages have found peace by turning to such guidelines for living.

Soothe Yourself: Wisdom from John

Drinking used to relax me. Without alcohol, life seemed unbearably stressful. Then I discovered that a good massage relieves stress better than alcohol ever did.

Now I track how much money I would have spent on alcohol if I was still drinking. Then I use that money to pay for therapeutic massages. It's a wonderful tradeoff!

John's best advice: Although it's important to learn to live frugally and simply, it's also vital to know when a splurge is absolutely required. For me, that needed indulgence is a massage once a month. For you it might be going to a movie, buying some special comfort food, or setting up a regular session with a psychologist. The key is not to confuse needs with wants. Look into your heart to discover what you truly need.

Bring Some Light into Your Life: Wisdom from Pablo

In my reading, I learned about a condition called SAD (seasonal affective disorder) and realized that I'd been suffering from this condition for years. It lasts throughout the fall and winter, during the time when the days are so short. Sometimes I awaken in the dark and return from work in the dark, and the gloom saps my energy.

Luckily, I learned that the condition is treatable. Light therapy (phototherapy) worked for me.

Pablo's best advice: If you find yourself feeling depressed in the wintertime, check with a medical doctor or psychiatrist. They can recommend the right type of light for you, and your insurance may even pay for it, as mine did. It's well worth getting the condition treated. You'll have more energy and motivation to improve your life.

Make Peace with Anger: Wisdom from Joshua

Alcohol, cocaine, heroin, meth—these were the shields I used to protect myself from the memories. While I was using, I could almost convince myself that I hadn't been sexually abused when I was twelve, raped by a man I trusted, a man who was a family friend. I could, for a few moments, forget how my parents refused to believe me about the abuse, a betrayal that somehow seemed even greater than the rape itself.

When I quit using, all the memories rose up, and with them the venomous emotions I'd buried for so long. I started lashing out at those who were trying to help me, those who wanted to befriend me, those I loved. My fury cost me several relationships before I got a handle on it.

Over time, I realized I was addicted to anger, which was just as toxic as my earlier drug habit. Ongoing therapy taught me to sit with my wrath and let it dissipate rather than act it out.

Like all feelings, anger lasts only a few minutes, and if I can keep from behaving rashly during that time, it makes life so much better. I came to realize that, although I had every right to feel rage toward my abuser, my anger didn't pay him back for what he'd done. It only perpetuated my own misery. Reducing the anger in my life has brought me a happiness I never knew existed.

Joshua's best advice: It's important to be in touch with your emotions, but you need to control them, not let them control you. Here are ways to manage anger rather than react in destructive or self-abusive ways:

- Name your emotion. Just telling yourself, "I'm furious" softens the harsh feeling and helps you find peace with it. When you sort out how you feel, you may discover you're sad, hurt, or jealous rather than angry.
- When you're mad, be slow and careful about what you do and say. Take deep breaths, count to ten, or walk away. Create a space between feeling anger and acting on it.
- Consider why you're angry. Often it's because you're expecting or demanding something from another person, yourself, or the world. When you pause to ask yourself what your expectation is, you'll mitigate your anger. Then you may be able to let go of the expectation or find a way to meet it. For instance, maybe you're expecting people to understand what you want. You're better off telling them exactly what you need from them rather than being upset because they can't read your mind.
- Don't suppress your fury or turn it inward. Acknowledge your feelings without judging or dwelling on them. Write in your journal or talk to a counselor, friend, or mentor. You can also use martial arts like boxing and karate to let out your poisonous feelings in a constructive, controlled way.
- Don't use derogatory language or put others down. You can be angry yet respectful at the same time. Understand that people have different viewpoints and that there doesn't have to be a right and a wrong answer.
- Rather than returning anger directed at you, let it pass over you like a breeze—as in judo, which lets you use the other person's energy to deplete itself. Buddhists tell us to view angry people as teachers, who give us the chance to practice tolerance and detachment.
- If you feel angry about an injustice or an issue that's important to you, speak up about it. But don't do so in the midst of a rage, or you'll be less than persuasive. Channel your anger into actions that will improve your situation, the lives of others, and the well-being of the planet.

- Experiment with different ways of reacting when you're mad rather than responding in a characteristic way. Just because you've always thrown things when you were in a temper, for example, doesn't mean you can't find a less violent way to express your emotions.
- Remember that your anger hurts you more than anyone else, and you have the power to leave it behind by changing your perspective. In *The Cow in the Parking Lot,* Leonard Scheff and Susan Edmiston ask you to imagine how you'd feel if you were waiting for a parking space when a driver cut in front of you and parked in "your" spot. Then picture the same scenario except that it's a cow that parks itself in front of you. Most likely you'd feel angry in the first case and amused in the second. Yet your circumstances are the same: You have to find a new place to park. The only difference is your attitude. In every situation, you have a myriad of choices. If you act out of anger, you shrink the buffet of possibilities into a beggar's bowl.

5

JUST CONNECT: SHYLOH'S STORY

Shyloh, the author's twenty-three-year-old granddaughter, gave up heroin in 2008. Since then she has relapsed and once again recovered. She believes that addiction can be a blessing, and so can relapse, as she explains in this chapter.

Author's Note:
I was forty-three when Andrea's first child was born. I'd never imagined being a grandma, so Shyloh was a complete gift and opened in me a reservoir of joy and laughter I never knew existed.
From the beginning, there was a sparkle to that girl that lit up every room. When we went to visit, she would be rocketing toward our car before we'd parked, beaming from ear to ear, ready to engulf us in hugs and kisses. She's still the most wonderful hugger—never in a perfunctory way but always with both her arms and all her heart.
To me, she hasn't changed much from that bright-eyed little girl with the infectious smile, even though today she sports various body piercings, death-defying heels, and mod hairstyles with the occasional purple streak. She works sometimes as a model and the camera loves her, but it's her giving heart that makes her so beautiful.
She shares green eyes with her mom and me, but instead of our shortish, stocky builds, she inherited a tall, lanky frame from Ed, her biological father. He moved away when she was two, just as her mom's biological dad (my first husband, John) disappeared soon after Andrea's second birthday. The parallels in the lives of the three of us—and my mother, too—were always startling, the threads that knit the generations together bold and bright. While Andrea and I had each struggled to undo those damaging patterns, neither of us had done so as early in life as Shyloh. Confronting that dark legacy at such a young age gave her an unequaled power over it, and her courage in breaking those knotted cords cascaded back to her mom and me.
Shyloh's dad, Andrea's dad, and my father's dad had all left when their children were young. I often wondered what might have happened had my father talked to me about the pain of his dad's abandonment instead of hiding that part of his life. I know it would have changed me, and maybe it would have altered what happened later.
I felt terrible that Shyloh became tangled in those ancient tethers and that it fell on her young shoulders to dismantle them. But I was in awe of the strength with which she tore off the bindings of the past that choked, ensnared, and nearly strangled us all.
Here is Shyloh's story.

– J.M.

✧ ✧ ✧

It was the worst day of my life. Or so I thought at the time, little knowing how much worse things could get.

I couldn't imagine then that anything could hurt as much as waking up in jail with no idea how I got there or how long I'd have to stay. I was twenty years old, a junior in college at the University of Wisconsin at Platteville, and now I was totally alone, surrounded by strangers, unable to see or talk to my friends or family, forced to come off drugs without any of the support a person might receive in a treatment center or detox facility. I'd seen jail depicted in countless movies so I thought I knew how bad it was, but it was far more frightening—and lonely—than I could have imagined.

Not remembering—that was gut-wrenching. But jail—that was the darkest of my fears coming true.

Jail had hung over my head for some time as I got into more and more scrapes because of my drinking and drugging. I'd lost my driver's license due to underage drinking and related offenses; driving drunk was a regular occurrence and, although I had only one "Operating Under the Influence" on my record, the number of times I risked my life and the lives of others was horrifying.

Each time I had a run-in with the cops, they made it clear that if I was caught drinking or doing drugs again, they would have no recourse but to put me in jail. Each time ended with me walking out of the courtroom with crocodile tears and an ineffectual tap on the wrist. I felt that I was invincible, that regardless of what happened, it was okay because I was "only" getting probation or fines. That changed when I violated probation (again) and found myself in the Rock County Jail on October 14, 2008.

Before being brought to jail, I'd been found in a coma and rushed to the emergency room. On the way to the hospital, my heart had stopped beating. But thanks to modern medicine, I'd been brought back to life after several minutes with no pulse.

I still don't know exactly what happened, because the previous day was wiped from my mind. One of the drugs I had taken was Rohypnol, the "date rape drug," which causes amnesia. That, in combination with my intravenous heroin use that night, had nearly killed me.

Lying on the narrow bed in isolation, detoxing from the heroin overdose, I thought at times that I'd died and been dispatched to hell. All the things that usually comforted me had been taken away. There were no drugs, of course, but there also was no paper, no utensils for writing or drawing, no one to talk to, laugh with, or put their arms around me and tell me it would be okay. I knew it wouldn't be okay, not this time.

✧ ✧ ✧

As the weeks went on, though, I began to find reasons to live, even to laugh and hope again. A trickle of relief began at the back of my mind. The court had mandated that I'd have to go to in-patient treatment as soon as a place opened up in a rehab facility in Madison, and I began to actually look forward to it. I knew my life was a mess, and maybe with professional help I could get back on track.

At the time, I thought I'd be out of jail and through with the four-week course of drug treatment before Christmas and back in school for the start of the new semester in January. I liked to plan ahead and had no idea how ridiculous those plans would seem to me later.

After being transferred to a different jail, I was allowed to have paper but no pencils. I made friends with a young girl who, because she was taking GED classes, was allowed pencils, and she snuck one to me. That was a great solace, because drawing and writing always helped me sort out my emotions and fears.

Another thing that made the days bearable was talking to my boyfriend, Tim, on the phone, calling him collect whenever I knew he had the time. He wasn't big on writing, but he did send me one letter, which I held on to like a buoy. Tim and I had moved in together a couple months before my overdose. It's true that we were heavily into drugs, but I felt I'd discovered what true love was all about.

✧ ✧ ✧

It wasn't till mid-December that a place opened up at Hope Haven, a Madison rehab center. Tim was about to start his own in-patient program in Rockford, Illinois. We would start a new life together—no heroin, just us.

The day I left jail, I was surprised at the anxiety I felt, as if a blanket I'd grown to count on had been plucked away. Rather than embracing my sudden freedom, I felt uneasy with it, going straight to my bedroom and staying there, as if hoping to guard myself against the vicissitudes of the world. But nothing could have prepared me for what happened next.

> *Growth means change and change involves risk, stepping from the known to the unknown.*
> —George Shinn

✧ ✧ ✧

I spent the night of December 14 at my grandparents' house in Madison so they could take me to Hope Haven the next morning. My parents lived thirty miles away in the Wisconsin countryside near Dodgeville, so my grandparents had offered to bring me to intake, which was at 8:00 a.m. sharp.

I was too nervous to sleep, so I was reading when my phone rang shortly after midnight. It was a friend asking if Tim was okay. It was an odd question, so I called Tim's mom, a woman who'd been endlessly kind to me and whom I loved like a second mom.

As the phone rang, I felt fear creep up. When she answered, I knew right away that I wasn't going to like what I heard. The unusual lack of emotion in her voice sent a shiver through me.

Then she was saying words I couldn't believe and couldn't bear to hear. She'd gone into Tim's bedroom to wake him and found him lifeless. It's hard to say if he died from an overdose or from the aspiration that occurred when he threw up while passed out on his back.

When she told me, I could hardly respond through my tears. I couldn't understand how this could happen to someone so smart, funny, handsome, talented, and kind, someone with the whole world in the palm of his hand. All I could say was, "No, no, no, no, no."

If I hadn't been stupid enough to get arrested, I wouldn't be hearing this news now. I would have been with him, and somehow we would have restarted his heart and brought him back to life, as had been done for me.

My grandma heard me crying and came in. She sat with me and held me for a long time as I sobbed.

I don't know what I would have done if I wasn't scheduled to report to Hope Haven the next morning. It was the last place I wanted to go, yet it turned out to be the best possible spot for me to be.

During those first days after Tim's death, I could barely speak without sobbing. The agony of those early days was like the pain of a wound when the anesthesia wears off. My heart felt cleaved in two. I'd used drugs to numb me from all kinds of pain, and now that cushion was gone.

For the first time, I understood the meaning of the words "never again." Those are without doubt the most terrifying words in the human language.

I longed to be with Tim's mom and our mutual friends so that we could share our grief, but Hope Haven didn't allow calls or visits at first. Luckily, I was surrounded by supportive counselors and therapists trained in helping people with trauma and loss. They encouraged me to talk about Tim and my anguish over his death.

I found that talking about what had happened helped others as well as me, because everyone at Hope Haven was dealing with grief, guilt, and pain. Soon they started to open up and cry over their own hurts. Reaching out to soothe them helped me comfort myself.

At first I put aside what everyone said about proceeding through stages of grief. I was sure it would be different for me. But I was shocked to discover that I wasn't as unique as I liked to think. I moved through the same stages Elizabeth Kubler-Ross and others had identified years ago—denial ("It can't be true, he can't be gone forever"); guilt ("I should have told him I loved him more often"); anger ("It's so unfair!"); bargaining ("I'll do anything if only I can see him one more time"); depression ("There's no point going on; I can't live without him"); reconstruction ("I have to build a new life for myself somehow"); and acceptance ("He really is gone forever, and it's time to move on").

Not that those steps happened in a tidy, linear way. My stages of grief went more like this: denial that he was gone, guilt for not being there when he died, fury at the fates, desolation and despair, certainty that I was going crazy, more guilt for all the drugs we'd done together, pleading with the universe to let me go back and redo the past, more denial that this could have happened, unbearable loneliness, extreme self-pity, wrenching guilt for having survived while he didn't, more denial and depression, guilt for all my crying and self-indulgence when others had things worse than I did, attempts to distract myself from my grief, a bit more guilt, a crumb of acceptance that things might be okay after all, lots of guilt for even thinking about letting go of my grief, defense mechanisms like distancing myself from my pain, a horrible realization of everyone's mortality, a nugget of forgiveness toward myself, a flitter of hope, guilt for feeling hopeful—and then the whole cycle over again but in a different order each time.

While my movement toward acceptance was chaotic rather than step by step, knowing about the stages of grief helped me anticipate what to expect and understand that these were natural feelings. Each time I grasped onto a piece of hope, I was able to hold onto it a little while longer.

In addition to talking about my emotions, I wrote about them in my journal. Writing from my heart was a way of grieving, of putting my shattered self back together.

> ## MOMENT OF TRUTH
>
> **A short course in sorrow**
>
> Unresolved grief hinders many people's recovery from addictions. Until you feel your losses fully, you'll have a hard time making progress toward a new life.
>
> *Grief is itself a medicine.*
> —William Cowper
>
> Consider these keys to working through your grief:
> - Keep in mind that everyone mourns differently. Do what feels right for you, on your own time table, no one else's.
> - Cry. Tears are your most healing elixir, not only emotionally but physically and spiritually. Jerry Bergman has written, "Tears are just one of many miracles which work so well that we take them for granted every day."
> - Talk to counselors, therapists, and grief support groups. You need to express your emotions to people who are willing to listen endlessly and with compassion.
> - Spend time with your favorite memories of your loved one. Memories may seem painful at first, but they will eventually bring comfort.
> - Laugh. It helps to remember the funny times, too, and it's not disrespectful to laugh. Consider laughter a remedy as healing as tears.
> - Use your creative spirit to heal yourself through music, art, and writing. Start a grief journal, and write in it each day.
> - Find a spiritual haven through meditation, prayer, church services, yoga, or other practices that take you away from your ego and link you to a vast universe.
> - Be willing to be happy. While it's essential to mourn your losses, it's also important to let hope and joy back into your life.
>
> – J.M.

✧ ✧ ✧

I put as much energy as I could into learning to live a new drug-free life. Tim's death focused everything down to one realization: If I was to go on living, I had to change my lifestyle completely.

My forced sobriety in jail had given me a head start. I had fifty-two days of sobriety when I started treatment. But not doing drugs was far different from learning to live a purposeful drug-free life.

I concentrated on doing the tasks we were given, sharing experiences in group therapy and attending the AA meetings that were held at Hope Haven. Although I'd never believed in God (my parents weren't religious beyond the basics of living a good, honest life), I knew it was vital to connect to something outside myself. I thought perhaps my higher power was my connection to other people, for I found my greatest strength when I let my authentic self link with others.

When it was time to leave treatment, I hated to go. Just as when I left jail, I was strangely uncomfortable with my new freedom and unsure how I would survive in the real world.

I knew I couldn't go back to the house Tim and I had shared in Platteville. The memories there were far too painful. I decided to stay in Madison, where I would be close to my new support system while starting to frame a new life for myself.

During the last few weeks in rehab, I had permission to leave for a few hours a day to apply for jobs. I could start working right away while continuing to live at Hope Haven and then look for my own place.

I was elated when I found a job doing captioning at a communications center. When someone called a deaf person, I would listen to the message and type it into our system, and it would appear on the screen attached to the deaf person's phone. I liked the idea that I was helping people connect.

Once I'd earned enough money to start paying rent, I found an apartment and a roommate and tearfully said good-bye to the people I'd grown to love at Hope Haven. In those first weeks, however, I returned to Hope Haven nearly every day for AA meetings or other support when I needed it. I learned to take the bus so I could visit other AA meetings around the city, too.

It was at one of those meetings that an unexpected door opened up for me, a miraculous portal that led to a whole new beginning. Just by chance, I sat next to a guy named Jackson and started talking with him; he too was a heroin addict and had been sober for nearly a year. We had a great deal besides heroin in common and hit it off right away. He told me about a place called Connections, headed by a woman named Shelly Dutch. There was an opiate group there for young people and he loved it. I promised him I'd attend the next one with him.

The group was led by a kind, empathetic woman named Skye. I connected with her at once, and when the meeting was over, I didn't want to leave.

Shortly after that first meeting, Skye became my counselor—and so much more. It was Skye who would walk side by side with me into my new life.

✻ ✻ ✻

Skye was forthright about her own experiences of using heroin and getting sober, which were similar to mine. Like me, she had lost someone close to her through drugs. She told me something that has resonated with me ever since: "Some must die for others to live." Hearing that, I realized that if Tim hadn't died and I'd gone back to him after treatment, I never could have stayed sober and would most likely be dead today.

Both Skye and I suffered from survivor's guilt, which sounds silly when you say it, but is torturous when you live with it. For me, it meant lying awake night after night asking myself:

Why was I the one who escaped with my life? What could I have done differently to save Tim? Those "why's" and "what if's" can destroy you if you let them.

But Skye reminded me that Tim would never blame me for his death and would want me to learn from it and move forward. Slowly, the guilt loosened its hold on my heart.

I found the best way to heal was to feel all the emotions fully, diving into the pain rather than hiding from it, and then taking slow, steady steps into the future, using everything that the pain had taught me.

I remember asking Skye, "How long does it take to get over it?"

"As long as it takes," she said.

As I grew to trust Skye, I confided things I'd never told anyone before. I found myself describing secrets that no one knew, that I'd concealed from everyone, some that I'd hidden even from myself.

✭ ✭ ✭

In many ways, it was a normal, loving home. To all appearances, things were fine with me growing up. But there was a great deal going on below the surface that no one in our family dealt with or even acknowledged.

Both my mom and dad can best be described as fierce. They were both very passionate about most things in their lives, which meant they gave me a lot of love but the house was filled with turmoil. They were both former alcoholics and addicts who, although they'd gotten sober, didn't believe in groups or therapy so hadn't addressed their addictions. Equally stubborn and opinionated, they'd get into loud, angry arguments, each refusing to give an inch. Those furious voices filled my head as a child, and I always wanted to make things better, to keep my family happy.

My biological father, Ed, left when I was two, and I had no memory of him beyond the dark space he left behind. My mother married a new man, who became the person I called "Dad." But when I was five and my brother was born, I became conscious of the fact that he belonged to both my parents, while I didn't. My brother and I constantly competed for affection, and the bedlam in our home mushroomed.

Ed's absence from my childhood caused me an abundance of pain and confusion. I believe this desertion was the root cause of my drug use. Having a dad who left me was the first traumatic experience of my life. This set the bar high, because practically any trauma that followed seemed unworthy of my concern. What could be worse than having the person who is supposed to love you the most decide that he doesn't care enough to stay—or even to keep in contact? I never heard from him, and I received the unspoken message that it was best not to talk about him. It was one of many things I filed in a corner of my heart and tried not to think about.

Before my brother was born, we moved frequently. If I put myself in my young shoes, it must have been stressful always changing houses, losing friends, and not understanding why nothing remained safe and secure.

It's not that we usually moved a great distance—a string of houses in Madison, a year in Phoenix, Arizona, then homes in several small Wisconsin towns before I started school, and finally our house near Dodgeville, Wisconsin. But to a little kid, the geographical distances don't matter. All she knows is that as soon as she has a good mental map of the important places in her life—her bedroom, her parents' bedroom, the kitchen, the bathroom, the back yard—it all changes. Pretty soon she begins to feel bewildered and insecure. Anyway, that's how it was for me.

When I was twelve and began experimenting with drugs and alcohol, both my parents told me about their drugging experiences, ending each tale with the ultimatum: Don't use drugs, or you'll be addicted! They described how both sides of my family go back generations with alcoholism, mental health issues, and drug addiction in the mix.

Their vigilant efforts to keep me from using backfired. Their warnings flipped a switch in me and made using seem both irresistible and inevitable. If I was going to be labeled as something, then I would earn the label. Just as they predicted, I became a chronic poly-substance addict. I'm not saying I wouldn't have become addicted if they'd used a different approach; it's just that, in my young mind, their stories made my path seem fated.

My using created a number of harrowing experiences. When I was fifteen, I was arrested at school for selling cocaine to a fellow student, after which I attempted suicide and was shipped off to a mental institution for seventy-two hours. Later we discovered that the antidepressant the doctor had prescribed (Prozac) wasn't intended for teens and had led to a manic spiral that caused the suicide attempt.

It only got worse from there.

One night I was babysitting for a woman who'd become a good friend. Before she left, she introduced me to someone who'd been visiting her. I was flattered when he stayed and seemed to enjoy talking with me. He was in his thirties and supposedly had a record company in Chicago, which, to a fifteen-year-old, sounded very glamorous. And then suddenly he was raping me, even though I kept saying, "No, no."

I was thankful that the kids were asleep and that my attacker eventually let me go. I ran and locked myself in the bathroom, praying for my friend to return. But when she arrived and I told her what had happened, she reacted not with the comfort I expected but with dismissal, telling me that, whatever had occurred, it wasn't rape and I should forget about it. What they tell you in school is to call the police, but with my growing track record and the cocaine in my system, I knew that if my friend didn't believe me, the cops surely wouldn't.

After I got over the initial shock, it seemed easier to move on than to deal with the horror and pain, although I didn't realize the true ramifications of trying to forget. While I didn't understand it at the time, the rape led to a wave of promiscuity and a huge dive in my feelings of confidence and worth. This would not be my only sexual assault, as I was a victim of the date rape drug in college as well. As one betrayal spiraled into the next, the shell around me grew thicker and more toxic.

> *You can hold back from the suffering of the world...but perhaps this very holding back is the one suffering that you could have avoided.*
> —Franz Kafka

I'd told no one about either of the rapes until I met Skye and grew to trust her. Just speaking the words "I was raped" was a crucial first step. There was something powerful in simply getting it out of my mind. Skye helped me see the shame I felt wasn't mine to bear.

I thought I'd put the rapes behind me, but now I realized they were related to a myriad of symptoms I'd been experiencing—nightmares, skin rashes, stomach problems, and susceptibility to every cold, flu, or other disease in my vicinity. These, it turned out, were all symptoms of post traumatic stress disorder (PTSD), which went beyond war veterans to encompass people like me who'd faced stressful events and never worked through them. Like all wounds, these untreated traumas had festered, and that's why I'd been so sick.

Skye referred me to a therapist who worked with PTSD victims, and, with his encouragement, I began identifying the buried feelings I'd never acknowledged—anger, fear, betrayal, sorrow, guilt. He told me it was natural to blame myself for the traumas in my life, starting with my father's desertion, and to feel helpless and hurt because I hadn't been able to keep those things from happening. Victims of broken homes and of rapes, he told me, can suffer all their lives from impaired self-esteem if they don't face the feelings involved. It's common for young women to become promiscuous after a rape, as I had, because of diminished self-respect and a twisted confusion between sex and love.

He emphasized that rape is a crime of violence and never the victim's fault. Flirting or dressing in sexy clothes doesn't cause rape, any more than carrying cash causes a mugging.

Talking about it with him and with Skye made me feel that perhaps I was a good person after all. As I began to leave my sense of shame behind and talked to other people about the rapes, I was astounded at how many women described similar experiences.

There is no agony like bearing an untold story inside of you.
—Zola Neale Hurston

TURNING POINT

Coping strategies after a trauma

Post traumatic stress disorder (PTSD) is a common response to a distressing event. It can show up in numerous physical symptoms, such as disordered sleep, stomachaches, headaches, and depression. It may disrupt your life many years after you thought you were over the trauma, especially if you didn't address it at the time. Here are some coping methods:

- Be aware of situations that trigger a stress response. Don't avoid them, but prepare for them. If you know you're heading into a trigger situation, focus on your breathing beforehand, taking ten deep, slow breaths to oxygenate your body. Wear a rubber band around your wrist, and if you feel a stress reaction begin, snap the rubber band to pull yourself out of it.
- Find a therapist experienced with PSTD. There are medications and treatments that are very effective. In *Secrets, Lies, Betrayals*, Maggie Scarf describes her miraculous recovery from PTSD symptoms through EMDR (eye movement desensitization and reprocessing) therapy. Studies show that rapid-eye-movement therapy is ninety-five percent successful in treating PTSD, as it makes new connections in the brain.

- Schedule fifteen to thirty minutes a day as your worry time. All your fears, obsessions, and worries need to fit into that time frame. Don't let yourself be anxious any other time of day or night. If something comes up, just tell yourself, "I'm putting that onto the list for my worry time."
- Write about your traumatic experience. Studies show that those who do so have fewer illnesses and less anxiety and depression in the future.

– J.M.

※ ※ ※

In addition to Skye, I became close to many others at Connections, including Shelly, the incredible woman who ran the counseling center. Shelly put me in charge of Connections' mentoring program, and my work helped pay some of my counseling fees. I discovered I was good at it—organizing social events, reminding people to check in with each other, and being available for anyone who needed to talk.

And, I loved doing it. It was wonderful having a network of people I could turn to whenever I needed, and I especially enjoyed connecting people to one another. Connection—that was the secret.

> *Everywhere, hands lie open to catch us when we fall.*
> —Anon.

A STEP ON THE JOURNEY

Appreciate the power of your network. Consider these research findings reported by Nicholas Christakis and James Fowler in *Connected* and Michael Dulworth in *The Connect Effect*:

- You shape your network, and your network shapes you, far beyond your direct social contacts. You're influenced not just by your friends but by the emotions, ideas, and habits of your friends' friends' friends through the "Three Degrees of Influence Rule." That means that people up to three degrees away from you—people you've never met—have a powerful effect on your life. "Your friends' friends' friend has more impact on your happiness than $5,000 in your pocket," as Christakis and Fowler put it.
- When you introduce your friends to one another, you become more central in your own network. That means you'll have more access to everything flowing through your network and will be more likely to achieve your goals.

- Networking involves more than just widening the circle of people you know. You need to build relationships with the right people—those you can turn to when you have problems, those you can trust. Although electronic communications facilitate networking, you can't eliminate face-to-face interaction if your connections are to be effective.

Who are the people in your support system? On a sheet of paper, write the names of everyone you count on. Next to each name, write a few words explaining how that person gives you the support you need. If you wish your network were stronger, think of steps you could take to add to it.

Draw a line between names to show who knows whom. Write down ways you could introduce your friends to one another to make your network more effective.

– J.M.

✭ ✭ ✭

When I attempted to transfer to the university in Madison, I found I didn't have a high enough grade point average to get in. That was hardly a surprise, considering I'd barely attended school during my past year in college, due to the constant drugging. If I applied to Madison's technical college and did well there, I'd be able to transfer to the university, but I decided I wasn't ready for that yet. First, I wanted to earn enough money to pay off my hospital bills and fines for all the times I was picked up drunk and high.

I had set up a payment schedule, but I was concerned about how I would make my deadlines. I asked to work more hours, but then I started getting overtired and sick. That wasn't good because I didn't have health insurance.

All these day-to-day frustrations were cushioned by a new relationship. I knew it was against all advice to begin a romance at this time, especially with someone who was also in early recovery, but I craved closeness so much that every piece of good counsel flew out the window when I met Alex.

This romance was different from any I'd had before, because I let Alex take care of me. Before, I'd always been the thoughtful, giving one, helping my partner in every way I could. It felt so comforting to have someone do those things for me.

During this time, I also started writing my autobiography. It began as an "assignment" in my support group but ended up as so much more. As I wrote my life story, I released feelings I'd held inside for a long, long time. It was like letting go of a balloon and seeing it waft into the sky.

There is a crack in everything, that's how the light gets in.
—Leonard Cohen

TURNING POINT

Tell your story. Begin the process of writing your life story. You don't have to write it all at once. Just jot down memories as they come to you. Here are some questions to jumpstart the process.

Your Early Life
- When and where were you born? Did you stay in one spot or move around while growing up? Did this have an impact on you?
- How many siblings do you have, and where are you in the birth order? How did this influence you?
- What were the personalities of your parents, siblings, and any other influential family members? How did their personalities affect you?
- What challenges did you face growing up?
- Describe some of your earliest memories.

Who You Are
- What are your strengths and weaknesses?
- What personality traits have been helpful in your life? Which ones have caused you problems?
- What do you like about yourself? What would you like to change about yourself?
- What is the main factor that has shaped your life and made you who you are?

Your Life So Far
- What have been the key successes and setbacks in your life?
- Briefly describe key relationships in your life.
- List the jobs you've had. What did you like and dislike about each one?

Addictive and Dysfunctional Behavior
- Discuss any addictions and other dysfunctions in your family.
- Consider your addictive behavior. When and why did it start?
- When did you first contemplate changing your life? Why?

Your Life Today
- Do you live a spiritual life? How do you "give back" to others?
- Who are your role models? Who do you aspire to be?
- Do you believe you have a purpose? If so, what is it?
- What do you like to do in your spare time? How are these things helpful to you?
- What are your plans for the future?

As you answer these questions, use old photos and videos to awaken your memories. Do some historical research to discover what was going on in the world in the years you were growing up. Who was President when you were born? Who's the first President you remember?

> Ask your family members about their lives, your ancestors, and your upbringing. The revelations you receive from them may be the most illuminating part of the autobiographical process.
>
> – J.M.

Writing a chronicle of my life also reconnected me with forgotten parts of myself.

I was reminded of what mattered most to me, of passions that had once sustained me, of pieces of the past that I could now incorporate into a new future.

I got back in touch with my love of drawing, which was a powerful way for me to express the truest part of who I was. Art was a form of alchemy for me, turning the monsters in my mind into something beautiful and enduring.

The same sense of fulfillment came when I finished scrubbing and straightening a room, so, in addition to my other work, I began taking jobs cleaning people's houses. It satisfied something deep within me to transform chaos and filth into something fresh and shining, and I liked the idea of turning my compulsive cleaning habits into cash.

> *Let yourself be silently drawn by the stronger pull of what you really love.*
> —Rumi

While I still wasn't religious, I began to feel the need to look beyond myself for answers to the mysteries of life. My mother gave me a book on Taoism, and I found I could pull a great deal of clarity from it. A friend of mine was a Buddhist and encouraged me to follow the "Zen path." I had to do a little research to figure out the basic differences between these spiritual practices.

Zen, I discovered, is a school of Buddhism that focuses on direct experience rather than theoretical knowledge. The Buddha said that we shouldn't believe what anyone said—even him!—unless we discovered it to be true and useful for us. I liked that.

Buddhists believe that all life is suffering, and their highest aim is Nirvana, a spiritual bliss free from pain that we can attain by living a moral life. On the other hand, Taoism (also called Daoism) emphasizes the joy that comes when we live in harmony with the natural way of the universe.

Despite the differences in these philosophies, I found useful lessons in all sorts of books by Taoist, Buddhist, and Zen teachers. Rather than choosing one, I could take what I needed from all these ancient spiritual seers, as many people do. I didn't need to believe in reincarnation, as these practices did, to gain insights from their teachings, such as accepting what is and being thankful for all that life offers.

> *You have to grow from the inside out. None can teach you, none can make you spiritual. There is no other teacher but your own soul.*
> —Swami Vivekananda

※ ※ ※

On my one-year sobriety anniversary that October, Shelly threw a party for me at Connections, and my family and friends came. Each of them stood and said something about their connection to me, and all of us cried.

The following weekend, Alex held another party for me at his place. His apartment overflowed with people I loved and who loved me with all my warts and bruises.

I had such wonderful friends, and my relationship with my family had grown stronger. Not long before I began recovery, my brother got sucked into a using lifestyle. Despite the pain in watching him flounder, I saw that his problems brought us together as a family as we helped him get back on track. Since then, he and I have built a close connection.

Alex and I loved each other, and I could see myself spending my life with him. My slowly burgeoning self-esteem made it possible for me to accept the love of such a kind, giving, and supportive guy.

During the celebration at Alex's apartment, I thought I would burst with the fullness of life. I would recall that day, surrounded by all the people I loved, many times in the coming months.

※ ※ ※

I'm not sure exactly when it all began to spiral downward. It must have been later that autumn when Alex sank into a deep depression. I'd known he was prone to depression, and I was no stranger to it myself, so I was understanding and patient with him. But it was hard to keep my own spirits up when nothing I did could draw him out or make him smile. His despair seeped into the air around me and into my pores. Our love was fragile, and rifts began to widen at the seams of our differences.

My financial life was going badly, too. I hadn't made much headway in paying off my debts from my using days, because just living was so expensive. Whenever I tried working more hours, I invariably got sick, leading to more doctors' bills. I wondered if there would ever be an end to the vicious circle.

Then something happened that was like a dream or a fairytale. My birth father, Ed, called me. Since he had no place in my memory, hearing his voice was like talking to a ghost.

I'd heard that Ed had moved to California, gotten sober (he had been a severe addict), become a fundamentalist minister, gotten married, and had twin daughters. But that's all I knew.

When I was little, I had tried to imagine what he might be like. When I asked Mom why he'd left, she told me he was too immature to live up to his responsibilities and it had nothing to do with me. Still, I thought he might have stayed if I'd done something differently. The fact that I never heard from him made me wonder why I mattered so little.

As a child and teen, I would withdraw into fantasies in which my "other family"—Ed and his wife and daughters—would ask me to live with them. Not that I would leave my current family, but it would warm my heart to be wanted. Those reveries shuttered off a place in my mind to keep me from looking at the reality—that Ed had left without a backward glance and had created a new family, none of whom cared about me at all.

Now not only was Ed calling me, but he was saying he'd like to send me an airline ticket to come visit him in California. It was like something that might happen on a poorly devised reality TV show. But it has actually happening to me.

Of course I said yes.

In the month before the trip, I talked constantly with my friends and family about meeting my biological dad and my sisters, who were five years younger than me. I loved saying those words, *my sisters*. All the daydreaming I'd done about having a different family was embodied in those three little syllables. After Ed called me, his daughters texted me, and we talked on the phone a few times, but I didn't have a real sense of what they would be like—or what Ed would be like, for that matter.

As the days fell away and the idea of the trip became real rather than a reverie, I felt as if my nerves would snap. I was thankful for the stress-busting tools I'd learned in therapy. I re-read my Taoist and Buddhist books, drinking in their message of living in the moment and letting the universe take care of the rest.

MOMENT OF TRUTH

Stop stressing, and start living. Tension is poison to your body. Here are some tools to combat it so you can live your most fulfilling life.

- Listen to soothing music or relaxation tapes.
- Sing or chant, either alone or with a group. Or repeat a word silently to yourself (words that end in "m" or "n" will increase the relaxation response).
- Visualize a serene spot. It could be an imaginary place by a mountain stream, in a forest clearing, or on a sandy beach. Or it could be an actual place where you've felt safe and comfortable, such as your grandmother's house when you were little, a favorite vacation spot, or your own bed. Keep that image in your mind so you can return to it whenever you face a stressful situation and want to relax yourself.

Is everything as urgent as your stress would imply?
—Carrie Latet

- Do a reality check. If you can't stop worrying about something, cross-examine that worrisome thought as if you were in a courtroom. What evidence is there that what you're worrying about will really happen? What would an objective witness say about it? What might other people do in similar situations?
- As you inhale, imagine breathing in serenity and peace. As you exhale, breathe out anxiety and worry. Continue to lengthen your inhale and exhale, filling your lungs as you breathe in and pushing all the air from your lungs as you breathe out.
- Take a long, hot bath. If you like, use bath oils with calming scents such as lavender. Or light a scented candle. After your bath, lavish your body with soothing lotions.

> *There must be quite a few things that a hot bath won't cure, but I don't know many of them.*
> —Sylvia Plath
>
> - Move your body. Aerobic exercise and weight lifting are great stress reducers. So are yoga, tai chi, qigong, and other meditative exercises from the East. Sometimes a quick walk, swim, or bike ride is all you need to refocus your mind and relax your body.
> - Build some quiet time into every day. Practice just sitting still and being in the moment, taking gentle notice of your environment and your body, reminding yourself that nothing in the world is so important that it needs to be done right now and that you can't accomplish any of your goals if you don't take time to renew yourself.
>
> – J.M.

✳ ✳ ✳

When I got off the plane in California, the feeling of living in a dream intensified. I'd left a bitterly cold, snowy, mid-December Wisconsin and landed in another galaxy, surrounded by Crayola-green grass, palm trees, people in shorts and tank tops, white teeth flashing in suntanned faces.

As I stood blinking in the sultry air, I saw coming toward me an older male version of myself. The way he smiled, the tall lankiness of him was so like a mirror of me it took my breath away. When he introduced me to his kids, I could see a little bit of myself in them too—more like a distant echo than a mirror, yet it was exciting to notice little parts of myself reverberating in the girls' smiles, laughter, and the tilt of their heads.

Moving as it was to feel that spark of recognition, and interesting as my time in California turned out to be, there were many things that bothered me about the whole experience. Ed's extreme religious views made it difficult for us to have any deep conversations, especially in regard to our addictions. He didn't seem to realize that he had cross-addicted from drugs to God. While not a life-threatening addiction and much more positive than narcotics, his Pentecostal views didn't leave room for much give-and-take discussion.

I never did ask the question that lay deepest in my heart: Why did you leave? I don't think it matters anymore; my resistance to asking and his to bringing it up solidified that fact.

What I learned on the trip made me think deeply about my sobriety and the kind of life a person needs to build in recovery. Although I know many people find comfort in religion when they get clean and it gives them the purpose they need to stay strong and sober, I had the sense that Ed was hiding behind his beliefs and that denial was one method of survival that he (and his wife and sadly my sisters, too) had mastered. I did feel a higher power in me that pushed me through each obstacle, but to me religion without self-awareness was sterile.

After my return to Wisconsin, I didn't speak much to Ed again, though I did stay in touch with my sisters. While it was satisfying to finally meet Ed, I didn't think much would come from it. The little girl in me wanted so badly to feel the connection, but the woman I'd become didn't dare to dream too big.

One thing life has taught me is that you cannot let your expectations deter you from forging on and finding happiness. But, at the time, without the perspective I have today, I let my broken expectations crush me, returning home disillusioned, resentful, and bitter. Everything felt wrenchingly wrong, and I began to slide downward into an agony of depression.

I had hoped my relationship with Alex would benefit from our time apart and that, when I returned, we could resolve the differences that had grown between us. But, instead, our problems intensified, and inevitably he left. It was best for both of us.

My growing depression was (in my eyes) the catalyst to this breakup. It's so true that if you don't love yourself, how can anyone else love you?

> *Someone I loved once gave me*
> *a box full of darkness.*
> *It took me years to understand*
> *that this, too, was a gift.*
> —Mary Oliver

✯ ✯ ✯

I continued with my life, but things didn't get better. To make ends meet, I added more cleaning jobs to my already overloaded schedule. Constantly exhausted, I felt like the whole world was collapsing on top of me.

I kept doing the footwork and going to meetings even though it all seemed too hard sometimes and I was bogged down by a burden I couldn't define. Months passed and soon it was summer again, but I was a ghost of the person I'd been, going through the motions more for the people around me than for myself.

In desperation, I decided to go on an Outward Bound trip. When I couldn't come up with the money, Shelly provided a scholarship for me through Connections' new Recovery Foundation. I'll always be thankful, because that expedition provided me some of the most valuable tools yet.

✯ ✯ ✯

It rained the entire trip. If I'd known beforehand that I would be portaging a canoe in a driving downpour, I probably would have found an excuse not to go. In retrospect, however, I see that the weather was one more thing for us to overcome, and the Outward Bound experience is all about facing what you thought you never could and finding hidden resources inside yourself.

In addition to Jessie, the wonderful woman who led the group, there were nine others. Working together under difficult conditions united us so that we were able to give voice to things we'd never uttered before.

We did a great amount of writing on that trip, answering questions Jessie gave us—soul-searching stuff. I wrote about how I grew up believing that weaknesses and failure weren't okay—weren't even options—for me. I confronted a key truth about myself that I'd never faced before—how I thrived on others' happiness and felt I'd failed when I couldn't fix people's sadness. Then, instead of filling me up, people sucked me of energy and spirit until I was left broken and alone.

I explored all the painful issues from my past and for the first time felt I could truly face up to the facts of my life. The reasons I didn't ask for help after I was raped made me so sad. I hated to think of any girl feeling so alone with her emotions that she couldn't tell her mom about something like that. It made me realize how dysfunctional our family was when I was growing up but how much closer we'd become.

After we wrote out our deepest wounds, we shared our writings with each other. Never before had I confessed so much in such an intense, concentrated way nor received such support. I felt surrounded by love and acceptance. As the others told their stories, I felt my heart swell with compassion for them. We'd all had similar challenges. Most of us were recovering addicts or had parents who were. Mine wasn't the only story of rape, and as we spilled out our secrets and regrets, we cried, embraced, and laughed together.

Tears, touch, and laughter—what essential ingredients for healing.

I felt happier and lighter than ever before. When I hugged my new friends good-bye, I felt as if we'd known each other forever and had bonded for life.

> ***If you want to get rid of something, you must first allow it to flourish. If you want to take something, you must first allow it to be given.***
> —Lao Tzu

✫ ✫ ✫

Returning to real life was a shock. None of my problems had evaporated while I was gone, and after the intensity of the Outward Bound experience, it took a while to get back into the swing of things.

Soon, however, I started working on the goals I'd created on the trip, the things I'd pinpointed that I wanted to change about my life. The first one, becoming physically healthier, required me to drop some things, because I knew I was stressing myself by doing too much. I decided to discontinue my cleaning business, not only to give myself respite but also because I suspected the chemicals in the cleaning supplies might have been causing my frequent illnesses.

I didn't become miraculously cured when I quit my cleaning jobs, but I did have more time to rest and care for myself. Occasionally I was even able to get eight hours of sleep a night, which was my aim. I also had time to buy and cook nutritious food. I began to feel better.

Another item on my list of goals was to find a more fulfilling job. I'd cared for mentally and physically disabled people in the past and knew it was well-paid, rewarding work. After a little searching, I found a job working for a quadriplegic woman who had been in a drunk driving accident at sixteen and was now in her fifties. Her difficulties put things into perspective for me, and in many ways, she helped me more than I did her.

That job so inspired and exhilarated me that I sought more work taking care of people in need. I found two part-time positions—one providing evening care to another quadriplegic woman (also a car accident survivor) and one caring for a ten-year-old autistic boy and his two younger sisters. I've always been a mother at heart and deeply enjoyed my time with those three kids, taking them to swim lessons and playing games. Children have an uncanny way of taking away the strains of life just by living and loving to laugh. I really needed that in my life.

Around that time, I did something else that made life feel more hopeful. I went to the Humane Society with a friend to help him pick out a cat and ended up going back and getting one for myself. I named her Serenity, for that's what her unwavering love brought me.

She was someone who was always glad to see me, someone to care for. Cuddling and petting her was the best stress reducer I'd found. She reminded me daily of the wisdom embedded in the Serenity Prayer—that we must accept what we can't change, change what we can, and understand the difference.

TURNING POINT

Learn from cats. Here are some things cats can teach you:
- Value your independence, and love yourself.
- If you're going to take a nap, make sure you really, really enjoy it.
- You can love someone without smothering them and being with them all the time.
- Observation and study are important. So are grooming and cleanliness.
- Trust and respect are to be earned, not expected.
- You can comfort someone with just your presence.
- Vomiting doesn't always happen at a convenient time or place—but it will happen.

— with gratitude to Tessa Lindsay

– J.M.

✯ ✯ ✯

Despite my new jobs, I was still struggling to dig myself out of debt. It seemed that the harder I tried, the further behind I fell, as large interest charges piled up atop the already mountainous obligations.

In addition, my mentoring work at Connections was threatening to drown me. By this time I had so many mentees that I was getting ten or more calls a day, and many were desperate cries from people in crisis. I did everything I could to help, sometimes going to their houses to talk with them for hours, and it was draining me. Whenever someone relapsed or my advice didn't work for them, I felt like a failure.

On one especially bad day, I wanted to vent my feelings at my Connections' support group, but instead of letting me talk, everyone wanted me to solve their problems. Finally I couldn't hold it in any longer and I exploded. I said I'd been trying for an hour to talk about what was on my mind and no one was listening. I was sick of everything. After a year and a half of sobriety, things were supposed to be getting better, but they weren't. In many ways, things were worse than ever. I couldn't envision ever being solvent enough to return to school and pursue my long-term goals. Being sober wasn't the utopia people made it out to be.

Then I started crying and had to leave.

I was too upset to go back to the Connections group after that. My friends in the group got hold of me and asked me to come back, but I just couldn't.

"That's all right," Skye said. "Take a break for a while. Continue leading the mentoring program if you want, but take some time off from the group. It's too much for you right now. And turn off your cell phone for a while. You don't have to be available to everybody every minute."

I knew it was my own fault for creating my support system almost entirely of people I was mentoring. Skye had warned me I needed to look for people who were further along in sobriety so that they could help me with my concerns rather than pull me into their own crises.

"It's not that your mentees don't care about you," Skye said. "They think of you as their leader, so they forget you have troubles, too. You need a place where people will listen to your feelings."

So I started going to more AA meetings. I also sought out my best friends, the ones I knew I could trust, and got together one on one with them. That gave us time to explore what was going on in both our lives.

By this time I'd discontinued counseling with Skye, as we both felt we'd become friends and peers. Having her for a friend was even better than having her as my counselor. She was always available when I needed help and gave me invaluable guidance.

> *In three words I can sum up everything I've learned about life: It goes on.*
> —Robert Frost

✯ ✯ ✯

Even when I was 100 percent sober, I liked the nightlife—going to bars, dancing, shooting pool. Now, with my new feelings of frustration and alienation, I started to go out and drink a beer or two. It was a terrible decision. An addict can find a drug dealer in a crowd like iron filings drawn to a magnet, and I was looking for trouble. I met an oxycontin dealer, started shooting oxy, and plummeted down the rabbit hole. Soon I was back with my true love, heroin.

What bitter sweetness it was to let myself slide into the nonjudgmental embrace of other heroin users, who had no expectations of me, none at all, except that I be there with them. There was no need to worry that I might let them down by not bettering myself, living up to my potential, or building a future.

Of course, the reason they asked nothing of me was that they didn't really care—a vast indifference that, to a tortured mind, could easily be misconstrued as acceptance, even love.

People always said they could tell when I was using because I didn't care about anything or anyone, especially not myself. A key example was using with the kids I mentored. People who had just started to see the light, and with my help had found new hope, became my using buddies. I'll never forget how horrible I felt when I saw the relapses of the kids I cared for, and by my own hands.

Most excruciating of all, I don't think their respect for me wavered once. You don't realize what impact you can have on someone's life, for good and for evil. Looking back, I think that was the keenest of all the pain, the lowest I could imagine falling, the most monstrous of all the unthinkable things I'd done in my life. Each day I felt myself wishing the shot would shut me down for good.

I shall tell you a great secret, my friend. Do not wait for the last judgment. It takes place every day.
—Albert Camus

✸ ✸ ✸

I asked my parents to let me come home for a while so I could save money. Their willingness to believe what I told them made it easier for me to convince myself that my using wasn't a problem.

But soon after I arrived back home, my dad decided he wanted a divorce from my mother and moved out. The one thing I had always counted on was my family, and when he left my whole world crashed down around me.

I'd given up all but one of my home-care jobs, and now I let the last one go. After that, there was nothing to keep me from sinking back into the using life full time.

My dad had bought me a car a few months earlier, telling me it was a reward for how well I was doing but that he would take it away if I used again. One day he spotted the track marks on my arms, and, true to his word, he took the car. Although I didn't appreciate it at the time, it was the best thing he could have done, and I'm grateful to him for forcing me to confront the consequences of my actions.

Not that I faced up to it right away. Being without wheels didn't slow me down much, as I'd reconnected with my using friends, who were always there when I needed a fix.

But, of course, my problems merely intensified, and finally I couldn't bear all the deception anymore. Lying to those I loved made me feel more and more alone.

Somehow, through my earlier recovery process, I'd learned to care for myself too much to continue the self-destruction. I told my mom I was ready to quit and, though it took a while after that first step to give up heroin for good, I could feel a faint warmth begin inside me.

I remember the last time I used. I'd just moved to my own apartment and started a new job in Dodgeville, and I was desperate to get my first paycheck. Aloud I kept saying I had quit drugs, but in the back of my mind I wanted a fix. Then another life changer happened, a reckoning I couldn't ignore. A close friend of mine died suddenly at twenty-eight from a brain aneurysm he'd had from birth; nobody could have seen it coming.

Devastated, I used heroin when I first heard the news, but the night of the funeral, I recalled what Tim's death had taught me: Some must die for others to live. When good people with so much to live for kept dying, how could I be selfish enough to waste my own precious life? Seeing the pain on his family's face and feeling it within my own heart, I knew I couldn't put my loved ones through that. I needed to stop squandering my life and start living it to the utmost.

I was starting over, but it wasn't quite like beginning at square one. All I'd learned through my earlier struggles would make this time easier.

Don't turn your head. Keep looking at the bandaged place. That is where the light enters you.
—Hafiz

TURNING POINT

Relapse is not failure: how to recover from a setback

- Be aware of warning signs that may lead to a relapse, These include mood swings, poor eating and sleeping habits, anxiety, anger, defensiveness, lying, thinking about using, and not asking for help. If you notice such signs, tell someone in recovery. They've been where you are and can help you ride out this dangerous period.
- If you do relapse, remind yourself that it isn't a sign of failure. It's a chance to regroup and continue to the next step.
- Be honest. Admit what's happened. Feel your feelings rather than denying them. Keep telling people where you are on the path to recovery so that they can help you.
- Don't be afraid to weep. Mourn your old vision of a perfect recovery in which you smoothly sail through life, as well as your false image of your drug as your friend. As John Bradshaw says in *Home Coming*, "All these feelings need to be felt. We need to stomp and storm; to sob and cry; to perspire and tremble."
- Banish thoughts of using. You have proof now that it's not the romantic life you may have fantasized about. Replay for yourself the parts of using that made you feel disappointed in yourself and the parts of a sober life that made you feel proud. When you compare the two, which holds the most promise?
- If you have cravings, take a walk, do some push-ups, make a pot of soup, clean the bathtub, or do something else to distract yourself. Most urges won't last more than half an hour, so if you can keep busy, they will pass.
- Don't think of your relapse as good or bad. You're not either a successful recovering person or an addicted loser. You're a soul on a journey.
- Instead of focusing on abstinence, concentrate on finding your own best, happiest, most productive and fulfilling life. A full life, not simply abstinence, is the goal.
- Make a point of getting enough sleep, eating healthy food at regular times, and using stress-reducing techniques like those in "Moment of Truth" earlier in this chapter.
- Ask the universe for help. There is boundless goodness and support available to you. You don't have to do this alone.
- Don't berate yourself for relapsing. Just get back on the right path as quickly as possible. Forgive yourself for being human, and live the best life you can today.

– J.M.

I made a decision that many of my friends disagreed with, but somehow I knew it was right for me: I didn't return to my support groups as people were urging me to do. I feared that if I did, I'd once again start focusing on other people's problems and avoiding my own.

Instead, I sought out people I knew would listen and understand. I made amends with my parents and the friends I'd hurt or disappointed with this last relapse. I dug inside to find the self-improvement tools I'd found helpful in the past, and I pushed forward.

With each day, I inched further away from that last high, and I could feel a bit of myself coming back, along with a sense of simple, comforting hope. While I wasn't sure what would happen next, I knew one thing: Every day I would focus, as much as possible, on the precious moments of being alive.

> *Our deepest fears are like dragons guarding our deepest treasure.*
> —Rainer Maria Rilke

✣ ✣ ✣

As I worked to pay down my debts, I came to a new understanding about my monetary problems: I was buying more things than I could afford. I realized that much of my shopping was a form of displacement. I was trying to substitute objects for needs I carried inside me. It was futile, because nothing I could buy was going to fill me with peace.

I began weighing in on my feelings before buying anything. I made a list of the needs I was trying to satisfy and other ways I could fill them so that when I was tempted to buy something, I could quickly turn to my list and find a healthier way to fulfill that craving. While not a foolproof plan, it made me more self-aware, reminding me that turning to material goods, drugs, sex, or any other external "fix" wasn't the way to staunch an inner woundedness. When I turned my energy to something more productive, the lure to spend dissipated and I could sense a feeling of control and even happiness come over me.

TURNING POINT

Fulfill yourself without shopping.

Remember that it's far easier to save than to earn money. Every time you resist the urge to buy something you don't need, you've just accomplished the equivalent of working for several hours.

Practice denying yourself things you want. This will help you get comfortable with feeling uncomfortable, which is an essential skill to develop. It's important to let yourself feel pain, discomfort, and frustration. Pain is the foil of joy. If you don't embrace feelings of distress, you can't feel happiness, either.

> ***To be without some of the things you want is an indispensable part of happiness.***
> —Bertrand Russell

Write down what you want to buy, what desires you might be trying to fill, and other ways to meet those needs without spending money. Examples:

Cosmetics, shoes, jewelry. NEED I'M TRYING TO FILL: I need to feel beautiful, sexy, and desirable. I need to be accepted and loved unconditionally. WHAT I COULD DO INSTEAD OF BUYING: Take a long, leisurely bath with my eyes closed, just feeling the buoyancy of my body, the smoothness of my skin, the perfection of every one of my body parts. Dress up in something colorful and fun. Smile at everyone I see, and watch my smile reflected back. Get together with someone who cares about me and won't judge me, and have an honest conversation about my fears and worries. Laugh with my friends.

Expensive business attire. NEED I'M TRYING TO FILL: I need a job in which I feel respected, professional, valued for the work I do, confident, and successful. WHAT I COULD DO INSTEAD OF BUYING: List things I love to do and feel passionate about. Brainstorm ways I could use my passions in a paying or volunteer job.

The latest fashions: NEED I'M TRYING TO FULFILL: I need a sense of belonging. WHAT I COULD DO INSTEAD OF BUYING: Join a group of people with a common purpose.

A new car. NEED I'M TRYING TO FILL: I need to feel strong, self-sufficient, and powerful. I need a sense of excitement and adventure. WHAT I COULD DO INSTEAD OF BUYING: Get some vigorous physical exercise. Take a boxing class, and get a punching bag to jab. Do some swimming, rowing, jogging, or skating. Join a sports team. Play racquetball with a friend. Learn to do something completely different. Explore new places. Take steps toward overcoming one of my greatest fears.

New furniture or a new house. NEED I'M TRYING TO FILL: I need warmth, intimacy, a feeling of being safe, protected, and nurtured. I yearn for a happy family and a place where I can feel at home. WHAT I COULD DO INSTEAD OF BUYING: Read to kids at a preschool or Head Start. Visit sick kids or older people in the hospital, and play games with them. Prepare food and bring it to someone who can use a home-cooked meal. Give away things to create space so that I can turn my home into the haven I want it to be. Add an altar or sacred space where I can meditate and find inner contentment.

– J.M.

✣ ✣ ✣

The desolate path I once walked has brought me into a bright, clear day. I used to despair when faced with obstacles. Now I ask, "What's the worst that can happen?" I've learned to laugh at my drama.

Once, I bent over backwards to please people, wanting them to be happy because of me. I had it all wrong. As soon as I flipped that around, I could feel the change and the influence it had on others. Now I realize that if I'm happy with myself, those around me will be happy (or, if they're not, I needn't let it affect me).

Although my mom and dad are divorcing, I've learned they're still there for me. This time I can see it's not my fault nor my responsibility to try to fix it.

I haven't reached all my goals, but one of the most critical things I've learned is patience. I'm no longer greedy for everything to happen right away.

Every day, I remember the enormity of small things, like watching birds at the feeder, the sunset, or the endless sky. I remind myself how insignificant an argument or hasty judgment really is. I try never to leave an argument without making sure the other person knows I care; we never know how life will surprise us and I don't want something dumb and frivolous to be anyone's last memory of me or my last memory of them. No matter what chaos swirls around me, it doesn't matter; I'm alive and sober; the world is beautiful.

> *When you face pain directly she will give you an ointment so the wounds don't fester.*
> —Ruth Gendler

I still want to go back to college someday and either teach or counsel young people. I've always felt that my destiny is to help others. Someday I want to get married and have kids. But for right now, I'm content. I'm in love with someone who is truly my soul's counterpart; he has a beautiful two-year-old son I'm proud to have in my life; and I've never been happier than I am right this minute.

My money and health troubles haven't disappeared, but they're part of life for everyone, and it's what you do in these situations that makes the difference. Today, I choose to let life happen, focus on the positive, and seek help when I need it. When I'm reluctant to ask for favors, I remind myself that the right people will understand and that I'll return the favor when it's my turn.

I feel gratitude for my addiction, relapse, and recovery, because they're what helped me get in touch with so many truths, including my true self. It's by probing my weaknesses that I've found my greatest strengths, and it's my gravest sorrows that have led to my deepest joy. I've surrounded myself with people who love me. I have become whole.

> *What is to give light must first endure burning.*
> —Victor Frankl

SHYLOH'S BEST ADVICE

- Befriend your grief rather than trying to distance yourself from it. If you walk side by side with it, it has much to teach you.
- Accept that your energy is finite and you can't do everything. Focus on the things that mean the most to you.
- Contrary to what many believe, peace of mind doesn't come from the absence of suffering.
- Your thoughts create your world. You *are* the world.
- Take responsibility for your life and everything in it. You may not have caused what happened to you, but you're responsible for how you react to it.

✮ ✮ ✮

I realize I can't ask you to learn from my mistakes. Everybody has to find out for themselves; I know I did. Even though my experiences have made me the strong woman I am today, nobody deserves to endure that pain. If one person can take what I've learned and choose a different path, my struggle has been worthwhile.

If addiction has a grip on you, reach out! Those in recovery are some of the most understanding and accepting people you could meet. Asking for help is the hardest step, but the sooner you do that, the closer you'll be to a healthy, happy life.

Life is full of possibility. It's a picture to be painted, not a puzzle to be solved. What does it look like when it's finished? That's yet to be determined.

✮ ✮ ✮

TOOLS FOR THE JOURNEY

List five traits that sum up who you think you are. (Example: I am dependable, timid, dutiful, kind, and helpful.) Now close your eyes, and envision each of those traits, one by one. If you consider the trait to be "negative" or unattractive, let your imagination turn it into a positive. For instance, if one of your words was "incompetent," think about how being imperfect makes you human, accessible to others, and a wonderful friend. Likewise, you could turn "timid" into words like "careful, mindful, observant, and thoughtful."

If you consider the trait to be "positive," imagine ways you can use it to enhance your life and the lives of others. If one of your words is "sensitive," for example, think of things you can do to be sensitive to other people's problems and be a friend to them.

Write down steps you can take to enhance each of the traits you identified as summing up who you are. Make a note to revisit this exercise often and add to it as you learn more about yourself.

Keep an ongoing list of things that interest you, no matter now insignificant they may seem. Add to this list every day, whenever you see or hear something that appeals to you. These things are clues that, when you put them together, will help reveal your true self—the person you can be when you put your passions to work in the world.

Practice seeing the lesson or unexpected insight that hides within every challenge. Try the following exercise to get started: List some hardships or troubles you're facing now or have encountered in the past. For each one, instead of thinking, "Who's to blame?" or "Why did this have to happen?" answer these questions: What can this teach me? What's the lesson in it for me?

If you lose someone, direct your pain and sorrow toward something positive. Change the world in that person's name. If a loved one dies of a drug overdose, for instance, you could channel your emotions into helping others with drug problems or donating time and money to recovery groups.

THINGS TO DO TODAY

Here are five stepping stones you can use today to move forward into a new life.

   1. **Answer these questions on paper:** What does "success" mean to you? Do you feel you've succeeded in your life? If not, when will you believe yourself to be a success? Realize that if you measure success in terms of money, status, or possessions, you're unlikely to ever accumulate enough to be happy. If you look for success within yourself, you're much more likely to have a successful life. How could you change your definition of success so that it includes true happiness and fulfillment? External markers like money can be part of a happy life, but they don't guarantee happiness the way inner peace does.

   2. **Let your worries float away today.** Life is full of anxieties, but they don't have to control you. See each worry as a dark cloud, then watch it drift away. Replace it with a fluffy white cloud to represent a good thing that could happen instead.

   3. **Write your favorite exercises or sayings** on pieces of paper, fold them up, and put them in a jar. Whenever you need a lift or a catalyst to creativity, you can pick one of these inspiration cards from the jar at random.

   4. **List five things** that give you feelings of joy and contentment. These can be the smallest of things, like stretching and yawning when you wake up in the morning, breathing in the scent of fresh coffee, layering cheese and bread and leaves of lettuce into a satisfying lunch. This list will underscore the fact that you don't have to look to someone else to fulfill you. Gladden your own heart by noticing the little things that please you.

   5. **Tidy your bedroom** before you go to sleep. Straightening up at the end of the day helps quiet your mind and improves your sleeping and dreaming.

– J.M.

WORDS OF WISDOM AND LIGHT

Here are more lessons you can put into action in your own life.

Don't Hide from Your Anxieties: Wisdom from Sonya

I've always had anxiety conditions, including obsessive-compulsive disorder and phobias. My therapist helped me deal with them by introducing me sequentially to the things that made me anxious. To deal with my fear of spiders, she first showed me drawings of them. When I became comfortable with those, we moved on to photographs and then videos of spiders. Then she showed me a small spider in a cage, moving on to larger spiders. Eventually, I could run across a spider unexpectedly without freaking out.

My therapist followed a similar procedure to help me accept being gay. I'd tried to pretend, to myself and others, that I wasn't gay, but that only made the feelings scarier and more overwhelming. Looking at photos and videos of gay couples, getting to know people who were gay, talking and listening to others talk openly about their sexuality—all these things helped me become comfortable with the idea of being gay and, eventually, feel free enough to come out of the closet. I had no idea how liberating it would be to finally stop hiding who I really was and come face to face with my fears.

Sonya's best advice: When you're anxious about something, move toward it bit by bit. Each time, come a little closer, until it loses its power over you. The key is to approach rather than avoid the things that upset you. When you evade them, they gain power. When you confront them, they subside. Don't forget to reward yourself whenever you make progress: Treat yourself to a special dinner, or tell others what you've accomplished so they can congratulate you. No matter how small the step, as long as you're advancing rather than retreating, it's a victory worth celebrating.

List Your Wonders: Wisdom from Tiasha

I keep a list of my own personal "Wonders of the World." I try to take one long trip a year to visit a place with a natural wonder, such as Niagara Falls, the Great Lakes, or the Rocky Mountains. But most of the wonders appear with no effort on my part, like the time a doe and two fawns walked in front of me or the morning after an ice storm when the whole world turned into diamonds.

Tiasha's best advice: Start your own list of wonders. Plan some adventures, and keep your eyes open for the many treasures life has to offer.

Talk Back to Your Addiction: Wisdom from Naomi

My drug use started when I was doing a craft project in fourth grade and got a wonderful feeling from breathing in the fumes of the glue I was using. Of course, I started doing a lot of craft projects after that. Next, I started drinking my mom's liquor and hanging out with a girl who was taking her mom's pills.

I had a nasty childhood, filled with terrible sexual abuse. My earliest memory is of being molested by an uncle when I was five years old. My cousins also raped me. The sexual trauma continued until I moved away in my teens.

Now, at eighteen, I'm finally getting a handle on my addictions—to all types of drugs but especially heroin. The tool that helps the most is writing. I carry notebooks with me everywhere and write whenever I have a spare moment. Writing out my sorrow and pain is the best way for me to face emotions that I've buried most of my life.

Naomi's best advice: Next time you hear your drug's wheedling whisper, don't listen. Put your addiction in a form outside yourself so you can take control of it. Rage at it. Tell it all the ways it has hurt you, lied to you, and ruined your life.

Turn your inner addict into a separate entity in your mind, and give it a physical form. Use an ugly troll doll or a squishy, spiky ball to represent your addiction. You can even name it if you want.

The point is to make it clear to yourself that your addiction isn't an intrinsic part of you, and you can free yourself from its insidious voice. When it murmurs to you that it can take away your pain and make you feel better, tell it you know it's lying and you won't be tricked. Throw it across the room; smash it against the floor; fling it out of your life for good.

The purpose of this exercise is to let you despise your addiction without loathing yourself. It separates you from your drugs so that you can accept that you're a good person. It's your addiction that's evil, not you.

Write a letter to your addiction, like this one:

TO MY ADDICTION:

Smack, you betrayed me. Once you were freedom and safety, but quickly you shackled me to the streets, to a life of poverty and sickness. You are disgusting, hideous, a silent killer coagulating on a spoon.

You were my greatest love, the strongest bond I ever forged. But what did you do to me? You made me frail, sleepless, sick, every single day. Just to get close to you, I stole, lied, cheated, committed credit card fraud, sold my most precious possessions for a fraction of their worth, lost every friend but you.

I've said no to you before—how many dozens of times? But this time is different, because I finally see you for the filthy beast you are. I realize you're stealing my soul and my life, and I don't want to die or be your slave any longer.

I want to live. I want to taste freedom again, to be a normal teenager for once. I want to see my baby sister's seventh birthday, to watch the light in her eyes when she blows out those pink candles. That wish is more powerful than you.

I tell you now, be forewarned. Run. Because I will fight you with every iota of strength I possess. When you beg for mercy, I will laugh. Demon, I am taking charge.

6

COURAGE DOESN'T ALWAYS ROAR: ANDREA'S STORY

Andrea, the author's daughter, quit drugs in her twenties. But only recently, in her forties, did she begin confronting the problems caused by her drug use and exploring the underlying issues. While she says she has "no answers" and is uncomfortable giving advice, she has a powerful story to tell.

Author's Note:
From the time she was a little girl, Andrea has danced to her own drum. That's part of what makes her so special. While I may be a bit biased because I'm her mom, everyone who knows her says the same thing. She's been written up in many magazine and newspaper articles for her accomplishments. Whatever she puts her mind to, she does with passion and a unique style.

An artist from the time she could hold a pencil, a musician, an inspiring athlete, and a caring mom, she acts according to what she believes is true and speaks straight from her heart. You always know where you stand with Andrea.

Drugs took over her life as a teenager, but she got back on track when her daughter was born and put her energy into being the best mother she could be. Her daughter, son, and husband became the center of her life, but she always found time for some sort of artistic pursuit—painting murals on garage doors, creating intricate beaded bags and necklaces, tattooing, making clothing out of leather she tanned herself, sculpting images into bones and antlers.

Her house in the Wisconsin countryside, tucked away in a valley, protected by a sheer rock wall, is just as she dreamed it as a child. It includes a dojo where she teaches martial arts and boxing, an art studio, and eighty acres of woods, creeks, birds, and prairie land that she restored herself. There, out of sight of the rest of the world, she has her own apple orchard, berry bushes, handcrafted log-cabin guesthouse, and a coop full of chattering chickens.

She has a way of turning each problem into a positive and immersing herself in whatever she's doing. To deal with her anger, she channeled it into karate, winning trophies and perfecting her skills with great passion. From karate she moved to kickboxing and then to boxing, becoming the state champion.

A movie producer in New York saw her in a photo spread of female boxers in Sports Illustrated, *loved her "look" and "attitude," decided she was perfect for the role he was casting, and flew her to New York to play the part of the boxer "Red Lennox" in the movie* The Opponent. *She did such an outstanding job in the movie that she was offered a job as a stunt artist. (She turned it down, thinking it would interfere with her mothering duties.)*

Perhaps she surprised herself most when she went back to school a few years ago at the age of thirty-eight and excelled at every class she took. As a teenager she had decided formal education wasn't for her, but now she enrolled in college, first at a technical school and then at the University of Wisconsin-Madison, deciding she wanted to be a physical therapist specializing in sports medicine. She threw herself into her studies and became a top student, winning awards and scholarships and discovering a deep love of learning.

I tell you these things not to brag as a mother, because I don't take credit for any of the myriad things Andrea has accomplished, but because I know she will downplay her successes when she tells her story. I'm just so glad she is in my life.

Here is her story, in her own words.

—J.M.

✵ ✵ ✵

I started using at thirteen—first cigarettes, pot, and alcohol, rapidly progressing into harder drugs. I used heavily throughout my teens and into my early twenties. I quit using years ago, but I didn't actually begin "recovery" until just recently, at age forty-three.

I've attempted to put my story into words multiple times, but it seems that the more I say, the more I end up focusing on what hasn't been said. I feel as though I need to tell everything, or nothing. I've tried here to find an honest middle ground.

Recovery for me has been the discovery of a new mode of travel less cumbersome, more forgiving, more open to trust. I am slowly learning to live in each moment with eyes and heart open. Some days I think I'm totally on top of it, other days I struggle. It's actually much harder than the "quitting" was.

I tend to be a person of extremes. Whatever I do, I do with intensity and often to excess. This has been a pattern for as long as I can remember, with my drug use and drinking but with my "healthy" activities as well. It feels as though I'm always trying to push things to their limits, to define the edges. How can you control your world when you don't know where the boundaries are? I never could seem to find them. The more I pushed, the further away they seemed to move.

There was always more to be endured, more that needed doing, always a steeper hill to climb.

Sometimes I would catch myself, as if looking in from the outside, doing whatever it was I was doing with a frantic, almost obsessive, intensity. I would know clearly in these moments that something was wrong, but could never quite define it. It felt as though I was running from something and if I stopped for even a moment to breathe, some horrible truth would catch up. I'm still not sure what it is I was running from, but I've finally decided to stop and let it come.

> *Searcher, there is no road. We make the road by walking.*
> —Antonio Machado

✵ ✵ ✵

I was born in Boulder, Colorado, in 1966. My mother married my biological father when she learned she was pregnant, but it lasted only a few years. After moving to Ann Arbor, she divorced him and met the wonderful man I call Dad; they married when I was three.

My dad was a professor and we moved from college town to college town. Moving so much inhibited my ability to form attachments with people, and I have always viewed myself as an outsider. In many ways I'm comfortable with this role, but it's at the same time very lonely.

I recall loneliness being a common theme to my childhood. True, I didn't have siblings I was forced to share with, but I always longed for a companion. I learned to amuse myself and stay busy, which built a competence and independence that has served me well throughout my life.

My parents were hard workers, one an academic and the other a freelance writer. They both did their writing and researching at home, and I remember being "shushed" out of the room regularly as a child, sent off to play alone, so that they could work. To this day I struggle with the sense of being a bother, of intruding, of people not wanting me around. I am so sensitive to this that I'll generally leave social situations with an excuse of some sort, preferring to be alone.

My early memories of my mother are confusing to me. Her emotional behavior, depression, and drinking had a deep impact on me. There was very little emotional consistency. I got such mixed messages from her, such incongruence of word and behavior that I learned to distrust words and my own emotions. I didn't understand that the glass of wine she always seemed to have in her hand or at her bedside may have been contributing to the confusion, or that she struggled with depression and a past of her own.

My dad on the other hand was my "rock." He taught me about the world, about nature, how to make things, to be curious, and how to look for answers. For him everything was logic and reason, and though he wasn't able to help me understand or deal with the undercurrent of painful emotion in our home, he did give my world enough order to keep me grounded for a while.

But if as children we believe the world revolves around us, then I also believed I must be responsible for all that felt "wrong" around me. I felt this burden overwhelmingly. There was an unspoken understanding that we not talk about what we were feeling, about anything negative. This I think fed my sense of guilt, that I was somehow to blame for all that didn't make sense to me, for my mother's obvious emotional pain, for all that was "unspeakable." I couldn't ask for clarification, so I created some pretty deep and dysfunctional beliefs and coping strategies. If I were to put words to what was scaring me, it would make it too real and I could no longer ignore it or hold on to my illusion of control. I had to keep what I was feeling hidden from even myself, so that I could readjust and redefine my reality to fit what I was experiencing. This became my modus operandi for most of my life. Emotions showed weakness, and I saw weakness as bad. I would not be weak.

Eighth grade is when I remember things really changing. I think it must've come with puberty. I remember starting to pay attention to how I looked, to how I was perceived by others. I was getting attention from boys, too, which was exciting and at the same time scary. To be perceived by others can make one feel very vulnerable, and for the first time I remember feeling self-conscious, aware of being judged.

It was in eighth grade that my friends and I first tried cigarettes. I don't remember why I started smoking. I had always hated the smell of cigarettes and complained terribly when my mother would smoke. But I felt pretty grown up doing it, cool and tough and in control. I was being a rebel, taking my stand against authority, and smoking cigarettes has long been a symbol of rebellion. Whatever the reason, we smoked. If I was going to do something, I would do it big. I smoked a lot.

Enter pot and alcohol. I never really liked smoking pot, it usually made me paranoid, but the pipe would come around, and I would take it anyway. Alcohol, on the other hand, felt like a long lost friend. Its effects were so immediate, so comforting, so empowering. I didn't feel judged, or alone, or awkward.

Besides the fact that I habitually do most things to excess, I think it may have been in my genetics that I couldn't use alcohol in moderation. Almost immediately I was a black-out drunk. At first friends would recount for me my wild, out-of-control behavior, but they soon got tired of watching out for me, and I would have to piece together the previous day and night on my own.

My first sexual encounter occurred when I was drunk, and I'm ashamed to admit that I hardly remember it. I was also drunk the night I was raped, remembering only pieces of that incident as well. Quite often I would wake up and not know where I was, who I was with, or how I got there. I felt flawed and disgusting and unlovable, so I rearranged my perspective and swallowed the pain with more booze.

By the time I was fifteen, I had overdosed twice on alcohol to the point that my heart had stopped. But waking up in the hospital wasn't enough to make me stop drinking. My world had become much too big for me to hold on to the illusion that I was in control of it, so I think I gave the control over to the drugs and alcohol instead.

My parents, my father, my rock, didn't know how to handle the teenage me. Neither did I! Looking back, I think I wanted so badly for him to be solid and confident and strong, to give me boundaries, and make the world less immense and ominous. But I was strong willed, independent, and unwilling to give in easily. I pulled away, hoping deep down that my parents could hold on, but they couldn't, or wouldn't. How could I trust my vulnerable self to be safe and protected if they weren't in control? They let me go. I more or less dropped out of school by the middle of my freshman year, and started hanging out downtown with the dealers and hippies and other lost youth. I met the boy who would be my "partner against the world" for the next several years. We discovered barbiturates and speed, acid and mushrooms. I was taken into the social services system as chronically truant and delinquent. I had just turned fifteen.

I spent just over a year in a residential treatment center for troubled teens, and actually flourished in the confinement and structure of the system, though I would never have admitted it at the time. But with the freedom of my release, I went straight back to the streets, the drugs, the drinking. I think my folks thought I would come home "cured," but nothing had changed except that I was a little older and had earned enough school credits to graduate. Whatever pain I was refusing to acknowledge to myself, whatever emotions were underlying my behavior, I still felt were mine to be endured alone and kept hidden. If those demons weren't acknowledged, I could still pretend to be in control of them.

I moved in with my boyfriend and his mother, a free spirit who let us do whatever we pleased. We started using cocaine, first snorting it, then shooting it. The users and dealers we hung out with weren't our friends. I don't think I had any friends, just a loyalty among users and thieves.

I remember distinctly, just before my eighteenth birthday, sitting in a circle with a group of people passing coke and a needle. Everyone but me had put in for the coke and I felt I would do anything for a hit, but no one was sharing. As I sat there watching each person's metamorphosis—from an animal-like anticipation, to the wash of the drug hitting their system—I was suddenly sickened to realize I was one of "them." I saw my reflection in their faces and it horrified me. I got up and left, and swore off needles for good. I've never touched one since.

COURAGE DOESN'T ALWAYS ROAR: ANDREA'S STORY   199

It was about this time that my boyfriend started to hit me. It wasn't unusual for an evening of drinking and getting high to end with him going off to jail and me there with eyes swollen shut, a lip split. This happened often enough that my nickname in the neighborhood was "Rocky." Part of me was ashamed that I would let this happen to me, but part of me was also strangely proud for being strong enough to stay and endure. I think I stayed for so long because I felt somehow I deserved it.

When I did finally move out and away from him, he stalked me. He broke into my apartment one night and tried to kill me. I think the neighbors must have called the police, and when he heard them coming he ran off. I remember being in a concussed haze for several days, and having flashbacks and nightmares, but it became another something to endure, to lock away in the recesses of my mind and ignore. I had become quite good at feeling nothing. I was finally rid of him when he was arrested for armed robbery (trying to finance his coke habit) and sent to prison.

I had sworn off needles, but not the drugs or drinking, and the next several years were a blur of bars and biker parties, coke and speed and booze. I did things I was deeply ashamed of, and I couldn't help but feel unspeakably flawed to have allowed any of it to happen. But I saw pain and fear, shame and vulnerability as signs of weakness, and I was determined to be strong. Instead of feeling anything, I would rearrange my perspective so I wouldn't need to confront how dysfunctional my view had become. I endured. I was strong and "in control."

During this period, quite by accident, I met a charming young carpenter named Ed. We eventually moved in together and, a year later, I found out I was pregnant. I was twenty-one.

I had never planned to have children or a family: If I "settled down," how would I keep running from whatever it was inside me that I worked so hard not to see?

But Ed convinced me we could be a family, and I decided to give it a try. I believe it was a decision that ultimately saved my life.

Being pregnant with my daughter, Shyloh, was a spiritual awakening. It inspired in me a feeling of love and connectedness I had never experienced. Even from my womb, my daughter was the first person I let completely into my heart with absolute trust and a fierce, unwavering love. To this day she holds a most sacred place there.

Ed also had a drug and alcohol habit, which inevitably kept our "family" from working. I left him when Shyloh was a year and a half to be with the man I would eventually marry. That man, my husband, had been a year sober when we met, which was huge for me. All the relationships I'd had to that point had been with drinkers and users and I needed desperately to have someone in my life I could trust, that I could count on, a "rock." With his strength to lean on, my world was less scary and more "controllable."

Over the next several years I quit drugs and cigarettes altogether. Since my husband didn't drink at all, getting drunk wasn't doing for me what it used to. I was starting to hate not being in control of myself, not remembering what I'd done the night before.

But my husband had a history of his own, full of abuse, violence, and trauma. It had made him strong but also gave him a violent temper. He never hit me, but the implied threat was scary for my daughter and me. There was that undercurrent of unspoken emotional pain and fear, which of course felt familiar to me. I never questioned it, and we were all very careful not to talk about it, not to "stir things up," to leave whatever lay below the surface alone.

After being married three years, I was pregnant again. By now my husband and I were ready and committed to setting down roots and raising a family, and we had a beautiful son.

I had traded drugs and cigarettes for exercise, throwing myself into it with customary immoderation. I became involved in martial arts and trained sometimes two to three hours a day. I'm told I was good, but I could never be satisfied with myself. I always had to be better, "perfect," but I had no sense of how to define perfection. I just knew that somehow my best would never be good enough.

I needed more challenge and began boxing competitively. I no longer drank at all, because it interfered with my training and diet. Training had become my "drug." To be a good boxer you have to train hard, so it was easy for me to rationalize my obsessive drive. I couldn't get enough of the rush of power and control I felt in the ring. It wasn't so much winning as controlling the fight that I loved. I didn't notice that I was still masking my pain, that instead of getting high, I worked out.

But after so many years of pushing myself nearly every day without a break, my body began to protest. I developed chronic back and shoulder pain, and I found myself loading up with ibuprofen and training anyway. I continued like this for another year until I realized I had to quit boxing. I was devastated. It seemed like such an ultimate admission of weakness and failure.

I took on a job as a general laborer doing prairie restorations at a local nursery. I was motivated, driven, and smart, I worked hard, fast, and efficiently. Within a year I was managing the plant and seed production and supervising work crews. From the outside I appeared in control, strong and proficient, in charge, what I'd worked so hard my whole life to be, but on the inside I was still always fighting the belief that my best would never be good enough, that if I slowed down for a moment my world would spiral out of control.

Though I truly loved the work, again my body began to protest from the intensity with which I exerted myself. At my husband's suggestion, I left the nursery and decided to go back to school.

Starting college at thirty-eight years old was exhilarating. When I was young, I'd found school tedious and confining, but as an adult I couldn't get enough. I loved stretching my mind in new directions, challenging the professors and myself with difficult questions. I could almost feel the new pathways being formed in my brain as I channeled my curiosity and grew.

A STEP ON THE JOURNEY

Gain a new brain. Research has proven the brain's neuroplasticity—its ability to reorganize itself to create new channels in response to injury, stress, and new situations or activities. Here are ways to help you sculpt the brain you want:
- Turn your full attention to what you're doing. This engages the brain's facility for plasticity and change.
- Protect your brain by not getting worked up about little things. Stress causes the release of cortisol, which in the short term is perfect for allowing us to deal with life-threatening situations, but over prolonged periods can actually kill brain cells and may lead to depression.
- Imagine yourself going through the specific motions of whatever it is you're wanting to do. Imagery can engage some of the same motor and sensory systems involved in the actual doing. Mental practice is a powerful way to rehearse a physical skill.

- Repeat beliefs to yourself mentally, orally, and in writing. Through repetition, you can change your thoughts by forging new passages in your brain, and this will become your brain's new reality.
- Do something different. Speak to someone you've never talked to before. Attend a class or read a book on an unfamiliar subject. Learn to juggle. Listen to a different kind of music. Each new thing you do makes your brain stronger.

—adapted from *Change the Mind, Change the Brain* and *The Brain That Changes Itself*

– J.M.

I falsely believed I had confronted my past and was "healed." I had regained control. I studied for hours each day and was able to maintain straight A's. I threw myself into my schoolwork the same way I had with my training and prairie work. I was home, but I wasn't there. I was falling into the same pattern, obsessing over perfection. If I earned all A's and one A-, all I could see was the minus. I stopped loving school, and again started to feel driven to perfection and control.

My family was more or less supportive of my endeavors, maybe even proud. But throwing myself into my passions came at the expense of attention to them. I didn't neglect my obvious duties; I prepared meals and did laundry, picked up the house and got the kids off to school, helped them with homework and drove them where they needed to go. We made things and I taught them about nature and the world. But I neglected to teach them to play, to be happy, to live in the moment, how to trust, how to fail, how to forgive themselves. With all my heart I regret this. But how could I teach what I myself didn't know how to do?

My daughter had started to struggle with drugs and alcohol at about thirteen, just about the time I'd retired from boxing. It felt like déjà vu, and I was suddenly forced to confront my past so I could keep her from repeating it. I took her to counselors, I told her stories detailing the horrors of drug use, I cried. I held on fiercely, determined to save her from herself.

She struggled throughout her teens, and I was there holding on with all my might. I didn't know how to stop it, and for the first time I was forced to admit to myself that I had no control, that I didn't have the power to save her. It was one of the hardest things I'd ever done. But I continued to hold on.

While his sister was getting the attention, my sweet and beautiful son faded into the background. It wasn't until Shyloh went off to college five years later that he began to shine, throwing himself into working out and playing football, his charm and wit coming through.

But without Shyloh at home as a constant reminder of her struggles, I think it was easy for us all to fall back into that comfortable rhythm. I rebuilt my illusion that my world was under control, and continued on.

Then my son too began to struggle with drugs and alcohol. He was fourteen, angry and violent, with a huge chip on his shoulder. Again I could see myself in my child's expressions of hopelessness. I was terrified and felt utterly helpless, and for the second time I was forced to admit absolutely that I had no control or power to save my child.

I could see that my husband began to feel the helplessness too. Our home, our family, was turning upside down. It became increasingly obvious that what was happening to our children, to our family, was a reflection of something there under the surface. My husband and I thought we had led well by example, not using or smoking, exercising and eating healthily, talking about the dangers of drugs and drinking. How was it that both our children had followed in our footsteps anyway?

One night we received a phone call from the police. Shyloh had overdosed on heroin, and I felt the bottom drop out of my world. They told us that the EMTs had administered a drug to counter the depressant effects, that her heart had been restarted, and she would be okay, though they were taking her to jail because of past drinking-related offenses. They would ultimately hold her there for three months while waiting for a spot to open at a residential drug rehab, a decision that I'm sure saved her life. Her boyfriend wasn't so lucky. The night before she entered rehab, she learned that he had overdosed and died. It was with that news that the following day my daughter went into treatment and began the painful process of recovery.

We took our son to counselors, and my husband and I started seeing a family counselor, too. At first it was in an effort to "fix" our son, but soon we both realized it was us that needed to change. We began to uncover dynamics in our marriage that had for years been burying pain and fear and insecurity. It was so humbling and sad to realize all we had unintentionally passed on to our children—dysfunction we thought was hidden deep and away. We had believed that if we didn't talk about or acknowledge it, we could go on ignoring it.

Around this time, browsing at a bookstore, I stumbled quite by accident across a book titled *A Path and a Practice*, a translation of the Tao Te Ching supplemented with suggestions for applying its wisdom. I'm turned off by organized religion, but am quite drawn to the eastern philosophies and had read translations of the Tao Te Ching as a young adult—several times, in fact. I found that Taoism made sense to me. But in the past I had tried to memorize and "perfect" the practice, to control it and use it to help me control my life. This approach had missed the point, and I would get frustrated, sidetracked, and put it aside.

I decided to look at it again. I bought the book and read it, and its message touched me as it never had before. I realized it wasn't about memorization and perfection and control. It was about acceptance and relinquishing control. The revelation was huge for me, though I still struggle to remember it day to day.

The primary theme throughout my life, weaving through all my dysfunctional turmoil, has been about "control"—or the illusion of it. As I learned to recognize old, unhealthy patterns, I went back to that little book. I was reminded to experience the moment, to accept myself and those around me, and to release myself of responsibility for things I could not change. I tried not to fret anymore that I wasn't yet able to hold on to these reminders for long. I knew I could come back any time I needed to.

I began to feel a "letting go," the releasing of a burden I hadn't even known I'd been carrying. So began my "recovery." As Shyloh got more and more into her own healing, I felt as though she were opening a door and making a path for me to follow. As odd as it may sound, she is one of my heroes. Her courage and strength seemed to be in her ability to let herself be vulnerable and open, and to give freely of herself to others. I truly admired that. My son was the absolute catalyst for change, his style being "in your face" confrontation. Where Shyloh had opened the door, I felt my son at my heels moving me through it. Children can sometimes be our greatest teachers.

Courage doesn't always roar; sometimes it is the quiet voice at the end of the day that says "I will try again tomorrow."
—Mary Anne Radmacher

> ## TURNING POINT
>
> **Accept everything.** The Tao teaches that wisdom comes not from controlling everything or understanding everything but from accepting everything. What some call suffering is wisdom ready to be transformed.
>
> What problems are frustrating you right now? What if they remained in your life but were no longer problems? As an experiment, pick an issue and spend a day pretending, just pretending, that it isn't a problem. Practice accepting it and appreciating the learning and wisdom embodied in it.
> —adapted from *A Path and a Practice*
>
> – J.M.

✣ ✣ ✣

I took the next step and found my own therapist. I asked her to help me learn to recognize and be okay with my emotions and vulnerabilities. With her help, I slowly dismantled no-longer-functional coping strategies and began to replace them with healthier ones. At times she had to restrain me from trying to rush ahead too fast in my attempts to get it all wrapped up and "under control." Old habits can die hard.

The counseling sessions with my husband didn't result in the progress I'd hoped for. At first I'd been encouraged as we faced our pasts together, knowing that it would likely get rockier before it got better, that it would take perseverance, but that it was crucial if we were to change. Looking back now, however, I see that my husband wasn't ready to confront his demons, and the more I tried to bring us together, to get him to open up to me, the more he pulled away and the angrier he became. There was such a lack of communication between us that ultimately all conversations ended in misunderstanding. Of course, in my typical way, I just pushed harder.

The next spring, in what would've been our twentieth year of marriage, he told me he was leaving and not coming back. It felt completely out of the blue. I honestly hadn't seen it coming, although, in retrospect, I believe he must've been planning it for a while. When my son learned we were splitting up, he chose to go with his dad.

That same week, our daughter Shyloh decided to move back home for a while. Almost immediately, we saw the fresh needle tracks on her arms and knew she had relapsed and had likely been using heroin again for at least four months. The signs had been there, but I hadn't wanted to believe what I knew in my heart. When I had questioned her, she had replied with proficient lies, an appropriate explanation for every suspicious situation. I had accepted her lies because I wanted to, because I couldn't bear the alternative.

So now here I was, my marriage broken, my home broken, my heart broken, and having to tell my daughter she would have to leave too if she was going to continue to use. I don't think she could bear watching me crumble emotionally. I know she loved me, but she loved the drugs more. She left.

To say I was devastated would feel like an understatement. My world had fallen out from under me and I could find nothing to hold on to.

By this time I'd built a pretty full life. In addition to a heavy load at school, I was teaching boxing and running my own gardening, landscaping, and prairie restoration business. I usually savored these jobs, but now I struggled through them in a daze.

I honestly don't know how I did it. I'd get up each day and put one foot in front of the other with no real thought of anything beyond that. I had thought I'd faced lows before, but this was the worst emotional pain I'd ever endured. I thought about killing myself almost daily, and came disturbingly close to following through more than once. I'm quite sure I'd fallen into a clinical depression but I'd lost my faith in everyone, especially therapists, and I certainly wasn't going to take antidepressants to "cure" me.

More than once I felt that old compulsion to go to the bar and drink myself to oblivion, but I resisted somehow. I felt I'd lost everything I'd believed in, everything that I'd cared about, the whole structure I'd based my life around. It felt as though my pain was all I had left; if I lost that, I'd have nothing. I wasn't going to dull it with medications or alcohol.

So every day I went through the motions out of habit and sheer faith that the sun was going to rise the next day. If I had thought I understood about relinquishing control before, I was getting a master lesson now.

In the past I would have turned my back on what I was feeling, compartmentalized it, drowned it with drugs and alcohol or obsessive activity, done all I could to be "strong" and keep my emotions under "control." But I think this was too overwhelming to run from, or perhaps the life lessons from the previous years had given me a new kind of strength.

Sometimes the grief would feel like a slow suffocation, squeezing tighter and tighter throughout the day. But often it would just hit me, crashing over me like a wave, and take my breath away. It would feel as though I'd been kicked in the gut. I found myself crying sometimes from a depth I hadn't known existed.

It wasn't just that my husband had left me, it went so much deeper than that. I felt absolutely betrayed by someone I'd allowed myself to trust so completely. All my fears as a child, my reluctance to trust or form bonds, being alone and abandoned, being flawed, unwanted, and unlovable, and of course having no sense of control, these demons stared me square in the eye now.

It might sound strange, but the night I came closest to killing myself, to really thinking it out, planning and imagining the details, was actually a turning point towards healing. It was like going to the edge of the abyss, looking down, and seeing it for what it was.

I called my mom that night and told her what I was thinking of doing, because I knew I needed to tell someone if I was going to live through that night. At first she tried to tell me not to feel that way, that everything would be fine, as though she could argue away my anguish. But then she paused and she told me she loved me, that she would be sad if I hurt myself, that she would miss me terribly, and somehow that's exactly what I needed to hear from her. I needed her to acknowledge my reality, to confirm that she'd "heard" me. From that moment and to this day, when I confide in her, my mother now hears me in a way I'd never felt from her before. I didn't feel quite so alone anymore.

When I let go of what I am, I become what I might be.
—Lao Tzu

✢ ✢ ✢

My entire life I had felt that emotions showed weakness, that they were something to deny to myself and others, and I had always been afraid to confront them completely. But now I had no choice but to let the emotions come, nameless and uncontrolled. It felt as though I would be swallowed alive, but when the waves would pass, there I'd still be.

I quit trying to put labels on what I was feeling, quit trying to rationalize or justify or even recognize it. I would just let the waves come and go, and let myself cry until the tears ran dry. I wish I could say that I'd feel miraculously better afterwards. Sometimes I did feel as though a cloud had lifted, but more often I just felt drained. Still, another day would pass, I'd keep putting one foot in front of the other, and honestly, after a while, it did get easier. Having truly let go, I felt just a little lighter and less burdened. I felt completely vulnerable, but not weak.

✢ ✢ ✢

The remainder of that year finally passed, one long painful day at a time, and a new year began. I slowly started to see the possibility of a new life, of loving again, of being loved.

In recent months I have met a man. We met for coffee and found ourselves talking for hours and hours, and a relationship grew from there. On the surface it seemed we had little in common but there was something about him that I was able to connect with. He is gentle and kind and patient, qualities that had always been seriously lacking in any of my previous relationships.

Over time I have made a conscious decision to open my heart to him, not because I've been promised that he'll care for it or because I need him to be my rock, but because I need to live my life honestly. For me that means allowing myself to be vulnerable to those I care about. It is terrifying, and yet I know that nothing in life is certain anyway. Even if there were promises made, there would be no guarantees that I wouldn't be hurt. One can't truly live if in constant fear of another's intentions, always on the defensive, building bigger and sturdier walls.

Walls may keep out the dangers, real or imagined. But they keep everything else out, too.

If there's one thing I've learned, it's the power of letting go. It would seem to be the easier thing to do, requiring so much less effort than holding on. We as humans seem to need to feel we're actively "doing" something in keeping to the illusion of having control over our world, our lives, our futures, our emotions, our children, our relationships. But I think that in letting go, in accepting and acknowledging things as they truly are and not holding onto preconceived notions of what we wish things to be, we can have much more influence on the direction we want our lives and hearts to go.

I've made the conscious decision to notice each day and to fully embrace each moment. It's so easy to fall into old patterns of behavior, and I do have to remind myself sometimes to stop and take notice, to inhale deeply of life. I don't want to miss anything. I don't ever want to look back with regret and realize I've been too safe, or too scared, or too busy planning for tomorrow, and have let that moment slip by unnoticed.

Happiness is not a state to arrive at but a manner of traveling.
—Margaret Lee Runbeck

From time to time there comes over me a feeling of dread that the earth is about to drop out from under me at any time, especially when life is going along smoothly and I'm feeling good. It's still a struggle not to panic and run. But I know I can never live that way again.

I want to feel all of life. I don't want to try to control it, or filter it, or box myself off in an effort of protection. I feel as though I've faced all my demons squarely, seen into the darkest recesses of my psyche. What is there to run from anymore?

✧ ✧ ✧

TOOLS FOR THE JOURNEY

In your journal, record a recent situation in which you had a strong emotional response. Next, identify the emotions that came up, no matter how irrational or insignificant. Then "listen" to the automatic thoughts associated with each emotion, following the threads of each thought to uncover its origin. Are these thoughts helpful and based on the reality of the moment, or are they linked to some past experience? Can you think of a more appropriate response? Do this exercise often, until you're able to catch yourself in the moment. Though the emotions may still arise you'll be free to make a conscious decision of how you want to respond.

Find a form of meditation that works for you, and be sure to set aside time each day, or at least several times a week for this. Make taking this time for yourself a priority! Not all meditation need be sitting quietly; there are many physical arts that are based on spiritual grounding and being centered, such as tai chi, aikido, and yoga. Dancing, running, and biking are other examples of activities in which you can deliberately be in the moment, at one with your body and breath.

The Dalai Lama has noted that the purpose of meditation is to make space in your brain to overturn old habits and learn new ones. In that sense, you're meditating when you read this book, perform the exercises, and practice new ways of viewing the world.

Make an effort to actively reach out to other people. Being true to yourself, find others who will accept you as you are.

Seek a source of spiritual inspiration. The Tao Te Ching is a book of poetic wisdom written hundreds of years ago by a Chinese Zen master, Lao Tzu. *A Path and a Practice* translates the ancient writing as well as offering helpful interpretations. It can be useful to read and re-read the poems when you're feeling ungrounded, as a spiritual reminder of acceptance and letting go.

Forgive yourself…and try again tomorrow.

THINGS TO DO TODAY

1. **If you're planning something** or looking forward to an event, examine your expectations about it. Are you imagining that it will turn out a certain way? That's fine, but remind yourself that if it doesn't go exactly as planned, that's okay. The way it unfolds may be even better than you dreamed.

2. **All day today, pay attention to the traits of the people you meet,** viewing them with compassion and without judgment. At the end of the day, ask yourself how these same qualities are present in you.

3. **Jot down four things** you would like to change about your life. These can be small (I would like to organize my desk drawers) or large (I would like more friends).

4. **Choose one of the items** in your list of things you'd like to change. Write a list of steps you could take to bring you closer to making that change. Do one of those things today.

5. **Congratulate yourself** for the progress you're making. Just picking up this book was an important step because it shows you want to change, and that's a huge stride forward. It makes everything possible.

WORDS OF WISDOM AND LIGHT

More lessons to guide you in your healing journey toward waking up happy every day.

Find Your Voice: Wisdom from Rachel

Two things happened recently to cause a major shift in my thinking. First, I was feeling unappreciated at work till I decided to make a case to my boss for why I deserved a higher salary. I was amazed to get an even bigger raise than I'd hoped.

Second, I'd been feeling indignant about doing all the caretaking for my sick mother while my sister, hundreds of miles away, did nothing. But when I told my sister how I felt, she was happy to pitch in and hire someone to help me. If I hadn't spoken up, I'd still be feeling victimized.

Rachel's best advice: Articulate what you want. You may not get everything you're looking for, but you'll likely get something and you'll feel stronger. Asking may feel risky, but you'll never hear "Yes!" if you don't pose the question.

Build Your EQ: Wisdom from Micky

I've discovered that a person's IQ (intelligence quotient) isn't nearly as important as their EQ (emotional intelligence quotient). Most of us who are recovering from addictions are highly intelligent people but, clearly, our intellect didn't keep us from making poor choices and messing up our lives.

I've found I'm better off if I get out of my head and work more from the heart and gut. That's where emotional intelligence comes in. Your EQ measures how well you manage your emotions, relate to others, and are true to yourself.

Micky's best advice: You can increase your emotional intelligence by aligning your instincts, emotions, and thoughts in ways that increase your self-awareness. In *It's Not How Smart You Are: It's How You Are Smart,* Jeanne Anne Craig describes ways to increase your emotional intelligence:

- Be an education junky. Make a special effort to learn things not directly related to your job or usual field of interest.
- Find "pacers"—people whose emotional intelligence is more highly developed than yours. They'll help you stretch yourself.
- Do neurobics—activities that are unusual for you, such as driving with mittens on or brushing your teeth with your non-dominant hand. They'll help create new circuits in your brain.
- Accept criticism for the gift that it is.
- Set small goals for yourself and make sure you fulfill them. If you decide to exercise for half an hour and feel like quitting after ten minutes, keep going till you meet your pre-planned goal. Then, when you face a large goal, you can tell yourself, "Remember all those times you kept going when you wanted to quit? You can do this!"
- Be willing to tolerate chaos and uncertainty. The Dalai Lama says that when everything seems to be going wrong at once, something wonderful is coming into being. When you feel uncomfortable trying something new, rejoice. Your new high-EQ self is being born.

Consider the Power of Negative Thinking: Wisdom from Warren

I'm what psychologists call a defensive pessimist. You keep hearing how important it is to be optimistic, but research shows that a positive-thinking strategy can be counter-productive for someone like me, who tends to worry a lot. I'm better off channeling my jitters into planning for the worst. After I've thought through all the possible bad outcomes and prepared for them, I'm more able to relax.

Optimists have an entirely different approach. They manage their anxiety by putting it aside and not focusing on it. Both tactics are valid, but you have to match the method to your personality type. If you're pessimistic by nature, like I am, it only makes you more upset if you try to deny your concerns.

It's important to accept defensive pessimists and not try to turn them into optimists. First of all, it won't happen, because you can't change someone's basic personality. Also, it's helpful to have us around because we introduce a healthy dose of reality into every situation.

You can be a defensive pessimist and still be hopeful about the future if you confront your anxiety and use it to improve yourself and the world. That's what I'm trying to do.

Warren's best advice: Don't blindly accept the advice you're given. In recovery, we're bombarded by platitudes like, "Always be positive." Maybe such truisms are right for you, but maybe not. What's best for you will be different from everyone else, because you're unique. Listen to the guidance you're offered, try it out, see if it fits, and listen to your heart.

7

MAKE ROOM FOR MIRACLES: MARILYN'S STORY

Marilyn and the author are close friends who met early in their recoveries. Marilyn quit drinking in 1983 and began an odyssey of self-discovery that continues today. In this chapter, she shares her hard-won keys to serenity and fulfillment.

Author's Note:

I met Marilyn at the first Women for Sobriety meeting I attended, where her warmth and caring shone through. We've been friends ever since and it's been an education to watch her transform herself.

When we met, she was as full of fears and self-doubts as I was. We worked hard to improve ourselves, doing exercises from self-help books, taking classes, reading widely about various belief systems, and discussing what we learned.

A few years younger than me, Marilyn was a year ahead in sobriety, and if you believed in past lives (and we liked to keep our minds open), you would call her an "old soul." I always had the feeling she'd lived many more lifetimes than I had. Because we have so many traits in common, and because I admire and love her, I learned to value those traits—like loyalty, sensitivity, kindness, and compassion—in myself.

Like me, she wore glasses and had brown, flyaway hair and green eyes that squinted nearly shut when she smiled. In the years to come, people would sometimes ask if we were sisters. "Soul sisters," we would reply. Or "Virgo sisters," since our birthdays were just a few days apart and we shared the Virgo sign.

Her wry sense of humor buoyed me up. Funny and irreverent, she seemed the embodiment of the adage that angels can fly because they take themselves lightly.

We both had "busy third eyes," as Marilyn put it—always seeking out new ways of looking at things. Because of our lonely childhoods, we were comfortable living in our imaginations.

We shared a love of books, words, art, and ethnic food, the spicier the better. Our tastes were so similar that the "drug of choice" for us both had been Carlo Rossi Chablis, which, in our drinking days, we would bring home in gallon jugs.

While not religious, Marilyn has a strong faith, which she has synthesized into everything she does. She doesn't simply espouse principles like justice, equality, and reverence for all living things, she assimilates them into her actions. She personifies her ideals, becoming a vegetarian because she feels that's best for our planet—and also, of course, best for the animals. More than just believing in a philosophy of service, mindfulness, and friendship, she lives and breathes it.

It was Marilyn who taught me to say no to things—even fun things—if they weren't what I wanted at the moment. Once, when I was wrestling with the idea of going to a party the following weekend, I dreamed of Marilyn sitting on her fluffy bed with a cat in her lap. With the insight from that dream—direct from Marilyn—I stayed home from the party and, instead, went to bed with a good book.

Although I can't say for sure why Marilyn and I have stayed sober for twenty-nine (for her) and twenty-eight years (for me) while many of our friends haven't, I believe one reason is that we never stop working on learning who we are and how we can put our strengths to best use in the world.

There's a theory that recovering addicts go through six stages, with only a very few reaching the final, sixth stage of enlightenment. Marilyn is the only person I know who has reached that highest step.

In *Many Roads, One Journey,* **Charlotte Davis Kasl** describes those six levels of recovery. Stage 1 is the innocent stage, in which people blindly do what they're told. In Stage 2, they "work the program" in a literal, single-minded way. In Stage 3, they reach out to others. It's in Stage 4 that they start asking questions about what's right for them. Stage 5 is an integrated version of Stage 4, in which people bring all parts of their life into alignment with their core beliefs. In the sixth stage, they attain wisdom. They're able to draw insights from different philosophies and incorporate them into their life.

Marilyn is the epitome of that utmost step. She knows who she is and what her values are. That knowledge is part of an inner compass that guides her every moment. She has attained an amazing level of peace, accepting herself and the world with humor and compassion. For her, living and believing have become one.

Here is her story.

—J.M.

✯ ✯ ✯

If I could tell you just one thing, it would be this: There's a place for you in this world.

I know because, for the longest time, I wondered if there was a place for me, somewhere I could feel safe to be myself.

When I was growing up, with a mentally ill mother, an alcoholic father, and three brothers who were valued because they were male, being me was lonely and scary. It was a traumatic childhood because I had no one I could trust to help or console me. As the oldest, I ended up doing much of the caretaking.

The deepest parts of me felt unacceptable, so I hid them away. I learned early that vulnerability, sensitivity, and empathy were mocked and scorned. I was called overly dramatic, high-strung, hyper-sensitive, self-centered, and too imaginative. I was told to toughen up and quit being such a crybaby.

Yet I knew those tender feelings were the realest thing about me, so I couldn't throw them away. Instead, I put them in a midnight-blue, velvet-lined, wooden box with a top carved with animals and birds and flowers that shape-shifted as needed. I carefully bundled that box in a rainbow-colored silk scarf. Then I wrapped that in a plain, brown, boring grocery bag. So if someone rifled through the layers of my former selves and got to the back of that long dark closet, they would be fooled by the plainness in which I hid my treasure box and give up and go away. Not even the cleverest of thieves and thugs would ever find it.

Years later, when I'd left home and was able to pull that box out of the closet, it wasn't dusty at all. I'd caressed it and cleaned it in my mind so many times over the years, whispering to it, "Just wait. The time will come when I can bring you out and you can take your rightful place in the world."

When I opened it, every single treasure was as sparkling and pristine and magical as the day I put it away. That box in which I'd stored all my feelings held my soul, my real self, and after I opened it again, I could begin putting that tender self out into the world.

It wasn't easy, because I had no practice in revealing myself to others. I think my drinking was a way to smooth that process. It was a very poor choice, and it did the opposite of what I intended, erecting barriers between me and others, between me and the world, between me and my self.

*My grandmother told me,
"Never hide your green hair—
They can see it anyway."*
—Angeles Arrien

✳ ✳ ✳

I have so few memories of myself as a child. I think I started out with a joyful spirit, but it got squashed. To my mother, who grew up on a Wisconsin farm, hard work was the most important thing. She was from a conservative sect of the Lutheran Church, so anything like drawing, reading, or putting on plays was considered foolishness.

Mom was severely bipolar (a condition people used to call manic-depression because it results in extreme mood swings from manic highs to depressive lows). She was sometimes so depressed that she would stay in bed all day and cry. Some days I'd come home from school and she wouldn't know who I was. Once I came home to find her walking around the house with a noose around her neck.

She was in and out of mental hospitals all through my childhood. Her depressions and manias colored everything.

We lived in Racine, a small manufacturing town in southeastern Wisconsin. My dad, a factory worker, was an alcoholic who drank every day, so he didn't provide much sense of security for us kids, either.

When Ted Kennedy died in 2009, his son described how he fell while skiing and couldn't get up. He told his dad, "I can't do it," and his dad said, "You *can* do it, and I will *help* you do it."

Those words amazed me. I thought: That's what I missed—that assurance that someone would be there to help. My parents were incapable of giving support. There was no ill intent, but they had a hard enough time dealing with their own lives.

I always frustrated my mother, even when I was a little girl. When I received a new doll as a gift, she'd suggest throwing away an old one. "No, no," I'd sob, "that's my blind doll. She can't see without my help. Not that one, Mommy, that's my crippled doll. Without her arm she can't feed herself and she has trouble walking without shoes."

I cried myself to sleep the night I got a new bed, heartbroken that my old bed was torn apart in the scary basement.

I graduated to stray animals, none of whom was allowed to stay, no matter how many times they followed me home.

It seems no matter what incarnation I am, I continue to be challenged with attachment. Just ask the purple plastic whale I dug out of a snowbank or the polka-dotted plastic frog whose head injury was so severe I violated my three-day rule (no bringing home strays of any kind for three days) and picked her up out of the bookstore parking lot. I like to think they're happier with me than in their former lives.

> *Everything I've ever let go of has claw marks on it.*
> —Michael Peake

✭ ✭ ✭

As an adolescent, I had terrible menstrual cramps. The doctors tried everything, but nothing helped. Then a doctor started giving me brandy, and it was the one thing that soothed the pain.

So, from the beginning, I saw alcohol as a miracle pain reliever. I used it only as medicine until I started college, but then I found that it could ease my emotional, social, and psychic pain as well as my physical distress.

Going to college was a huge step for me. My parents didn't want any of us kids to rise above our family's working-class station. We should be satisfied with factory jobs, not think about educating ourselves.

But school was the one thing I was good at, the only place I got any praise or encouragement. My teachers said enough positive things about me and offered me enough support that I gathered my courage and enrolled at the University of Wisconsin Extension in Racine while continuing to live at home.

It was 1966, a tumultuous, challenging time, and the campus was filled with excitement and new ideas. I was drawn to the civil rights movement, horrified by discrimination against people because of the color of their skin. Since kindergarten I'd gone to school with black and Mexican kids whose fathers, like mine, worked in factories. This was a cause dear to my heart.

I wasn't aware of the underlying racism in my own neighborhood and family. When Martin Luther King, Jr., was assassinated, I participated in a march from a black church to downtown Racine. My father heard that I'd linked arms with people of color and was so enraged that I had to leave home to protect myself from physical violence. A family for whom I did childcare at the college took me in for two months, then helped me set up in an efficiency apartment near campus. My parents disowned me and forbade me to see my brothers.

That's when I started using alcohol to cover my pain. I tried marijuana, but the hallucinogenic effects reminded me too much of witnessing my mother's psychotic breaks.

In the fall of 1968, I moved to Madison to escape the scrutiny and small-town gossip of Racine. An old friend from Racine lived in Madison with three roommates, and I slept on their living room floor. Until I found a job, I wrote term papers for money so I could buy flats of unmarked, dented cans of fruits and vegetables to eat.

I bought wine with money from collecting returnable glass bottles and aluminum cans. That's how I coped.

✯ ✯ ✯

Being away from my family gave me the chance to live according to my own beliefs instead of the ones my parents imposed on me. Soon after moving to Madison, I gave up meat, because of my love of animals. One of the deciding moments in my life was seeing chickens slaughtered on my grandma's farm when I was nine years old. I probably would have become a vegetarian then, if I could have, but my parents would never have permitted it.

But moving to Madison also deepened my many anxieties and insecurities. Alcohol tamed those demons and made them bearable. It was a magic potion. Or so it seemed.

> *Leaving home in a sense involves a kind of second birth in which we give birth to ourselves.*
> —Robert Neelly Bellah

✯ ✯ ✯

I'd received the strong message from my family and the culture: Boys are powerful and have important careers, unlike girls. That message was so ingrained in me that I couldn't escape it. I believe that's why I never finished college.

During my first years in Madison, I was in and out of college, a semester here and there, working part-time for the state and as a waitress. I was a lost soul wandering from major to major—sociology, social work, child development, botany, and probably others I've forgotten.

Finally I dropped out of college for good and got a state job keeping the records needed by social services to pay welfare benefits. It didn't pay a lot, but the job suited me. I'm detail-oriented, and I appreciated the security of a government job.

When I got my own apartment, I became famous as a bed and breakfast. I once tallied up between twenty and thirty roommates I let move in with me during this period (not counting the animals), including: my former boyfriend, his new pregnant wife and two kids; Jim, the man everyone thought I would marry, who came out as gay a few years into our relationship; his partner, Bob; a homeless couple whose names I've forgotten; and the former boyfriend of a former roommate who had one semester of grad school left and whom I finally had to kick out three years later because he wouldn't leave on his own.

Saying no, setting boundaries, considering my own wants and needs—all those things were completely foreign to me. Like when I was growing up in a chaotic home, I yearned to make everyone happy.

> *Some people choose suicide. Some choose alcohol.*
> —Anon.

✯ ✯ ✯

As the years passed, alcohol lost its magic properties and, rather than enlarging the world around me, began to shrink it. My fears and anxieties became overwhelming. The goblins that alcohol had once subdued hurtled out of control.

When the bedlam became unbearable, I looked for a therapist and was lucky enough to find a kind woman who helped me see how I was sabotaging myself by drinking. After months of therapy, it became clear that I needed to get sober if I were to have any kind of peace in my life.

The very idea of giving up drinking was terrifying. I'd been using alcohol for so long—nearly two decades by this time—to cover so many painful feelings, I was petrified to think what would appear once I was unmasked.

My therapist advised me to go to Alcoholics Anonymous, and I agreed to give it a try. But that AA meeting was like one of Dante's inner rings of hell. The room was filled with men, all smoking and trying to outdo each other with macho drinking stories. I couldn't identify with anyone there.

I was also alienated by all the talk about God. I remember someone saying, "God doesn't have to be up in the sky. God can be anything you want. God can be a coffeepot." I thought, "Well, I don't want God to be a coffeepot."

Afterwards, I said to myself, "I would rather die in a gutter than go to another AA meeting."

Luckily, I heard about Women for Sobriety, and I started going to those meetings. I know AA is a lifeline for many people, and I don't want to denigrate it. It just wasn't for me. I'm so fortunate that I was living in a city that had alternatives.

At Women for Sobriety, I found many kindred souls. Instead of drinking stories, we revealed our hopes and dreams as we supported each other gently through our troubles.

We started using a deck of Motherpeace cards along with the book *Motherpeace*, which explained each card's meaning. Motherpeace is based on tarot cards, but it's much more positive. It's impossible to get negative cards, although they do nudge you toward making constructive changes.

The cards acted, I thought, like a Rorschach test. Like people who discussed what they saw in ink blots, we used the cards as springboards to talk about ourselves.

One of the cards I drew that first non-drinking spring was the Star card. It softly urged me to do something nurturing and self-loving, such as getting into a hot tub, sauna, or bath. It suggested I might take a new, special, spiritual name—perhaps the name of my favorite flower—as in the Navaho Changing Woman ceremony.

I'm fond of all flowers and couldn't pick a favorite, but irises were in bloom and I admired them every day, so I chose Iris as my spiritual name. I took some fresh irises into my bath that night and thought about the way they and I were part of the same life force. It was hard for me at that time to feel beautiful, as the Star card counseled, but I did feel a new kind of opening inside, which made the bath special. That's what life is, really—making as many moments special as you possibly can.

All of us in the group enjoyed using tools like these to open our intuitive sides. We appreciated the way the cards freed us up and made it easier to share painful things.

But when a new woman joined the group and was uncomfortable with our practice, calling it "black magic," a few of us left and started our own, smaller group. It's not that we took our ritual too seriously. Just the opposite: we preferred playing with the cards and seeing where they might lead us. Those of us who started our new "Motherpeace" group, however, were annoyed to be labeled witches when all we wanted was to experiment with new ways of viewing things.

✫ ✫ ✫

One of my fears when I quit drinking was that my friends wouldn't think I was funny anymore. Luckily, that worry turned out to be baseless. I could still make my friends laugh.

But my foreboding about all the buried feelings rising up to haunt me was well-founded. Life became a roller coaster of emotions from one hour or minute to the next. I started having horrible, incapacitating panic attacks. My heart raced so fast and pounded so hard I felt like I was having a heart attack. Sometimes I was sure I was going to die.

> *Anxiety is the dread of our own daring.*
> —Paul Goodman

My therapist knew I had a strong spiritual side, although I didn't believe in a traditional God. She taught me to say, when I felt a panic attack coming on, "I give thanks for help unknown that is already on the way."

She also helped me learn to be a friend to myself—gently reassuring and comforting myself. She encouraged me to become not happy with who I was, because that was asking too much at the time, but supportive of myself. She advised me to do what good parents do for their children—talking them through hard things, reassuring them that they're doing okay and that things will get better.

Each week, she gave me "homework." One of her assignments was to spend the week with my head up, taking in everything around me, looking people in the eyes, seeing, not looking down and away. That was hard, but it slowly became a habit, and I found I felt better about myself as a result.

During that time, I focused on ways to counter tension, because I couldn't make progress on changing myself if I was too frazzled. There are two ways to cope with stress, my therapist explained. The first is to do nothing except relax and let go. The second is to do something—work on a project, plan for the future, accomplish something.

I was pretty good at the second, more active solution. Much harder was doing nothing. Whenever I tried to escape anxiety through relaxation, I heard my parents' voices calling me lazy.

My new Women for Sobriety friends helped me counter those voices. Since many of them had similar problems with stress, we fortified each other. In a way, we gave each other permission to be a little slothful—to miss a day of work, to skip exercising for a day, to take a nap after lunch instead of doing the laundry, to turn off our phones all evening.

> *How beautiful it is to do nothing, and then rest afterward.*
> —Spanish proverb

Cooking was another thing that brought me comfort. I loved asking myself: What are you hungry for right now? I would go through the possibilities in my mind until I hit on the perfect answer. Then I would start chopping, dicing, sautéing, and simmering. I enjoyed the whole experience—the crackle of vegetables, herbs, and spices in the pan, the aromas filling the kitchen, the tastes on my tongue. Cooking was an outlet for my feelings, a way to express myself, and a chance to be creative without worrying too much about the results.

A STEP ON THE JOURNEY

View cooking as therapy. Whether you're a novice or an accomplished chef, a slight change in attitude can reduce stress and deepen self-awareness. Here are some ways to use cooking as therapy:

- Vent your emotions and mitigate excess energy through kitchen activities such as cutting, chopping, scrubbing, and pounding. Smash some garlic, beat some eggs, tear the husks off ears of corn, and notice how much better you feel afterward—plus you can reward yourself with a tasty dinner.
- Think of the kitchen as a testing place. Challenge yourself with recipes and ingredients you haven't tried before.
- When you're having a difficult day, cook something comforting. Leave experimentation for times when you're ready for adventure.
- Foster your creative nature by making up new recipes or putting new twists on old ones.
- Experience failure in a safe place. The kitchen is a great environment in which to recover from the disease of perfectionism.
- Indulge the senses. The colors, shapes, and textures of food can rival any still life. The scents that engulf you when chopping garlic, cilantro, basil, or other herbs are the most natural form of aroma therapy.

—adapted from *Cooking as Therapy* by Louis Parrish

– J.M.

✧ ✧ ✧

By this time, I was in my thirties and had saved enough money to buy a townhouse. Having a home of my own felt like an absolute necessity to me, so I had slowly accumulated enough money to make that dream come true. I lived a very frugal lifestyle, which made it possible for me to save enough for a down payment.

Shortly before I bought my house, my boyfriend Jim told me he was gay and in love with a man named Bob. For some reason I let them both move into the new place with me. As I may have mentioned, I've always had a hard time letting go of things.

Living with Jim and Bob was harrowing. I found myself acting as a mediator between them when they were arguing, which was often. I did hear faint echoes of the peacemaking role I'd taken in my family of origin. It seemed to be a role I couldn't relinquish.

MAKE ROOM FOR MIRACLES: MARILYN'S STORY

The constants in my life, the things that kept me from going berserk, were my meetings with my therapist and my Women for Sobriety friends. And laughter. I made it a point to laugh every day.

When I couldn't get to a meeting and had no one to talk to, I spoke to myself in my journal. Writing helped me clarify my childhood and work through the pain of it. I realized that my family members and I had loved one another in our own ways, with all our shortcomings and limitations.

Jill, my good friend from Women for Sobriety, and I did a lot of reading, especially books with exercises we could complete to learn more about ourselves. We would do the exercises and then get together to share our answers and talk about the issues they brought up for us. This was the best kind of therapy.

An exercise that had an especially powerful impact was one that asked us to list our parents' good qualities. As I made my list, I had an epiphany that reshaped my perspective. I realized that, through all the craziness of growing up with a mentally ill mother and alcoholic father, the one saving grace—the life raft that allowed me to survive—was my mom's sense of humor. If you learn to laugh at yourself, she used to say, you'll never run out of good material.

She was very funny, and nothing was too dark or serious that we couldn't joke about it, even death. On her gravestone, she said she wanted the epitaph "I like to dance, but I'm no floozy."

I decided the epitaph I wanted was "Alone at last."

Many of my mother's humorous quips had kernels of truth at their core. For example: "Your mind is a mansion, and most people only live in the lobby." The older I get, the more wisdom I find in remarks like that one, and the more they make me smile.

As someone said—I think it was Carol Burnett—"Comedy is tragedy—plus time." That saving sense of humor has carried me through many a storm. Without it, I would never have made it through.

A person without a sense of humor is like a wagon without springs—jolted by every pebble in the road.
　—Henry Ward Beecher

❈ ❈ ❈

I also remember completing an exercise about building a new family. I was learning that I could create my own family through my friends. In addition, this exercise advised putting together an imaginary group of people I'd like to have in my family.

That part of the exercise was fun for me. The second part was harder. I had to imagine why those new family members admired *me*.

It turned out to be a helpful activity, giving me a new way of seeing myself. Here's who I chose and what I imagined them telling me about myself:

MY FAMILY MEMBERS AND WHAT THEY ADMIRE ABOUT ME:

1. Morgaine le Fay (King Arthur's half-sister and a powerful healer in the Arthurian legend): "It's difficult having a druid soul in a Christian world, isn't it? I'm pleased that you're seeking your true essence even though it may not be in step with the society around you. You have the makings of a priestess; you're interested in healing, both psychic and physical, in natural ways, and have an abiding respect for the earth. Your reawakened interest in flowers and gardening will keep you grounded and centered, as will your love of cooking."

2. Calamity Jane (an adventurous woman in the Old West who wore men's clothing, performed trick shooting in the Wild West show, nursed victims of smallpox, and was a chronic alcoholic): "What I admire about you is that you were able to quit drinking and change your life as a result. I never managed it for myself so I appreciate the difficulty of the feat. Your independence and resourcefulness are just beginning to bloom. You are forging ahead, taking risks in a more civilized, socialized way than I did, but it's pioneering nonetheless. I sure can identify with your shyness among strangers. It's okay."

3. Eleanor Roosevelt (First Lady of the U.S., who supported the New Deal policies of her husband, Franklin Roosevelt, and was an advocate for civil rights): "We've both suffered from being adult children of alcoholics and from not being what our partners needed from us. Your political, civic, social consciousness is strong. You've used your caring for the disenfranchised to protest inequality and work with your friends in feminism. Continue to use your caring for the betterment of the world. Learn from me to overcome stage fright and become more vocal in your involvement."

4. Lassie (a fictional collie in the book *Lassie Come Home* and in a number of movies based on the book): "You have the makings of a good dog. You're fiercely loyal to your friends. You're intelligent enough to follow the good rules and to ignore or disobey the bad ones. You watch over your friends and try to protect them from harm. You speak up when someone threatens those you love. You dislike people who try to dominate others. Your instincts in such areas are good. You like to go for walks and always find your way back home."

I still have the paper on which I created this family. I have to say that I'd probably pick the same people today with a couple of additions. I would add Buddhist teacher Pema Chodron, whose spiritual philosophy is closest to mine, and cellist Yo-Yo Ma for his creation of beautiful music, his graciousness toward his fellow musicians, his curiosity, and his humility. (And I need at least one man in my family.)

A STEP ON THE JOURNEY

Create a virtual family for yourself. Choose anyone—living or dead, someone real or a character from a book, TV, or the movies—whose qualities you appreciate and would like to emulate. Now, for each one, write down a message from them to you. Have each one tell you what they value about you and why they're glad to be in your family.

Keep your new family members in your mind to turn to when you want advice or comfort. You can continue to add people throughout your life, making your family as big as you want.

Jot down your ideas here:_____
_____
_____
_____

– J.M.

✰ ✰ ✰

A year after we started our informal "Motherpeace Women for Sobriety" group, everyone drifted away except Jill and me, so the two of us kept meeting on our own. We made it a point to meet frequently to talk, take walks, eat spicy food, explore art fairs, and discuss books.

We often referred to a concept Lillian Rubin had introduced to us in her book *Just Friends*—the idea that there are friends of the road and friends of the heart. The others in our group had been friends of the road—women who had touched our lives and then traveled on. Jill and I were friends of the heart. We knew that no matter what happened, we always would be.

Another book we discussed was *Goddesses in Everywoman* by Jean Shinoda Bolen, which describes the archetypal goddesses or personalities portrayed in ancient mythology. In her book, Bolen urges us to tap into these archetypes to become heroines of our own life stories.

The goddess I identified with most was Hestia, the goddess of hearth, home, and temple—the solitary seeker of sanctuary, the maiden aunt. That's me to a T. Hearth-keepers stay in the background, and that's where I'm happiest.

When Bolen talks about Hestia, she might be detailing my own life. Hestia women, she says, tend to come from traumatic households with tyrannical fathers and depressed mothers where the needs of the children are discounted and individual expression is swallowed up by the father's need to dominate. Such children feel as alienated from their siblings as from their parents. They truly are different, and they survive by turning inward, becoming as unobtrusive as possible, and cultivating solitude even in the midst of others.

As adults, we Hestia women are drawn more toward a spiritual than a romantic life. We try to avoid large gatherings, which make us feel painfully awkward. But we're faithful friends who express our concern for others through thoughtful acts.

Just describing Hestia makes me feel better about myself. Those qualities that often make me feel inadequate and inept—they're goddess qualities.

What struck me as I read about the mythical goddesses was how, for each one, their greatest strength was, at the same time, their greatest weakness. It's a matter of cultivating those strengths and becoming adept at using them for the best possible good. For me, my introverted tendencies could isolate me if I wasn't careful, but they could also help me find the inner self that I'd kept hidden for so long.

✽ ✽ ✽

Three years into my recovery, Jim and Bob, the gay couple, were still living in my house with me. Children of alcoholics have a special problem with boundaries, and I'm no exception. But this was the biggest boundary crisis I'd ever had. I knew it was ludicrous to let Jim stay with me even after he'd come out as gay and paired up with Bob, yet I couldn't find my way out of the situation.

Jill reminded me what Bolen said in *Goddesses in Everywoman* about my inner goddess: A Hestia woman needs to acquire assertiveness to take care of herself in the world. With Hestia as my guide, I mustered the courage to tell Jim and Bob they had to leave. I let them know I cared about them and wanted them in my life. Using "I" rather than "you" statements, I told them how the situation was affecting me: "I'm finding I don't have as much alone time as I need. I've learned that quiet time is central to my well-being. If I don't have it, I can't function properly. I have the feeling I'm meant to live by myself."

Jim and Bob were fine with it. There was none of the drama I'd feared. They said they'd be out in a week, and I told them to take all the time they wanted. The relief I felt was incalculable, even though it was mixed with loss, guilt, and sorrow.

Difficult as that experience was, it was a durable foundation for the years to come and the boundary issues I faced over and over again. It was valuable training for being able to say, "This is not right for me," or "That wouldn't be in my best interests, so I'm going to say no."

✽ ✽ ✽

A week after I asked them to move out, Jim and Bob said good-bye and told me they were moving to New Mexico. That was quite a jolt. I'd expected them to move somewhere in the same neighborhood, or maybe across town, but not all the way across the country. I felt terrible about it.

For weeks after they left, I cried every day. But this crying was a little different from the crying I'd been doing on and off for years. I had a feeling that eventually there would be an end to it.

I started a ritual of calling Jim and Bob once a week, and they called me often, too. I saw that, while they were out of the house, they weren't out of my life. We would always have a connection. I could actually love them better from a thousand miles away.

We were able to joke about it. I would ask, "Seriously, did you have to move all the way to New Mexico?" and they would make some kind of jokey answer. I began to realize that my asking them to leave wasn't only a watershed moment for me. It also released them to follow a dream they'd had for a long time.

As the months went by, I discovered I was far happier and more at peace on my own. When I was living with someone, I tended to lose sight of myself and my needs. That's the adult child of an alcoholic in me, the "caretaker" I am to my core. I was always too quick to abandon myself. Of course, even a caretaker-type person can learn not to do that, but it's hard.

Also, because I'm an introvert, I always needed more time to myself than an extrovert would. Living alone assured that I didn't have to fight for that time.

My animal companions were enough for me. Ever since I'd left my childhood home, I'd always had a dog, a cat, or sometimes both at once. I can't imagine not having an animal companion. That's how I think of them—as companions. They have such accepting, nonjudgmental natures. There's a purity to that connection that gets muddled in human relationships.

And there's nothing like coming home and having someone so glad to see you.

I want to live with animals: They do not lie awake in the dark and weep for their sins.
—Walt Whitman

When I first got sober, I had two dogs and a cat. They were all strays I'd brought home because they had no one to love them—which made me love them all the more fiercely. Cindy was a Sheltie, Gerta was a giant Schnauzer-Airedale mix, and Moses was a brown-and-white tabby cat. He was very shy, maybe because the female dogs took up so much room.

Although I'm fond of all animals and don't like to say I prefer any one species, there's something about dogs. What a gift to be in the presence of such an accepting, forgiving being when one is struggling to accept and forgive oneself.

Dogs know what friendship is all about. I second the notion of one of my favorite philosophers, Gilda Radner, who considered dogs "the role model for being alive."

The greatest pleasure of a dog is that you may make a fool of yourself with him, and not only will he not scold you, but he will make a fool of himself, too.
—Samuel Butler

❈ ❈ ❈

After Jim and Bob left, I never had another serious romantic relationship, and it was something I never missed. I felt more complete, more myself, living on my own than I ever felt when I tried to make myself fit with a romantic partner.

My friends (both human and animal) fulfilled me. I had a wide constellation of friends, which was a good thing, because I've always felt you need all kinds of beings in your life. You need people you have to clean your house for, and you need those for whom you don't need to bother.

A STEP ON THE JOURNEY

Build friendship into your life. Friends are crucial to your well-being. Luckily, friendship is an art you can learn. Here are a few tips:

- You need to practice friendship. It doesn't happen all at once. Start by working on acquaintanceship. Friendship takes time, but acquaintances lead to friends. Make overtures. Invite an acquaintance to coffee. Join clubs, and make an effort to get to know people there. You need to do this active building work to forge the basis for friendship.
- Friendship is about honesty. Your friends like you because you share your true feelings and let them do the same. Friendship can't grow unless you risk being candid and vulnerable with another person.
- Make a list of your "really close friends," "close friends," and "people who may become good friends." Write a few lines describing what you can expect from each one. Can you call them whenever you need to talk? Can you count on them in a crisis? Do they always do what they say, or do they tend to cancel plans? Don't judge them but accept them as they are. There are many valid reasons why some friends can't be as available to you as others. If you know what to anticipate, you won't be disappointed, frustrated, or angry if they can't give you what you want. Appreciate them for what they offer.
- Remember, there are seasons in friendship. When people first get married, have a child, start a new job, or go through a crisis, they may become less available. Keep in touch without demanding more than they're able to provide, and the friendship may blossom again in a new season.
- Be open to friendship with many different kinds of people. Those with beliefs and attitudes different from yours can add valuable new dimensions to your life.

– J.M.

✣ ✣ ✣

My friend Jill and I explored our inner selves by taking personality tests, such as the Myers-Briggs Type Indicator (you can take the test yourself at Keirsey.com). The personality that emerged for me was "the Quester" or spiritual seeker. Such types apparently make excellent monks.

Actually, I would probably do well in a monastery. I crave stillness, solitude, and time for contemplation. Embracing my "monkness" meant no longer feeling odd about my quiet life.

One does not become enlightened by imagining figures of light but by making the darkness conscious.
    —Carl Jung

MOMENT OF TRUTH

How to find balance in your life:
- Be sure your life is balanced among four spheres: (1) Love. Learn to love yourself and give of yourself to others. Try not to focus all your love on a partner or other loved one. If you have a spectrum of folks to love, you won't demand too much of one person. (2) Work. Do work that uses your talents and strengths. Be passionate about what you do, but don't let it overwhelm other spheres of your life. (3) Significance. Connect to something greater than yourself, and take continual steps toward enhancing that connection. (4) Legacy. Decide what positive change you want to leave behind after you die. Do something every day that will add to that legacy.
- Be flexible, ready to change directions when conditions warrant. That may mean switching from linear thinking to more creative, holistic thought or balancing your reasoning side with the feeling and sensing realms.
- Look to the wisdom of yoga, which is all about finding balance—between inhaling and exhaling, pointing and flexing your feet, leaning backward and forward, paying attention and stilling the mind. Yoga teaches us to stretch ourselves a little more each time but never force it—and this guidance is as true for mind, spirit, and emotions as for body.
- Occasionally switch character, and go against your nature. If you're an introvert, try reaching out to others. If you're an extrovert, experiment with spending time alone. If you usually arrive late, come early, and vice versa. After trying this exercise for a day, write about how it made you feel and what you learned. _____
_____
_____

– J.M.

Balance was what I was reaching for—that counterweight between depression and mania, solitude and companionship, passion and detachment, the avoidance of extremes the Buddha so often advised. It was about yin and yang—honoring both sides of my nature. Our culture is slanted more toward the yang, masculine energy, than the yin, or feminine, yet it's the feminine that most encourages wholeness and healing. Accepting my feminine side meant paying attention to friendships, feelings, softness. But I also needed to be attuned to the yang—the reasoning, doing, acting part of myself. I had to temper the heart and spirit with the thinking brain.

While I weighed reason and emotion before making decisions, in the end I always went with my instinct, that small inner voice that warned me when something wasn't right. It was a matter of listening to my whole self—my body, intellect, and emotions—as well as everything in my environment, and then letting my subconscious merge all the pieces together. Intuition was an everyday kind of miracle that I grew to trust.

> ## TURNING POINT
>
> **Hone your intuition.** In "Intuition in Decision-Making" (*Nonprofit World*, Vol. 25, No. 4, snpo.org), Erika Oliver (erikaoliver.com) offers these steps to strengthening your intuition:
>
> 1. **Trust your gut feelings.** Realize that they come from your ability to compile many sources of information without consciously knowing how you're reaching your conclusion.
>
> 2. **When you need to make a decision,** visualize a spectrum of solutions in as much detail as possible. Notice how your body responds to each possibility. Does the idea relax you, or does it cause your body to tighten up with resistance?
>
> 3. **Practice.** Think of ways to test your intuition. For example, while you're in the checkout line at the grocery store, guess how much the bill will be. You may be amazed at how close you come to the actual amount, and your guesses will get better the more you practice. It may seem otherworldly, but it's not. It's a consequence of the way your intuition lets you speed-sort information. Your brain is processing, comparing, and counting all the time. Listening to that inner voice and trusting what you hear will bring remarkably accurate information.
>
> – *J.M.*

Happiness is not a matter of intensity but of balance, order, rhythm, and harmony.
    —Thomas Merton

I found that when my mind, body, and emotions got disconnected, that's when there was illness, whether mental, spiritual, or physical. The more I focused on connecting all those parts of myself, the healthier I was.

Self-care was one of my hardest lessons. I tended to spend time either working or taking care of other people's needs. But I realized I couldn't help anyone if I didn't care for myself first.

I created a list of things I could do to make myself feel cared for. They included writing in my journal, getting massages, napping in the afternoon, and taking time to meditate, read, and listen to music. I bought a bath pillow that fastened onto my tub so I could lean back and daydream—one of my favorite things to do.

A STEP ON THE JOURNEY

Give yourself the love and care you need. Take care of yourself with some little luxuries. Don't call them guilty pleasures, because there's no reason to feel guilty about taking time for yourself. Some counselors and clients at Connections suggested these creative indulgences:
- Soak your feet in warm water with epsom salts.
- Pamper yourself with a hot stone massage.
- Brew a cup of antioxidant-rich green tea.
- Just one word: Chocolate!
- Curl up with a soft blanket and take a nap.
- Spray yourself with a new scent at a department store's sample perfume counter.
- Read comics.
- Spread toast with butter and cinnamon.
- Treat yourself to a facial.
- Put real whipped cream in your coffee.

Write down three things you will do for yourself today: _____
_____
_____

– J.M.

Women need real moments of solitude and self-reflection to balance out how much of ourselves we give away.
—Barbara De Angelis

Practical and skeptical by nature, I began paying more attention to my spiritual, mystical side. Spirituality was vital to me but not in the sense of going to church or adhering to any one creed. For me it meant being open to a kaleidoscope of ways of knowing the world.

As I read and explored different faiths, I found myself taking a little from each one. Since I was attracted to yoga, which is associated with Hinduism, Buddhism, and Jainism, I searched into those traditions and found much to admire. Like them, I believed in looking deep within to find my spiritual core, seeing my connectedness to everything else, and tolerating all perspectives as long as they harmed no one.

At any moment, you have a choice that either leads you closer to your spirit or further away from it.
—Thich Nhat Hanh

Because I was part of this world, I wanted to respect it by using renewable resources and being aware of what I consumed. Shopping at the farmers' market and co-op helped assure that I knew what I was buying, where it came from, and its true cost in terms of fossil fuels and environmental impact. Also, the things I bought there were unpackaged (I carried my own bag with me), so there was less trash.

It helped that I didn't drive a car. I'd never learned to drive and didn't feel I missed much. I made a point of living in neighborhoods with nearby stores so I would be self-sufficient. I kept myself in shape by walking practically everywhere.

When I had to go somewhere beyond my walking abilities, I carpooled or took public transportation. I liked riding the bus because it made me feel grounded, connected, an integral part of humanity. In an age of rootlessness, walking and taking the bus kept me tethered to my community.

Those who rode the bus in Madison tended to be disenfranchised—poor, mentally ill, challenged in many ways, not the ritziest characters in the world. Some people avoided riding the bus for that reason. But those down-and-outers didn't cease to exist when we averted our eyes. Sitting with them every day exercised my capacity for empathy, gratitude, and humility.

MOMENT OF TRUTH

Be kind to yourself and the planet. You're part of the environment and human race, so taking care of them is a good way to take care of yourself. Here are a few simple ways to do so:

- Remember the four Rs of how to treat your trash—reduce, recycle, reuse, and repurpose—and the three Rs of how to treat the planet—with respect, reverence, and responsibility. Instead of throwing out an old jar or box, for instance, you might decorate it and give it to a friend, filled with pieces of paper on which you've written memories of times you spent together. You'll reduce the quantity of stuff in the landfill, give new life to something old, and increase the amount of love in the world.
- Practice empathy. When you feel annoyed at someone cutting you off in traffic or taking forever to write a check in the checkout line, imagine being them. Maybe they've been through a trauma, are caring for sick loved ones, or are just overwhelmed. Consider how you would feel in those situations and how much you would appreciate others cutting you some slack. Once you start exercising your empathy muscle, you'll realize that it makes you feel better, act better, and become the kind of person you want to be.
- Make decisions based on ethical principles. When choosing between two options, ask: Which decision will result in the most good and least harm to the most people? Which decision fits best with the person I want to be?
- Buy products that help rather than harm the environment (those made with renewable resources, such as fast-growing bamboo rather than slow-growing hardwoods, for example).
- Show kindness to all living beings, great and small. Consider giving up some or all meat to reduce animal suffering. Start with one or two meat-free days a week. You can find vegetarian recipes on line (try vegetariantimes.com), or simply use meat substitutes (give nut burgers and tofu sausage a try).

- Consider the Buddhist idea of "right livelihood"—choosing an occupation that helps people and lets you earn an adequate amount without accumulating too much excess wealth.

What one thing could you do today that would help the planet? ________________
____
____

– J.M.

☼ ☼ ☼

After several years of sobriety, I'd become much better at managing my stress, although life did keep throwing up roadblocks to keep me on my toes. My dog Cindy had died, and Gerta and Moses were so old that I knew they wouldn't be with me much longer. It has always been in my nature to have a "back-up dog" so that when one died, I would have another in my house and wouldn't need to look for a new one while grieving the old one.

That's why I brought home a handful of dark-chocolate-colored fluff I named Casey. He was a standard poodle, a breed I'd always admired. They're gentle yet large enough to be good protectors, with soft, curly hair that's perfect for petting.

There is no psychiatrist in the world like a puppy licking your face.
—Bern Williams

☼ ☼ ☼

From the very first day, Casey brought me boundless joy, along with unimaginable exhaustion. My fairly sedate life, which I'd managed to arrange into a semblance of order, was turned inside out. Part of it was the chaos a puppy always brings, and part of it was Casey's personality. He bubbled over with energy, mischief, and *joie de vivre.*

Casey kept me laughing and helped me get in touch with my playful side. He was truly "the god of frolic" (as Henry Ward Beecher once defined a dog).

I was grateful to have Casey's ebullience to buoy me up, because my dog Gerta died the following year. She was sick for months. Finally I could tell she was no longer enjoying life, and it was time to let her go.

My veterinarian, Joanne, came to the house. I prepared a special place for Gerta, where she and I could lie together in a cluster of pillows, and I held her and whispered good-byes as Joanne gave Gerta the shot that ended her life.

Joanne was also there with me a month later when my cat Moses died. I knew I had to provide company for the young, social Casey immediately, so my new kitten, Maude, came home with me that same day.

Maude had as much energy as Casey and bounced around the house as if she had springs on her toes. Watching the two of them cavort together could dissolve me into laughter. But I also remember being seriously sleep-deprived during that time, as I trained my two new companions while continuing to work full time and trying to have a life.

During times like that, it became clear to me how desperately I needed oases of rest, peace, and stillness. I captured such moments when I could.

I knew the only way to survive this stressful time was by paring away as many responsibilities as I possibly could. That turned out to be a good chance for me to practice something that had always been one of my greatest challenges—saying no.

> *Saying no can be the ultimate self-care.*
> —Claudia Black

I remember one mid-winter Saturday when Casey and Maude were both sick, and we'd all been up most of the night together. The next morning, all I wanted was to stay home and curl up with my animal companions. I had to call and cancel a meeting I'd promised to attend as well as lunch with a friend and dinner with some acquaintances. I hated to disappoint them, but every inch of me rebelled against going out.

When I finished my phone calls, I made myself a cup of tea. How sweet it was to sit with a blanket around me, sipping my tea, Casey's head on my lap, Maude purring against my leg. The entire world breathed a sigh of relief.

> *Bed, its utter inactivity, offers a glimpse of eternity, without the drawback of being dead.*
> —Lynne Sharon Schwartz

MOMENT OF TRUTH

Learn the art of "no."
- Practice saying no. Say, "No thanks. Sorry. I can't. But thanks for thinking of me." Keep saying it till it comes easily to you.
- Be clear on your priorities. It's easier to say no if you're sure a request doesn't fit with your main goals. Be realistic about what adding one more thing to your schedule will do to your well-being.
- Pause before replying. Say, "Let me think it over and get back to you tomorrow." If the request is via email, compose your reply and read it over the next day before sending it.
- If you can think of a possible "yes," propose it. Offer another option—a way to meet both your needs. If you must say "no" to joining a board of directors, for instance, can you suggest someone else who might love the opportunity?

– J.M.

✯ ✯ ✯

Around this time, my brother Sam moved from Racine to Madison. As I helped him get settled and introduced him to the city, I could see that he looked to me as a role model, and that meant a lot to me. He was having some of the same problems with alcohol that I'd once had, and I helped him get into treatment. I was surprised to discover how much we had in common now that we were adults.

Sam and I started a regular pattern of driving back to Racine every few weeks to see our family, which brought all of us closer. I enjoyed getting to know my brother Ted's wife and children, a boy and a girl. My niece and nephew nestled into the center of my heart. Being the doting aunt was a role I was made for. Repairing my relationship with my family was a vital part of my recovery and growth.

✯ ✯ ✯

The following year, I made a new friend who worked in the same building I did. I was still keeping Wisconsin's welfare records, and Susie also worked for the state but in another department. The first time I met her I had gone into the bathroom and thrown open a stall, and she was sitting there. I was so embarrassed that I tried to avoid her after that.

But a few months later, Susie heard I was looking for someone to take care of Casey and Maude while I was on a weekend trip, and she said she'd be glad to do it for me. After that, we quickly became friends. She had a wonderful sense of humor, and we laughed often about our inauspicious meeting.

Susie was looking for a place to live, and I wanted to move to a different neighborhood. We discussed getting a place together, but I knew I didn't want to live with anyone except my animals. Then I got the idea of buying a duplex and renting half of it to Susie. She was all for it.

It took us two months to find a duplex we both liked. It was an old building, and the apartments themselves were tiny, under a thousand square feet, but there was a huge back yard, just made for dogs to run and play, and it was a few short blocks from a grocery store, theater, and several excellent restaurants. I fell in love with the leafy, quiet, old-timey neighborhood.

Shortly after we moved in, Susie began dating a guy named Jerry, they married, and he moved in with her. That was a total surprise to me. I was exceedingly glad that we each had our own half of the duplex to ourselves, although I enjoyed having her nearby. It was also handy to have a man around to fix things, as long as I didn't have to actually live with him.

Jerry helped us build another bedroom in the basement, where Molly, Susie's daughter from her first marriage, came to live. He also did most of the work when we turned the garage in our back yard into a gazebo. It was a fairytale spot, where I could lounge with a book and glass of lemonade beside me.

Susie and I planted a perennial flower garden and took care of it together. Every year, we added a few new flowers. I loved having that piece of earth to work in.

A few months later, I found the courage to take an art class (remember, my mom's religion forbade any frivolity like art, so this was a huge step). Although it felt risky, I wanted to reconnect with the creative part of me that was crushed when I was a child.

That art class opened a new world for me. Actually, it was more of an art therapy class, because it was about expressing ourselves rather than learning art technique. That was perfect, because I didn't want to worry about doing things "right," but I did want to explore new things.

I'd suppressed that part of myself so long that it was a struggle to get in touch with my "inner artist." Luckily, I had an excellent teacher. She was nonjudgmental, encouraging us to use art to free up our feelings rather than worrying about the final product. That was such a critical step for me.

One evening, our teacher asked each of us to create a picture of our greatest fear. I used shapes of things I found and traced, along with photos cut from magazines, to represent my fear of abandonment.

Then I created another picture of how I could overcome that fear. I wanted to depict the fact that I was a healthy adult who could heal the childhood parts of myself that felt cast out. I arranged photos of myself now, as a baby, and as a nine-year-old girl, along with words cut from magazines—words like hope, loyalty, and compassion—to show all I could offer those forsaken pieces of my psyche.

A STEP ON THE JOURNEY

Use art as therapy. Here are ways to use artistic expression to get in touch with your feelings, face your fears, and heal your psychic wounds.
- Listen to different kinds of music, and use paint, charcoal, or pastel chalks to show how each one makes you feel. You can do the same thing with scents. Take a whiff of cocoa, sage, lemon, or basil, and draw or paint the emotions they evoke in you.
- Take a stack of old magazines and cut out pictures and words that appeal to you. Paste them onto a piece of paper in whatever arrangement you like. When you're done, you'll have a "self-portrait" that communicates what's important to you.
- Think of someone close to you and create a piece of art, using whatever materials you like, that represents how you feel about that person.
- Draw or paint a picture with your eyes closed.
- Create a found-object collage by bringing home things you find lying around—anything from leaves and flowers to matchbooks, tinfoil, and candy wrappers—and gluing them onto paper.
- Draw (or use clay to sculpt) yourself as a god, goddess, warrior, or superhero.
- Take a picture you've drawn, and tear it up. Then use the pieces to assemble a new piece of art.
- Draw a cartoon or comic strip about something that happened to you or that you'd like to have happen.

– J.M.

✧ ✧ ✧

After that first course, in which I became less self-conscious about my artistic attempts, I continued to take classes that gave me the chance to create, mostly workshops that were just a few hours long. While creating, I kept reminding myself of something one of my teachers told me—that it was my job to do the work, not to judge it.

Art? You just do it.
—Martin Ritt

Another class I enjoyed was one on dreams. There are times when I have vivid, interesting dreams and other periods when it seems as if I'm not dreaming at all. Unfortunately, I didn't seem to be dreaming much during the time I took the course.

On the first evening of class, the teacher had us each take a letter of the alphabet, at random, from a box. We were supposed to dream about something beginning with that letter sometime during the six-week course and share that dream with others in the class. I drew a V.

As the weeks passed, the other students shared their dreams. One woman, who'd picked an A, dreamed about angels. A man who'd gotten an S dreamed of snakes. I was amazed that they'd been able to do what seemed so impossible to me.

Then, the night before our last class, I dreamed my house was full of people I didn't know. They were chatting, laughing, eating, and having a good time. I was distraught about what these strangers were doing in my house. Then one woman smiled at me, leaned in closer, and whispered in my ear, "We're visitors."

Isn't it magical, the way the mind works?

By replacing "No Way!" with "Maybe," we open the door to mystery and to magic.
—Julia Cameron

✧ ✧ ✧

I began to join other women for ceremonies to commemorate passages such as the turning of the seasons. We held many of these celebrations outside during the full moon. We would chant, pound on drums, rattle gourds, and dance under the moon and stars.

I've read that chanting unlocks some part of your brain that helps you feel part of the greater whole. I relished that feeling.

MOMENT OF TRUTH

Tap the power of rituals. You can perform rituals alone or with others. They provide a sense of continuity while honoring what's important to you. Some suggestions:
- Commemorate any beginning or ending—the winter's first snowfall, the end of a love affair, a move into a new home. Your ritual might include dancing, chanting, or singing, or be as simple as lighting a candle and saying a few words.
- Set up an altar. A space the size of a scarf or towel will do. On the cloth, arrange objects to represent the four elements that make up life on this planet, as defined by the ancient Greeks: air, earth, water, and fire. For example, you could use a feather to represent air, a stone for earth, a seashell for water, and a candle for fire. Add other things with special or symbolic meaning, such as photos of loved ones. You can meditate or pray at your altar, or use it as a comforting way to honor your deepest self and your place in the universe.
- On a date that's memorable for you (your birthday, New Year's Eve, or your sobriety anniversary, for instance), write a letter to the person you'll be next year at the same time. Then read the letter you wrote to yourself last year. This ritual will emphasize how much you're changing and growing.
- Create a morning and evening ritual for yourself. For example, you could do a few yoga moves when you get up and write in your gratitude journal before bed.
- Choose a weekly practice to calm and restore you. Once a week, for instance, you could attend a tai chi class, spend an hour in a church or other sanctuary, walk in nature, sing in a choir, or volunteer in the community.

What life passages or natural cycles are coming up that you could commemorate with a ritual? _____

What rituals could you integrate into your life every day? _____

What weekly practices appeal to you? _____

– J.M.

After a while, my attendance at group rituals slowed down, as I found it more meaningful to perform rituals by myself. On the day of the winter solstice, for example, I lit candles and played music to welcome back the light.

I also started a ritual that I followed from 5:30 to 6:30 every morning. I meditated, read something inspirational, wrote in my journal, and sent wishes out into the universe for anyone who needed a special boost of some kind. My favorite inspirational readings came from *The Book of Awakening*, which includes a quotation, affirmation, and exercise for each day of the year. I liked the way the author embraced all different philosophies. You didn't have to be religious or even believe in God to read it.

> ## TURNING POINT
>
> **Create a wish list.** When you wish for something, ask for what you want and then add "or something better, for the highest good of all concerned." Then release the outcome, and tell yourself that you'll be happy with whatever comes.
>
> You may not always get what you want, but by asking for the highest good, you open the door to receiving something even better. The universe may have more in store for you than you can dream of.
>
> Begin your wish list here: _____
> _____
> _____
>
> – J.M.

A few years later, after taking a one-on-one class from a Reiki master, I added Reiki—a spiritual healing practice that promotes physical, mental, emotional, and spiritual harmony—to my morning ritual. I began by repeating, "I am a clear and loving pathway for Reiki healing energy. I call upon Divine Spirit to encircle me with love. I ask for healing in all parts of my being, known and unknown, for the greater good of myself and the world." Then I laid my hands on my head, eyes, ears, throat, chest, stomach, and hips (the body's chakras, or energy centers).

This ritual touching reminded me to return to my body when my mind wandered. When you're traumatized as a child, you get good at leaving your body, and Reiki helped me stay grounded. I always felt better afterward in a quiet, calm way.

> *Always we hope someone else has the answer, some other place will be better, some other time it will all turn out.*
> *This is it; no one else has the answer, no other place will be better, and it has already turned out.*
> —Lao Tzu

> ## MOMENT OF TRUTH
>
> **Use your fingertips to shift your energy.** Sit in a comfortable position, and gently touch (rub or tap with your fingertips) your head, eyes, throat, chest, stomach, and hips as you say affirmations to yourself, either out loud or silently. (For affirmation ideas, see "Turning Point: Use Affirmations to Claim your Power" in Chapter 1 and "Moment of Truth: Perform a Mirror Mantra" later in this chapter.) Begin with the

top of your head and, after a few minutes, slowly move to your eyes, and so on, down your body. Combining affirmations with ritual touching will help you tap into your most positive energy.

Try this exercise now and write about how you feel when you're done: _________
____
____

– J.M.

✲ ✲ ✲

Casey, Maude, and I had settled into a routine that made us happy. I liked to walk with Casey before I left for work and again after I got home. Casey had many friends and admirers in the neighborhood, and we had to stop often to let them fuss over him. An exuberant goofball with a perpetual smile on his face, Casey lived for the attention.

Casey and Maude were well-suited and enjoyed each other's company. Nothing gave me more satisfaction than watching them play together.

When I had a chance to buy another poodle pup, I debated for a while. Things were on such an even keel I hated to add the havoc of a puppy to the mix. But my instincts told me it was the right thing to do.

I brought home the little pup I named Hannah in August. She was the opposite of Casey in every way—creamy white instead of chocolate brown, shy instead of outgoing, a serious girl rather than a brash clown.

Casey had always had a lot of illnesses. I was constantly taking him to the vet and worrying about his health. I had the feeling he wouldn't be with me much longer.

I was right. Casey died shortly after I brought Hannah home. He was only seven years old.

A friend told me that when someone dies, you can take something of your loved one inside yourself and make it part of you. I decided the part I would take of Casey was his ability to indulge himself without feeling the least bit contrite. One of my favorite memories was of how, at a Thanksgiving party one year, he ate all the caviar while no one was looking. When we confronted him later, he wagged his tail happily, refusing to waste any energy on shame or guilt.

While Casey had kept me laughing with his antics, Hannah was more quiet and timid—more like me. Caring for her helped me work through my grief over losing Casey. She brought out my mothering instincts.

✲ ✲ ✲

Those next years passed quickly, as Hannah, Maude, and I adjusted to life without Casey. There were the usual ups and downs that life throws at all of us, but I'd gotten pretty good at riding those out without losing my balance too badly. I loved so many things about my life—my friends, my house, my neighborhood, the classes I took, all the routines that gave meaning to each day.

But then everything started to go terribly wrong. I think it all began when Maude died and I brought home Ella, a tiny black kitten. A spitfire, Ella intimidated sweet, shy Hannah. My friends assured me that, in time, Hannah and Ella would become friends. I'd introduced cats into households with dogs before, and it was true that they eventually got along, but, meanwhile, struggling to make them both happy was nerve-wracking. How did I always end up trying to make peace between two creatures who seemed destined to clash?

Things were going badly at my job, too. By this time, I'd worked for the state of Wisconsin for almost thirty years. As the economy tightened, the state laid off people without hiring anyone to replace them. When those in my department left, I was expected to take up the slack. Pretty soon I was doing the work of two others in addition to my own job.

I was so frustrated I could have cried. Actually, I did cry. I didn't want to weep at work or even at home where Susie, Jerry, or Molly might hear me. My friend Sara told me I could use her office, not far from my house, in the morning before anyone was in the building, so every day I went there and sobbed.

To add to the anguish, my mother, who'd been struggling with Parkinson's disease, was growing weaker and sicker. Realizing her time with me was coming to an end, I was taking the bus to Racine every weekend to see her.

One morning, I stopped at a bookstore to find something to read on the bus. My eye was drawn to a photo of Pema Chodron on the cover of her book, *Awakening Lovingkindness*. She had a kind face and looked like she might understand me.

I bought the book and started reading it right away. Her words were plain and sincere, her message simple: No matter how overwhelming life is, start where you are. I thought to myself: I can do that! Another one of her messages was a little harder, but it, too, was attainable: Make friends with yourself, every part of you, even (or perhaps especially) the parts you don't like.

On bad days, I'm okay. On good days, I'm also okay.
—Pema Chodron

That book, with its message of equanimity and acceptance, helped me withstand my mother's death. Although it was hard to say good-bye, I had many months to come to terms with her leaving.

But what happened next came out of the blue. Only one month after my mother's funeral, Susie died suddenly of a stroke. She was in her forties, and, although she was overweight, there had been no hint of impending death.

One evening we were laughing together, and the next afternoon, she was gone.

Susie's husband and daughter were devastated, and I spent every spare moment trying to help them come to terms with the unexpected death. I felt I had to hold myself together so I could console Jerry and Molly.

I think it's because I couldn't handle Susie's death on a conscious level that I did so subconsciously. She started visiting me in my dreams. I would tell her what was going on with Molly, Jerry, and me, and she would assure me that she missed us but was doing all right.

> ## A STEP ON THE JOURNEY
>
> **Reconnect with those who have died.** Before you go to sleep, think about deceased loved ones you'd like to meet in your dreams. Hold pictures of them or objects of theirs, or close your eyes and call up images of them in your mind. Write down questions you'd like to ask and things you'd like to tell them. (For more on connecting to your dreams, see Chapter 1.) If it doesn't work the first few times, keep trying.
>
> With whom would you like to reconnect? What would you like to say?
> _____
> _____
>
> – J.M.

Seeing Susie in my dreams was a balm for my grief. Her sudden death left so many loose ends, and I was able to tie them up by spending time with her in my dreaming life. Every night she came, and she comforted me.

I was glad to have that consolation because coming up was a terrible year, the worst so far.

✫ ✫ ✫

At work, the tension was making me sick. I'd planned to retire in five years, but suddenly I realized I couldn't wait. I told my bosses I'd be retiring on my birthday that year.

Although I knew I'd made the right decision, things didn't get any easier at work. In fact, they got much harder. Now it was up to me to train my replacement and try to put my job's complex requirements into a clear-cut job description. I was working longer hours than ever before, and the strain was torturous. The only way I survived was to add a once-a-week massage to my schedule and keep to my routine of meditating, doing yoga, writing in my journal, seeing friends.

Things weren't any better at home either. Ella was still bullying Hannah, and I would come home from work, see how dispirited Hannah was, gather her into my arms, and weep.

Those six months leading up to retirement plunged me into such misery that I reverted to many of my old ways—worrying endlessly, isolating myself, letting stress poison my body, mind, and spirit.

Then it happened—the worst thing imaginable. One soft spring morning, Hannah died.

She was youthful and had rarely been sick, so the cause of her death was unclear, but I felt I knew the unspeakable truth. The stress she'd felt from Ella's presence and my own anxiety, which always affected her deeply, had killed her. I had killed her.

While all the deaths in my life had been painful, I'd been able to make peace with them because I didn't blame myself. But I felt utterly responsible for Hannah's death, and that's what I couldn't live with. It was my fault for bringing Ella into the household and being unable to mediate between her and Hannah. By adding my own unhappiness, I'd made it even worse for Hannah, sealing the fate of the sweetest, most innocent creature imaginable.

During those next few months I think I cried more than I'd ever cried before—and, as you know by now, I'm a prolific crier. I started going earlier to Sara's office, long before anyone else arrived, so that I could bawl as loudly and long as I wanted.

I also scrawled incessantly in my journal, castigating myself for what I'd done, grieving for what I'd lost. I didn't think there would ever be an end to my tears, my guilt, my grief.

Then, a few months later, I heard about a self-forgiveness workshop and signed up. It took place over a weekend that summer, and I think it may have saved my life.

The workshop taught me to do two things that helped heal me. First, I limited the time I spent writing about what was bothering me. I wrote on a hurtful subject for only fifteen minutes and then put my journal away. A few hours later, I re-read what I'd written and reframed it by thinking of other ways to say the same things that were kinder toward myself.

The second thing I learned was to look in the mirror, directly into my eyes, and tell myself I was a worthy person and that I loved myself just the way I was. When we were first "forced" to do this in the workshop, I thought, *Oh, God, no.* But it turned out to be a moving thing to do. It did help me forgive myself.

MOMENT OF TRUTH

Perform a mirror mantra. Stand in front of your mirror—naked if possible, though it may take time for you to be ready for that—and give yourself positive feedback about how you look. For example: "I have soft, silky hair. My eyes are bright and soulful. I have a friendly smile. My hands are graceful." Work your way down your body, finding something good to say about every part of yourself. Tell yourself at the end, "I'm beautiful in every way, just as I am."

After a while, if you do this mantra every day, you'll believe what you're saying. As you become comfortable with this exercise, you'll think of new affirmations to tell yourself.

While positive self-talk helps most people if they stick with it, some people feel worse after such exercises, at least at first. If you're one of them, it's important to recognize the negative feelings undermining your messages, understand they aren't the truth, and realize you can let go of their power over you. You determine the truth of your life by what you choose to believe.

Perform the exercise now, and write down how it makes you feel: _____
_____

– *J.M.*

✵ ✵ ✵

Soon Hannah was visiting me in my dreams along with Susie and Casey. Like them, she assured me she was doing fine. Of course she forgave me, once I'd absolved myself.

When I finally retired and put the weight of my job behind me, it was like coming out of a tunnel into fresh, sparkling air. At first, I needed time to recover from the long months of exhaustion. I moved slowly, focusing on the delights of daily life—the first sip of strong coffee in the morning, a hot bath after coming in from the cold, a piece of dark chocolate melting on my tongue.

I began giving or throwing things away, simplifying my life, no longer needing to hold on to everything so tightly. I grew to love the sense of possibility reflected by an empty shelf.

About a year later, I tossed out all my old journals. Those pages, brimming with sorrow, rage, and shame, had served their purpose, and getting rid of them was as cathartic as writing them had been. Finally, finally, I was letting go.

As I thought about all I'd learned about attachment, I recalled a story about how people in India caught monkeys. They cut a small hole in a coconut and put candy inside. A monkey would reach in, grab the sweet, and then be unable to remove its fist. Rather than release the treasure, the monkey would let itself be captured.

How often I'd grabbed on to what I loved with clenched fists. How good it felt now to relax my hands.

> *Dust on diamonds, tears we cry. First we walk, then we fly.*
> —Mark Chapple

TURNING POINT

Slow down and live. Do one thing with all your attention and mindfulness. For example, you might decide to pay total attention to making yourself a cup of tea. Put thought into choosing what type of tea to brew and which cup you'll use—a heavy mug or a delicate teacup, your favorite cup or one you've never tried before. Appreciate every motion that goes into making the tea and taking the first sip. Breathe in the smell of it. Savor its warmth and flavor. Notice how the cup feels in your hand.

Try the same technique with other things you usually do without thinking—things like getting dressed, brushing your teeth, or washing the dishes. Cherishing simple things is the secret to a life of waking up happy.

– J.M.

✽ ✽ ✽

The best part of being retired was having time to volunteer more regularly. My favorite volunteer job, which is still an integral part of my life, is at a food pantry. I put groceries on the shelves and help people find the food they need. It's deeply fulfilling work.

The job brings my passion for food together with my desire to help others. I receive such satisfaction from stocking the shelves, walking side by side with people to choose the groceries they want, sharing their pleasure as they carry out boxes of healthy, nourishing provisions. My soul feels nurtured as well.

I feel like there's no way to tell who is the helper and who is being helped. We are the same. We are each other.

Everybody can be great. Because anybody can serve. You don't have to have a college degree to serve. You don't have to make your subject and your verb agree to serve. You only need a heart full of grace. A soul generated by love.
—Martin Luther King, Jr.

It's important to me to give my time and money to causes I believe in, such as animal and human rights. I support places like the elephant sanctuary in Tennessee, where the animals have lots of land and don't need to interact with the public, so their integrity as wild creatures isn't compromised. I enjoy going to elephants.com, where I can watch the elephants and keep up on how they're doing.

I've always had a special affinity for elephants. They're vegetarians. They're communal, living together and working in unity to raise their young. And they kick the men out if they don't behave!

I like the Native American belief in animal totems—animals who act as our teachers. I think of a number of animals as my guides, because they have characteristics I admire and am drawn to. The elephant is my main guardian spirit, but I have many others, which change depending on what life lesson I'm learning or need to learn.

A STEP ON THE JOURNEY

Choose a totem animal—a creature whose traits you admire. Read some books and search online to find out as much about your totem animal as you can. List the animal's qualities that you want to emulate. Find a picture, emblem, figurine, or anything else that depicts your animal guide, and carry it with you. Touch or look at it whenever you want to remind yourself how the animal's positive characteristics align with your own power.

What animal do you feel drawn to?_____

How would you describe its personality? _____

_____

– J.M.

✯ ✯ ✯

About five years ago, I decided to mother the little girl inside me who didn't get good parenting. Since I grew up with a mother who was fragile and in need of protection, I ended up being the parent in a way, which robbed me of parts of my childhood. Now that I was (relatively) mentally healthy, I realized I could take care of that neglected child.

I named her Zoe, which means "life." When she first came to me, she was five; these days she's closer to eight. She's curious and creative in the way I originally was but didn't get to express.

Every day during my birthday month, I asked Zoe what she wanted and then did whatever she said. She told me to do things like blowing bubbles in the back yard, staying in my pajamas all day, or eating dessert before the main course. Once it was to go to the butterfly exhibit at the botanical garden. Another time, when I was shopping and couldn't choose between two things, Zoe insisted I buy them both.

By the day of my birthday, I'd taken such good care of myself that I felt totally fulfilled. I still do this ritual every year, but now I only need to do it for a week rather than a month, because I've integrated Zoe's wishes into my life and listen to her whenever she speaks up.

TURNING POINT

Parent the child within. Find a quiet place, close your eyes, and summon your inner child.

Visualize your inner parent as well. This parent loves unconditionally, listens without judgment, and nurtures completely—a parent none of us actually had, because it's an ideal, but one we can bring into being through imagination.

Have your inner parent ask your child, "What are you feeling?" Listen carefully, and don't dismiss your child's fears. Don't say, "It's okay. There's nothing to feel bad about." You need to validate your child's feelings—something your parents may have been unable to do for you.

Feel your child's emotions fully. If it becomes too painful, tell your child you need to stop but you'll return later. You may want to set the alarm for five minutes during these early sessions so you won't become overwhelmed. Your child has been starved for parental affection and may be very demanding at first. Be patient and go slowly.

Some people like to make an image of their internal child out of soft material or use a stuffed animal or cloth doll for the purpose. You can hold this representation of your child while you sing, rock, hum, or whatever else feels comforting.

Once you've felt your child's emotions, ask, "Do you have any idea why you feel this way? Is there anything I can do to make you feel better?" Listen to what your child needs.

You may want to start a dialogue in your journal between yourself and your inner child. Or write a letter to yourself from your inner child, explaining what you need and why.

To begin, think of a name for your inner child (a name you've always liked, a word that's inspirational, the name of someone you admire, or whatever sounds right to you). Write it here:_____

– J.M.

I grew bolder. I asked my hairdresser to add a purple streak to my hair. I ventured farther from home, attending meditation and yoga camps. Last year I took an especially big leap when I decided to visit a friend in Portland, Oregon.

It wasn't the first time I'd taken a long trip. Soon after getting sober, I flew to Seattle, Los Angeles, and even Spain with some friends. All these excursions were disasters. The crushing crowds, dizzying pace, and the blunder of packing too much into too short a time triggered panic attacks and episodes of disabling exhaustion.

This time I took steps to prevent a similar catastrophe. First of all, I decided to take the train instead of flying. The journey would take several days each way, which would provide a gentle transition. I would stay for only a few days and take care not to schedule too many things. My pace would be unhurried. Serenity would be my aim.

TURNING POINT

Stretch yourself. Ask yourself this: When was the last time you did something that seemed scary and stretched you beyond your comfort zone? Write about what you did, how you felt afterwards, and what that experience tells you about how to challenge yourself. Use your insights to do something a little intimidating today. Draw strength from memories of other times you triumphed over fear.

Promise yourself you'll try to do something every day that stretches you past what feels comfortable. Examples: Say hi to someone you don't know. Stop to help a person who needs a hand. Sign up for a course or workshop to learn a new skill. Volunteer at a nursing home, preschool, hospital, animal shelter, or charity of your choice.

– *J.M.*

As I boarded the train and nestled into my seat, I imagined myself as a rabbit in its hole. It was important to honor my rabbit-like timidity. My mistake on earlier trips was to ignore it or shove it down.

After the first night, I woke earlier than the other passengers and quietly explored the train. That helped me feel safer.

I was relaxed and calm when I arrived in Portland and was able to keep my equilibrium throughout the trip. I was proud of my rabbit self. I'd read that rabbits represent fears in some Native American cultures and opportunities in others. That struck a chord with me, because I was learning that only by facing my fears could I open myself to new opportunities.

The wonder, the terror, the exultation of being on the edge of being.
—Anatole Broyard

✭ ✭ ✭

It's been nearly three decades since I quit drinking and attended my first Women for Sobriety meeting. I'm far from that enlightened being the Buddhists talk about, free from desire and attachment. But I do feel I'm making progress.

I see Jill often, and we still draw Motherpeace cards together. One of us picks a card and the other reads aloud what the book *Motherpeace* says it means. Then we discuss the relevance of those messages in our lives.

It's uncanny how the cards always give us exactly the lesson we need to hear. It's one of those mysterious things that's hard to explain. Maybe we draw from the cards what we need at any given moment. Or maybe it's magic!

I like to leave a little room for magic in my life.

There was a time when I thought liquor was the fairytale potion that charmed away all problems. Now I know that magic and miracles don't come from the outside. The more time I spend looking inside myself, the more I marvel at the wonders that lie there and connect me to all the treasures of the world.

✭ ✭ ✭

MARILYN'S BEST ADVICE

- Treat the environment with care. Remember, we *are* the environment, and we need to be tender with ourselves.
- Go slowly through the day. Nothing is so important that you can't move toward it with peace and tranquility.
- Don't forget to put yourself on your to-do list. In a time of crisis, I'll spend extra time with a friend who needs it. But afterwards, I'll add more time for myself so I can recharge, relax, and find the right balance.
- When life gives you lemons, sit with them awhile. Maybe you don't want lemonade. Maybe you want to make tabooli instead.
- Be mindful of each minute and the beauty, wonder, and magic it holds. Once you learn to live with mindfulness, gratitude, and laugher, you hold the keys to waking up happy every day.

TOOLS FOR THE JOURNEY

Use these tools to help you put the lessons in this chapter to use in your own life:

Grow your own vegetables. You can nurture them on your windowsill, start a garden in your yard, or use a neighborhood plot. Start by visiting a nursery or garden center and asking questions, or talk to someone you know who's a gardener. If it's not spring yet, you can begin by reading books on the subject, getting on the mailing list to receive seed catalogs, and dreaming about how wonderful your freshly grown vegetables will be. Some good veggies to begin with: peas, beans, carrots, lettuce, beets, and cucumbers.

Eat what you love. When you force yourself to eat certain things and not others, you set yourself up for emotional eating. Staying in balance with your eating habits starts with eating the things you enjoy most, savoring every bite. Pay attention to your foods' color, taste, texture, and smell. Feel gratitude for it, for those who raised and prepared it, and for the elements—air, earth, water—that joined together to create it.

Laugh at yourself. Don't take yourself too seriously. If you can turn painful experiences into funny stories, you've given yourself an immeasurable gift. There's always a twist, an irony, a reason to laugh, if you look hard enough within the pain.

Imagine that what has happened to you occurred in a novel. What would the novelist want the book's hero to learn from it? Perhaps the hero needed to learn not to hold on to things too tightly, to let go, to find inner strength, or to ask for help.

Put up a bulletin board, and start filling it with things that interest you—poems, quotations, photos, colorful images, whatever catches your eye or touches your heart. Then, on New Year's day—or another day that's meaningful for you, such as your birthday, sobriety anniversary, or simply when you feel it's time to move on—hold a taking-down ceremony, and remove everything from the board. Use some of the items to create a collage. Picking what you want to include will give you insights into how you've changed throughout the year—which things are still meaningful and which you may have outgrown. Paste bits of the things you've chosen onto your collage in whatever pattern you like. Now your bulletin board is free for you to fill with all the new things that strike your fancy.

Do small things to change the world around you. Little ideas are the only ones that work. Ask yourself how you could make your neighborhood a better place. Look at ways you can connect with others in your area and work together to improve things.

Clean out one closet, drawer, or cupboard, and put aside items you haven't used in a year. Give them to thrift stores or others who can use them.

THINGS TO DO TODAY

1. The next time you're hungry, think about what you're most hungry for, and eat what satisfies you. Studies have shown that your body is better at metabolizing food you enjoy. (And you will feel happier.)

2. Ask the child inside you, "What do you need to help you feel cared for?" Do whatever your inner child suggests (as long as it's legal and doesn't hurt you or anyone else!).

3. Focus attention on your breath, inhaling for a count of four and exhaling for a count of eight. As you inhale, imagine yourself breathing in beauty, contentment, and joy. As you exhale, think of releasing any resentment, bitterness, or worry you're holding on to.

4. Pick one of the resources listed in the Appendix, and take a look at it today.

5. Write down three good qualities about each of your parents. What do your answers tell you about yourself and your formative years?

6. Bake a pie, and eat a big slice right out of the oven. Forget what your mother told you about letting it cool first.

WORDS OF WISDOM AND LIGHT

More guidance for the soul.

Forgive, Forgive, Forgive: Wisdom from Roger

When I was young, I was an altar boy at the Catholic church, and the priest molested me. The sexual abuse went on for years, and when I told my parents about it, they didn't believe me. They were staunch Catholics and couldn't fathom the idea that a priest would do such an evil, depraved thing to an innocent child.

The pain of those years changed me into another person. I have no idea who I might have become if my feelings about myself hadn't been destroyed at such a young age, if my soul hadn't been murdered. I was just ten when it began.

The worst thing was that the priest made me feel complicit in my own abuse. I thought I must have done something to cause it. I was filled with a bottomless well of self-loathing and despair, as well as a fearful anger.

When I quit drinking, all those emotions bubbled up as if to drown me. I knew I had to deal with them somehow. You can't fill your heart with love, gratitude, and joy when it smolders with wrath, contempt, and malice. Learning to forgive is key.

I used a creative imaging approach to make peace with the ghosts of the past. First, I wrote out my feelings about the priest who abused me. Then I took deep breaths, inhaling compassion for him and exhaling bitterness. I told myself that his behavior came from a place of pain within himself. His torture of me was born of his own wounds. Picturing him as a hurt child lashing out at the world in agony, I tried to see the world through his unhappy eyes.

I reminded myself that my inability to forgive was hurting no one but myself—that the caustic poison I'd concocted was sickening me, not him. While I couldn't change him, I could make any changes I wished within myself.

Then I ripped up the pages on which I'd described that cauldron of emotions. After I threw them away, I closed my eyes, called up my imagination once again, and visualized those vile feelings disintegrating, falling away, and losing their grip on me.

All my rage and resentment didn't disappear at once, but I continued performing this exercise every day. Each time, more of my malignant feelings wafted away.

After I forgave the priest, I moved on to forgiving my parents for not believing or protecting me. It took me still more time to forgive the church and Catholicism itself.

Then I still had to forgive myself for letting it happen and for allowing my body to respond to the sexual stimuli even though I knew it was wrong. That's one of the dirtiest secrets about being abused by someone you love and trust: It can actually feel good to the body. The shame becomes so deep it's entwined in your very being. You become part of that darkness.

I repeated this letting-go exercise over and over. Little by little, I began to feel more peaceful. I was astounded to find that it actually was possible to forgive what seemed unforgivable.

I didn't forgive the priest for his sake. I did it for me. It was the only way I could begin to feel happiness.

Forgiveness doesn't mean that I believe what that priest did was okay. It means I won't let him hold the reins of my life any more. It means giving up the hope that the past could have been any different from what it was. It means letting go of guilt, malice, and regret. It means taking back my power.

The world is full of dreadful things—things so intolerable you don't know how you can possibly go on. But you do. You go on, one hour, one footfall at a time. You speak about the unspeakable, you endure the unendurable. The thing is, there's beauty, too. There is such beauty.

Now, at last, I can feel love for myself and others. I finally know what happiness is.

Roger's best advice: Forgive those who have hurt you. Do so for your own sake. Experiments show that people who take classes in how to forgive others have better physical and mental health, less stress, and more joy.

If you're having trouble forgiving someone, you can try the creative imaging technique I used, by itself or in combination with Martin E. P. Seligman's five-step process, called REACH, which he describes in *Authentic Happiness*: **1. Remembrance:** Recall the hurt, objectively. **2. Empathy:** Look at what happened from the perpetrator's point of view. **3. Altruism:** Give the gift of forgiveness to the person who hurt you. **4. Commitment:** Commit yourself in writing. Write a certificate of forgiveness, a letter to the offender, a poem or song. These are all contracts that lead to the final step. **5. Holding on to forgiveness:** Memories will recur, but don't wallow in them. Remind yourself that you have forgiven, and read the documents you composed.

> **When you hold resentment toward another, you are bound to that person or condition by an emotional link that is stronger than steel. Forgiveness is the only way to dissolve that link and get free.**
> —Catherine Ponder

I Can Still Be Amazing: Wisdom from Sara

I used to judge everything I did as either perfect or imperfect. I didn't think there was any middle ground. If I didn't do a perfect job, I was a failure.

Then I started to think about the possibilities that existed between those two poles. I found I could identify shades between perfect and imperfect. I asked myself: What's perfect? What's amazing? What's acceptable? What's unacceptable? It was a huge relief to think that I could be amazing even if I wasn't perfect. If I couldn't be amazing, I could still be acceptable.

Sara's best advice: Be proud of being imperfect. It's one of the most human things you can be.

Embrace Your Orchid Soul: Wisdom from Elena

An article in *Atlantic* magazine changed the world for me. "The Science of Success," by David Dobbs, describes research with profound significance for all of us who suffer from depression and addiction. Those of us with propensities toward addictive behavior tend to be more sensitive to bad environments, Dobbs writes, but we also have greater resilience when we're in good surroundings.

In the article, Dobbs categorizes people as either dandelions or orchids. Most people are dandelions. They have genes that make them hardy, able to take root and survive almost anywhere. A few of us, however, are more like orchids—delicate, sensitive, and fragile. If planted in poor soil and neglected, we wither. But if tended carefully in a greenhouse, we can burst into spectacular blooms.

If we're orchid personalities and grow up in a toxic environment with poor parenting, we can end up depressed and drug-addicted. But when transplanted into nourishing surroundings, we can thrive in phenomenal ways. We're more creative, intuitive, and adaptable than dandelion people when we receive the care we need.

The article helped me view my infirmities as a blessing. I now see that the genes underlying my addictive behavior are helping me be successful now that I've put my mind to recovery. Each time I reach out to someone who can nurture my orchid soul, I'm creating that greenhouse atmosphere that will help me flourish.

My lesson from the article is that when I feel particularly sensitive to something that happens, I'm going to appreciate that reaction instead of questioning it, judging it, or regretting the suffering it may cause me. I know that in other areas of my life my ability to react with sensitivity and intensity makes me special, valuable, and brilliant.

I'm an orchid, and I embrace that! The wonderful thing is that I'm surrounded with other orchid people. Together, it's unbelievable how beautifully we can blossom.

Elena's best advice: Accept all sides of yourself, understanding that your shortcomings hold within them your greatest power. There would be no light without shadow, and you need to get to know your dark as well as your bright aspects. Bring those darker facets of yourself into the daylight where you can learn to appreciate them and use them for the greater good.

SUMMARY

WHAT WORKS AND WHAT DOESN'T

All of us in this book have tried a myriad of strategies to mold lives of contentment, serenity, and joyful adventure. Through pain and struggle, we've learned what's worth trying and what's unlikely to be effective. Here are truths culled from our experience:

TACTICS THAT DON'T WORK AND ARE COUNTER-PRODUCTIVE
- the geographic cure (moving to a new location, across town or across the globe)
- defining success as making money, accumulating things, or becoming the person someone else wants you to be
- keeping secrets
- aiming for perfection in yourself and others
- focusing on your appearance
- seeing mistakes, failures, and setbacks as things to hide and feel shameful about rather than invaluable lessons
- keeping your feelings and deepest beliefs inside
- comparing yourself to anyone else
- having no plan at all or such an inflexible plan that you can't take advantage of the little miracles that come along when least expected
- thinking you can go it alone, tough it out, and prevail through sheer willpower
- boxing off your pain, grief, and anger rather than facing your emotions
- trying to keep complete control over what's going to happen in the future
- rigidly following the tenets of religion or some other belief system. (Slavishly following a list of rules may work at first, but eventually you must let go of them and create your own life lessons and principles to live by. It's all about flexibility and openness to possibilities.)

KEYS THAT WORK BEST
The stories in this book reinforce these keys to forging a full, rich, happy life:
- Find people you can talk to from your heart, and get together with them regularly. Support them, and lean on them when you need to.
- Make friends with yourself. Get to know and like the person you are. Use personality tests, therapy, and self-help exercises to pinpoint, develop, and use your strengths.
- Learn to recognize irrational, negative, hurtful messages you give yourself. Replace them with helpful, positive messages.
- Give to other people and the community.
- Laugh often, especially at yourself.

- Feel your emotions without letting them dictate your behavior. After you've felt them fully, let them go.
- Count your blessings frequently.
- Speak the words you think you cannot say. Getting those deep truths out of yourself, having someone hear and accept them, is a powerful step toward accepting yourself and moving forward.
- Connect to something larger than yourself. Formulate a philosophy that adds meaning to your life by answering the questions of why you're alive and what life and death mean to you.
- Keep a journal of your life, feelings, and the dreams you have each night. Re-read your words regularly to gain insight and perspective.
- Pay attention. Many of the exercises in this book come back to this piece of wisdom, urging you to focus on the concrete, the tangible, the beauty right beneath your feet.
- Face your fears and phobias. Confronting monsters takes away their power and infuses you with courage.
- Practice mindful meditation or yoga, slowing down your thoughts and your breathing.
- Be kind, forgiving, nonjudgmental, and compassionate to yourself and others.
- Focus on the journey, not the destination. Remember that life is about living the questions, not coming up with answers.
- Find activities that nurture your soul, and do them every day.
- Form a relationship with the natural world.
- Be patient, and remind yourself that it took a long time to solidify your bad habits, so reversing them won't happen overnight.
- Live with hope that, with time, patience, and perseverance, the future will be better than your deepest dreams. There is always hope. Things do change. You can create a future in which waking up happy is not only a metaphor but a way of life. Nothing is impossible when you have the will, the energy, and the understanding. Move forward, just that one small bit, today.

CONCLUSION

NEVER, NEVER, NEVER GIVE UP

Those of us who've told our stories here had different time schedules for changing our lives and have taken varied pathways, but all of us were—and are—on the same odyssey. Moving away from our addictions was just one step on that road to a new life.

Before we could create lasting change, we needed to find the root causes that made us turn to drugs—and other addictions—for relief—childhood abuse, neglect, mental illness in the family, secrets and fears that stifled honest communication as we were growing up and made us doubt ourselves and our worth. Confronting those ghosts, we learned to care for ourselves and find peace in our hearts.

Education was vital: Learning about our disease and accepting that it *was* a disease helped us brave our guilt and self-blame.

Asking others to forgive us for things we did in our pasts helped us forgive ourselves, bathe away bitterness for bygone wounds, and move forward into a life of purpose.

Support groups were essential. Sharing our pain with others, listening to them express their own feelings, and knowing there was someone there to hear, accept, and understand us was the salve that healed us.

Gail Caldwell has written of "that empty room in the heart that is the essence of addiction." We all had to learn to fill that emptiness and longing with a consciousness greater than our own, whether it was the support group itself or a spiritual presence that sustained us. We learned to turn to that higher power to express our gratitude for all the rewards of our new lives.

We also filled those places of emptiness, doubt, and self-loathing by pinpointing our strengths. Then we used those aptitudes to find our true selves, home in on our life's purpose, and give of ourselves to others.

It wasn't about the drugs. There was always something missing at the core. What was missing was love. We had to learn to love ourselves, the people and environment around us, and finally the larger world.

The more miserable we felt, the more important we found it to make lists of all the blessings in our life. At first, we could find little to be thankful for other than the fact that we were alive, we were sober, and the sun was shining. But as we kept our journals and opened our minds, we started to see multitudes of gifts around us.

There were many secrets being kept. To lead an authentic life, we had to stop keeping secrets and become totally honest. We learned to communicate with candor, empathy, genuine caring, and an open heart. We discovered how to listen.

The first step for each of us was a new sense of self-esteem, a belief that life was worth living, the confidence that we could change. This feeling often came from a relationship with a higher power or a connection to someone who said, "I believe in you. You can do it, and your life is worth fighting for."

We grew to comprehend the secret that Aristotle called the golden mean. It was a matter of finding the middle ground. It sounds simple, but it was extremely hard for those of us in this book, all self-described people of extremes. Instead of see-sawing from high to low, from too much to not enough, we had to make a conscious effort to find balance—between activity and reflection, companionship and solitude, emotion and reason. Each day, we had to point ourselves toward that slow and easy middle way, and as we became more limber on the balance beam, we found joy.

Along the way, we lowered our expectations of others, accepted our own imperfections, learned to laugh at our mistakes, and found satisfaction in just being ourselves, living our lives, and accepting those things we could not change. After we learned to care for ourselves, we were able to look outward and found that helping others, living lives of service, and contributing to society deepened our sense of joy and hope.

The afflictions that went along with addictions—depression, eating disorders, sexual compulsions—complicated our voyage. We had to be vigilant that we didn't slip back into those secondary disorders. Doing so required us to become detectives in unraveling the mystery of our own lives, and digging for those answers became one of the most exhilarating parts of the journey. The only thing more magical was sharing our discoveries with others and listening to their stories of self-discovery.

Thus, we found that our disease gave us a gift few receive—the absolute necessity of starting over, building new lives from the foundation up. In the process, we re-evaluated our spiritual beliefs and ended up with different ones from those we started with, ones that resonated more clearly in our hearts and solidified a paradoxical truth: The darkness itself had become the light that showed us the way.

We have come full circle but have discovered that life isn't really a circle but, rather, a spiral. Each time we come around to what seems like the same place, we're on a different level, with greater ability to apply the lessons we've learned before.

We ask ourselves: How many times do I have to learn this lesson? The answer is: You will be learning your life lessons forever. But each time, you embed that lesson within your psyche a little more fully.

Step by step is the way. Slow and steady is the speed. That's how change happens—by inches. By millimeters. By micrometers.

It is our brokenness, the jagged parts of ourselves that catch the light like crystal. It's the glitter of those pointed pieces that beams a light for us and for others.

Taking these lessons to heart, we're stronger than we ever thought possible. And yet we're stronger still—immeasurably strong—when we join with others on the pilgrimage. We're like beads of water falling on stone. Together, we transform the stone into something altogether new. We will never give up.

Keep in touch with us at jill@snpo.org, wakinguphappybook.com, and on Waking Up Happy's Facebook page, where we hope you'll share your own story and connect with other readers who are beginning this voyage with you. We look forward to hearing from you!

365 STEPS ON YOUR JOURNEY

Here is a strategy for every day of the year to help keep you on your path. Remember, that's all you need to do—take one small step at a time. Each one will take you closer to a new life.

I've arranged the exercises in four phases, with each phase building on the next. If you do the Phase 1 "Setting the Foundation" exercises first, they'll lay the groundwork for the second phase. Phase 2, "Building and Growing," leads into the third phase, "Expanding Your Consciousness." That will take you to the highest phase—a place of peace, equilibrium, and enlightenment.

Of course, you needn't do the exercises in order. You can pick out those that appeal to you and skip those that don't. Do remember, though, that the exercises you put off may be the ones from which you'll gain the most. The important thing is to make a habit of looking at this list on a regular basis.

When you find an exercise that helps you, do it often. It's through repetition that transformation occurs. What you do becomes part of you.

If you can't complete an exercise to your satisfaction, don't see it as a failure but as valuable information about yourself, what challenges you, and how you can grow. Write TD (To Do) next to it to remind yourself to try it again later.

Keep in mind that these ideas are suggestions, not prescriptions. The aim is for you to find strategies that work in your own unique circumstances to keep your mind, spirit, and body balanced and open to all the universe has to offer.

Put a check mark next to each exercise as you finish it. Put stars next to those you find especially helpful.

Phase 1: SETTING THE FOUNDATION

____**1. Ask someone** to be your "Waking Up Happy Buddy" and do these exercises so you can get together regularly, discuss your results, and share your thoughts.

____**2. Spend three minutes** sitting quietly in a comfortable position. Close your eyes, concentrate on your breathing, and practice doing nothing.

____**3. As you walk today**, focus on extending the top of your head toward the sky, keeping your shoulders relaxed, and smiling.

____**4. Choose five adjectives** to describe yourself or the self you'd like to be. Write about why you chose each one and how you could enhance those traits in yourself.

____**5. Put on some soothing music.** Shut your eyes, and just listen.

____**6. Toward the end of the day today, write** about how things went (or speak into a recorder)—what went well, what challenged you, what surprised you, what you learned, and what you want to do differently in the future.

____**7. Stand up right now** and stretch your body.

___8. **Create a quick list of five things you could do that would make you feel good about yourself.** (Examples: do the laundry, volunteer at a food bank, sign up for classes, do some sit-ups.) Take one of those actions now.

___9. **Do something you loved to do as a child**—visit a playground and swing on the swings, make sand castles or snow angels, play with clay…

___ 10. **Plan to get together with a group** (any sort of support or interest group). Find out when the group meets and write the date in your datebook. If you don't have a datebook, daily planner, calendar, or other scheduling tool, buy one or find one online so you won't lose track of your important plans.

___11. **Make yourself a smoothie** with a little milk and lots of fruit, water, and ice.

___12. **Laugh at least three times** today. Watch a comedy, rent a DVD or CD of a stand-up comedian's act, exchange jokes with friends, or just laugh out loud over nothing.

___13. **Eat something you love.** Eat it slowly, mindfully, with total attention. Concentrate on nothing but the food and its color, flavor, aroma, texture, and beauty.

___14. **Kneel next to your bed,** and close your eyes. Thank the universe for all the good things in your life.

___15. **Go outside**. Feel the breeze on your cheek, the warmth of the sun, or whatever nature offers.

___16. **Lie on your back,** on your bed or a blanket on the floor, with bent knees. Press your lower back into the bed or blanket as you exhale. Relax your back as you inhale. Repeat ten times, taking deep breaths. With each inhale, breathe in love and acceptance for your body.

___17. **For one hour today, turn off all devices**—phones, TV, computer, and so on—and use the quiet time to think, regenerate, and appreciate the beauty of stillness.

___18. **Take a hot foamy bubble bath**, and let the water dissolve any tension.

___19. **Near the end of the day, share with someone** your answers to these questions: What was the best thing about the day? Why? What was the worst? Why? Listen to their answers to these questions, too.

___20. **Hold a pity party** for yourself. Find a time when you can be alone and out of the hearing of others. Decide how much time you want to spend, and set a timer to go off at the end of your "party." Then feel sorry for yourself, wallow in your misery, cry and pound your pillow, be dramatic. Bemoan the tragedy not only of your own plight but of the whole human condition—the "whole catastrophe," as Zorba the Greek once called it. When the timer goes off, end your pity party, and do something constructive with the rest of your day.

___21. **Yawn deeply** as you raise your arms overhead and gently lean back a little. Repeat.

___22. **Peruse one of the websites** in "Resources to Guide and Inspire You" near the end of this book.

___23. **Make the decision not to watch TV** today or tonight. Instead, write in your journal. If you don't yet have a journal, start one. (For journaling suggestions, see "A Step on the Journey: The Best Cure—Words from Your Heart" in Chapter 1.)

___24. **Rub your hands** together briskly to warm and energize them. Then use slow, purposeful circles to massage your shoulders, face, neck, head, ears, and knees.

___25. **Jot down things that comfort and restore you**—a cup of jasmine tea, soft music, a nap. Do one of those things today.

___26. **What was your first thought** when you woke up this morning? If it wasn't a thought that made you feel good, think of something you're grateful for and something you're looking forward to. End your day the same way. Reserve your unhappy thoughts for a specific half hour of "worry time" in which you set a timer and quit worrying when the buzzer goes off.

____**27. Take a deep breath** and as you let it out, say, "Aaaah, all is well." Repeat throughout the day.

____**28. Break your routine**—eat something different for breakfast, turn your radio to a new station, shake things up with a type of exercise you've never tried before, sprinkle some unusual spices in your coffee.

____**29. Think of three types of physical activity** you might enjoy (walking, running, dancing, swimming, jumping rope). Try one of them today.

____**30. Call the laughter hotline** (1-712-432-3900; enter pin number 6071292#). For more information, visit followthelaughter.com.

____**31. List the four most breathtaking things** you've seen. How could you add more such beauty to your life?

____**32. Incorporate pockets of rest** throughout your day. Take a few minutes between activities to sit down, breathe deeply, and unwind.

____**33. Tonight, go to bed early enough** to get eight hours of sleep. A good night's rest is key to physical, mental, and emotional health.

____**34. Dance** to your favorite music.

____**35. Whatever you're doing right now, take a pause, and smile!** Smile for no reason except that it feels good and will improve your mood. All day today, smile at least once every hour, no matter what. It will make you and everyone around you feel better.

____**36. Lie on your stomach** (on a rug or mat) with your arms at your sides. Lift your head and feet just a few inches as you inhale. As you exhale, release the pose and relax. Repeat six times. This gentle back bend (called the locust in yoga) is the perfect antidote to our busy lives, in which we're bending forward most of the time.

____**37. Check out a thrift store**, garage sale, or resale shop and buy something that's a luxurious bargain.

____**38. Make a list of people and resources you can turn to for support** (friends, counselors, support groups, websites, toll-free numbers). Keep this list handy so you can reach for it whenever you need help, reassurance, or someone to talk to.

____**39. Stop by a shop** where something is made fresh daily (pastries, coffee, smoothies, sandwiches). Choose a small treat, and linger over it.

____**40. Go barefoot** as often as possible today. Jot down words to describe the textures you feel under your feet.

____**41. Reach overhead as you inhale.** Exhale as you bring your hands down your body, inch by inch, to the ground (or as close to the ground as possible). Let your head hang as you inhale and exhale five times. Then gradually stand up.

____**42. List five things** you're grateful for.

____**43. Strive to be fully present** in one situation today. If you find your attention wandering, tenderly bring it back to what you're doing.

____**44. Pet a dog or cat.** If you don't have one, go to an animal shelter or ask friends to let you pet theirs.

____**45. Look in the mirror** without letting your eyes go to any specific part of your body. See yourself as a whole, beautiful person, the way others see you. Realize that no one who looks at you zeroes in on your flaws. They see you as a whole. They see your inner light.

____**46. Take a shower.** Appreciate everything about the experience—the temperature of the water, the feel of your body as you soap it, the scent of your shampoo, the fact that you live in a place and time where showers are possible.

____**47. Raise your shoulders**, then pull them back, bringing your shoulder blades together. Now relax your shoulders. Repeat.

____**48. Meditate for five minutes.** Simply concentrate on nothing but your breathing. If your thoughts drift away, patiently bring your mind back to a focus on your breath.

____**49. Take a walk, and pay attention** to everything you see along the way.

____**50. Think of someone** who has been important in your life—a friend, relative, or even someone you've never met but consider a hero or role model. Write a letter thanking this person.

____**51. Make eye contact** with everyone you see today.

____**52. Envision a perfect day** from the time you wake up until you go to sleep. Write it all down. Now pick one part of your ideal day that you could add to your life. Write about how you'll move closer to the life of your dreams.

____**53. Wear something colorful**—maybe an orange scarf, a red hat, or some brightly patterned socks.

____**54. Laugh** while at the same time saying out loud (the words won't be understandable, but that's okay) all the things that anger, worry, and upset you. Release all those stressors, with your laughter, into the solar system.

____**55. Think of someone who cares about you**. In moments of your greatest self-doubt, what would you like that person to say to you? Now, say those words to yourself.

____**56. Go slowly** all day, being attentive of everything around you. Put a rubber band around your wrist, and snap it every time you find yourself rushing. Tonight, write a few paragraphs about what you learned from this exercise.

____**57. Talk aloud to yourself** in the mirror about your problems, anxieties, and joys (or talk to a pet, plant, or statue). You'll receive information you can't get by talking to yourself in your head.

____**58. Lie on your back.** One by one, relax each part of your body, starting with your toes and moving up your legs, torso, arms, shoulders, all the way to your forehead. Breathe slowly. Each time you exhale, soften your body a little more.

____**59. Search the library for books and CDs** that describe yoga and other mind-body techniques. Peruse these resources, and see if you discover anything you'd like to try.

____**60. All day, act as if you can achieve everything you want,** no matter how impossible it might seem. At the end of the day, write about how this sense of possibility influenced your day.

____**61. Stop by the market** and buy some fruit (a type you've never tried before if possible). Cut it up, put it in a bowl, and eat it with some milk or honey.

____**62. Have you made any promises** that you haven't fulfilled? Follow up on them today. If you make any new promises, note them in your datebook to assure you'll follow through.

____**63. Make some music.** Sing, hum, whistle, play an instrument, or drum with your hands.

____**64. Surround yourself** with a scent you like, such as fresh flowers, cinnamon sticks simmering on the stove, an apple pie in the oven, freshly chopped herbs, vanilla candles, or incense.

____65. **Throughout the day, notice** how often you say or think "That's not right," "That should be different from what it is," and similar negatives. Each time such a statement comes to mind, replace it with a positive.

____66. **Buy a sleeping mask.** Wear it when you go to sleep tonight and while you're meditating or doing yoga. Pure darkness is a key ingredient for true rest and relaxation.

____67. **Write down some tactile sensations** that soothed you in the past—the softness of a favorite quilt, an old T-shirt, fresh sheets against your skin, a puppy's fur, and the like. Comfort yourself with one of those sensations today.

____68. **What three parts of your body** do you feel best about? Write down your answers. What insights do your choices give you?

____69. **Do something that goes against the grain** for you. If you're right-handed, write with your left hand. If you're shy, speak up, and if you're usually effusive, stay silent. If you always do something a certain way, try the opposite approach.

____70. **Go on a news fast today.** Don't read newspapers, watch the TV news, or check the news online. Instead, write in your journal about how you're feeling. You may find you feel more positive and uplifted without being bombarded by negative information.

____71. **Call a friend**, and just talk and listen.

____72. **Take a mini-vacation** to a garden, park, river, cemetery, lake, or other restorative spot. While you're there, whether it's for ten minutes or three hours, do whatever you like. Tonight, write a few paragraphs about the experience.

____73. **Notice whether you compare yourself** to anyone today. If you do, tell yourself, "I am who I am." Remind yourself that you're unique and valuable. Comparisons serve no one.

____74. **Listen to classical music**—at a concert, on the radio, in your car, or on a CD. It's a good way to expand your brain.

____75. **Make a tally of ways to take care of your health and safety**—flossing your teeth, wearing your seatbelt, and so on. Make a conscious choice to do these things today.

____76. **Give yourself a yoga facelift.** Bring your hands to your neck, then slowly up your face to the very top of your head. Grab hold of your hair, gently pull it upwards, and as you let go of it, release all your tension into the sky.

____77. **At the library, find a memoir, biography, or autobiography** of someone you admire. As you read it, note how that person overcame adversity.

____78. **Make room for one hour** of pure, sweet silence.

____79. **Take the quiz at moodscope.com** to measure your happiness and see how to improve it.

____80. **What emotions do you feel right now?** Sit with those feelings, without judging or trying to fix them. Just feel them. Then let them go, and turn your mind to something else.

____81. **Find or create an affirmation** you like. ("I am healthy and happy"; "I am learning and growing every day"; "I am filled with joy"; see more examples in Chapter 1.) Write it down and put it where you'll see it often. Repeat it to yourself frequently today and before you go to sleep tonight.

____82. **Do something that requires getting your hands dirty.** Ideas: Plant flowers or vegetables. Pull weeds. Play with mud, clay, or paste. Knead dough.

____83. **Start your heart pumping.** Take a brisk walk, ride your bicycle, or run up and down the stairs.

____84. **Choose a mantra**—a word or phrase you can repeat to calm yourself or focus your mind. Examples: "Om" (the sound of infinity), "Shanti" (peace), "Yes," "I believe." Recite your mantra aloud or silently for several minutes.

____85. **Cut some vegetables** into bite-sized pieces, and keep them at hand to snack on.

____86. **Check out some library books** on birds, plants, and trees. Learn about the natural world that surrounds you.

____87. **Send an online greeting card** to let someone know you're thinking of them.

____88. **Take a personality test** to give you insights into who you are. See, for example, yourpersonality.net.

____89. **Use crayons or paints** to draw colorful pictures without worrying about how they look.

____90. **Create a drawing** of your parents, siblings, and yourself. Make a note to look at it again in a few weeks and see what insights you can glean from it. Share it with others to gain their perspective, too.

____91. **Do the "happy-baby pose."** Lie on your back. Hold your hands and feet in the air and wiggle them as if you're a baby discovering the joy of moving your body.

____92. **Turn up the car radio, and sing** along at the top of your lungs. If you're not going to be in a car today, sing in the shower.

____93. **Do something to organize your life**—tidy a drawer, arrange your bookshelf, throw away old papers, make a schedule for the week, or the like.

____94. **List six things** that bring you pure joy. Put one of those things on today's to-do list.

Phase 2: BUILDING AND GROWING

____95. **Draw a picture** of the way your perfect future would look.

____96. **Use a bulletin board as your inspiration canvas.** Tack photos, pieces of fabric, cartoons, quotations—anything that interests you—onto the board. You'll discover connections that will provide important clues to your true self.

____97. **Listen to someone** today without trying to decide if they're right or wrong. Just seek to understand them and their perspective.

____98. **Take a camera or some paper** with you on a walk, and photograph or draw whatever strikes your fancy.

____99. **Ask at least one "dumb question"** today. You'll likely be surprised to find that it's not so dumb after all and may, in fact, be profound and revelatory.

____100. **Make two columns,** headed "Like" and "Dislike." List five things you like and five things you dislike about yourself. Plan to focus on your strengths and stop worrying about the things you don't like.

____101. **All day today, watch people's eyes.** Where are they looking? What can you learn about them by noting what they focus on, and how, and for how long? Notice how much people tell each other through their eyes.

____102. **Make a conscious decision not to multi-task** today. Do one thing at a time, with your full attention.

____103. **Make cookies**, and share them with a friend.

____104. **Draw up a list of your needs**. For each one, think of a healthy way to fulfill that need. For instance, food is a need you can fill by preparing a meal from scratch. Intimacy is a need you can meet by building strong, caring relationships.

____**105. Who are your heroes?** Why? What qualities do you admire in them? How can you become like them? Write about your answers.

____**106. List the things that are most important** to you. Then prioritize the items on your list. Put a 1 next to the most important, a 2 by the second most important, and so on. Now, do something to enhance one of your highest-priority things.

____**107. When are you most energetic and productive**—first thing in the morning, later in the afternoon, or in the evening? Whatever your best time is, use it today to make progress toward your highest priorities (see the list you made in the previous exercise).

____**108. Notice any "negative" emotions** you feel today—anger, fear, resentment, guilt, worry, etc. Write them down. Note the beliefs that may be at work when you feel this way. Then jot down an alternative belief that might change your response. For example, suppose you feel embarrassed and anxious when someone cries in a group meeting. You're probably reacting to long-held beliefs that tears are related to pain and that it's unseemly to show your pain in public. You might replace it with a belief that tears can be healing and that crying with other people cements bonds and mends wounds.

____**109. Take some time to listen to your body.** Where is it tight? Where does it hurt? What mental and emotional things in your life might be contributing to your body's tension and pain?

____**110. Use playdough or some other form of clay** to mold a statue of your favorite animal. Remind yourself that you have the same strengths as it does, and you can draw on them at any time.

____ **111. Ask yourself these questions**: Who am I? What is my purpose? What do I really want? Or ask yourself another question you want to answer for yourself. Set a timer for ten minutes, and start writing, quickly and without stopping until the timer goes off. The process is what's important, not the end result.

____**112. Make a list of what you're passionate** about, what you're good at, and your positive personality traits (such as creativity, loyalty). Note actions you can take to use those things in your life. Follow through on one of those actions today.

____**113. Do something relaxing.** If you can't think of anything, see the examples in "Moment of Truth: Stop Stressing and Start Living" (Chapter 5) and "A Step on the Journey: Give Yourself the Love and Care You Need" (Chapter 7).

____**114. Make basic human contact today** with people you don't know. Smile and say "good morning" to a passerby. Take time to chat with a salesperson. Realize that such encounters can enrich the soul without "accomplishing" anything.

____**115. Select something in your life you believe is essential to improve or change**. Take an action that will further that purpose.

____**116. Identify a mistake** you recently made, and think about what you learned from it. Tell someone about your mistake and what it taught you.

____**117. Compliment** someone today.

____**118. Picture yourself walking** into your house, apartment, or wherever you live. Look at it as a stranger would, and write down your impressions. What does this space tell you about the person who lives here? Would you like it to say something different? What steps could you take to make your space what you'd like it to be?

____**119. Prepare a delicious meal.** If possible, use a recipe or an ingredient you've never tried before.

____**120. Think of an afternoon ritual** you could perform to break up your day and quiet your busy thoughts (make yourself a cup of tea, do some stretching, read a verse of poetry). Add it to your life today.

____**121. Reply to this question** in writing: What would you attempt if you knew you could not fail?

____**122. Look at your answer** to the previous question. Whatever you said you'd like to attempt, take the first step to doing it, knowing that there's no such thing as failure, only lessons to be learned. The secret is to make that first step small—for example, ask others their ideas for how you might fulfill your dream, research it online, ask at your library for books that might help, look for classes in your area of interest. Make a note in your datebook to take a second small step in a few weeks.

____**123. Ask three people** where they were born or what their favorite city is.

____**124. List things you'd like to do**, hobbies you'd like to try, classes you'd like to take, and fun things you'd like to experience. Pledge to take action toward one of those desires this month. Write it in your datebook so you won't forget.

____**125. Practice some breathing exercises.** Inhale on a count of four, exhale on a count of eight. Repeat. Then fill your lungs with air, and let it out slowly. Breathe in through your nose and out through your mouth. Spend a few minutes doing these exercises.

____**126. Truly connect** with people today. Look directly into their eyes. Pay attention not only to what they're saying but also to what they're feeling.

____**127. Write a letter to an imaginary pen pal** from another country, introducing yourself and explaining who you are and what your life is like. Then read the letter as if someone wrote it to you. What are your reactions?

____**128. Choose a book** from "Resources to Guide and Inspire You" (in Appendix). Ask for it at the library.

____**129. Draw a line across a piece of paper** to represent your life. Arrange key events from your life along this line. If you were happy at the time, place the event above the line. If sad, put it as far below the line as you wish, to indicate your feelings. Is your life a series of peaks and valleys, or is it fairly even? What does this lifeline tell you about yourself?

____**130. Say "no"** to one thing you'd rather not do—something that complicates your life while adding little benefit, that won't help you reach your goals, or that doesn't fit with your core values.

____**131. Take the humor test** at queendom.com to see if you need more laughter in your life.

____**132. Spend a few minutes** letting your mind wander. Write down the thoughts that come to you.

____**133. Work on a jigsaw** or crossword puzzle.

____**134. Take some small pieces of paper**, and on each one write something you love to do. Put them in a box. When it's time to reward yourself for something—for meeting a goal, taking a positive step, or persevering for one more day—draw one of these cards, and follow its instructions. It's a good way to acknowledge all the progress you're making while adding extra joy to your life.

____**135. Treat every conversation today** as a learning experience. Be open to what others have to teach you. This evening, write down what you gained from every dialogue.

_____**136. Visit an art museum.** Pick one work of art that intrigues you, and view it from different angles. What's its title? Why do you think the artist chose that name? What do you think was in the artist's mind?

_____**137. Get a bath pillow**, some bath toys, and a jar of soap bubbles, and play in your tub. It's as good as a spa visit.

_____**138. Find a photo of yourself** when you were small. Think of the person you were then as a friend who needs your protection and love. Keep the photo with you as a reminder to take care of that innocent child.

_____**139. Browse at a grocery store,** and buy only health-enhancing food. Eat some of that food later today.

_____**140. Begin putting together a laughter folder** in which you store cartoons, jokes, funny quotations, and memories that make you laugh. Keep it close by to consult whenever you need a boost.

_____**141. Take a trip to the library**, and pick up some new books to read.

_____**142. Do three helpful things** today—throw away litter, straighten a room after a meeting, smile at someone who's down. Using your ingenuity to discover how to help is half the fun.

_____**143. Set up an altar** in a corner of your house to display objects that are special or symbolic to you. Use it as a place to meditate, pray, or simply to be still.

_____**144. Brainstorm ways to cut back** on some things to make time for new practices you want to develop. Ideas: Don't work overtime or through the lunch break except on rare occasions. Check your text messages and emails no more than twice a day. Watch only one hour of TV a night. Write down your ideas, and try one of them today. Use your extra time for self-enhancing practices like doing the exercises in this book.

_____**145. Ask someone** to recommend a book or movie. Plan to read or see whatever they suggest and then discuss it with them.

_____**146. Write down a situation** that's worrying you. Separate what you can do to change it from what you can't. Let go of what you can't change, and move forward on changing what you can.

_____**147. Find out how well you read people's emotions**, using the BBC's ten-question "Spot the Fake Smile Test" (bbc.co.uk/science/humanbody/mind/surveys/smiles/).

_____**148. Add color to your life.** Scour a thrift shop or flea market for blankets, rugs, baskets, and other items in vivid hues.

_____**149. Carry a small notebook**, and jot down everything that makes you smile or laugh.

_____**150. Buy a type of tea or coffee** you've never tried before, and relish every sip.

_____**151. Close your eyes,** and tell yourself that when you open them, you'll see something you didn't notice before.

_____**152. Make a resolution** to be honest in every word you speak, write, and think today—with others but, above all, with yourself. Consider whether your words, thoughts, and actions match your values, whether you're candid about what you think and feel, and whether you fulfill your promises to yourself as well as to others.

_____**153. Ask a few friends or acquaintances** what their favorite things are, and see how much you have in common.

_____**154. If you discovered you were going to die tomorrow**, what would you do differently today? With whom would you talk? What would you tell them? Today, do and say some of those things.

____**155. Put a notebook and pen** (or tape recorder) by your bed, and record any dreams you have tonight. (See Chapter 1 for tips on remembering and learning from your dreams.) Plan to keep an ongoing diary of your dreams, writing down any scraps you remember from your dreaming life.

____**156. Ask yourself questions to boost your health**: What nutritious foods can you introduce into your life? How can you improve the quality of your sleep? Jot down your answers. Add more to your list as you think of things.

____**157. Use finger paints** to create a picture that expresses your feelings.

____**158.** Take the "What Animal Are You?" quiz (gotoquiz.com/animology_what_animal_are_you) to discover what animal most matches your personality.

____**159. Find or draw a picture** of the animal in the above exercise. What four positive qualities do you associate with that creature? How could you enhance those attributes in yourself?

____**160. As you go through the day, watch yourself** from the viewpoint of someone else. Watch with interest and without judgment.

____**161. Read an article** or book chapter. Write a few sentences about your reactions to what you've read. Then discuss it with someone.

____**162. List people, places, and things** that nurture you. Get in touch with one of them today.

____**163. Think of something** you've been putting off, and do the minimal amount to get started. If you've been meaning to read a book, read the first page. If you want to tidy your garage, sort one box. If you need to wash the floor, clean just one tile. That's how all projects get done—by starting small.

____**164. Read over your journal** for the past month and notice any patterns that emerge.

____**165. Every time you want something badly today,** put it off for an hour. Remind yourself that there are few things that can't be delayed. Waiting will open up a space for new possibilities while making you more resilient.

____**166. Write about a time** you've overcome difficult circumstances. What inner strengths helped you prevail? How can you use that same fortitude today?

____**167. Make a list of five things** that are going right in your life.

____**168. Name three qualities** you like about yourself and three things you'd like to change. List some actions you could take to build on what you like and make the changes you want.

____**169. Imagine you've attained** your greatest dream. Write a letter to a friend describing what things are like now that you're living your ideal life. Put in as many details as you can. Having a clear picture of what you want will help make it come true.

____**170. Ponder your short-term and long-term future.** What do you want to accomplish this week? This month? Where do you want to be in six months? A year? Two years? Five years? Create a plan that includes answers to these questions. Write down steps you can take to bring your plan to fruition.

____**171. Share your insights** with someone recovering from an addiction or trying to change their life. Savor the joy of collaborating in transformation.

____**172. Write a story** about an incident in your life, viewing yourself in the third person (using he or she rather than I). Later, read over your story. How does this new vantage point make you feel about yourself?

____**173. Pinpoint four times in your life** that you were at a crossroads. How did you react? What did you learn? Write your thoughts in your journal.

____**174. Check out halfbakery.com**, where people have contributed all manner of innovative ideas to jumpstart your creativity.

____**175. For ten minutes, write** about a problem in your life. When the time is up, put the problem out of your mind. Make a note to re-read your journal in a few days and see if a solution has come to you.

____**176. Give away one thing** to a thrift store or to someone who needs it more than you.

____**177. Be a detective** today, and find out one new thing about each person with whom you talk.

____**178. Spend some time** writing about your emotions—what you're feeling now and what you've been feeling lately.

____**179. Take the first steps toward learning another language.** Find a book or some tapes you can listen to. Sign up for a course. Ask friends if they know another language and if they'll speak it with you.

____**180. Attend services** at a church, synagogue, temple, or other sanctuary you've never visited before.

____**181. Be open to surprises** today, and consider how they can enrich your life and help you grow.

____**182. Think of a creative outlet** you'd like to try—playing an instrument, singing, writing, sewing, painting, making jewelry, juggling, acting, dancing, scrapbooking. Find a class or group of people interested in the same thing. Make a note in your calendar to follow up on this.

____**183. Go to a public place** where you can people-watch. Pick out someone you don't know, and make up a story about them, either in your mind or on paper. From the person's age, dress, manner, and other clues, create an imaginary scenario about who they are, what they do, and why they're where they are.

____**184. Check a book of poems out of the library.** Choose a poem with a subject that interests you, and read it. If you don't understand it, read it again. Close your eyes and let the poem's images fill your imagination. Continue to re-read it until it makes sense to you. Realize there's not just one meaning but many possible meanings, and figure out what the poem says to you.

____**185. Spend time with a child**, following their lead about what to do. If you don't have a child of your own, visit a friend's child or volunteer to help out at a preschool.

____**186. List changes you'd like to make** in your life and what's keeping you from realizing them. For example: "I'd like to read more, but I rarely have time to sit down with a book." Now, replace the word "but" with "and." This little change will move you out of excuse-making mode into problem-solving mode.

Phase 3: EXPANDING YOUR CONSCIOUSNESS

____**187. Begin adding your friends' important dates** to your calendar—their birthdays, sobriety anniversaries, and any other days that are meaningful to them. Start by asking one or two friends for this information today. Plan to send a card or note to let them know you're thinking of them on these occasions.

____**188. Choose one goal** to focus on. Decide on three action steps you can take to move toward that goal. Put reminders where you'll see them (for example, write each action on a sticky note and arrange them on your mirror). Mark dates in your calendar when you'll review your progress. To increase your commitment, share your goal and planned action steps with someone.

____**189. Remember things you've done well** in the past. Visualize what you did and how you felt. Recalling past successes builds your skills and confidence for the future.

____**190. Today, taste something delicious**, notice something beautiful, feel something sensuous, and listen to something soothing.

____**191. Take stock** of your life. Ask yourself: What's possible for me right now? What's holding me back? What do I want to change? What do I long to do or be?

____**192. Ask someone for a cutting** from one of their house plants. Put it in a glass of water so you can watch its roots develop. Make a note to move it into a pot of soil when it has roots, then water it once a week and admire it as it grows.

____**193. Tonight, after dark, find a place** where you can see the night sky. (Hint: For true darkness, get away from city lights.) Spend an hour gazing at the stars and contemplating your place in the universe.

____**194. Think about a change going on** in your life. How can you use that change to stimulate your learning and growth? Answer that question in writing.

____**195. Lend or recommend a favorite book or DVD** to a friend, and make plans to discuss it.

____**196. Take a route** you've never traveled before. Keep your eyes open. When you get home, write about what you discovered.

____**197. Assess the spirit** in your life with the index of core spiritual experience at spiritualityhealth.com.

____**198. What emotion** are you least comfortable expressing? Write about it. When do you remember feeling it? How do you tend to respond to it? What healthy things could you do to deal with it?

____**199. Ask yourself, "What would be meaningful** for me to do today?" Keep asking that question throughout the day, looking for things to do that will increase your feeling of purpose, passion, and service to others.

____**200. Join the Levity Project** at thelevityproject.com to bring more joy, play, and levity to the world.

____**201. Make a card** for someone, expressing your gratitude for the person they are.

____**202. What you focus on** determines how you live your life. What do you pay attention to? What might you focus more on? Write down your answers.

____**203. In a dictionary,** find a word you've never used before. Make a point of using it in conversation sometime today.

____**204. Seek to understand** how you may be contributing to your own troubles. Think of a problem you're wrestling with, and imagine for a moment that you're completely responsible for causing and continuing that problem. What new ways of seeing does such an approach open up for you? From that vantage point, what possible solutions come to mind? Move forward on one of those solutions today.

____**205. Plan to spend some time** alone in a peaceful place where you can get in touch with nature.

____**206. You become the average of the five people** you associate with most, according to author Jim Rohn. Who are these five people in your life? Do they represent the kind of person you want to become? If not, whom would you rather emulate? Make a resolution to spend more time with those whose example you most want to follow.

____**207. Create a wishing ritual** for yourself. For example, hold a shell, feather, stone, or other object that's meaningful to you while closing your eyes and sending your wish out into the world.

____**208. Spend twenty minutes** writing about the underlying causes of your addictions. What did you fear so much that you had to numb yourself to hide from it? What was missing inside you that you tried to fill with drugs, food, or other addictions? If this is too difficult to think about, find a therapist to help you unravel the answers.

____**209. Approach the day with a sense of adventure** about everything. Go into stores and public buildings you've never entered before. Talk to someone different. Explore everything interesting that catches your eye. Tonight, describe your day in your journal.

____**210. Join a group of people** who do something you enjoy—hiking, bowling, knitting, playing board games, sampling ethnic restaurants, discussing philosophy, and so on. Meetup.com will give you ideas for groups meeting in your area, or start your own group.

____**211. Send a thank-you note** to someone who has given you help, advice, inspiration, or anything else you're grateful for.

____**212. Jot down six blessings** you've received from your sobriety and new way of life.

____**213. Take fifteen minutes to watch a living creature**—a pet, a bird or squirrel in the park, even an ant or spider.

____**214. Think of a message you received in childhood** that didn't serve you well. What message could you replace it with that would be more helpful to you?

____**215. Go on a hike,** bicycle ride, or other adventure in the outdoors. Invite a friend to join you, or make it a time for yourself.

____**216. Call someone** who has the qualities you'd like in your own life, and suggest getting together.

____**217. Find four small stones,** and name each one for something you want more of, be it courage, serenity, love, compassion, forgiveness, or something else that's important to you. Hold these stones, and imagine them giving you strength to create what you want in your life.

____**218. Go out of your way to talk to someone** you don't know well.

____**219. Check some joke books** out of the library. Write down jokes you think are funny, and share them with friends. Be sure these jokes aren't mean-spirited or derogatory toward any group of people.

____**220. On paper, explore your relationships**. Which are satisfying and nurturing? Which would you like to change? How could you make your relationships healthier? Is it time to set firmer boundaries? To speak up and make clear what you want? To let go of a relationship and build a new one with someone who'll treat you as you deserve? Decide on a step you can take to improve one of your relationships.

____**221. What are your core beliefs**? What values do you live by? Answer these questions in writing. (For more on core values, see Chapter 4.)

____**222. Draft a list of messages you sometimes tell yourself** about what you should do, must do, ought to do, are expected to do. Then change them to messages without the "shoulds." In place of "I should…," say, "I want to…," "I would probably feel better if I…," and other more affirming messages.

____**223. Write about the losses** in your life—people who've died, changes you've had to make, wounds from your childhood, dreams you had to let go of, experiences you've missed, things that have hurt you. Let yourself cry as you pour it out on paper. Then take some deep breaths, let the sadness go, and turn your mind to all the positive things in your life.

_____224. **Broach a series of "What if?" questions**. What if you could do anything? What if you had all the time and money you could ever want? What if you could make your greatest dream come true? What if there were no limits or restrictions to your goals? What if you aimed as high as possible? What if you could spend your day doing what you loved? Write down an action you could take to make one of those "What if's?" real.

_____225. **Think of someone you consider wise**. Invite that person to meet for coffee. Plan to do more listening than talking.

_____226. **Pay attention to your inner voice** all day today. Speak and act on what you think and feel, not what others say or what you think others want.

_____227. **Ask someone for what you need**—a hug, help with a project, or perhaps a listening ear.

_____228. **Use paper and pencil** to sort out anything that's bothering you, and ask yourself what will make you feel better. Perhaps you need to take some time off from work, look for a job you love, or find someone to talk to. Whatever it is, take a step now toward doing it.

_____229. **Invite a friend** to go bowling, play tennis, try some other sport, or take a walk.

_____230. **Create a rough blueprint** of your ideal house. Then write about what your dream house says about you and what's important to you.

_____231. **Ask** one of your parents or other relatives what they remember about you as a child. Write down their responses and your reactions. Do their memories sound familiar? Do they reinforce the way you see yourself? Would you like to overturn that view of yourself or build on it? How could you do so?

_____232. **Measure your ability to empathize**, using Simon Baron-Cohen's 60-question quiz (glennrowe.net/BaronCohen/EmpathyQuotient.aspx).

_____233. **Think about your mentors**. (If you don't have any yet, it's time to find at least one.) What can you do to give back to them? Be sure your mentoring relationship is a two-way street.

_____234. **Find a class in dance**, karate, aerobics, or any other form of movement. Make a note in your datebook to sign up as soon as possible.

_____235. **Choose three people you'd like to know better**. Do one thing that will move you closer to getting to know one of them (send them an email, find an excuse to talk with them, ask them a question).

_____236. **What are some of your earliest memories?** Write about them and the emotions they bring up for you. What clues do they give you about yourself?

_____237. **List things you could do to enhance your relationship** with the people in your life. For example, perhaps you could call someone, stop by to see a friend, or invite an acquaintance to do something with you. Take one of those actions now, and make a note in your datebook to take another action within the next week.

_____238. **Do something that will give you a sense of accomplishment**, enjoyment, or adventure. Examples: Try a new recipe, invite a friend over, go someplace you've never been before.

_____239. **Sit in a relaxed position**. Close your eyes and visualize yourself walking down a path to a building. Open the door, knowing that inside is the truth you need to move your life forward. Write about (or draw a picture of) what you might find on the other side of that door.

_____240. **Consider a problem** that's bothering you. Write it down. Before going to sleep tonight, read over what you've written, and reflect on the problem. When you wake up, lie still, think of your problem, and see if your dreams have offered you some solutions.

____**241. Thank as many people as possible today** for what they do.

____**242. Find a buddy** to do something with you on a regular basis, such as walking your dogs together, visiting places of worship, or doing self-improvement exercises and discussing the results. Give someone a call right now and ask if they'd be interested.

____**243. What five things do you need or want** from other people? Put them down on paper. Now think of ways you could do those things for yourself.

____**244. Take half an hour to write about your spiritual life.** How would you define your higher power? What spiritual beliefs are you sure of? How might you intensify your spiritual life? Who could you talk to about such matters?

____**245. Think of a happy couple** who've been together for years. Ask them their secrets for staying together.

____**246. Invite some friends over**, and ask each of them to bring a favorite game to play.

____**247. Treat all the people** you come in contact with today as if they're close relatives whom you respect, care about, and want the best for. Tonight, write about how that shift in perspective felt.

____**248. Print a word or name** that means something special to you (your own name, for example, or a friend's name). For each letter of the name, write a sentence beginning with that letter. Then combine the sentences to create a mini-poem.

____**249. Take it easy** on yourself all day today. Don't push yourself to the limit or strain for perfection. Let good be good enough, and relax into each moment.

____**250. Name five people whose lives you've changed** in any way, no matter how small.

____**251. Create stories in your mind** about how your future could unfold. Imagine what it would be like to live in each of these possible futures.

____**252. Go someplace** that has meaning for you that you haven't visited for a while. Write about the experience.

____**253. Practice speaking to others with respect and caring.** For instance, begin statements with "I" rather than "you" to avoid a perception of blaming. ("I feel inadequate when you yell at me," rather than "You make me feel horrible!")

____**254. Name something you'd like to change** about yourself. Then behave as if that change has already taken place. Research shows that your thoughts can change your behavior. In one study, for example, when people were asked to smile artificially, they felt happier as a result.

____**255. If you meet anyone today who annoys you**, step back and take a "helicopter" view. Imagine what it might feel like to be that person. Ask yourself what lesson that person holds for you. The more uncomfortable someone makes you, the more profound the lesson is likely to be.

____**256. Prepare two lists**—one of things you'd like more of in your life and another of things you'd like less of. Create goals to add and subtract these thing from your life.

____**257. Tell someone a true story** about an event in your life.

____**258. Find a quiet place** to relax, reflect, and write about the changes you've made. How is your life different today from what it was before you started your journey of change?

____**259. Imagine you're a friend describing you** to another friend. Write down the way you think someone would describe you. Is it different from how you see yourself? What could you do to bring the two descriptions closer together in a positive way?

____**260. Practice patience** throughout the day. Look at "down time"—such as waiting in line or at a red light—as a chance to do some deep breathing, reflecting, or communing with your inner muse.

____261. **Instead of walking today**, try skipping, marching, tiptoeing, or walking backwards.

____262. **Close your eyes,** and picture the sun above you. Imagine its color changing from gold to orange to red to purple to deep blue to green. See it coming out of the sky and into your body so it's part of you. Visualize it lifting you into the air. You are all the colors of the rainbow, part of the sky and the universe. Breathe deeply as you envision this.

____263. **Alter your physical relationship** to the world. Sit in a different chair. Lie on the opposite side of the bed from usual. Look for similar opportunities to give your body new perspectives throughout the day.

____264. **Create a picture of your desired future in your mind.** What will people around you be saying? What will your environment look, sound, and feel like? Make this image as vivid, clear, and beautiful as you can. Remember that you can return to it in your mind whenever you want. Imagining the life you'll lead will help bring it into being.

____265. **Tell someone a mystifying dream** you've had. Describing it may make the meaning clear to you, and other people may provide fresh insights.

____266. **Write about the childhood** you wish you'd had. Ask yourself what you could do now to give yourself some of what you missed then.

____267. **Re-read a book** you liked when you first read it. Then write about the ways it seems different this time. Remember, it's not the book that has changed, it's you. What does the re-reading tell you about the person you've become?

____268. **Ask someone to play a childhood game** (such as jacks, jump-rope, marbles, or hopscotch) with you.

____269. **Be completely present for one person** today. Communicate your caring with a smile, a nod, a reassuring touch. Your simple presence has the power to promote well-being. Just be there, without any agenda.

____270. **Find a thesaurus** online, at the library, or at a used book store. Use it to find a synonym for a word you often use. Sometime today, use the new word instead of your usual one.

____271. **Look inside yourself and ask:** What would you have become if you had been fully supported with all the encouragement and opportunities in the world? How can you give those things to yourself? How can you find supportive people to help you? You can't change the past, but you can create the future you want.

____272. **Recall a time** when someone helped you. Pay it forward by doing something helpful for someone else.

____273. **Examine a problem** you're facing, and shift your attitude toward it. Instead of seeing it as an insurmountable obstacle, view it as an opportunity to deepen your creativity. See how many innovative solutions you can come up with.

____274. **What habits** do you have that enhance wellness in your life? What are your unhealthy habits? Commit yourself to replacing one bad habit with a good one. Write down the specific steps you'll take each day to cement your new habit and eliminate your old one.

____275. **If you're having trouble relating to someone,** envision the characteristics you wish that person had. Pretend that the person actually does have those attributes. Doing so will help you be more accepting while developing those qualities in yourself. For example, if someone seems cold and distant, imagine that they're friendly. You may begin to glimpse a hidden warmth in them and be friendlier to them, which will bring out their friendly nature in turn.

____276. **Sign up for a CPR or other first-aid course** (the Red Cross holds free ones) to empower yourself as well as to help others.

____**277. List foods** you eat when you're not hungry but are trying to fill some other longing. Note the emotional needs you might be trying to meet with those foods. Think of ways you could fulfill each of these needs in ways that don't involve food. (See "Clarify Your Feelings around Food" in Chapter 2 for ideas.)

____**278. Share your feelings, joys, and concerns** with one or more people today.

____**279. Sketch a floor plan** of a house you lived in as a child. Label the rooms, and note places that were especially meaningful to you. When you're done, write about how this exercise made you feel. What good and bad memories does the house bring to mind?

____**280. Pose these questions** to yourself, and write down your answers: What are you accepting in your life that you wish you could refuse? What do you wish you had more of? What is superfluous that you could get rid of? What is your heart's yearning?

Phase 4: REACHING ENLIGHTENMENT

____**281. Look for someone you can mentor**—someone who could use your advice from time to time. Ask this person to meet for coffee, and suggest getting together every month or so. (You don't have to identify yourself as a potential mentor; just act like a friend.)

____**282. Write a letter to your childhood self.** Tell that child what you wish someone had told you when you were little. From the place of wisdom you hold today, answer any questions you had back then. Give yourself all the love you deserved.

____**283. Read a newspaper**, news magazine, or online news source. Write a letter to someone in the news who inspires you, makes you angry, or incites other feelings in you. You don't have to send the letter, but you'll get extra points if you do (and perhaps have the fun of receiving a reply).

____**284. Tell someone you're sorry** for what you did to hurt them.

____**285. List things that make you angry.** For each one, write down the unmet demand underlying it. Then think of a way to meet that demand without getting angry. (Example: I get angry when my partner ignores me. Unmet demand: To be validated and respected. Other way to meet the demand: Find self-nurturing things to do so that I needn't look to others for validation.)

____**286. Sign up to volunteer** for a cause you believe in. If nothing comes to mind, contact your local United Way to see what volunteer jobs are available.

____**287. Write in your journal or talk to someone** about your greatest fear. What strategies could you use to diminish your anxiety? If this exercise feels too scary, make an appointment with a therapist who can help you conquer your fear.

____**288. In all your relationships today,** follow the 100/0 principle: Give 100 percent of yourself, and expect nothing at all from the other person. You may be surprised to find how quickly this approach can strengthen a connection, leading eventually to the perfect 100/100 relationship.

____**289. Has anything ever happened to you** that you can't explain rationally? Describe one or more such experiences on paper. Share them with a friend. Discuss the idea of a realm beyond the logical, factual, and verifiable.

____**290. What losses** have you experienced lately? How could you turn each loss into a gain? Write about how your losses can enhance your life.

____**291. Reach out to someone** who seems shy, withdrawn, or in need of a friend. Ask questions about their life and what they've been up to, and listen to what they have to say.

____**292. If you feel any envy** for anyone, remember that we all have troubles. Those who seem to have everything have pain hidden inside. If you could switch places with them, you probably wouldn't want to—not if you knew all the things they have to bear. You're better off working on your own situation. That way, you can turn life into exactly what you want it to be. Notice today if you have any twinges of envy and see if this exercise helps. Write about it when you get home this evening.

____**293. Write out a statement** of what you believe to be your fundamental purpose—the thing you most want to accomplish in your life.

____**294. Give out awards for the "best of the day."** Take notes on the best thing you have to eat today, the biggest smile you see, the most beautiful sight, the most colorful outfit, etc. You can keep these awards private or share them with others.

____**295. Are you able to trust life's unfolding**, or do you try to control everything? Are you lonely, or do you feel connected to a larger whole? Talk to your journal and your higher power about your answers.

____**296. Draw pictures** of your outer self (how you appear to others) and your inner self. Now write a few words about what these drawings tell you.

____**297. Draw your ideal self**—how your inner and outer selves would look if you were the person you want to be. Write about steps you could take toward becoming your ideal self.

____**298. Contemplate the Buddhist wisdom** that without expectations there would be no pain. Are you holding any expectations? Remind yourself that nothing you anticipate is likely to turn out as you plan—and that's something to celebrate!

____**299. Give someone a small gift.** Write about how you chose the gift, how you felt when you gave it, and what you learned from the act of giving.

____**300. What do you need to forgive yourself for?** What shame do you hold in your heart? Write it down, then burn or shred the paper along with your guilt. If you don't feel absolved, plan to repeat this exercise once a week.

____**301. Visit a labyrinth.** (To find one, see labyrinthsociety.org.) Moving meditation can be centering and profound.

____**302. Join a group working to solve a problem** in your community, your state, the nation, or the world.

____**303. Write about a dream** you had recently. Underline the key words, and note the associations each one has for you. For instance, if a key word is closet, you might write: skeletons, darkness, secrets. Keep free-associating until you get an idea of how the word pertains to your life and what message it might be sending you.

____**304. What do you want your legacy** to be? How do you want to be remembered? What difference will your having lived make in the world? Put your thoughts into several paragraphs.

____**305. Describe yourself** as if you're a journalist writing about a famous person. What insights might an objective reporter have about you?

____**306. Pretend you're on your death bed**, and all your loved ones are gathered around you. You have time to say one thing to each of them. Who is there, and what will you say to each one? Consider saying those things to your loved ones today.

____**307. Envision someone who loves and approves of you** standing in front of you. Look at yourself through their eyes and see the positive things about yourself that they see.

____**308. How do you feel** about life? How do you feel about death? Are you happy with your answers? Or do you need to shift your attitude in order to live life fully and face death peacefully?

____**309. Write a message** to your spiritual power, asking for help with a problem, question, or situation. Then put it out of your mind and turn it over to the universe. Make a note in your datebook to re-read your letter in a month to see how the universe responded.

____**310. Do your relationships** include people of different races, ages, and backgrounds? If not, plan to visit a place where you'll find people different from you. (Examples: Volunteer at a nursing home or kindergarten. Attend events at a community center.) The more different you are from someone, the more you can teach each other.

____**311. Answer these questions:** What do you want to contribute to the world? Who do you want to be? What three steps would help you fulfill those wishes?

____**312. Write a letter** to your spouse, partner, or someone else who is important in your life. Describe the relationship as it is and as you wish it could be. Don't send the letter; use it to clarify your own feelings.

____**313. Who is the oldest person** you know? Ask that person: What's the most important lesson you've learned about life? What's the secret of your longevity? What's your best advice? If you can't think of anyone, go to a nursing home and ask if there's someone there who enjoys talking and would like a visitor.

____**314. Think of a topic that you've avoided** discussing with someone but that needs to be aired. Meet with that person, and lovingly bring up the subject. Be open to listening to their views as well as expressing your own.

____**315. List five ways** you can take care of your emotional health. Examples: Read an uplifting book. Keep a feelings log and a gratitude journal. Meditate. Attend a support group. Do one of those things today.

____**316. Meditate on the good qualities of someone you don't like** or someone who upsets you. Try giving them what you wish they would give to you. If you feel they're not listening to you, for instance, take special care to listen to them. If you want their forgiveness, forgive them.

____**317. Write about the role luck has played in your life.** Do you consider yourself lucky or unlucky? What do you think about the idea that lucky people tend to be more prepared to take advantage of promising situations when they occur? In what ways could you prepare yourself so that when luck comes along you'll be ready?

____**318. Draw a circle big enough to fill a piece of paper.** Divide it into six sections to represent (1) work, (2) family and friends, (3) spiritual life, (4) physical and emotional health, (5) mental growth, and (6) service to others. Make each piece of the "pie" a size that corresponds to the proportion of time you give to that element. Are these six realms of your life in balance? If not, which parts need more attention? How could you enhance those neglected pieces of yourself?

____**319. Work some magic.** Carry a notebook and an imaginary magic wand with you today. Whenever you see something you'd like to change, write it in your notebook and wave your wand. Tonight, look over your list of wishes. Write some steps you could take to make them come true.

____**320. Visualize your life as a movie** and yourself as the hero. Think of today as the opening scene. As you move through the day, what is the hero learning from each thing that happens?

Tonight, write about the experience. Did you meet anyone who might be an important character in the movie? If so, how will you make sure that person remains part of the narrative? How will you follow up on all the possibilities of today to make sure there is a triumphant ending to the plot?

____**321. List problems you have**, challenges you face, and questions for which you seek answers. Now see if you can find the answer to a question in one of your challenges. When you bring together parts of your life that seem unrelated, you'll often discover remarkable connections.

____**322. Read through** your dream diary. Do you notice any patterns?

____**323. Write a letter to someone who has hurt you.** When you've expressed all your feelings, put it aside. In a few days, re-read it and decide if you want to send it or tear it up. Either way, let the feelings go, and fill your heart with forgiveness. Then move on.

____**324. Look for a situation today** that could be turned into a short, short story. This evening, take ten minutes to write that story.

____**325. Ask someone for feedback** about an aspect of yourself you'd like to improve. Receive the feedback with gratitude—especially if it seems negative. Consider ways you can use the advice to become stronger.

____**326. Send a letter, card, text message, or email** to a friend (or someone you'd like to have as a friend). Give that person a compliment, or tell them why you appreciate them.

____**327. Ask someone for a favor.** Think of a way to show your appreciation.

____**328. Do something bold today**—something you're nervous about doing but that will stretch you, expand your comfort zone, and help you grow as a person.

____**329. Practice thinking of metaphors.** Start by using metaphors to describe what you see, hear, and feel right now. (Examples: The music is a salve to my soul. The night air is a velvet cloak. I'm so relaxed I'm a limp rag.) Seeing likenesses between dissimilar things and linking them together is a wonderfully mind-expanding practice.

____**330. Start a creative-failure notebook.** Write about times you failed at something. What did you learn? What creative lessons does failure teach?

____**331. Make a favorite dish** and take it to someone who can use a home-cooked meal—a neighbor, busy friend, someone who's lost a spouse or is caring for a sick relative.

____**332. Think of a decision you need to make.** Toss a coin—heads for yes, tails for no. When the coin lands, notice how you feel when you see the results. Glad, relieved, disappointed? Your feelings will tell you which decision your subconscious wants you to make.

____**333. Write about your beliefs.** What are you absolutely sure of? How have your assumptions changed over the last few years? What convictions from your childhood do you still hold today? What inside you is solid and unchangeable?

____**334. Itemize things** that you've always wanted to try or that would broaden your world for you. (Travel someplace new. Take flying lessons. Go up in a hot-air balloon.) Take a first step toward doing one of those things.

____**335. Find a way** to give some sort of caring physical touch—a hug, a pat on the arm, a squeeze of the hand—to three people sometime during the day.

____**336. Think of three people who can benefit from this book**, and tell them about it. Share with them one of the things you've learned from it.

____**337. Use one of your signature strengths** in your work or relationships today. If you haven't yet learned your signature strengths, take the self-assessment at authentichappiness.

org. Another way to figure out your signature strengths is to ask yourself the following questions: What did you enjoy doing when you were around eight years old? What would you do all day if you could do anything you liked? What's your idea of the perfect job? When are you most joyful and enthusiastic?

____**338. All day, look at everyone and everything** through eyes of love. See the hope, beauty, and wonder that surround you. Open your heart. This evening, write about the experience.

____**339. List three activities that deeply involve you** while building your inner strengths—things that engage you so totally that time flies while you're doing them. (Examples: drawing, cooking, talking to a friend, taking photographs.) Make time for one of these activities today.

____**340. Describe your philosophy of life.** Why are you alive? What do you think will happen to you after you die? Make a plan to discuss your philosophy with others and see how it differs from theirs. Be open to their ideas, realizing that there is not one "Truth" but many valid truths.

____**341. Do one tiny thing today** that will change some part of the world around you.

____**342. Perform a letting-go ritual**, either alone or with friends. (Some ideas: Let go of a habit, attitude, or relationship. Free yourself from trying to control anyone besides yourself. Release old burdens of guilt, resentment, or pain.) Say aloud and in writing what you're giving up and why. Then rip up the paper on which it's written to represent the fact that you're letting go for good.

____**343. Read through your journal and your dream diary.** Does reading them together bring new revelations about your dreams' meanings?

____**344. Give a small amount of money** to a cause you care about.

____**345. Is your life changing** the way you'd like? Can you feel yourself becoming the person you want to be? Reflect and write about your answers. Ask your higher power for help in continuing to change and grow.

____**346. Imagine what people might say about you at your funeral.** What would you like them to say? What actions could you take to increase the chances that someday they may say those things? Take one of those actions today.

____**347. Assess yourself** with these questions as you go through your day: What are you feeling and thinking? How many of those feelings and thoughts are you expressing to others? What are you keeping hidden inside? What are you saying that doesn't match what you believe? How can you reduce the discrepancies between what's inside you and what you show to the world?

____**348. Is there anything from your past** that bothers you? Write about it; then write these words: That was then, this is now. I can let it go. The past isn't me. I am reborn and continue to be reborn each day.

____**349. Tell someone a funny story** about something that happened to you. If possible, make the story about a fallibility or foible of yours, a blunder you made, or a time you misunderstood something. For instance, what erroneous childhood beliefs did you hold? (See IUsedtoBelieve.com for examples.)

____**350. Add three action steps** to your daily planner—steps that will move you closer to fulfilling your goals and dreams.

____**351. Look at photos of your parents** before you were born. See them as people who once were separate from you with their own hopes, problems, and needs. Write about how it feels to view your parents as human beings with their own lives. Does it make you feel more compassion for them? Does it expand your reality?

____**352. Visit someone** who could use a listening ear. Perhaps you know someone who's ill, housebound, or lonely. Or visit a nursing home, hospital, or hospice.

____**353. Reflect on what matters most** to you. What do you care about beyond all else? What are you living to do? Write down the answers that come to you.

____**354. Sign up to go to a conference, workshop, or retreat** on any topic you choose. Check bulletin boards or newspapers, or ask people for suggestions.

____**355. Write about patterns** in your family. What behaviors do you see occurring and re-occurring? What addictions run in your family? What secrets? What hidden shames? What unhealthy ways of dealing with food, money, sex? What dysfunctional relationships? Are there ways you're recreating your parents' lives against your will? What steps could you take to end one of these patterns?

____**356. Introduce yourself to one or more of your neighbors**. Ask if they have time for a chat. If so, take a few minutes to get to know them. Exchange contact information so you and they will have someone to turn to in an emergency.

____**357. Read over what you've written in your journal** for the past year or so. Summarize the main points—the key things you've learned, the threads that run through everything.

____**358. Is there something you've been wanting to do** but were afraid to try? Do it, or make a start toward doing it, today. Feel the fear, but move beyond it. You can't help your feelings, but you can control your behavior.

____**359. Some time today, show or tell someone** that they matter.

____**360. List five injustices** in the world. For each one, decide if there's anything you can do about it. Could you join a group working to end world hunger, volunteer at a homeless shelter, donate money to fight child abuse, or do something else to mitigate one of the injustices you've identified? If so, make a note to take a step toward doing so. If not, release any anger or unhappiness you feel about the injustice, and let it go.

____**361. Look at your schedule** to see if it contains enough "white space" for reflection, self-improvement, and spontaneity. If not, find ways to open up your schedule so it's not too tightly packed with things to do.

____**362. What is the biggest life lesson** you've learned? Share it with someone and ask them to share their most valuable life lesson with you.

____**363. Pick one of these 365 exercises** that you enjoyed. Do that exercise again today.

____**364. Which of these exercises** taught you the most? What did you learn? Write a few paragraphs describing how you've put that learning into practice in your daily life.

____**365. Did you skip any of these 365 exercises**? If so, why? Write a sentence for each skipped exercise, explaining why you didn't do it. If you think it's too hard or you're too resistant, ask someone to help you. That's how you'll change your life—one step at a time.

APPENDIX

RESOURCES TO GUIDE AND INSPIRE YOU

Chapter 1. Trust Your Inner Guide: My Story
Websites

Alcoholics-Anonymous.org and **na.org** (Narcotics Anonymous) are good places to start.

Womenforsobriety.org is a nonprofit organization dedicated to helping women overcome alcoholism and other addictions.

Positscience.com and **sharpbrains.com** have exercises you can practice to strengthen new parts of your brain and make your mind more flexible so that it will be easier for you to make changes in your life.

Nami.org is the site for the National Alliance on Mental Illness.

DoYourGiving.com provides insights on how you can share your blessings with others.

The-emotions.com delineates different feelings and helps you learn to identify them.

Cfiwest.org/sos (Secular Organizations for Sobriety) takes a secular approach to recovery.

Smartrecovery.org teaches recovery based on the latest scientific research.

Rational.org uses cognitive therapy techniques in recovery.

Passionaries.org will encourage you to make a difference in the lives of others, which is an important part of changing yourself.

IUsedtoBelieve.com is a funny and bizarre collection of ideas that adults thought were true when they were children. It will remind you what it was like to be a child, fascinated and horrified by the world in equal parts. Some recent examples from the site: "I used to believe that the things rattling around in spray paint cans were baby teeth that the tooth fairy sold to the paint company, and that's how she got her money." "I used to think there were live beetles inside each speaker playing every song because the only band I'd heard of was the Beatles." Conjure up the beliefs you held as a child, and add them to the list on the website.

SuccessConsciousness.com gives practical information on awakening your inner power through visualization.

43things.com helps answer the question, "What do you want to do with your life?" It also helps you attain your goals and connects you with others with similar goals.

StickK.com is a free site where you can set a goal, establish milestones in meeting it, and put down money that you'll have to forfeit if you don't attain it. It has helped millions of people give up smoking and other bad habits.

Books

The Wisdom of the Five Messengers: Learning to Follow the Guidance of Feelings by Kerry Paul Altman

Toxic Parents by Susan Forward

Hidden Victims by Julie Tallard

How to Refuse to Make Yourself Miserable about Anything by Albert Ellis

Cognitive Therapy: Basics and Beyond by Judith Beck

Cognitive Therapy of Substance Abuse by Aaron Beck

Mother-Daughter Revolution by Elizabeth Debold

Change Your Mind, Change Your Brain by Sharon Begley

Dream Power: How to Use Your Night Dreams to Change Your Life by Cynthia Richmond

The Power of Coincidence by David Richo

Chapter 2. Connect to the Earth: Shelly's Story

Websites

Connectionscounseling.com is the site for Connections Counseling Clinic, focused on creating a recovery community conducive to hope and healing.

Edap.org is the National Eating Disorders Association (NEDA) site, which includes information, referrals, support, prevention, and newsletters.

Overeatersanonymous.org offers a program of recovery from compulsive overeating using the twelve-step model.

GivewithGratitude.com and **KatieKrueger.com/blog** offer snippets of gratitude to remind you of all you have to celebrate.

Hazelden.org provides books, resources, and treatment for addiction; sign up for "Today's Gift" and receive an inspiring message every day.

CourageRenewal.org aims to help you become more wholehearted in your life and work.

Emotionsanonymous.org is the site for a group working toward recovery from emotional difficulties such as depression, loneliness, low self-esteem, and anxiety.

Laughteryoga.org describes what laughter yoga is, where you can find laughter yoga clubs, and even includes videos of laughter yoga sessions.

Books

Walden by Henry David Thoreau

Voluntary Simplicity by Duane Elgin

Secrets of Serenity: Timeless Wisdom to Soothe the Soul by Running Press

Life Is Hard, Food Is Easy by Linda Spangle

Addicted to Stress by Debbie Mandel

Conquer CyberOverload by Joanne Cantor

Driven to Distraction: Recognizing and Coping with ADD by Edward M. Hallowell

The Wisdom of Wilderness: Experiencing the Healing Power of Nature by Gerald G. May

Wild Chickens and Petty Tyrants: 108 Metaphors for Mindfulness by Arnold Kozak

Chapter 3. Humbly Ask for Help: Adam's Story
Websites

Depressionabout.com includes many resources and information to help deal with the disease of depression and to understand how antidepressant medication works.

29gifts.org has the mission of reviving the giving movement in the world—one gift at a time.

Writeexpress.com explains how to write letters of apology, acceptance, appreciation, and much more.

Wearewhatwedo.org is a global movement of ordinary people who want to change the world.

Getamused.com has a collection of jokes and funny stories guaranteed to help you laugh.

TheMoth.org is a nonprofit storytelling site where you can learn to put the power of stories to good use in your life.

Books
  Being Generous by Theodore Roosevelt Malloch
  Why We Love the Dogs We Do by Stanley Coren
  No Death, No Fear by Thich Nhat Hanh
  Listening to Prozac by Peter Kramer
  The Happiness Hypothesis: Finding Modern Truth in Ancient Wisdom by Jonathan Haidt

Words of Wisdom and Light
  The Liar in Your Life by Robert Feldman

Chapter 4. Make Yourself Happy: Skye's Story
Websites

Erikaoliver.com will inspire you to keep finding good things in your life.

StopYourStressNow.com provides a free teleseminar on overcoming stress and anxiety.

Buddhanet.net and **Beliefnet.com** offer good descriptions of loving-kindness meditation.

Self-directed-search.com will help you choose the career that's right for you.

AuthenticHappiness.org shows how you can attain genuine happiness by discovering your signature strengths. The key to well-being is to find your core strengths and use them, every day, in work you love to do. Take the quiz at this website to pinpoint these strengths for yourself.

Gratefulness.org provides resources for living a grateful life. You can sign up to receive an inspirational quote each day.

Books
  Three Good Things by Erika K. Oliver
  Repotting by Diana Holman and Ginger Pape
  Perfectionism: What's Bad about Being Too Good by Miriam Adderholdt and Jan Goldberg
  Moments of Clarity by Christopher Kennedy Lawford
  Authentic Happiness by Martin E.P. Seligman

Gross National Happiness by Arthur C. Brooks
The Geography of Bliss by Eric Weiner

Words of Wisdom and Light
The Cow in the Parking Lot by Leonard Scheff

Chapter 5. Just Connect: Shyloh's Story
Websites

Grief.net, the site of the Grief Recovery Institute, includes many articles and resources about recovering from grief and loss.

Ptsdinfo.org is a gateway to a number of sites about post traumatic stress disorder.

Addictionsandrecovery.org has many helpful articles on relapse prevention.

Books

Finding Your Strength in Difficult Times: A Book of Meditations by David Viscott
Secrets, Lies, Betrayals by Maggie Scarf
Connected by Nicholas Christakis and James Fowler
The Connect Effect by Michael Dulworth

Chapter 6. Courage Doesn't Always Roar: Andrea's Story
Websites

Taoteching.org offers translations from Taoist literature such as the Tao Te Ching.

Moodscope.com helps you keep track of your moods and learn what triggers them.

Books

The Book of the Heart: Embracing the Tao by Trevor Carolan and Bella Chen
A Path and a Practice by William Martin

Words of Wisdom and Light
It's Not How Smart You Are: It's How You Are Smart by Jeanne Anne Craig
My Start-Up Life by Ben Casnocha

Chapter 7. Make Room for Miracles: Marilyn's Story
Websites

Motherpeace.com is the site of the Motherpeace cards, co-created by Karen Vogel and Vicki Noble. The seventy-eight cards in this round deck are beautiful, vivid images celebrating Goddess cultures throughout the world.

At **Elephants.com**, you can donate money to the elephant sanctuary, sign up for their newsletter, and watch the elephants as they interact in the wild.

Gotoquiz.com/animology_what_animal_are_you provides a quiz that identifies your totem animal based on your personality.

Evolvingbeings.com features spiritual topics that inspire you to expand your consciousness.

Vegetariantimes.com has a starter kit to help you switch to a vegetarian diet, along with tips and recipes.

DailyOm.com is dedicated to whole-self well-being, helping you put your mind and body into balance.

Dharmaseed.org offers talks about Buddhist teachings you can download for free.

Keirsey.com is the site for one of the most acclaimed personality tests in the world, the Keirsey Temperament Sorter.

Books

Motherpeace by Vicki Noble
Please Understand Me by David Keirsey and Marilyn Bates
The Book of Awakening by Mark Nepo
Eating Well for Optimum Health by Andrew Weil
Many Roads, One Journey by Charlotte Davis Kasl
Faith Is a Verb by Kenneth Stokes
Stages of Faith by James Fowler
Goddesses in Everywoman by Jean Shinoda Bolen
Just Friends by Lillian Rubin
Awakening Lovingkindness by Pema Chodron
Healing Ceremonies by Carl Hammerschlag and Howard Silverman

A NOTE OF THANKS

Writing this book required the help of many friends—and many strangers who became friends along the way. Heartfelt thanks to my incredible team of readers—Dawn, Mary, Karen, Gail, and Marla—and writing group—Sandra, Chris, Dan, Katherine, and Richard: Your suggestions, encouragement, and ever-present laughter mean more to me than you'll ever know.

To Phillip, my true love, who has been by my side every step of the way, and to my incomparable women friends: You have blessed my life with your support, understanding, and love.

To the Recovery Foundation's incredible board members for their financial support and belief in the need for this book. Your good work helps untold people find their way, and I am pleased to donate book proceeds to the Foundation, knowing you will use it well to help many others.

My undying gratitude to those who shared their stories and insights: Your courage is an inspiration and will help countless people. Deepest appreciation for all those wonderful contributors who aren't recognized with their real names in these pages: Your wisdom and light illuminate these pages. The fact that I couldn't include every one of your words is a reflection not of their worth but of the frustrating confines of space.

A special thanks to my daughter Andrea, granddaughter Shyloh, grandson Zeke, and friends Marilyn and Adam. And, finally, to Shelly and Skye, my guardian angels: If it weren't for you, there would be no book. Thank you for trusting me.

INDEX TO TIPS, EXERCISES, & RESOURCES

This alphabetical listing of *Waking Up Happy's* exercises, tips, and resources is arranged according to subject and activity so that you can find them when you need them. The exercises in "365 Steps on Your Journey" aren't included here, but those 365 steps all build on earlier exercises in the book, so if you need more information on a subject, you can find it in this index.

AA: see Support groups, Twelve steps
AA, alternatives to: 277
Acceptance: 84, 159, 203, 224
Acting as if: 67
Addiction, talking back to: 192-193
Affirmations & mantras: 44, 239
Anger: 162-163, 280
Ancient Wisdom: 161
Animals & nature: 83, 106, 117-118, 183, 228-229, 241, 245, 279, 280
Anxieties: 192
Apologizing: 35-36, 133-134
Attention Deficit Disorder (ADD): 278
Authenticity: 137-138, 148, 190, 279
Body & movement: 65, 82, 84, 235-236
Books & libraries: 65
Boundaries: 52, 230
Brainstorming: 96
Breathing: 37, 246
Buddhist teachings: 162, 229, 279-281
Change: 151, 160, 200-201, 207, 245, 277-279
Childhood & inner child: 22, 65, 242, 246, 277
Cognitive therapy: see Thinking.
Connecting with others: 19, 34, 64, 102, 106, 107, 138, 159, 174-175, 206, 220-221, 280; see Friendship
Coping skills: 64, 73-74, 173-174
Creativity: 96, 106, 191, 218, 232, 245
Death: 123, 238, 279
Defensive pessimism: 209
Depression: 130-131, 278
Dreams: 46-47, 65, 238, 278
Eating healthy: 82, 88-89, 278, 281
Emotions: 23-24, 63, 73-74, 84, 87, 130-131, 162-163, 169, 206, 208, 277-280
Emotional Intelligence: 208
Fears: 48, 192
Forgiveness: 53, 87, 131, 134, 207, 247-248
Friendship: 25, 126-127, 224, 281

Giving: 53, 62, 131, 136, 277-279
Goal-setting: 65-67, 92, 108-109, 159-160, 277
Goddesses: 281
Gratitude: 73, 93, 136, 160, 234, 244-245, 278-279
Grieving: 31, 169, 191, 280
Happiness: 74, 95, 104, 135, 157-160, 169, 174, 187, 191-192, 207, 279-280
Hope: 92, 130-131, 169, 235, 252
Intuition: 226
Laughter: 25, 74, 95-96, 136, 157, 169, 188, 244-245, 251, 278-279
Learning: 51, 66-67, 121, 126, 200-201, 208, 280
Lying: 137-138, 279; see Authenticity
Meditation & mindfulness: 80, 84, 105-106, 131, 134, 136, 169, 180, 206, 234, 240, 244, 252, 278-281
Mental illness: 277
Moods: 73-74, 106, 134, 186, 280
Motherpeace cards: 280-281
Orchids vs. dandelions: 248-249
Parents: 57, 242, 246, 278
Planning & prioritizing: 64-66; see Goal-setting
Perfectionism: 159, 218, 248, 251, 279
Personality tests: 251, 281
Post traumatic stress (PTSD): 173-174, 280
Problem solving: 66, 203
Puzzles: 107-108
Reiki: 235-236
Relapsing: 186, 280
Relaxation: see Self-care.
Resilience: 248-249
Rituals: 88, 131, 234
Scheduling: 64
Seasonal Affective Disorder (SAD): 161
Self-care: 37, 64, 73-74, 84, 88-89, 94-95, 97-98, 101, 105-108, 124, 161, 179-180, 191, 206-207, 227, 240, 245-246, 251-252, 278-280; see Serenity & silence)
Self-esteem: 40, 208

Serenity & silence: 85-86, 97-98, 101, 134, 179, 278
Shortcomings as strengths: 248-249
Signature strengths: see Happiness.
Simplicity: 278
Singing: 108
Smoking: 155
Spirituality: 25, 85, 107, 119, 132-136, 144, 169, 206-207, 280-281
Story-telling: 121, 279
Stress: see Self-care.
Support groups: 19, 34, 155, 169, 277-278; see Connecting with others
Surrendering: 116, 132-133
Taoism: 161, 280
Therapy: 78
Thinking: 39, 66-67, 151, 158-161, 200-201, 208-209, 277-278
Twelve steps: 131-135
Vegetarianism: 280-281
Visualization: 105, 179, 226, 278
Wonders of the world: 192
Writing: 20-21, 57, 74, 87, 100, 158, 160, 169, 174, 176-177, 206-207, 234, 242

www.ingramcontent.com/pod-product-compliance
Lightning Source LLC
Chambersburg PA
CBHW080727230426
43665CB00020B/2642